For Michele

THE
TROUBLE
WITH
TIGERS

The Rise and Fall
of South-East Asia

VICTOR MALLET

HarperCollinsBusiness

HarperCollins*Publishers*
An imprint of HarperCollins*Publishers*
77–85 Fulham Palace Road,
Hammersmith, London w6 8jb

www.harpercollinsbusiness.com

This paperback edition 2000
1 3 5 7 9 8 6 4 2

First published in Great Britain by
HarperCollins*Publishers* 1999

isbn 0 00 638888 4

Set in PostScript Linotype New Baskerville

Printed and bound in Great Britain by
Caledonian International Book Manufacturing Ltd, Glasgow

Contents

Acknowledgements

This book would not have been possible without the assistance and advice of scores of people across the ten countries of south-east Asia, as well as the contributions of a few others scattered around the globe from Britain to Australia. In some cases, the help spanned several years; in others, it was a matter of a single interview or piece of information. In particular, I was supported by the constant encouragement (and fluent Thai) of my wife Michele and the intelligent suggestions and stimulating conversation of Toby Mundy and Lucinda McNeile at HarperCollins.

I must thank the *Financial Times* on several counts. First, it sent me to south-east Asia. Second, it takes the whole world seriously and continues to publish daily news and analysis about developing Asia, Latin America and Africa as well as Europe, Japan and the US. Third, the *FT* granted me a year's leave of absence to research and write the book. My *FT* colleagues, meanwhile, were generous with their hospitality and with their contacts. I am grateful to *The Economist* in general and Gideon Rachman in particular for their inspired coverage of the 'Asian values' debate and of Singapore, which earned *The Economist* a torrent of letters from an irritable Singapore government. I relied heavily on other media as well. It is obviously impossible for one person to cover ten countries day to day simultaneously, and like other journalists in the region, I devoured the *Far Eastern Economic Review* each week in search of news and ideas from its excellent network of correspondents.

Above all, I thank the people who took the time to talk to me. Some were busy government ministers. Some were dissidents who have subsequently been jailed. Still others were businessmen and women, academics, diplomats, farmers, factory workers, stockbrokers and people working for small non-governmental organizations or large international institutions such as the Asian Development Bank.

Those who helped me during my more than three years as a correspondent in south-east Asia are too numerous to mention by name. What follows is a list of those who helped me in the research and writing of the book in 1997 and 1998. Sadly, some of my most important contacts cannot be named, either because it might expose them to political persecution in countries such as Vietnam or Burma or because – as diplomats or entrepreneurs in sensitive positions – they asked to remain anonymous. I fear it is also inevitable that one or two people will have been omitted inadvertently, and I apologise for that in advance. My thanks to: Geni Achnas, Abdul Rahman Adnan, Teodoro Añana, Dewi Fortuna Anwar, Zaina Anwar, Bradley Babson, Karen Bakker, Gopal Baratham, Ted Bardacke, William Barnes, Hasan Basar, Priya Basu, Jonathan Birchall, Stephen Brookes, Chan Yat, Chea Vannath, Philip Cheah, Chee Soon Juan, David Chew, Chia Thye Poh, Victor Chin, Korn Chatikavanij, Kavi Chongkittavorn, Nick Cumming-Bruce, Ja'afar Daud, Do Duc Dinh, Leo Dobbs, Fan Yew Teng, Juan Flavier, Mary Flipse, Nirmal Ghosh, Ian Gill, Goon Kok Loon, Mark Graham, Jeremy Grant, Arnaud Guinard, Paul Handley, Jerry Harmer, Julian Hartland-Swann, Lao Mong Hay, William Hioe, Hishamuddin Rais, Hla Min, Michael Holman, Philip Jeyaretnam, Kao Kim Hourn, Aristides Katoppo, William Keeling, Khieu Kanharith, William Klausner, Sarwono Kusumatmaatmadja, Kwik Kian Gie, Kyi Maung, James, Lucy and Tom Kynge, Philippe Le Billon, Lee Hsien Loong, Lee May Lin, Jon Liden, Christopher Lingle, Bertil Lintner, Bindu Lohani, Simon Long, Ed Luce, Gloria Macapagal-Arroyo, John McBeth, Dave McCaughan, Vincent McClean, Sheila McNulty, Bernadette Madrid, Mary-Kay Magistad, Alex Magno, Kishore Mahbubani, Mak Jun Nam, Philip and Mary Mallet, Peter Mares, Justin Marozzi, Julinda Mega, Din Merican, James Michener, Jonathan, Cory and Zoe Miller, Emmanuel Miñana, Somsanouk Mixay, Goenawan Mohammed, Jatti Mohammed, Chandra Muzaffar, Palaniappan Narayanan, Luong Thanh Nghi, Huu Ngoc, Le Do Ngoc, Abdul-Aziz Nordin, Cynthia Owens, Bernard Pe-Win, Virachit Philaphandeth, Epifania Piadoche, R. J. Pillay, Surin Pitsuwan, H. J. C. Princen, Raphael Pura, Johnny Quiap, Gideon Rachman, Roberto Romulo, Pham Bich San, Manuela Saragosa, Adi Sasono, Seng Teak, Ammar Siamwalla, Marsillam Simandjuntak, David Sparkes, Suraphol Sudara, Juwono Sudarsono, Rizal Sukma, Marinee Suwanmoli, Tan Kim Hooi, Tan Lian Choo, Nguyen Trung

Acknowledgements

Thanh, Thani Thongpakdi, Thein Tun, Tran Quoc Thuan, Edgardo Tongson, Jimmy and Emily Traya, Panwadee Uraisin, Michael Vatikiotis, Abhisit Vejjajiva, Cita Vendiola, Abdurrahman Wahid, Sofjan Wanandi, Paiboon Wattanasiritham, Denise Weldon, Peter Weldon, Evan Williams, Dawn Wong, Jenny Wong, Kean Wong, Ahmad Yahya, Yee Khim Chong, Nguyen Thi Le Yen, George Yeo, Mohammed Yunus Pathi Mohammed.

*

It is with great sadness that I pay tribute to two people who helped to make this book possible and who died after it was first published. Sander Thoenes, the *Financial Times* correspondent in Indonesia, was killed by gunmen in East Timor while reporting the conflict there. Mark Graham, my Bangkok neighbour who devoted himself to the cause of wildlife in Asia, died in an air crash in Thailand. They are both sorely missed.

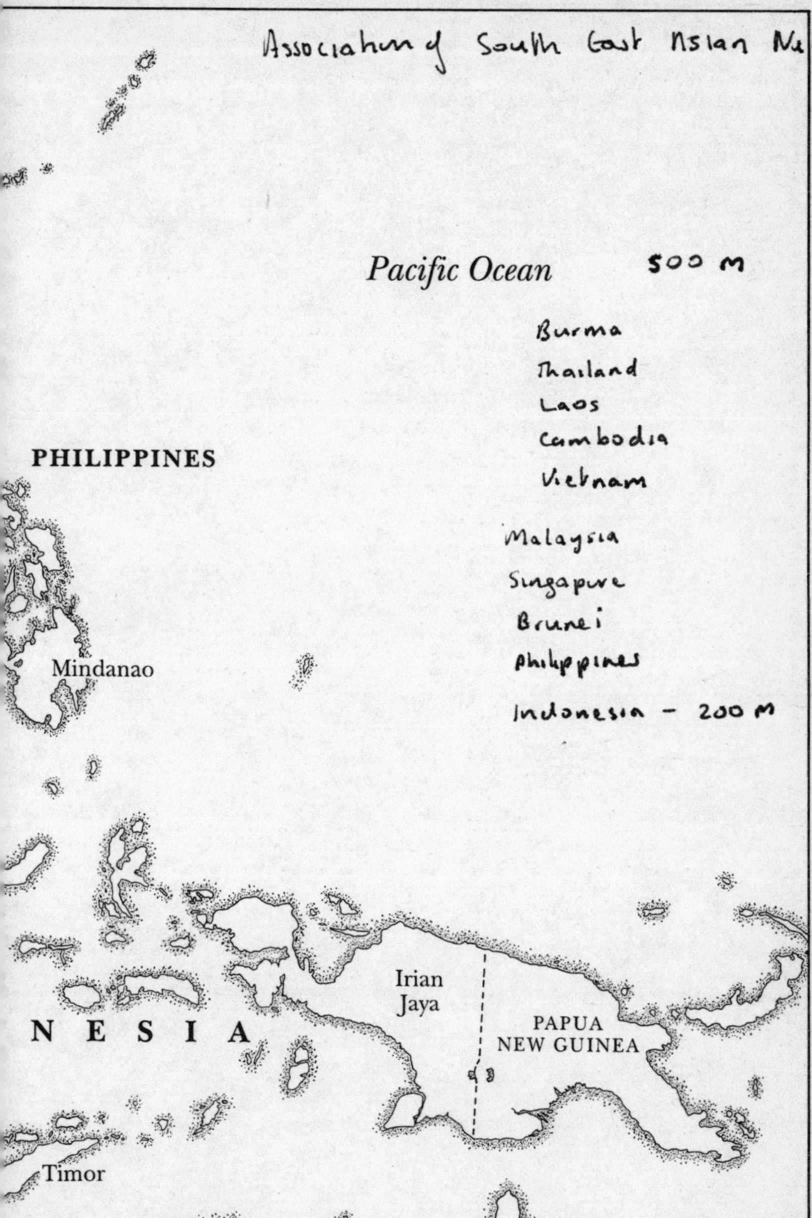
Association of South East Asian Nations
Pacific Ocean
500 M
Burma
Thailand
Laos
Cambodia
Vietnam
Malaysia
Singapore
Brunei
Philippines
Indonesia - 200 M
PHILIPPINES
Mindanao
Irian
Jaya
PAPUA
NEW GUINEA
NESIA
Timor
AUSTRALIA

Preface

Asia can be disconcertingly modern for a westerner. One day a couple of years ago I was reverently approaching the centre of the ancient temple of Angkor Wat in Cambodia – apparently alone as I admired this 900-year-old work of art – when I heard a strange, high-pitched burbling noise. I soon found the cause. A Cambodian woman was sitting in the centre of the temple playing furiously with her hand-held electronic Game Boy. Perhaps I should not have been surprised. Europeans and Americans, not to mention Asian tourist boards, are still guilty of 'Orientalism', the practice of portraying eastern lands as exotic, sensual and mystical, rather than as part of the modern world. Asians themselves, meanwhile, have been taking part in the fastest industrial revolution in history, completing in a few decades a modernization that took 150 years or more for the first such revolution in England in the eighteenth and nineteenth centuries. And they have been doing so at a time when technology has advanced far beyond steam engines to computers and electronics, allowing them to leapfrog whole stages of the industrial revolutions experienced by others. It is not uncommon for Asian men and women to move straight from working in the family's paddy fields to a factory producing microchips.

The world was rightly fascinated by this post-war transformation of agrarian Asian societies into fast-growing, industrial exporters, a process which came to be called the 'Asian miracle'. Much has been written about the economics behind Asia's success in the last four decades. But there is less literature on the risks presented by the extraordinary social and political upheavals accompanying this 'miracle' – risks that were vividly illustrated by the financial crash of the late 1990s. That is a gap I hope to fill. Likewise, there have been many books of general interest published about Japan and China, but not enough about the countries of south-east Asia. Indonesia –

the fourth most populous nation and the largest Moslem one – has been correctly described as the most under-reported country on the globe.

I hope this book, by addressing these issues, will help to explain the financial crisis which erupted in Thailand in mid-1997, spread to the rest of Asia and eventually disrupted economies as far away as South Africa and Latin America. I trust it also shows that the continuing confrontation between the Malaysian government and its opponents and the Indonesian popular uprising in 1998 were not isolated events triggered solely by the crash of Asian markets, but part of a pattern of political reform throughout the region.

There has been no slackening in the pace of Asia's industrial revolution in recent months. South-east Asian economies began to recover in 1999, although (as discussed in the final chapter) there are doubts about whether they will return to the high growth rates of the past. Over-reaction has been a consistent theme of short-term foreign investment in Asia, to the detriment of the investors as well as the recipients of the money. In the 1980s and early 1990s, over-optimistic investors thought south-east Asian economies could do no wrong. In 1997 and 1998, they withdrew their money in a pessimistic panic, consigning hundreds of companies to bankruptcy and millions of diligent workers to unemployment. Then they regained their confidence in the first half of 1999, pumping money back into the region in spite of warnings that governments had failed to tackle the 'crony capitalism', corruption and poor banking practices that had precipitated the crisis in the first place.

Politicians have been busy, too. In Indonesia, President B.J. Habibie, the interim leader who succeeded the deposed Suharto, allowed the country to hold its first democratic election in nearly half a century in June 1999. The party of Megawati Sukarnoputri, a former opposition leader, won the most votes, but it was Abdurrahman Wahid, the ailing Moslem leader, who was later elected president. Still more remarkable was the Habibie government's decision to grant the people of East Timor – brutally invaded by Indonesia in 1975 – the chance to secede. A referendum on independence was held under UN auspices in August 1999, amid frequent outbreaks of violence in East Timor itself and other far-flung parts of the Indonesian archipelago. The East Timorese voted overwhelmingly for independence, but pro-Indonesian militiamen backed by the security forces immediately unleashed a campaign of terror on the largely defenceless population.

In Malaysia, Anwar Ibrahim, the reformist deputy prime minister and heir apparent to Mahathir Mohamad, was sacked by Mahathir, expelled from the ruling party, arrested on charges of sodomy and corruption and beaten in detention. He was sentenced to six years in jail. Mahathir also imposed controls on the flow of short-term capital for a year and declared that 'the free market system has failed'. But Anwar's supporters took to the streets with the same cries of 'Reformasi!' ('Reform!') that helped bring down Suharto in Indonesia, and Anwar's wife Wan Azizah Wan Ismail formed a new opposition party ahead of a general election. A couple of other south-east Asian governments broke with a tradition of polite non-interference to condemn publicly Mahathir's treatment of his former deputy.

In Cambodia, the main political parties reached a compromise to end a violent dispute over the outcome of the 1998 election, in which Hun Sen's ruling party won the biggest share of the vote with the help of widespread intimidation of voters. In Burma, the military junta sought once again to crush its opponents with hundreds of arrests. In Vietnam, tensions increased within the Communist Party over corruption and the need for political reform. Joseph Estrada, the action movie star who became president of the Philippines, was criticized for allowing the rehabilitation of business cronies of the late dictator Ferdinand Marcos.

This book is about the ten countries which are regarded – and which regard themselves – as 'south-east Asia', the region lying between India to the west and Japan and China to the east and north. In alphabetical order they are Brunei, Burma (Myanmar), Cambodia, Indonesia, Laos, Malaysia, the Philippines, Singapore, Thailand and Vietnam. All ten are members of the Association of South East Asian Nations (Asean), an organization originally established as a security umbrella at the time of the Vietnam war but which now focuses on trade as well. This is a region with more than 500 million inhabitants and a plethora of cultures and languages; where France, the US and China all came to grief fighting in Vietnam; where Pol Pot murdered more than a million people in Cambodia; which produces much of the world's opium; which has inflicted on itself some of the worst traffic jams and most polluted rivers; which has (briefly) the tallest buildings on earth in Malaysia; and which boasts in Singapore one of the most computerized cities on the globe. The ten countries are at very different stages of development, but they see themselves as a distinct group with common interests and they are all undergoing industrial revolutions. All have been affected, to a greater or lesser degree, by the region's financial crisis, and all have undergone convulsive change since World War II.

Some of the changes of the past decades, good and bad, would be familiar to nineteenth century Americans or to the English of the eighteenth century: the migration of men and women from the countryside to the cities in search of factory work, increased crime and pollution and the rise of 'robber barons' or 'gangster capitalists'. But nowadays the process is much faster and there are many new factors: the rapid spread of television and computers; the growth of consumerism; imports of foreign films and music; the use of drugs such as heroin and Ecstasy; new sexual habits; and much else besides. It is hardly surprising that Asians feel bewildered as well as elated by the changes in their lives as they enter the new millennium.

Nor is it surprising that Asian leaders, especially south-east Asian ones, became more assertive on the international stage as they became wealthier and more powerful in the 1990s. The last European colonies in Asia have been handed back to China (Britain returned Hong Kong in 1997, and Portugal was due to leave Macao at the end of 1999). Lee Kuan Yew, the architect of modern Singapore, and Mahathir of Malaysia both remember the colonial era and attribute their economic success since independence to 'Asian values'. They argue that Asians work hard and respect their families and communities, in contrast to individualistic, liberal and decadent westerners. Opponents of the 'Asian values' school, on the other hand, say the argument is a false one deployed merely to justify authoritarian Asian governments.

I have devoted space to this lively debate because it explains much about what went wrong with south-east Asia's 'tiger' economies, and because its outcome should make it easier to predict the region's future. One of the few benefits of the financial crisis is that it has prompted Asians to ask questions about their own societies. How much of what is happening is peculiarly 'Asian' and how much is merely 'modern'? Do richer and better educated citizens always demand more democracy and better human rights? What is the point of all this economic growth if our quality of life is getting worse?

Few of the answers are simple, but my conclusion is that industrialization itself has proved to be a much more powerful force for change than any particularly 'Asian' values. The industrial revolutions of south-east Asia have remarkably similar effects to those that have gone before in Britain, America and Japan. It could be argued that as a western-educated person, it was inevitable that I would come to this conclusion, just as it was inevitable that Francis Fukuyama of the US would assert the primacy of liberal democracy as a political system in *The End of History and the Last Man*. I do not believe the languages and cultural traditions of south-east Asia will suddenly disappear, any more than they have in France, Germany or Britain. But I was surprised by how few ordinary Asians – and I asked the question of almost everyone I met while researching this book – subscribed to the theory of 'Asian values' as voiced by Asian political leaders and millionaires, and by some western business executives too.

In the aftermath of the financial crisis, south-east Asia will resume the race to catch up with the industrialized world. In the process more and more of its inhabitants will enjoy the benefits of prosperity – better education and healthcare, more material goods and more leisure. But this time around, as they emerge from the humbling experience of the economic crash, they will also be more inclined to tackle the challenges of industrialization: pollution, crime, social disorder, cultural confusion and the urgent need to build effective political institutions. In places as different as Burma, Vietnam and Malaysia, lifestyles are changing rapidly and democrats are already demanding a say in the way their countries are run. The revolution in Indonesia was not the first in the region, and it will not be the last.

Victor Mallet
September 1999

Introduction:
A miracle that turned sour

Bangkok in the early 1990s was an extraordinarily energetic city. The peaceful chaos of the streets, where Mercedes-Benzes and BMWs jostled with motorcycles and three-wheel *tuktuks* for hire, where hawkers cooked noodle soup next to newly-constructed sky-scrapers, epitomized the south-east Asian economic boom. When I first set foot in Thailand in 1991, I was impressed not just by the energy but by the easy mixing of new and old, rich and poor, western and Asian. On Ploenchit Road outside my office, a statue of the Buddha, wreathed in incense and garlands of flowers, sat only yards away from a slightly bigger, plastic statue of Colonel Sanders outside a Kentucky Fried Chicken store. On the crowded pavements, foreign backpackers dodged between Thai businessmen talking stock prices into their mobile telephones and disabled women selling lottery tickets to passers-by.

South-east Asia's dynamism was seductive for a journalist accustomed to other continents. Europe seemed almost lethargic by comparison, and the sense of purpose in Asia's cities was a refreshing change from the despair in much of Africa and the Middle East. Books about the east Asian economic 'miracle' proliferated. It was impossible not to be impressed.

But from the beginning I had doubts – both about the supposedly miraculous nature of what was happening and about how long it could be sustained. I do not claim to be alone in this, for my doubts were sparked and then fuelled by the south-east Asians I met and interviewed throughout the region. Most governments and many business executives were supremely confident, but opposition politicians, academics and others repeatedly warned of the dangers ahead: governments were authoritarian or corrupt or both and

1

would be challenged by their subjects; many Asian businesses were successful not because they were well managed but because they were in league with the same corrupt governments; the environment was being destroyed; and the societies and cultures that seemed so stable were actually in the throes of an enormous upheaval. I confess that my scepticism about the 'miracle' soon began to waver in the face of accusations that I and some of my journalistic colleagues were too pessimistic and were mistakenly viewing events through 'western' eyes. Several more years of rapid economic growth made our doubts seem even more unreasonable.

Then came the financial crash of 1997. This book was conceived in 1996, so neither the region-wide economic crisis nor the overthrow of President Suharto in Indonesia came as a shock to me or to those Asians who had long advocated political and economic reform. But these events – particularly the abrupt end of the economic boom – did come as a nasty surprise to many south-east Asians and foreign investors. They had assumed that rapid economic growth would continue indefinitely, although they argued about the precise rate of expansion. In the mid-1990s, if you asked anyone in a south-east Asian city a casual question about how things were going, it was surprising how often the reply was a cheerful '7.6 per cent', '9 per cent' or some similarly precise number. Europeans or Americans usually know if their economy is doing well or badly, but most would struggle to remember a recent estimate for the growth of their gross domestic product. For Malaysians, Thais and Singaporeans, however, economic expansion had become an obsession.

There were good reasons for this. The rapid economic growth these countries had enjoyed in the previous three decades had a palpable effect on people's lives, whether they were cabinet ministers or factory workers; an economy growing at 8 per cent a year doubles in size in nine years, and most people have correspondingly more money to spend and save. South-east Asia's success – one of the great achievements of the second half of the twentieth century – was also a source of pride to politicians and ordinary citizens alike. The ten countries of south-east Asia have been involved in the most rapid industrial revolution in history. For the half a billion people who live there, this means being catapulted out of traditional and largely rural societies into the new world of big cities, factories, offices, cars, telephones and mass entertainment. Much has been written

2

about the economic causes of this 'miracle'. This book is about its effects on the people of south-east Asia, and about how it went wrong.

Many of the results of rapid industrialization are self-evidently good: people now live longer, and they live better. But some of the leaders who supervised south-east Asia's industrial revolution became arrogant. They began to believe that their societies were imbued with special 'Asian values', and were therefore immune to the political and social pressures that had accompanied previous industrial revolutions. They failed to deal with increasing demands for democracy; the spread of crime and drugs; the ultimately disastrous rise of a class of businessmen better at making friends with politicians than at managing their balance sheets; the destruction of the region's environment and natural resources; or the need to fend for themselves diplomatically and militarily after the end of the Cold War.

Whether or not south-east Asia recovers economically – as most economists believe it will after the recent financial crisis – the need to manage these challenges will make the bare statistics of growth seem much less important in the early years of the twenty-first century than they did in the 1990s. Most of the challenges are new to the region, but not to the world. As people become educated, they tend to become more vocal in defending their interests and confronting unrepresentative governments. As they move out of villages into impersonal cities, they loosen the ties to families and small communities. Politics, social life, religion, culture and business are all transformed. But south-east Asia's industrial revolution has been much more rapid than those that went before in Europe, the US and Japan. The result is a delay of many years between the superficial changes – the arrival of television and mobile telephones – and the more profound shifts in the way people think about their families, their communities, their governments and their gods. South-east Asian leaders made a mistake. Instead of seeing this time lag for what it was, they interpreted the continuing weakness of their political opponents and the strength of social traditions as signs that Asia was different and that they would be spared the trauma of modernization.

It was an oversight they would later regret. But even after the collapse of confidence in the region's developing economies in 1997, there is plenty to boast about in the scale and extent of the south-east Asian 'miracle'. One country, the city state that is the island of Singapore, has completed the industrial revolution, in the sense that it has caught up with other industrialized nations and even started to overtake them. The average Singaporean is already richer than the average Briton. Singaporeans live in an efficient and highly computerized urban society, eat at expensive restaurants, buy expensive clothes and travel widely, just like their fellow consumers in Japan, the US or Italy.

In Vietnam, Laos, Cambodia and Burma, on the other hand, the revolution has hardly begun. Most people in these countries are still peasant farmers barely able to subsist on what they grow. But even here the trappings and habits of modern life – motorcycles, tarred roads, televisions, discotheques, tall buildings, toilets, shampoo, banks, advertising, passenger aircraft – are spreading fast. As recently as 1992, the Vietnamese capital Hanoi was a quiet town of elegant but dilapidated French villas where the swish of bicycle tyres was only occasionally drowned by the noise of an army truck; peasant women defecated openly on the pavements. There were no taxis and hardly any cars. The few simple restaurants that existed in what was then a typically dour, communist-run city rarely had names – they were known by their street numbers. Today, the city seethes with noisy activity; the streets are crowded with new motorcycles, cars and taxis, and they echo to the sound of construction as new hotels and office blocks spring up alongside bars and karaoke parlours. In northern Cambodia, far from the capital Phnom Penh, villagers watch videos at night on black and white televisions powered by twelve-volt car batteries which are recharged each day in the nearest town. In communist Laos, young women play cheap, hand-held computer games on the banks of the Mekong river.

Halfway up the ladder come Malaysia, Thailand, the Philippines and Indonesia. They have a large middle class of relatively wealthy, well-travelled and well-educated citizens living in the big cities; but also millions of poorer people, urban and rural, who are able to enjoy only some of the fruits of the continuing revolution. Malaysia, once known for its plantations of rubber and palm-oil trees, has become the world's biggest exporter of air conditioners; the world's tallest buildings, originally designed for Chicago, now tower over the capital Kuala Lumpur. In Thailand, nine tenths of the population live in homes with television; in the Bangkok metropolis, the figure is 97 per cent. If you visit one of the new shopping malls in Jakarta, the Indonesian capital, only the faces of the shoppers and the occasional sign in Bahasa Indonesia betray the fact that you are in Asia rather than Europe or America; there are 'cybercafés' serving refreshments and access to the Internet, McDonald's burger bars, cinemas showing Hollywood films and shops selling the same brand-name clothes you can find in Paris or New York.

The reasons behind south-east Asia's success – 'probably the most amazing and beneficent revolution in history', as one author called the whole east Asian experience[1] – are now generally agreed. Governments adopted sensible economic policies and promoted exports; most of them also provided a reasonably stable political environment which allowed growth to proceed unhindered; ordinary people worked hard and saved a high proportion of their earnings, permitting investment in education and in further industrial expansion; foreign countries helped too, principally by opening their markets to imports from south-east Asia (in the case of the US), and by investing heavily in industry (in the case of Japan). In the 1980s, the end of the Cold War – which had pitted 'pro-western' nations such as Thailand against the communist states of Indochina – provided an additional boost to the regional economy. South-east Asia's success was all the more remarkable because it was not foreseen, and because other parts of the world failed where south-east Asia appeared to have triumphed. Gunnar Myrdal, a Nobel Prize-winning Swedish economist, has become the butt of jokes among Asia experts as a result of his gloomy predictions about south-east Asia in a three-volume, 2,700-page book in the 1960s.[2] Another academic wrote in 1962 of the 'desperate, and in most cases to date, the losing race to achieve economic growth in the face of consistently mounting population pressure on already inadequate resources'; he also lamented the failure of south-east Asia's ruling elites to show 'any notable capacity to solve the problems involved' in modernizing politics and society.[3] Today, much of Africa is afflicted by war, poverty and disease. Latin America has only recently begun to recover from a long period of stagnation. The Middle East continues to struggle with political instability. Yet south-east Asian countries, after as many as thirty years of strong economic growth, have been extraordinarily successful and – until the crisis that began in 1997 – increasingly self-confident.

Their economic triumphs – preceded by the success of Japan, South Korea, Taiwan and Hong Kong and accompanied by that of China – led to a flurry of predictions about the rise of Asia and the relative decline of the West. The twenty-first century, it was argued, would be the 'Pacific Century'. Extrapolating recent economic growth rates far into the future, Asians and foreigners forecast – triumphantly, gloomily or with a shrug depending on their point of view – that such and such a group of Asian countries would overtake Europe or the US in the year 2025 or 2020 or 2015. The dangers of extrapolation are well known. In the 1950s the World Bank had made optimistic predictions about both Burma and the Philippines, because they seemed to have the best skills and resources for economic expansion, but they turned out to be among the worst performing south-east Asian economies. Likewise both assumptions on which the 'Pacific Century' calculation was based – that Asia would continue to grow and that the West was stagnating or declining – were doubtful; the US and Europe may do better than expected, and Asia may do worse. Two other important points were forgotten in the euphoria over Asia's performance. First, Asian economies were simply catching up the ground lost to the West in the previous two centuries – and it is easier and quicker to catch up than to take the lead. In 1820 Asia accounted for about 58 per cent of the world economy, a figure which fell steeply to 19 per cent in 1940 after the western industrial revolution before rising again to about 37 per cent in 1992. Even before the crisis of 1997 it was assumed that Asia's share of the global economy would reach 57 per cent only in the year 2025 – back where it was near the beginning of the industrial age. Second, some of Asia's economic growth has simply been the result of a temporary 'bulge' in the number of people of working age as a proportion of the total population – a typical quirk of modern industrial revolutions. Better healthcare and the fact that death rates fell quickly while birth rates initially remained high mean that there are now large numbers of Asians of working age supporting relatively few elderly dependants. This demographic 'gift' to the region's economies will eventually disappear as the 'bulge' moves up the age scale. It will then become a burden as birth rates decline, populations age, and the number of young people in work starts to fall as a proportion of a country's inhabitants.[4]

South-east Asia's political leaders, and many of the region's businessmen, had a completely different explanation for their success: it was, they said, the result of 'Asian values'. Chapter 1 looks at the rise of the 'Asian values' philosophy and why it is being discredited. According to its proponents, Asians are different from westerners in that they are hardworking and have a greater respect for education, family, community and government. The people of Singapore or Burma are thus more concerned about collective rights than individual rights and will therefore not necessarily demand the same things as westerners did at the various stages of economic development: free trade unions, liberal democracy, an independent judiciary, religious and sexual freedom and so on. Strong, even authoritarian governments – the argument goes – have meanwhile delivered both economic growth and political stability for the benefit of all. They should continue to do so unimpeded by meddling foreigners or domestic dissidents who want to impose alien values on Asians. The argument has struck a chord for some American and European politicians and business executives, who not only agree that it is right for Asia but believe that some of its tenets should be applied in western countries afflicted by chaotically inefficient democracy, violent crime and moral decay. But the 'Asian values' theory has been dismissed as nonsense by its critics in Asia and the West. They say it is merely an excuse for authoritarian governments to stay in power, depriving their subjects of rights which are not 'western' but universal. They also point out that it is bizarre suddenly to attribute south-east Asia's recent success to Asian culture, when for centuries western intellectuals put the opposite case: that Asia's economic backwardness was the fault of supposedly Asian cultural traits such as laziness and lack of enterprise. By 1997, support for the idea of attributing the region's success to 'Asian values' was in decline, eroded by economic and environmental disasters in southeast Asia and by growing evidence of a popular desire for democracy. Yet much damage had already been done. Blinded by pride in their new Asian identity, south-east Asian leaders had failed to prepare for the political, social and commercial crises about to erupt in front of them.

Political upheaval in the region, the subject of chapter 2, is proving to be as exciting and unsettling as the slow rise of liberal democracy in industrial Britain. Greater wealth has swollen the middle class in countries such as the Philippines and Thailand, and these well-educated people quickly lose patience with heavy-handed governments. The crowds of pro-democracy demonstrators in Bangkok who helped to bring down a military-led Thai government in 1992 (after a coup d'état the previous year) were notable for the number of young professionals – stockbrokers, lawyers, university professors – carrying mobile telephones. Five years later, that process led to the formulation of a new, more liberal constitution for Thailand. Granted, middle-class activism is not automatic. As long as governments are delivering stability and economic growth, the more prosperous citizens of countries such as Indonesia, Singapore and Malaysia will happily forgo political liberties while they enjoy the benefits of a modern consumer society. Indeed, they are frightened of losing what they have already gained. But such conservatism is fragile, because it depends on the belief that the existing regime is better for economic growth and political stability than any alternative. The systems of patronage binding politicians and businessmen are fragile too, because the deals on everything from road-building contracts to the allocation of cheap shares in privatized telephone companies are all built on the assumption of rapid and continued economic growth. What happens when the gravy train stops? In Indonesia, the urban elite, including ethnic Chinese business magnates and Indonesian yuppies, quietly supported President Suharto's leadership for decades while the economy expanded. But by the time south-east Asian financial markets crashed in 1997 they were understandably nervous about whether the economy could sustain the corruption, nepotism and cronyism to which Indonesia was particularly prone. In 1998 Suharto was ousted after pro-democracy demonstrations and outbreaks of looting in which hundreds of people were killed. Investors who had done deals with the president's children and friends began to regret their alliances with discredited people who only months before had been the most influential business contacts in Indonesia.

It is not only the middle classes who are pushing for change. The poor have benefited from the industrial revolution, but not nearly as much as the rich. Throughout south-east Asia, peasant farmers and the urban underclass have started to complain about the widening gap between them and their richer compatriots. In Thailand, hundreds of peasants camped repeatedly outside parliament in Bangkok in the 1990s demanding redress for a range of grievances: low crop prices, for example, and the government's failure to pay compensation for land submerged by reservoirs for hydro-electric dams. In Indonesia, people have staged demonstrations against the building of supermarkets; big new shops are said to be of use only to the rich and to put local traders and hawkers out of work. Such protests often take on disturbing religious or ethnic overtones, and there are plenty of real or imagined grievances for people to seize on as an excuse for violence. Most big businessmen in south-east Asia are ethnic Chinese, so it is usually the Chinese who build the supermarkets and suffer the consequences if shops are destroyed or looted. Rioters frequently burn down churches in Indonesia, too, identifying them with the minority Christians in a country where most people are Moslems. Neither the rural nor the urban poor feel they can hope to taste the fruits of industrialization that the rich – with their big cars, private schools, foreign travel, expensive night-life and mobile telephones – so ostentatiously relish. The situation is bearable when the economy is growing fast, unemployment is low and wages are rising faster than inflation – in other words when even the poor feel that this year is better than last. But the hitherto remarkable equanimity of the underclass could easily vanish in a real economic recession. (Until 1997 south-east Asia became so accustomed to rapid growth that 'recession' was loosely used in the region – it could mean annual growth of 5 per cent rather than an actual contraction of the economy.)

Another reason to expect political change is that a handover from one generation of leaders to the next is imminent. Those who experienced British, French or Dutch colonial rule and fought or campaigned for independence – such as Mahathir Mohamad of Malaysia, Lee Kuan Yew of Singapore, the elderly communists of Vietnam and Laos and ex-President Suharto of Indonesia – have sought to differentiate themselves from their former colonial masters. They inherited parliaments, courts and civil services (or, in the case of the communists, imported their models from the Soviet Union), but they moulded them to suit their own ambitions, suppressing dissent and arguing that strong government was essential for nation-building. Younger citizens, including the new generation of politicians, tend to be more liberal. From Burma in the west to Vietnam in the east, there was intense public interest in news of the South Korean trial of the former presidents Chun Doo-hwan and his successor Roh Tae-woo; the two generals, quintessential Asian authoritarians who pursued economic growth with ruthless determination, were condemned to death and prison respectively (though both were subsequently pardoned and released) for their corrupt and brutal rule of South Korea in the 1980s and early 1990s. The question asked in south-east Asia, sometimes openly, sometimes *sotto voce*, was: 'Will there not come a time when we can do the same in our country to bring our leaders to account and usher in a better society?'

All three of the forces for political change mentioned above – the rise of the middle class, the resentment of the poor and the arrival of a new generation of politicians – were as significant in previous industrial revolutions as they are in south-east Asia's. But there is a fourth phenomenon which is particularly relevant in the world of today: the speed with which information and ideas can be transmitted around the globe, even to the remotest corners of rural Burma or Borneo. It has become very difficult for governments, however dictatorial, to suppress news and views from abroad, as the trial of South Korea's former leaders showed. Burmese villagers listen to the BBC or Voice of America on their radios, learning not only about international affairs but also about events in their own country that the military authorities have chosen to suppress or distort. Indonesian students download information from the World Wide Web via telephone lines in Jakarta – that is, if they are not pursuing their studies at American or Australian universities. Thai accountants watch satellite television. Singaporean computer engineers can afford to travel abroad and get access to any information they please. Nevertheless most governments in south-east Asia (Thailand and the Philippines are the notable exceptions) do try to restrict what their citizens can see, hear and read. They win the occasional battle with the help of censorship or lawsuits, but they are slowly losing the information war. They are overwhelmed both by the supply of information and by the demand for it from their citizens as the cost of information technology falls and the sophistication of readers and viewers increases. Already people can watch live television discussions with all their unpredictable consequences, participate in free-for-all Internet debating forums and choose from an array of new magazines in English and vernacular languages covering every subject from fashion to foreign policy.

*   *   *

Introduction: A miracle that turned sour

The unprecedented speed of south-east Asia's industrial revolution has not just affected politics. It has had a dramatic – some would say devastating – effect on societies and cultures. Chapter 3 looks at how tastes, habits, languages, religious beliefs and more are being reshaped, leaving people bewildered, broken – and occasionally happy. Proponents of 'Asian values' argued that south-east Asia would be spared the criminality and family breakdowns that normally accompany the migration of millions of people from small villages to impersonal towns during industrial revolutions. The evidence suggests otherwise. Drug abuse is just one example of the modern ills that south-east Asian societies now have to face. Even authoritarian governments admit the region has a serious drugs problem. Not only does it produce much of the world's heroin – derived from the poppy fields of Burma and Laos and exported with the connivance of powerful businessmen and officials through Thailand, Cambodia and Vietnam – it has also become a big consumer of drugs. Teenagers sniff glue in the Lao capital Vientiane; truck drivers take amphetamines to keep themselves awake on the roads of Thailand; heroin addicts have multiplied in Malaysia and Vietnam, where the drug is sold at the base of Lenin's statue in central Hanoi; and the children of the new rich pop Ecstasy pills or snort cocaine in the discotheques of Bangkok and Jakarta. Alcoholism is a problem too, even among Moslems for whom alcohol is forbidden by the Koran. The reasons given for crime and drug-taking, and the tales of how each feeds on the other, rarely seem particularly 'Asian'. In fact they would be wearisomely familiar to newspaper readers in the US or Europe. Heroin addicts and 'street-children', the youngsters who beg, shine shoes or prostitute themselves to earn a living, speak of broken homes and the despair of those who are left out of the economic race. The richer kids who hang around shopping malls in Malaysia or race their motorcycles around the lakes in Hanoi complain about the ennui of modern city life and the inability of their parents to understand them. Concerned governments in Vietnam and Malaysia have mounted strident campaigns against 'social evils', but they have met with cynicism from their teenage targets, who fail to see why governments are more concerned about youthful misdemeanours than corruption in high places.

Not all social changes are the object of outright condemnation. Some are welcomed, others are merely controversial. The most visible aspects of the social revolution are the goods and services that people have started to consume. In the cities, they drink wine and eat take-away pizzas as well as local food and drink. Irish theme pubs have sprung up in Phnom Penh, Hanoi and Bangkok. People shop at 7–11 corner stores and in shopping malls ('I went malling', said one Filipina recently when asked what she had done at the weekend) as well as at market stalls. They watch soccer on television, and play golf in addition to badminton. They drive Toyotas and Volvos. They go to Michael Jackson concerts in Bangkok and listen to Hootie and the Blowfish in Jakarta. They watch dubbed or subtitled Hollywood movies. They work and live in concrete buildings indistinguishable from those in London, Frankfurt or Oklahoma, and inside them they use computers with software made by Microsoft. They sit on modern toilets manufactured by American Standard or its Japanese rivals. Even in the countryside, farmers drive Honda motorcycles and watch televisions made by Mitsubishi. It is true that each Asian market remains distinctive, that very few Asians watch television programmes in English, and that a truly global sense of culture lies far in the future: Thais do not become American just because they go to American fast food outlets, any more than the inhabitants of San Francisco adopt Thai habits after eating a Thai meal. Still, cultures are heavily influenced by the increasing contact between south-east Asia and the rest of the world. Languages absorb words from America just as they used to co-opt the Dutch, French and English vocabulary of the colonial powers. Modern south-east Asian music, architecture and fashion often draw on the traditions of both east and west.

Family relationships and attitudes to sex are changing too, although at a much slower pace than shopping habits. Loyalty to an extended family of cousins and in-laws is gradually giving way to the nuclear family of mother, father and children more typical of modern cities. Single men and women independent of spouses or parents are beginning to make an appearance on the radar screens of market research companies, even if most people continue to live with their parents until marriage. The anonymity of city life and the availability of contraceptives have removed most of the impediments to pre-marital and casual sex. For liberals, this is all good news. Young people enjoy more freedom and are no longer constrained by the old-fashioned customs of their ancestors. Women are less likely to be regarded as subordinate to men, and some are beginning to shine as bankers, businesswomen and politicians. Homosexuality is more widely accepted, too.

But there is a bad side to these new-found freedoms. The young feel insecure because they can no longer rely on numerous relatives to look after them, find them jobs or lend them money when times are hard. The old begin to worry that their offspring will not provide for them in old age (hence the Singaporean law of 1995 – the Maintenance of Parents Act – making it compulsory for children to support needy parents in old age). Divorce rates are rising in several countries in the region. Worse, there is evidence in Indonesia and elsewhere that young girls, amoral and materialistic, have begun to engage in casual prostitution with older men in order to buy the designer clothes they could not otherwise afford, a phenomenon previously noticed in Japan. Professional prostitution, meanwhile, continues to flourish in the region on a grand scale, while gigolos in Bali ply their trade with foreign women much as Tunisian men do at the beach resorts of North Africa. Some sociologists argue that what they call 'contractual sex' has always been an integral part of life in, say, Thailand and Vietnam.[5] Yet the increased mobility within and between countries that is the inevitable result of the industrial revolution has raised some new and disturbing issues. The disease AIDS is wreaking silent havoc in countries where both intravenous drug abuse and casual sex are common. Paedophiles from the West and from other Asian countries such as Taiwan have Cambodia, Thailand and the Philippines high on their list of destinations. Pornographic videos are widely distributed in Indochina. Rape is common. Such problems afflict other countries where half the population has moved from villages to cities. But the Asian leaders who have convinced themselves that these issues are 'western' in origin rather than simply modern are finding them particularly difficult to solve.

Rapid modernization is affecting people's spiritual lives as well as their personal relationships. Religion is the subject of two contradictory trends: on the one hand, religious observance often declines as the young loosen their ties to the traditions of their forefathers and spend their time on the two activities into which life is divided in the modern mind – work and leisure; on the other hand, people feel so insecure when they see the collapse of the customs which previously framed their lives that they seek the solid comfort of religious dogma and even of fundamentalism. Both trends are evident, sometimes in the same country or even the same family. Indonesians, for example, are struggling to explain the simultaneous increase of both decadence and religiosity among Moslems in Jakarta. Islam, Buddhism, Hinduism, Christianity and Taoism (ancestor worship) are the principal religions of south-east Asia, but they often thrive alongside – or in combination with – older forms of superstition and animism. In 1994 I stumbled on the sacrifice of a dog in an Akha hill-tribe village in northern Thailand. In all, a dog, two chickens and two pigs had been killed, and grains of rice and freshly cut leaves piled near the dog's bleeding corpse in the hot afternoon sun. It turned out to be a routine sacrifice. Some villagers in the community of Paka Sukjai had fallen sick, and they paid a spirit-man fifty-two baht (in those days about two US dollars) to perform a ceremony to cure them. Elsewhere in Thailand, the Thais, like the Romans of old and many pre-industrial civilizations the world over, believe in household gods; almost every home and office has a small 'spirit house' to which offerings of food and incense are made. People pray to statues of the Buddha in the hope of winning the lottery; and occasionally they pray for fertility at shrines of great wooden phalluses.

In terms of numbers, Islam is south-east Asia's dominant religion. It has long been asserted that Islam in Asia is 'milder' and less troublesome as a political force than it is in the Middle East, partly because many of Indonesia's millions of Javanese Moslems have a more mystical and less rigid interpretation of Islam than their co-religionists. Yet the religion does loom large in political calculations, posing as it does a dilemma for governments which see it both as an enemy of modernization and a friend of moral, non-western 'Asian values'. In Indonesia, Islamic separatists are confronting the government in Aceh in northern Sumatra, and Javanese Moslems regularly burn down Christian churches. Malaysia banned a fundamentalist Islamic sect called al-Arqam in 1994. Moslem guerrillas in southern Thailand and the southern Philippines, where they are minorities in predominantly Buddhist and Christian countries respectively, have fought sporadic battles against their rulers for years. The Indonesian and Malaysian governments – like their counterparts in the Middle East – have been forced to perform tricky balancing acts to defuse any Moslem opposition to their rule. They crack down hard on those they regard as extremists, but they also try to co-opt Moslems by making concessions and by appearing more religious themselves. As the ruling families and politicians of the Gulf states and Egypt have discovered, this can be a dangerous game. Once you have introduced a law that satisfies devout Moslems, it is very difficult to repeal or relax it without being condemned as an irreligious backslider. There is no question that Islam is the religion that has the most difficulty accepting the social and economic changes that appear to accompany every modern industrial revolution. But Malaysians such as Anwar Ibrahim, the former deputy prime minister who was an Islamic firebrand in his youth, are convinced that they can forge a society that is simultaneously Moslem, democratic and technologically advanced[6]. If they succeed, they believe they could become a model for other Islamic countries, which find themselves in a state of turmoil and decline 1,000 years after the time when they were at the forefront of science and civilization.

Even when south-east Asians agree on the need for a moral compass, however, there is no agreement on which way it should point. Like Europeans and Americans, Asians are tempted by the trivial, the sensational and the material. But the same governments which rail against the West for infecting Asia with liberalism and decadence are accused by their fiercest domestic opponents of being too 'western' themselves. Particularly among the region's intellectuals, there is mounting disgust with the crude materialism of south-east Asia's political leaders and their often boorish business associates. What was the point of all those magnificent economic growth statistics if the quality of life is not improved, if the poor simply swap rural misery for its urban equivalent, if the rich are stuck in traffic jams in their BMWs, if the great new cities of Asia are ugly and polluted, and if art and language are bastardized by quasi-American global culture? As in the Victorian England of Charles Dickens, there is a nostalgia for good things lost and a fear of recently created evils – as well as pride in the new prosperity and power.

The 'Asian values' argument is thus being turned against its creators. South-east Asian political leaders, their critics say, are guilty of taking the worst aspects of westernization and industrialization (materialism and consumerism) while ignoring the best (political reform, social idealism and philanthropy); at the same time they are keeping the worst aspects of the old order (authoritarianism and institutionalized corruption) while abandoning the best (the village sense of community, harmony with nature and traditional artistic sensibilities). Politicians are sensitive to such criticisms. Singapore's leaders speak openly of the need to file down the rough edges of the coarsely materialistic *nouveaux riches*. They mount campaigns to promote the arts, protect the environment and encourage good table manners. The region's poorer inhabitants, meanwhile, have their appetite for unaffordable consumer goods whetted by advertising and by the lifestyles portrayed in television soap operas. Parents in the hills of northern Thailand still sell their children for cash to brokers who send them into prostitution in the big cities. Moralizing does not suit south-east Asia's leaders or its elders. When teenagers are criticized by their governments or their parents for their taste in music or their lax morals, they are able to point out bitterly that many of the politicians and entrepreneurs who should be their role models are at best amoral and opportunist and at worst drug-traffickers and gangsters.

The extraordinary influence of big business in the running of south-east Asia in the past three decades is examined in chapter 4. Close connections between unscrupulous businessmen and governments are not unprecedented at times of headlong economic growth: Britain and America also had their capitalist 'robber barons' in the heyday of industrialization, and they and their descendants were soon cloaked with respectability. Indonesian, Malaysian and Thai tycoons – starting with the sale of agricultural commodities such as rice and tapioca, moving through the manufacture of industrial products such as cars and computers and on to services such as retailing and airlines – have never been afraid to use the money they make to buy political influence and a comfortable place in high society. They make alliances with army generals and presidents' children; indeed, sometimes they *are* army generals and presidents' children. They have been involved in everything from drug-trafficking and illegal logging to lucrative and corrupt infrastructure projects for roads and telephone lines. In the early days, the businessmen can be openly thuggish, as they were in Cambodia in the early 1990s. But before long the drug barons and gangsters are dressed in Savile Row suits, their children are educated overseas, the family business is engaged in banking and finance and the past is all but forgotten.

The fate of business in south-east Asia is inseparable from the fate of the various ethnic Chinese communities which dominate trade and industry. Although some of the Chinese in south-east Asia suffered grievously at the hands of the invading Japanese during the Second World War, they quickly re-established themselves after the war and soon occupied the commercial territory abandoned by the departing colonial powers. Chinese minorities run the biggest conglomerates in Indonesia, the smallest shops in Cambodia and much in between. Needless to say, they are often resented. If they invest too much of their profits in their home markets, they are accused of dominating local business; if they invest overseas, in mainland China for example, they are accused of disloyalty to their adopted country. In Indonesia, where tens of thousands of Chinese were murdered in anti-communist massacres in the mid-1960s, some of the wealthiest Chinese businessmen threw in their lot with Suharto and his relatives. This ensured favourable treatment for a time, but leaves them vulnerable now that Suharto has been forced out of the presidency. The Malaysian government, alarmed by clashes between Chinese and Malays which left scores of people dead after an election in 1969, adopted a deliberate policy of favouritism called the New Economic Policy designed to transfer wealth, opportunity and skills to Malays; in Malaysia, it is the Chinese who feel resentment, although even Malays think the discriminatory policies may have outlived their usefulness. Thailand has taken a different approach, slowly assimilating the Chinese over hundreds of years to the extent that many of them think of themselves as Thai. In the Philippines, the ethnic Chinese share the upper reaches of society with another elite – the professionals and business families of Spanish descent.

However much the 'indigenous' – or, more accurately, non-Chinese – peoples of south-east Asia succeed in improving themselves, ethnic Chinese business will remain crucial for economic progress in the foreseeable future. But businesses will need to change fast if south-east Asia is to resume the spectacular economic growth of earlier years. That is because many of them are old-fashioned organizations. They can make money at the early stages of an industrial revolution, when they are able to exploit unregulated markets in natural resources and cheap labour, create domestic monopolies and make products for the local market behind a protective barrier of high import duties. But they are ill equipped for genuine competition in the modern global economy. Frequently they are centralized, family-run businesses that have made money the easy way, initially using government connections to win road-building or other infrastructure contracts or to gain logging concessions in virgin forests, before graduating to joint ventures or franchise agreements with foreign companies from car manufacturers to pizza parlour managers (the foreign companies provide the technical expertise and the local companies contribute their political influence and local knowledge). Finally, they buy land and become property speculators and developers. In spite of all the praise heaped on south-east Asian economies for their liberal economic policies and their successful penetration of export markets, many of the region's own markets remain protected in reality if not by law. Foreigners cannot just buy a house in Thailand or set up a bank in Singapore or sell noodles in Indonesia, although the recent economic upheaval and the need for foreign capital has forced several countries to liberalize protectionist regulations.

The limitations of rough and ready pre-modern capitalism are quickly becoming apparent. Investments made by south-east Asian companies in the more competitive markets of Europe and America often run into trouble. But such failures have been dwarfed by the problems at home. The currency and stock market crisis which affected Thailand, Indonesia and Malaysia in particular in 1997 and 1998 showed that these economies, and many of the businesses in them, were managed by people who were too complacent, over-dependent on short-term borrowings and more reliant than they should have been on government largesse. Fortunately for south-east Asia, a new generation of entrepreneurs is eager to meet the challenge. Many of them are the sons of old-fashioned capitalists, but they are often educated at universities and business schools in the US or elsewhere in the West. They have learned modern management methods and they know that south-east Asia is quickly losing the advantage of cheap labour as wages increase; they are starting to believe in creativity and innovation, backed by higher spending on research and development, instead of copying something done elsewhere and trying to do it cheaper; and they know that trade liberalization in the region and internationally will expose their businesses to more competition than ever.

One of the depressing results of industrialization, population growth and the success of businesses greedy for growth has been the destruction of the natural environment, the subject of chapter 5. Such damage is by no means unique to south-east Asia, but the speed and scale of the abuse since the 1960s is unparalleled. Governments insist, in spite of evidence to the contrary, that it is cheaper to get rich first and use the money to repair the environmental damage later. And they suggest – or at least Mahathir Mohamad of Malaysia does – that foreign environmentalists are motivated by foolish sentimentalism or by a protectionist desire to weaken Asia's economies. But the situation is so severe that even unsentimental locals are starting to take notice. Filthy, noisy and congested metropolitan cities such as Manila, Jakarta and Bangkok have become nightmarish for the poor and difficult even for the rich. Countryside that was once lush and green has become scarred and barren.

The damage is done in many ways. Population growth and indiscriminate tree-felling have shrunk south-east Asia's forests to a fraction of their former size. Malaysia, Indonesia and Thailand complain that they are not given recognition for having set aside vast areas of their territory as national parks. It is true that such legally protected areas are much larger than those in most developed countries. But legal protection does not always mean real protection. In Cambodian national parks, soldiers with chainsaws can be seen today happily cutting down trees. Some of Thailand's 'forest areas' are actually devoid of trees. In Indonesian and Malaysian Borneo logging continues on such a large scale that even government officials admit it is unsustainable. With the Philippines, Thailand and Vietnam already devastated, Asian logging companies have moved on to Cambodia, Laos and Burma or further afield to South America, where their rapacity is as controversial as it is at home.

Wild animals have had their habitats destroyed, and the survivors are hunted down so that their body parts can be incorporated into Chinese medicines and aphrodisiacs. The tiger became a symbol of the economic strength of east Asia, but these 'tiger economies' have few real tigers left. Likewise, the elephant has long been associated with the traditions of Burma, Thailand, Laos and Cambodia, but wild elephants are increasingly rare. There is little sentimentality about the loss of wild creatures which kill farm animals and damage crops, any more than Europeans mourned the disappearance of wolves and bears. Nor is there much concern about 'biodiversity'. But millions of people suffer too: deforestation has contributed to soil erosion, landslides, droughts and devastating floods. The sea has fared no better than the land. Fishermen, like their counterparts in Europe and North America, have overfished their waters. They poach in their neighbours' fishing grounds, prompting armed clashes and frequent seizures of fishing boats – and arrests of fishermen – by the governments concerned. The coastal mangrove forests where fish and shrimp once bred have been uprooted by property developers and commercial prawn farmers, while coral reefs are killed by sewage or blown apart by fishermen using dynamite to catch the few remaining fish.

Neither the depredation of land and sea nor the pollution typical of the early stages of industrialization have received much attention from wealthy city-dwellers. They are much more concerned with the critical state of their cities. The air is thick with dust and toxic gases generated by the trucks, cars, factories and building sites that are the accompaniments to economic success; pedestrians in Manila or Bangkok vainly hold handkerchiefs to their noses and mouths to try to filter out the filth. To call rivers and canals polluted is an understatement; they are black and empty of life. Drivers sit for so long in traffic jams that some have bought portable toilets and office equipment for their cars. Elegant old buildings are torn down and green spaces paved over to make way for unremarkable office blocks and apartment buildings. The urban rich react to this assault in the time-honoured way – by moving out to the suburbs.

A backlash against environmental destruction has begun, although there is still more talk than action. Pressure groups have appeared. Businesses declare their green intentions. Governments have set up environment ministries. Politicians campaign, and sometimes win elections, by espousing green issues. And although most of the region's big cities remain dirty, noisy and ugly, the most economically advanced – Singapore – has cleaned up its principal river, resurrected old buildings and started to boast of its green credentials. Some economists and environmentalists have calculated that a substantial proportion of south-east Asia's impressive economic growth in the past three decades can be attributed to a one-off fire-sale of natural resources, which means that it may be harder for economies to grow so fast when the trees, the fish and the soil are all depleted. For the individual Indonesian or Thai citizen there are more personal concerns. They remember fishing in a river or drinking from a stream as a child. They see its poisonous waters today and regret what they have lost.

Wealth has not only made south-east Asia dirtier. It has also made it more powerful. Chapter 6 looks at the uncertain state of regional security after the end of the Cold War. Several countries have bought weapons from the US, Europe and Russia, including American F-16 and Russian MiG-29 jet aircraft; Indonesia bought most of the old East German navy. There has been talk in academic journals and the media of 'a regional arms race'. But the Association of South East Asian Nations (Asean) is striving to present a united front to the world. It has quickly embraced Burma and the former communist states of Vietnam and Laos and is expected to incorporate Cambodia shortly to bring its final complement to ten. Asean, founded by five countries in Bangkok in 1967, is a motley collection of rich countries, poor countries, liberal democracies, not-so-liberal democracies, communist states, a military junta and a sultanate, and it has begun to exert its influence on everything from world trade negotiations to security policy. In 1993, it founded the Asean Regional Forum to bring together all the countries concerned with maintaining peace in Asia, including China, Russia and the US.

A prominent part of the Asean agenda hitherto has been to promote the so-called 'Asian value' of consensus. In foreign relations, this approach means compromise rather than confrontation. But the agenda is starting to look dangerously out of date. Consensus is not easy to reach with an increasingly assertive China which, like Asean, is translating its new-found economic muscle into increased military might. In the past few years China has made repeated naval incursions into Vietnamese offshore oil exploration zones (and it invaded Vietnam by land as recently as 1979); it has also occupied disputed atolls of the Spratly Islands off the Philippines, again in pursuit of its claim to almost the whole of the South China Sea; and it has alarmed Asean members such as Thailand and Singapore, as well as India, by developing close military and commercial ties with the Burmese junta. Asean was forced to confront the Chinese over the South China Sea incursions with un-Asean directness: they told the Chinese to stop. Asean members, especially the vulnerable island of Singapore, have had to acknowledge their continuing dependence on the security umbrella provided by the US, however unpalatable American views on democracy may be.

Asean has also espoused the 'Asian value' of communal (as opposed to individual) rights. It has rejected western complaints about human rights abuses or environmental damage on the grounds that political stability and economic growth for all are more important to developing Asian countries than the complaints of a few dissidents. But the populations of the Asean countries become more sophisticated with every year that passes, and younger Asians can no longer be relied upon to accept their governments' definitions of right and wrong. Siding with Burma's notorious military junta against the West in the interests of Asean solidarity is enough to test the diplomatic skills of even the most hardened adherent of 'Asian values'. Asean thus risks being seen as a complacent clique of governments whose main aim is to keep themselves in power, a sort of 'regime survival club'. Meanwhile, there are plenty of real dangers for the organization and its member states to avert if they want to proceed smoothly down the path of modernization. There are the problems on the fringes of Asean – the stand-off between North and South Korea, the assertiveness of China, the dependence of the whole area on oil and gas imported from the Middle East – as well as conflicts within it over secession movements, drug-trafficking, border disputes, piracy at sea, and the over-exploitation of natural resources. The south-east Asian states are quickly discovering that wealth and power do not merely confer the right to push forward one's own views; the powerful must also share the burden of keeping the peace.

Chapter 7 looks at the ten countries in turn and analyses the part played by each in the modernization of politics and society. Like central America or southern Africa, south-east Asia sees itself, and is increasingly seen by others, as a distinct region. But it contains an exceptionally wide variety of races, religions, colonial experiences and styles of economic development. Each country is affected by the industrial revolution in different ways.

* * *

Modernization and the prosperity that comes with it, chapter 8 concludes, have nevertheless made life better for the overwhelming majority of south-east Asia's 500 million people. Some have yet to benefit, a few are worse off than before, but many have moved from a hand-to-mouth existence in the countryside to the financial security of paid employment in the towns. South-east Asia today is no longer simply a place of golden temples and rice-farmers in emerald-green paddy fields. Those images are slowly being replaced by the modern reality of factories and city streets. Asian nations are becoming part of the industrialized world. To have this happen in one country is an achievement; to have it happen in ten neighbouring countries simultaneously is nothing less than extraordinary. But there is a long way to go. Some governments have convinced themselves that Asian political violence and social decay exist only in the imagination of jealous western observers, but they are wrong. More and more Asians recognize that there are big obstacles to overcome if the next twenty years are to be as successful as the last twenty. The biggest mistakes their leaders made in the 1990s were to try to suppress the popular urge for political and social change while boasting about their economic achievements in a mood of premature triumph.

ONE

The rise and fall of 'Asian values'

Datuk Seri Dr Mahathir Mohamad has asked Malaysians not to accept western-style democracy as it could result in negative effects. The prime minister said such an extreme principle had caused moral decay, homosexual activities, single parents and economic slowdown because of poor work ethics.

– Voice of Malaysia radio, 29 May 1993.

Some people have the illusion that things are different in Asia because the spirit of feudalism still prevails and peasants are politically inactive. This is not true. Asians and Vietnamese are changing. They are desperate for democracy, freedom and development. Nothing can restrain them any longer and it is only a matter of time before the situation erupts. The political stability which appears to exist in Vietnam at the moment is a fake.

– Bui Tin, a former Vietnamese army officer and self-exiled dissident.[1]

For centuries, Europeans regarded Asia with a mixture of horror and jealous fascination. Schooled since the Enlightenment of the eighteenth century to believe in the power of reason and discipline, Europeans saw Asia as exotic, irrational, unreliable and decadent. To them, Asia was a world of cruelty and sensuality, of despots and harems. The real Asia was often submerged in the European mind by the fears and feverish imaginings of the Europeans themselves. These delusions later became known collectively as 'Orientalism' – a word used to describe the western habit of simultaneously glamorizing and demonizing the east.[2] This is not to deny that the countries of Asia were very different from those of post-Enlightenment Europe, both socially and politically. Asians themselves – whether in power or in opposition – often sought to modernize their societies by emulating the commercial, administrative and social practices of the colonial powers with which they came into contact; King Chulalongkorn of Thailand, for example, is credited with turning his country into a modern bureaucratic state, complete with railways, roads and canals, during his rule from 1868 to 1910.

But in the 1980s and 1990s Asian leaders, especially in south-east Asia, decided to turn the tables on the West. Independence from the European powers had been won three decades before, and had been followed by a period of rapid economic growth in much of east Asia. Men like Mahathir Mohamad of Malaysia and Lee Kuan Yew of Singapore declared that Asia was indeed different from the West. But this time it was the *Asians* who were disciplined, hardworking and moral, while the West was a place of unreason – a morass of crime, decadence and loose sexual habits. By the early 1990s a lively debate was under way in east Asia and among politicians and academics in the US and Europe.[3]

Supporters of the concept of 'Asian values' argued that east Asians, although ethnically diverse, shared certain core beliefs. They were loyal to their families and communities, whereas westerners were obsessed with the rights of individuals to the extent that their societies were starting to fall apart. Lee Kuan Yew, the architect of modern Singapore, its prime minister from 1959 to 1990 and now with the title of senior minister, told an interviewer in 1994 that he liked the informality and openness of American society. 'But as a total system, I find parts of it totally unacceptable: guns, drugs, violent crime, vagrancy, unbecoming behaviour in public – in sum the breakdown of civil society,' he said. 'The expansion of the right of the individual to behave or misbehave as he pleases has come at the expense of orderly society. In the East the main object is to have a well-ordered society so that everybody can have maximum enjoyment of his freedoms. This freedom can only exist in an ordered state and not in a natural state of contention and anarchy.'[4]

The philosophy of 'Asian values', developed principally in Singapore and Malaysia, is much more than a set of abstruse social theories. From Burma to China and beyond, it has a direct bearing on everything from attitudes towards human rights abuses and film censorship to international trade negotiations and deforestation.

After three decades of political stability and extraordinarily rapid economic expansion, some of Asia's leaders feel that they have earned the right to run their countries according to their own rules. They have had enough of being lectured on how to run their political systems, look after the rights of their factory workers and protect their tigers and elephants by former colonial powers such as England and France, and by a United States made arrogant by its victory over communism in the Cold War. The coming century, they believe, will be the 'Pacific Century' – an era in which confident Asians will finally be able to discard the western baggage left behind by the colonial era.

Such emotions are most deeply felt by the older generation of leaders who remember colonial rule and who still hold sway in much of the region. Mahathir, the septuagenarian Malaysian prime minister who has led the country since 1981, has courted Japan in his efforts to advance the cause of 'Asian values', both because of Japan's present influence as an economic superpower and because of its historical role in sweeping aside the colonial powers in south-east Asia during the Second World War. Although the British, the French and the Dutch returned after Japan's defeat in 1945, the mystique of the all-powerful European was shattered for ever, and they soon departed again, leaving behind the newly independent countries of Asia.[5] The forthright Mahathir has found favour in Japan by urging the Japanese to stop apologizing for the war and to take pride in the resurgent Asia of the late twentieth century. In 1995 he co-authored *The Asia that can say No: a Card against the West* with the right-wing Japanese politician Shintaro Ishihara, and in it he laid out the basic tenets of the new Asian philosophy: the West is suffering from 'moral degeneration' and hedonism in the form of incest, cohabitation, sensual gratification, avarice and lack of respect for family or religion; Asia is in the ascendant economically and morally; and the jealous West is therefore trying to stifle Asia's growth. 'Fearing that one day they will have to face Asian countries as competitors, some western nations are doing their utmost to keep us at bay,' he wrote. 'They constantly wag accusing fingers in Asia's direction, claiming that it has benefited from unacceptable practices, such as denial of human rights and workers' rights, undemocratic government, and disregard for the environment.' For Mahathir, Asian values were not just different, they were better. The West 'should

27

accept our values, not the other way round'. Ishihara joined in with enthusiasm along similarly anti-western and anti-liberal lines. Among other declarations, he made the controversial assertion that westerners sought depraved sex and child sex in south-east Asia while Japanese visitors just wanted normal sex with prostitutes. More significantly, he aired the idea of 'a new economic co-prosperity sphere' for Asia, echoing the wartime Japanese concept of the 'Greater East Asia Co-Prosperity Sphere' which justified Japan's invasion of other Asian lands.[6]

All this harked back to Japanese Second World War propaganda about undesirable Anglo-American values – individualism, liberalism, democracy, hedonism and materialism – that should not be allowed to pollute the pure spirit of Japan.[7] But the memories of Japanese atrocities against both prisoners-of-war and civilians meant that a new 'Asian Way' so closely associated with Japan was never going to be popular in south-east Asia, let alone China. Mahathir said the Japanese troops in Malaya had done nothing 'improper', but other Asians of his generation – including Filipinos and Chinese – remember all too well the gruesome massacres, rapes, torture and other atrocities committed by Japanese troops. Lee Kuan Yew has repeatedly mentioned the dark days of the Japanese occupation of Singapore and used it to warn his people of the need for constant vigilance. The idea of an 'Asian Way' for the 1990s with Japan taking the lead was further impeded by the reluctance of Japanese politicians more cautious than the swashbuckling Ishihara to antagonize their American allies.

Another way for east Asian leaders to cement 'Asian values' into a coherent philosophy was to summon the help of Confucius. The Chinese sage, who lived 2,500 years ago and whose thoughts on government and morality are recorded in *The Analects*, at first seemed ideally suited to the task of uniting east Asians behind a common value-system. Like modern east Asians, he revered the power of education and preached filial piety. As early as 1977, the University of Singapore hosted a symposium on Asian Values and Modernization. Academics bemoaned the rise of juvenile delinquency and the increasing divorce rate and suggested that western values should be inspected – as if by customs officials – before being imported. They discussed the need to build an ethos based on supposedly Asian values such as 'group solidarity', 'community life' and the belief in extended families.[8] By 1983, Singapore had established the Institute of East Asian Philosophies. Sponsored by Lee's ruling People's Action Party, it was designed to revive Confucianism and adapt it to modern life, and was explicitly aimed at countering the westernization of Singaporeans. A new theory of government based on harmony and consensus was outlined: debate and criticism would not take place in public but among members of the government behind closed doors. As one western academic put it in 1996, in Indonesia and Singapore 'consensus means conformity with the wishes of the regime'.[9]

The appeal of Confucian conservatism is understandable, particularly in societies with pre-existing Confucian traditions such as Vietnam and among the minority ethnic Chinese communities widely spread throughout south-east Asia. At a time of tumultuous social and political change, Confucianism seems to offer clear guidelines for maintaining civilized values. 'Criminality is on the rise, opium and drugs are on the rise too and morality is in decline – such things as would make the hair of the ancestors stand on end,' says Huu Ngoc, a Vietnamese writer living in the capital Hanoi. For him, the chaos caused by modernization is damaging a community spirit based on the co-operative cultivation of rice – a spirit which he sees as spreading out in concentric circles from family to village to nation. The result, he says, is that 'Confucianism – which is the basis for this community solidarity of family, village and state – is breached.'[10]

By the late 1990s, however, it was clear that Confucianism was an unsuitable glue for holding east Asians together in the name of 'Asian values'. There were three main reasons for this. First, the non-Chinese who form the majority of south-east Asians could not identify with an essentially Chinese philosophy; just as Singaporeans found it impossible to espouse an 'Asian Way' linked to Japanese wartime imperialism, so Malays and Indonesians – who sometimes fear China as an external power and resent the Chinese communities in their midst – were unable to accept one so explicitly connected to China.

Second, it emerged that Confucianism was an exceptionally weak card for Asians to play against the West in order to proclaim Asian supremacy. This was because both western and Asian thinkers had for a century or more been blaming traditional Confucian values, with their rigid respect for hierarchy and disdain of commerce, for the *failure* of Asia to make economic progress following the European industrial revolutions. It was absurd for Asian leaders suddenly to attribute their success to Confucius when it had long been argued that he was one of the causes of Asia's relative economic decline in the previous 1,000 years. For Max Weber, the nineteenth- and early twentieth-century German sociologist, Asian values were inimical to economic success because they discouraged innovation and competition; it was the northern Europeans, with their 'Protestant Ethic', who were succeeding. Kishore Mahbubani, permanent secretary at the Singapore Ministry of Foreign Affairs and one of the most forceful proponents of Asian values, is convinced that the region fell behind because Asian minds became 'ossified'. 'After centuries of inertia resulting from oppressive feudal rule,' Mahbubani wrote, 'the work ethic is coming back in full force in most East Asian societies.'[11]

The third, and perhaps most important, reason why Confucius was confined to the sidelines is that a close reading of Confucian texts reveals a philosophy not quite as politically convenient for present-day south-east Asian leaders as previously thought. It was not merely his dismissal of women, his snobbish disdain for manual labour or his anti-commercial instincts; neo-Confucianists had in any case embraced business from the sixteenth century. It was much worse. Although it was true that Confucius and his followers, such as Mencius, encouraged respect for authority, it turned out that they also insisted on good government and social justice and sometimes accepted the need for subjects to rebel against unjust rulers. Confucianism quickly became less popular with several east Asian governments.

But some of south-east Asia's rulers still felt the need to unite their peoples behind a common set of 'Asian values', partly to promote stability in their own multi-ethnic region and partly to confront outsiders with a coherent philosophy that explains their actions and arguments when they are engaged in international negotiations. In 1993, Tommy Koh, a senior Singapore diplomat, outlined ten basic 'Asian values' in 1993 that still hold good for adherents to the 'Asian Way' today. They are: an absence of extreme individualism; a belief in strong families; a reverence for education; frugality; hard work; 'national teamwork' between unions and employers; an Asian 'social contract' between people and the state, whereby governments provide law and order and citizens behave well in return; a belief in citizens as 'stakeholders', for example through home-ownership –

this only applied to some Asian countries; moral wholesomeness; and a free but responsible press. 'Taken together,' Koh wrote, 'these ten values form a framework that has enabled societies in East Asia to achieve economic prosperity, progress, harmonious relations between citizens and law and order.'[12]

It is perhaps not surprising that many south-east Asian leaders should believe in a set of values that simultaneously justifies their own forms of government and suggests that they are culturally different from – if not superior to – westerners. What is remarkable is how many westerners agree. In a book urging European businesses to become more involved in the then fast-growing markets of south-east Asia, Corrado Letta, an Italian business consultant, drew up a table comparing 'cultural values' in Europe and Asia. Europeans were characterized by 'reluctance to learn', Asians by 'willingness to learn/ respect for learning'; Europeans had 'complacency', while Asians had 'creativity'; Europeans liked 'taking it easy', whereas Asians preferred 'hard work'; Europe was full of 'doom and gloom', but Asia enjoyed 'booming confidence'; and so on.[13] Letta is not alone. It is common to hear both westerners and Asians declare that Asians are more hardworking than Africans; more concerned about losing 'face' than Americans; or more gentle than Europeans. 'Asians,' wrote one western commentator bluntly, 'believe in consensus.'[14] This is about as meaningful as the nineteenth-century Orientalist generalization that Asians enjoy cruelty, and most such hard-and-fast cultural distinctions can be dismissed as neo-Orientalist.[15]

A more realistic view is that the people of south-east Asia – because they have only recently undergone or are still undergoing their rapid industrial revolutions – still retain some of the values of an earlier, pre-industrial age. Like many Asians today, Europeans and Americans used to live in extended families, work hard, show respect for their elders and live by stern moral codes. Western politicians often play to ordinary people's nostalgia about this aspect of their past, and declare that there is much westerners can learn from those Asian societies which appear to be both prosperous (in a modern way) and law-abiding (in an old-fashioned way). This is why Margaret Thatcher was enthusiastic about 'Victorian values' and why Tony Blair, within weeks of becoming prime minister, invited Lee Kuan Yew to his office at Downing Street in London to discuss such matters as welfare reform and education. It is also why it was – in political terms, at least – so ill-advised of President Bill Clinton to take up his human rights cudgels on behalf of Michael Fay, an eighteen-year-old American sentenced in Singapore in 1994 to be flogged with a rattan cane for various acts of vandalism, including spray-painting cars. US administration officials and several American newspaper columnists expressed outrage at the punishment, which can leave permanent scars. But many ordinary Americans, fed up with crime in their own country, thought Singapore was taking the right approach and told the Singaporeans – in the words of at least one caller to a US radio phone-in programme – to 'whip his butt'. The Michael Fay affair played straight into the hands of Asian leaders who reject the idea that the US has anything to teach them about human rights. Lee Kuan Yew responded to US criticism by saying that America might be rich but it was also chaotic, and neither safe nor peaceful. 'If you like it that way, that is your problem,' he said. 'But that is not the path we choose. They always talk about human rights. I think it is just a convenient slogan.'[16]

But only the most stubborn defenders of 'Asian values' would argue that they are immutable. Brigadier-General Lee Hsien Loong, Singapore's deputy prime minister and the son of Lee Kuan Yew, commented recently on the failure of western policies on welfare and crime and the spread of social problems to countries such as Taiwan, and said: 'If we do not watch the way we go we could become like the West.' He said Chinese, Malays and Indians (the three main ethnic groups in Singapore) did have a different 'world view' from westerners. But when asked whether values could not change dramatically from generation to generation as they do in the West, he replied: 'The answer is we don't know. They are not unchanging. They will evolve, but if we can't preserve the essence of them into the next generation then we think we are finished.'[17]

In the eyes of certain Asian leaders, 'Asian values' are not immutable but have a cultural basis – representing a different world view – and are worth defending in the name of social cohesion. Some of the ten values listed by Tommy Koh are unremarkable, and are accepted as good whether or not they are actually adopted in the rest of the world as well: frugality and hard work, for example. Others are more controversial. They suggest curbing the rights of the individual in the interests of society as a whole; they hint at tame trade unions and an uncritical press; and they support the idea of strong government. These are not just theories. They are put into practice by the authoritarian governments of south-east Asia. In Indonesia, Singapore, Malaysia, Vietnam and Burma, independent trade unions and newspapers have been restricted, tamed or banned. Political systems are designed and controlled so that opposition parties can exist to preserve the image of democracy but not actually take power. Few of the region's governments are embarrassed when challenged on these points. On the contrary, they cite 'Asian values' to support restrictions on individual freedoms. Economic growth and political stability, which benefit all citizens, take priority over failed 'western' concepts of individual rights, they say, especially during the early stages of industrialization when a smaller proportion of the population is educated sufficiently to take on the responsibility of voting. They also compare Russia to China, condemning Russian governments since the collapse of communism for causing chaos and poverty by democratizing politics before liberalizing the economy, and praising China for embarking on economic reform while maintaining firm political control. This kind of analysis often finds favour outside Asia as well. The corruption and poverty of African countries following independence from the colonial powers were held up by African authoritarians, and their supporters in the West, as reasons not to impose western-style democratic institutions on alien cultures where people are supposedly 'not ready' for democracy.

However, just as it is easy to find Europeans or Americans who sympathize with the concept of 'Asian values' because they bemoan the problems in their own societies, it is notable that there are plenty of Asians who bitterly oppose the whole idea. For these people, the 'Asian Way' is an elaborate fraud which does not stand up to serious analysis and whose main purpose is to provide authoritarian governments with a rationale for staying in power indefinitely. In south-east Asia, it is the leaders of Malaysia and Singapore who have talked loudest about 'Asian values'. Others, including the governments of Burma and Vietnam and individual politicians and businessmen throughout south-east Asia, have followed suit with varying degrees of enthusiasm. But in the Philippines and Thailand – the two most democratic countries in the region – many influential people scoff at 'Asian values' and the people who espouse them.

The Philippines, which was one of the most advanced Asian economies after the Second World War, is the favourite target of authoritarians;

they say it has lagged behind its neighbours and fallen prey to poverty and crime largely because of the government's inability to take hard decisions – to raise fuel prices, for example, or enforce tax collection – in a US-style democracy notable for bickering, lobbying and countless legal challenges. Unlike the orderly streets of Singapore, those of Manila are congested by overloaded and unroadworthy vehicles belching black smoke. Instead of Singapore's neat, high-rise housing estates, filthy slums sprawl around the city and its garbage dumps. Law and order scarcely exist: patrons of bars and restaurants are urged by signs to leave their 'deadly weapons' at the front desk, and policemen have been among those implicated in the frequent kidnappings of ethnic Chinese businessmen and their relatives. Perhaps it is not surprising that Alfredo Lim, the mayor of central Manila who cracked down on drug-dealers and cleared Manila's streets of overt prostitution and go-go bars (they moved to another district of the Manila metropolis), is an admirer of Lee Kuan Yew.[18] George Yeo, Singapore's Minister for Information and the Arts, uses the Philippines as a salutary example of how things can go wrong without strong government to 'keep the body politic whole'. He said:

> Look at the Philippines – a few decades of mismanagement and what happens? Their womenfolk are being sent to the Middle East, to Hong Kong, to Singapore, to Malaysia. They become domestic maids – highly educated, very intelligent people – why? Because their own country, their own economy, cannot make use of the value they are able to add to the whole economy so they end up choosing other jurisdictions. It's an absurd situation. I think all of us see that, all of us do not want to be like the Philippines of a few years ago. And they [were like this] despite the fact that after the war they were the most educated, the most literate, the best founded of any of the nation states newly independent in south-east Asia.[19]

Filipino democrats cannot dispute the facts. The Philippines has been badly mismanaged and its people do suffer the humiliation of going overseas as migrant workers. But they bitterly reject the Singaporean analysis that democracy is in some way to blame. The real problem, they say, is not democracy but the years of dictatorship

34

they suffered under the late Ferdinand Marcos, who favoured his business cronies and entrenched protectionism and corruption in the economy. When Lee Kuan Yew himself came to the Philippines and told a meeting of Filipino business executives that their country needed discipline more than democracy, President Fidel Ramos – under whose leadership the economy had started to recover – had a tart reply: 'This prescription fails to consider our ill-fated flirtation with authoritarianism not so long ago.'[20] Corazon Aquino, who preceded Ramos as president after leading the democratic uprising which overthrew Marcos in 1986, was once so incensed by one of Lee's lectures that she was heard muttering: 'That arrogant bastard, I feel like kicking his shins.'[21]

Such feelings are not confined to the Philippines. When Suharto was president of Indonesia, he was happy to benefit from the increased international legitimacy afforded to authoritarian governments by the 'Asian values' argument without making any significant public contributions to the debate himself. 'Indonesia,' says Rizal Sukma, a researcher at the Centre for Strategic and International Studies in Jakarta, 'has become some sort of free rider in this debate.' But he adds: 'Among young intellectuals there is resentment about why the Singaporeans and Malaysians want to be spokespersons for the whole region. Not everyone agrees with Lee Kuan Yew's formula.'

The disagreement extends to the ordinary citizens of Singapore and Malaysia as well. 'It's mind-boggling this Asian values thing. What are Asian values?' asks Hishamuddin Rais, a Malaysian filmmaker and political dissident who has lived in exile but recently returned home after negotiations with the authorities. Rais – with his brown felt hat, beard and long hair in a bun – is a far cry from the typical Malaysian factory worker or bureaucrat. He accepts that there are cultural differences between Asians and westerners, but says 'Asian values' have become an excuse for totalitarianism and the stifling of free expression. 'They say, "we want to develop economically first", but this is a danger – develop until when? Have we started sowing the seeds of free debate? . . . Have you created a fertile ground, a field where ideas can grow? No, you haven't.'[22] As he was making these comments to the author outside a hotel in Kuala Lumpur, two men from the Malaysian police special branch were seen unobtrusively taking photographs of the meeting.

* * *

When the debate heated up in the 1990s, each side accused the other of misrepresenting their arguments. As Mahbubani of the Singapore foreign ministry complains: 'The caricature of the Asian value position is that "Oh, this is purely a sophisticated way of justifying authoritarian governments. This is a very sophisticated way of saying the Asians are not ready for democracy, the Asians like to be ruled by dictators and so on." That's a caricature of what it's all about. It reflects a western tendency to believe that Asians cannot have supple philosophical minds . . . in fact I would say a fair amount of thought is going into the "Asian values" position.' Mahbubani says the 'Asian values' argument arose partly as a reaction to western arrogance after the collapse of communism. 'At the end of the Cold War there was a sense – as part of the mood of triumphalism in the West – that history had ended and that the rest of the world would grow up and become copies of western societies. And that was basically what the Asian values debate was all about – to say . . . they might evolve into the kinds of societies that may not necessarily be clones or copies of what you find in the West.'[23]

For liberals, Asian and western, this explanation is itself a misrepresentation. The point for them is not whether they should have particular kinds of political or electoral systems, but whether governments are legitimate and people are treated justly. Certain rights, in other words, are neither western nor eastern but universal. As Marsillam Simandjuntak, an Indonesian political activist and former medical doctor, puts it: 'If I want some kind of justice, being an Asian, isn't that an Asian value? . . . I demand it because I need justice, not because it's similar to what there is in the West.'[24]

An important weakness of the 'Asian values' argument is the difficulty of drawing sensible distinctions between 'Asian' and 'western' cultures, particularly during a period of rapid modernization in Asia. 'Those people who said "let's reject western values" said it while playing golf,' comments Marsillam drily. 'The problem with Lee Kuan Yew,' adds Ammar Siamwalla, a political analyst at the Thailand Development Research Institute in Bangkok, 'is that he's not saying it's a Singapore way; it's an Asian way. The very term [Asia] was handed to us by the bloody Europeans!'[25] Asians may be different from Europeans, but then the Thais are very different from the Vietnamese, just as the French are from the English. In fact there is more variety within the vast expanse of Asia than within Europe.

The Indonesian archipelago alone is 5,000km from end to end and is home to about 200 million people. There are few similarities between a tribesman wearing a penis sheath in Irian Jaya and a businessman in a suit in Jakarta. Many of the nation states of Asia are recent creations, and a large number of their inhabitants are as likely to identify themselves with a clan, region, religion or ethnic group as with their countries – let alone a continent.

The same objection can be raised against the use of the words 'West' and 'western' to define the type of society which is supposedly the antithesis of 'Asian values'. For the 'Asian values' argument to work well, it helps to believe in a homogeneous 'West' in social and political decline and apparently unable to reform itself. This means using state-controlled media to emphasize the bad, especially crime and poverty, while playing down the good – and gathering the bad news, it need hardly be said, from the independent western media in much the same way as Soviet anti-western propaganda operated during the Cold War. Thus Major Hla Min, a spokesman for the Burmese military junta, is able to compare Burmese housing policy favourably with the situation in the US. 'There are people living in the United States in cardboard boxes,' he says.[26] That is the truth, but not the whole truth. And it is easy to demonize the thinking behind liberalism as well as its effects. In the words of Mahbubani: 'To any Asian, it is obvious that the breakdown of the family and social order in the US owes itself to a mindless ideology that maintains that the freedom of a small number of individuals who are known to pose a threat to society (criminals, terrorists, street-gang members, drug-dealers) should not be constrained (for example, through detention without trial), even if to do so would enhance the freedom of the majority. In short, principle takes precedence over people's well-being.'[27] Many Americans would find the words 'mindless ideology' an offensive way to describe their belief in individual rights, especially when they are engaged in painful debates about how to improve a society which almost all admit has serious flaws.

Gloomy Americans and Europeans – harking back to a mythically crime-free, pre-industrial past – are almost as eager as south-east Asian leaders to condemn the social ills afflicting the West. Yet not all the news is bad. According to statistics on labour strikes from the Organization for Economic Co-operation and Development, industrial conflict in the western industrialized countries fell in 1996 to its lowest level for more than fifty years.[28] By 1998, the US was enjoying its seventh consecutive year of uninterrupted economic growth, and unemployment was at its lowest for twenty-five years. Again in the US, drug abuse seems to have stabilized; deaths from Acquired Immune Deficiency Syndrome (AIDS) have started to fall for the first time since the epidemic began in 1981; and serious and violent crime has been declining for five years. Americans are far from being complacent about such trends; one newspaper even had the headline 'Major Crime Falls Again, But Why?'.[29] In the longer term, sociologists believe that the West will benefit from a reduction in crime because of lower birth rates and the consequent increase in the average age of its populations – a characteristic of prosperous industrial societies – while south-east Asia may for a few decades suffer the opposite; the obvious reason for this is that it is the young, not the elderly, who tend to break the law. In short, it is as foolish for Asian leaders today to stereotype western societies as crime-ridden and amoral as it was for Europeans in the past to dismiss Asians as 'sensual' and 'cruel'. As Edward Said wrote, 'the answer to Orientalism is not Occidentalism'.[30]

Even the proponents of 'Asian values' have difficulties explaining what they mean. Almost as soon as the term came into popular use in the 1980s and 1990s, their arguments were plagued by inconsistencies which seemed to be more than the growing pains of a new philosophy. 'Flexibility' and 'pragmatism', for instance, are supposed to be among the advantages of Asian societies in both politics and business. So whereas a western business person would insist on contractual obligations, an east Asian would rely on personal contacts and informal relationships that would allow the deal to be done quickly. Leaving aside for a moment the question of whether the informality is simply left over from an earlier age when business was less complicated, this notion was seized upon in various south-east Asian countries to justify the kind of 'informal' contacts which are otherwise recognizable as corruption. Westerners are told not to inquire too closely into 'Asian' business practices: they cannot possibly understand them because of their different cultural background. A Thai army colonel, quoted in a ground-breaking independent academic survey of corruption in Thailand, justified the frequent exchanges of favours between military officers, politicians and businessmen by saying that 'in our society we are not so individualistic like westerners. Thai people live together like relatives. Favour requires gratitude in return. Today we help him, in future days he helps us. It may not be proper in the whole process. But it is necessary.'[31]

Such self-serving interpretations of 'Asian values' do not go unchallenged. Anand Panyarachun, a former Thai prime minister who has been active in both business and politics, recently lamented the decline of ethical standards in Asia and what he called the 'grim' role models presented to the public: 'Military figures negotiating business deals, narcotics traffickers serving as parliamentarians, respected business personalities consorting with shady characters, professors offering snake-oil remedies to age-old problems, clerics caught under the covers – laughable, were it all not so deplorable.' Anand went on to heap scorn on 'the current wave of support for our so-called Asian values'. He said: 'As if a long-hidden treasure-trove had suddenly been discovered, Asian values are the fashionable topic of the day. Without specifying what, precisely, is being referred to, political leaders region-wide have grasped this fashionable term as a useful rhetorical device. They have used it to champion special interests, to oppose foreign competition, to curry favour with an all-too-often gullible public.'[32] Anand proposed his own set of 'Asian values' – good governance, ensured by visionary, vigorous and responsible leadership; moral integrity; and service to others. There was nothing about 'flexibility' or curbing the press.

Another problem with 'Asian values' is the very different characters of the people who espouse them. In politics, for example, it would be hard to find two people more different than Malaysia's Mahathir and Lee Kuan Yew of Singapore – the two best-known voices of the 'Asian Way'. They are rivals, not friends. Mahathir is dynamic but erratic and given to emotional outbursts, boasting of the superior qualities of Asians and particularly Malaysians when things are going well, but bitterly blaming foreigners for conspiring against Asia when they go badly – as he did during the south-east Asian financial crisis of 1997. Lee is much more calculating. In the 1950s, when he was pressing Britain to end its colonial occupation of Singapore, he said: 'If you believe in democracy, you must believe in it unconditionally. If you believe that men should be free, then, they should have the right of free association, of free speech, of free publication.'[33] After taking power, he and his followers carefully modified their views as they slowly built the edifice of the 'Asian Way'. They emphasized the importance of cultural differences between peoples, stressing the need for Asian governments to be respected rather than suffer the noisy and unproductive harassment typical of debates in the West. Unconditional democracy was out. But Lee, a lawyer by profession, reads more widely and thinks more deeply than the energetic but unreliable Mahathir. He and other Singaporean government ministers do not take simplistic anti-western postures, and are usually ready to give credit where they feel it is due. They openly praise the US for having opened its markets to Asian exporters after the Second World War, an action which was a vital contribution to the Asian economic 'miracle'. And, without embarrassment, they publicly support a continued US military presence in the region to ensure security.

For all the debate in Malaysia, Singapore and the rest of south-east Asia, there is little chance that a coherent value-system will emerge. The historical and cultural arguments for 'Asian values' are weak, and there is little popular support for a philosophy that seems to be the narrow preserve of governments. When the authoritative *Far Eastern Economic Review* published a series of profiles of its more influential readers to mark its fiftieth anniversary in 1996, it was remarkable how many Asians – business people, academics, bureaucrats – cited 'Asian values' as the greatest cliché about Asia before going on to say why they thought it was nonsense.[34] And yet 'Asian values' still exert a powerful influence in south-east Asia, not just in the politics of individual countries (where these values are used to underpin the authority of particular governments) but also in the region as a whole: it is significant that the members of Asean pursue a co-ordinated foreign policy based largely on 'Asian values'.

Asean foreign policy is supposed to operate on the basis of the 'Asian values' of consensus, by which it is meant that differences between member states should not be aired in public but resolved by governments behind closed doors; communiqués and public statements thus tend to be exceptionally bland, even by the anodyne standards of international meetings the world over. The search for consensus, however, does not apply to relations between Asean and the outside world. For Asean is eager to confront what its members see as foreign interference in the way they run their countries. The governments object to being told how to run their domestic politics and how to formulate laws on labour rights and environmental protection. In 1993, Asian governments, including Asean, even went so far as to qualify the notion of universal human rights. At a meeting in Bangkok before the UN World Conference on Human Rights, they implied that the UN standards to which most countries, including themselves, had formally subscribed were 'western'. They argued that more attention should be given to an 'Asian' interpretation of human rights, which stressed economic growth and political stability for the benefit of whole communities more than individual freedom. Lee Kuan Yew endorses this view, belittling the UN's Universal Declaration of Human Rights on the grounds that it was drawn up by the victorious powers after the Second World War and that neither China nor Russia believed in the document they signed.[35] The growing confidence of Asean governments in the early 1990s, and their desire to protect each other from challenges to their authority, made work increasingly difficult for local pressure groups on issues such as human rights and the environment. These groups, known as non-governmental organizations (NGOs), had never been popular with the governments they challenged; but now they found their meetings banned or restricted if they attempted to discuss human-rights abuses in another Asean member state. This occurred even in Thailand and the Philippines, the two most democratic Asean members and the two with the greatest respect for freedom of speech, when NGOs tried to discuss the Indonesian occupation of East Timor – a territory abandoned by Portugal, invaded by Indonesia with great brutality in 1975 and forcibly incorporated into Indonesia the following year. Just as China tries to force other Asian countries to refuse entry to the Dalai Lama, the exiled Tibetan leader, Indonesia, the largest Asean member, does not hesitate to put pressure on other member governments to suppress embarrassing meetings. In 1994, angered by a planned conference on East Timor in Manila, Indonesia temporarily withdrew from an economic co-operation programme with the Philippines and suspended its efforts to mediate between the Philippine government and Moslem rebels.[36]

The attempts by Asean governments to monopolize debate do not go unchallenged. NGOs, liberal politicians and academics in all

Asean countries have vigorously re-asserted their belief in minimum universal standards of human rights and continued to protest against everything from poor factory conditions to environmental abuses in the region. In a car park outside a hotel hosting an Asean meeting in Bangkok in 1994, Cecilia Jimenez, a human-rights lawyer from the Philippines, complained about the Thai government's decision to disrupt a human-rights meeting taking place in the city at the same time and bitterly condemned the Asean governments for 'cultural relativity'. She said: 'I think that's so racist, so insulting to say that we Asians deserve less human rights than you guys from the West . . . The Philippines and the Thai government are under tremendous pressure from the Indonesian government. That's why we object to the bully tactics of the Indonesian government.'[37]

The biggest test of Asean's unity, however, is not Indonesia but Burma. It is one thing to use the concept of 'Asian values' to defend the rights of, say, Singapore and Malaysia to restrict personal freedoms in the interest of economic growth and political stability: such countries have been labelled 'soft authoritarian' by political scientists. But Burma is by no means soft. It is ruled by a military junta which has tortured and killed hundreds of its opponents, and which has condemned what should be one of Asia's wealthiest countries – fertile, rich in minerals, attractive to tourists and home to fifty million people – to poverty and oppression. The junta was so out of touch with its own people that it was convinced it would win a democratic election it organized in 1990. When it was resoundingly defeated at the polls, the generals ignored the result and continued to rule. Meanwhile they kept Aung San Suu Kyi, one of the founders and leaders of the National League for Democracy, the party that won the election, under house arrest for six years. She won the Nobel Peace Prize. They eventually freed her, but went on to arrest many of her allies and soon re-imposed restrictions on her movements that were almost as effective as house arrest. All of this was hard for south-east Asian leaders to justify, even with the most extreme interpretation of 'Asian values'.

Asean nevertheless welcomed Burma as a member in 1997, overcoming the reluctance of some of its own members, including Thailand and the Philippines, and overruling the objections of western governments and both Asian and western human-rights movements. (One Asian NGO, meanwhile, distributed a colourful poster asking the question 'Should Asean welcome Slorc [the junta]?' in six south-east Asian languages. It showed a fat, beaming Burmese military officer being greeted by obsequious officials of other Asean countries, all standing on a plinth made out of the Asean symbol, a stylized sheaf of rice stalks; a couple of the Asean officials were frowning as they looked down to where Burmese soldiers were standing guard over manacled prisoners and kicking a woman with a baby.) There were three main reasons for Asean's decision to grant Burma membership. The most pressing was the need to counter the growing Chinese influence in Burma. The Chinese have been developing both military and commercial links with Burma's military rulers. Second, the Asean governments, and particularly the Malaysians who were hosting the 1997 summit, wanted to expand Asean to include all ten south-east Asian countries to give the organization added authority in international negotiations – only Cambodia was excluded and this was at the last minute because of a coup d'état. Third, Asean wanted to help protect the increasing investments being made in Burma by both state-controlled and private south-east Asian companies.

Even Asean leaders who supported Burma's entry into their organization, such as Mahathir, could not pretend that all was well inside the country. They therefore declared that they recognized the need for economic and political reform in Burma and would work quietly behind the scenes to achieve it. With unconscious irony, they labelled their policy 'constructive engagement'. This was the phrase used by the US and Britain in the 1980s to describe their dealings with the white minority government of South Africa at a time when others – including developing countries in Asia – were demanding economic sanctions against Pretoria. 'Constructive engagement' was just as controversial when applied to Burma as it was when applied to South Africa.[38] One Burmese man in Rangoon – whose punishment for being elected as a member of parliament for Aung San Suu Kyi's NLD was to be jailed in a ten foot by ten foot cell with several others – eloquently expressed the bitterness felt by Burmese democrats towards the junta's regional allies after his release from prison. Asking to remain anonymous for fear of reprisals, he spoke of his party's regret about the rapprochement between Burma and such countries as Singapore, Thailand and Malaysia. 'Constructive engagement is not constructive,' he said. 'It's destructive opportunism. We are in a time of trouble. When the government is oppressing its own people, they shouldn't do it.'[39] Another Burmese intellectual declared: 'There's no Asian way. There's totalitarian ways and democratic ways.'[40] Singapore, as a big investor in Burma, a supplier of weapons and above all a public defender of authoritarianism, is particularly loathed by Burmese liberals. 'Singaporeans are all set to make money,' says Kyi Maung, an elderly and shrewd NLD leader and confidant of Suu Kyi. 'They have no moral conscience at all.'[41]

Singapore's defence against these accusations is twofold. It repeats that Singapore and Asean are in fact trying to introduce reforms in Burma, albeit through gentle persuasion rather than confrontation with the regime. Second, it deploys the 'Asian values' argument in favour of strong government: this means that the army is an appropriate institution to run the country because Burma is ethnically diverse and would be in danger of disaster under any other system. 'Imagine what happens in Burma if you dismantle the *tatmadaw* [Burmese army],' says George Yeo of the Singapore government. 'What you have left will be like Cambodia in "year zero" [when the Khmers Rouges took over] because there is no institution in Burma which can hold the whole country together.'[42] There is no question that Burma has problems with ethnic divisions – two dozen different ethnic guerrilla armies have fought against the central government since independence in 1948 – but there are doubts about the long-term effectiveness of the junta's political strategy. The guerrilla armies fighting the regime have been either defeated by military force or persuaded to sign peace deals in exchange for the right to continue operating as drug barons in their own territories. Reconciliation and real national unity still seem a long way off. So the ideal solution for Singapore and Asean would be for Burma to combine political reform with continued military control. Under this so-called 'Indonesian' method (discussed in more detail in chapter 2), democratic-looking institutions are introduced and the army withdraws into the background while still retaining much of its influence.

Unfortunately for the supporters of 'Asian values', there have been few signs that the Burmese junta has any inclination to embark on even the mildest of reforms. Instead, they have turned Asean's support for authoritarian governments to their own advantage, using it to justify the continuation of their regime. Major Hla Min of the Burmese defence ministry explained that the countries of south-east

Asia understood Burma well because they had had military governments in the past and in some cases still had them. 'Even Singapore – it's a police state,' he said. 'Everybody admits it's a police state.'[43]

This is hardly a ringing endorsement of the ethics of the 'Asian Way'. But until now Asean, and Asian governments as a whole, have been surprisingly successful in promoting 'Asian' versions of human rights in international forums – or at least in stopping western countries imposing their versions on Asia. The reasons for the West's diffidence are all too obvious. As Asian economies continued to grow, western governments and companies became ever more reluctant to jeopardize their commercial interests for the sake of their liberal principles. This often obliged them to adopt postures in favour of human rights at home for domestic political purposes, while appeasing Asian governments overseas. Confusion and hypocrisy were the inevitable result. 'When they come here they [western politicians] talk about the environment, human rights and democracy in public,' says Sarwono Kusumaatmadja, the former Indonesian minister responsible for the environment. 'But in private they talk business . . . so we listen politely to their exhortations and then we do our own thing. Some of them are very insincere.'[44] In the case of Burma, Asean governments rightly point out that it is hypocritical of the US to impose economic sanctions on Burma, which has a small and relatively unimportant economy, because of its human rights abuses, while simultaneously turning a blind eye to similar abuses in China because it has a very large economy. To which the honest, if unedifying, response from a senior US diplomat is: 'Being a superpower means we don't have to be consistent.'[45]

So successful were Asian authoritarians in promoting their own version of human rights that they almost turned the tables on the western countries they had accused of bullying them. Chris Patten, the last colonial governor of Hong Kong, said shortly before the territory was handed over to China in July 1997 that he believed the West should pursue both its commercial and political objectives energetically, but as separately as possible: trade, in other words, should not be a political lever. He added a warning: 'If we are not to mix them up, then we should not permit Asian countries to play the same game in reverse, threatening that access to their markets can be allowed only to the politically correct, to those prepared to be muzzled over human rights. We should not allow ourselves to be demeaned in this way – with Europe played off against America and one European country played off against another, and with all of us treading gingerly around the sensitivities of one or two countries, deferring to the proposition that open and vigorous discussion should be avoided at all costs.'[46] It is not only westerners who feel uncomfortable about the use of 'Asian values' in foreign policy. Asean defends its members' human-rights policies – or lack of them – on the basis of supposedly distinctive Asian cultural traditions, but Thai and Filipino diplomats have complained that they do not share in these purported traditions: on the contrary, they regard their own democratic values to be at least as valid as the authoritarian ones of Singapore or Indonesia.

In 1993, at the height of the 'Asian values' debate, it was pointed out that one reason for doubting the widely-held view that the twenty-first century would be a 'Pacific Century' was the lack of a genuine Asian value system with international appeal. 'A strong economy is a precondition for domestic health, military strength, and global influence,' wrote Morton Abramowitz, President of the Carnegie Endowment for International Peace, in a perceptive analysis of Asian hubris. 'But in an interdependent world, those that aspire to lend their name to centuries must also have political strengths and value-systems that enable them to project influence persuasively. Economic power without acceptance of the responsibilities and burdens of leadership ultimately engenders divisiveness and hostility.'[47] For all the speeches and articles extolling 'Asian values', there is little sign of an emerging Asian ethic that appeals to the peoples of Asia, let alone the outside world. However, the search for a stronger value system, whether it is labelled 'The Asian Way' or something else, will doubtless continue. Singapore's Kishore Mahbubani says the debate has only just begun, and will continue for another hundred years or more. Anand Panyarachun, who was twice prime minister of Thailand in the 1990s, bemoans the greed and consumerism of present-day south-east Asia but has not given up the search for something better. 'Asian values today appear to be glorifying personal interest,' he said. 'Yet the essential objective of any ethical society must be the realization of public aspirations. In that quest, ethics cannot be divorced from good governance.'[48]

* * *

When governments pursue immoral or foolish policies cloaked in specious ethics, it is not just nasty. It may be dangerous for the countries concerned. Take the environment debate in south-east Asia. In 1994, Christopher Lingle, an American professor at the National University of Singapore, responded to a rather triumphalist article by Mahbubani that extolled the virtues of Asia and belittled Europe for its inability to extinguish the 'ring of fire' on its borders caused by political upheavals. Lingle thought this image more appropriate for south-east Asia because – as he pointed out in his article – Singapore and parts of Malaysia and Indonesia were at that moment choking from the smoke from Indonesian forest fires raging out of control. More significant than the fires themselves was the refusal of south-east Asian governments to do anything about them or the consequent pollution affecting their citizens because members of Asean are not supposed to interfere in each others' affairs. 'These Asian states seem more interested in allowing fellow governments to save face than in saving the lives of their citizens or preserving the environment,' he wrote.[49] He went on to discuss the dangers of not having a free media. As it happened, Lingle fled from Singapore because he was taken to court over the same article for questioning the independence of the judiciary. But his comments on the forest fires proved prophetic. Three years later, the fires – an annual occurrence typically started by logging companies, plantation developers and slash-and-burn farmers – were so severe that vast areas of south-east Asia were shrouded in smoke and some people suffered serious breathing difficulties. In Sarawak, one of the Malaysian territories on the island of Borneo, visibility was reduced to a few metres, airports, offices and schools were closed and the government declared a state of emergency. President Suharto of Indonesia apologized, but there was no immediate sign of a change of attitude among the proponents of 'Asian values'; according to them, neither foreigners nor environmental groups within south-east Asia have any business interfering with the rights of governments and their business partners to cut down forests at an unsustainable rate and sell the wood.

The myopia of 'Asian values' theorists is not confined to environmental issues. Tommy Koh of Singapore visited Cambodia in 1996 and returned, he wrote, 'with fewer criticisms than other recent observers'. He acknowledged that Cambodia had a long way to go on the journey to democracy and the rule of law, but implicitly criticized Michael Leifer of the London School of Economics for saying that Cambodia had regressed politically since a UN-organized election in 1993 and for calling the Cambodian government 'a strong-arm regime that intimidates opponents and lets unscrupulous foreign interests exploit natural resources'.[50] Yet Leifer was right. That is exactly what the regime was doing. And just over a year later, the Cambodian leader Hun Sen demonstrated the truth of Leifer's assertions by staging a coup d'état to seize power fully and remove his co-prime minister Prince Norodom Ranariddh, whose party had won the biggest share of the vote in the election. Some of Hun Sen's opponents were murdered, others fled. Asian timber companies continued to cut down Cambodian forests.

A worse shock for south-east Asia's leaders than the Cambodian coup – which for them simply meant an embarrassing delay in admitting Cambodia to Asean – was the regional economic crisis which began in mid-1997. South-east Asian stock markets and currencies plunged after Thailand floated its currency, the baht, and its value fell sharply. There were unremarkable economic reasons for this chain of events. In Thailand itself, they included a stagnation of exports, too much short-term foreign borrowing by Thai companies, an overpriced property market with too many new buildings, too much debt and not enough buyers, and inadequate regulation of the plethora of finance companies which sprang up in Bangkok when the economy was booming. (The business aspects of this are discussed in chapter 4.) Instead of accepting that they had to address their economic problems, however, many south-east Asian leaders instinctively assumed that they were doing a fine job – it was well known, after all, that they were in charge of an economic 'miracle' – and that therefore the problems must be the work of outside conspirators. Asean foreign ministers even issued a communiqué blaming 'well co-ordinated efforts to destabilize Asean currencies for self-serving purposes'.[51] Such statements, especially the vigorous condemnations and threats coming from Prime Minister Mahathir of Malaysia, made matters worse, convincing international speculators, currency traders and stock market investors that their money would be safer elsewhere.

The financial crisis, the misunderstandings about events in Burma and Cambodia and the environmental crisis over Indonesia's forest fires brought to light some of the dangers of 'Asian values' as applied in south-east Asia in the 1990s. Sometimes politicians cynically used 'Asian values' to justify their own shortcomings; sometimes – overwhelmed by the attentions of foreign investors as their economies grew at 8 per cent a year or more – they actually believed what they were saying. Triumphal assertions of Asia's superiority blinded them to failings and difficulties which in reality affect industrializing Asian countries as much as European or American ones: a reluctance to offend Asian neighbours meant that even if a government recognized a problem it was reluctant to raise it in public; and even if it did so, government attempts to control the media in much of the region limited the free debate which might elsewhere produce a solution. It will probably not be long before south-east Asia's social problems – widespread drug abuse, for example – begin to tarnish its shiny self-image as surely as the economic crises and environmental damage of recent years have already done.

This is not to say that south-east Asian leaders are inflexible or incapable of learning from their mistakes. In the midst of the financial crisis, Thai politicians and bureaucrats were forced to acknowledge their economic weaknesses and strike a deal with the International Monetary Fund. Having insisted that Malaysia's big infrastructure projects would not be affected by the crisis, Mahathir did a U-turn and suspended some of his most prized projects – including the huge Bakun dam in Borneo and a new capital city – to rescue the Malaysian currency and the Kuala Lumpur stock market. After Indonesia's apology for its forest fires, Malaysia sent 1,200 firefighters to Sumatra to help tackle the blazes. Circumstances – in this case, smoke so thick that Malaysians were ending up in hospital on respirators – obliged south-east Asian governments to accept that they had a regional problem and do something about it, even if it meant breaking the Asean taboo on interfering in the affairs of neighbouring countries. This doctrine of non-interference had always been shaky in any case; regional 'consensus' quickly dissolves when national or religious interests are at stake. Thailand has spent decades interfering in Burma and Cambodia by supporting rebels on its borders. Malaysia, which sees itself as a champion of Moslem causes, was happy to remain silent about the Burmese junta's persecution of its predominantly Buddhist people but protested when thousands of Burmese Moslems fled into Bangladesh in 1992 with tales of forced labour, torture, rape and killings at the hands of Burmese troops.

The more prudent supporters of 'Asian values' say that while the past three decades of economic growth have revitalized Asia after centuries of stagnation – and given Asian countries some much-needed confidence and hope after the colonial era – there is still plenty of thinking to be done. 'It would be very dangerous for Asian societies to adopt any sort of triumphant mood,' says Mahbubani. 'We have a long way to go. Asian societies ... have lots of major questions to address themselves, what kind of society they want to have, what kind of political system will work for them, what kind of social environment they want, how do they arrive at the checks and balances every society has to evolve and so on.' He continues: 'I think in private there isn't the sense of absolute confidence that "Hey, we've arrived". I don't get that sense at all. What you do get a sense of is "Hey, maybe we can make it", whereas twenty years ago if you had come to this region, or ten years ago, there wasn't the sense of confidence that societies in this part of the world could become as developed or as affluent as those you find in western Europe or north America. Today the realization is coming in, "Maybe we can do it", and that's the psychological change that has taken place.'[52]

A change of generations is also imminent. Suharto has already been ousted. And the remaining south-east Asian leaders brought up in the colonial era – including Ne Win in Burma, Mahathir in Malaysia, Lee Kuan Yew in Singapore and the elderly politburo members in Vietnam – will not last for ever. Their thinking was shaped by the region's struggles for independence and by the urge to differentiate their new countries from the old world that used to dominate them. This has been the impetus behind many aspects of the 'Asian values' debate, including the rejection of 'western' human rights and environmental standards. As Mahathir put it in a speech to university students in Japan: 'Having lost their globe-girdling colonies, the Europeans now want to continue their dominance through dictating the terms of trade, the systems of government and the whole value-system of the world including human rights and environmental protection.'[53]

But the up-and-coming generation of Asian politicians brought up after independence lack their elders' obsession with colonialism. They believe they have more freedom to pursue policies on their merits – regardless of the provenance of those policies. Many of the views expressed by Anwar Ibrahim, Mahathir's former deputy, would be endorsed by those who pour scorn on 'Asian values' as defined by south-east Asian governments. In the preface to his book *The Asian Renaissance* – a collection of his speeches and articles – Anwar says he detects a resurgence of art and science as well as an economic revival. But he rejects 'cultural jingoism' whether from the West or the East. 'Asians too, in their xenophobic obsession to denounce certain Western ideas as alien, may end up denouncing their own fundamental values and ideals. This is because in the realm of ideas founded upon the humanistic tradition, neither the East nor the West can lay exclusive claim to them.' He goes on:

> If the term Asian values is not to ring hollow, Asians must be prepared to champion ideals which are universal. It is altogether shameful, if ingenious, to cite Asian values as an excuse for autocratic practices and denial of basic rights and civil liberties. To say that freedom is Western or unAsian is to offend our own traditions as well as our forefathers who gave their lives in the struggle against tyranny and injustice. It is true that Asians lay great emphasis on order and societal stability. But it is certainly wrong to regard society as a kind of deity upon whose altar the individual must constantly be sacrificed. No Asian tradition can be cited to support the proposition that in Asia, the individual must melt into a faceless community.[54]

Anwar is a living example of how quickly south-east Asian societies are changing. In his youth, he was regarded as an Islamic firebrand and was detained without trial by the government after leading a demonstration. By the time of the financial crisis in 1997, Anwar – as deputy prime minister and finance minister – was the government figure who reassured foreign investors and sought to limit the damage done by Mahathir's anti-foreign outbursts and threats of exchange controls. His supporters express disgust at the abuse of the term 'Asian values' to justify corrupt connections between politicians and businessmen, and draw explicit contrasts between

Anwar's contemporaries and the older generation of south-east Asian leaders. 'We reached maturity after independence,' says Abdul Rahman Adnan, director of the Institut Kajian Dasar (Institute for Policy Research), a think-tank in Kuala Lumpur which pushes forward Anwar's agenda. 'Everything was already Malaysian. You can't really blame the nasty colonial power for all the ills of society.' Adnan and others like him believe that Malaysians are now sufficiently educated to be allowed a more energetic and independent press and more say in how their country is run. 'They expect the government to be more accountable,' he says.[55]

Admiration for Anwar is not confined to Malaysia. 'He represents what the generation of my age would like to see as the new set of values for the future . . . Anwar Ibrahim does not fit into the stereotypes of Asean today because of the generation gap,' says Adi Sasono, secretary general of the Moslem Intellectuals Society of Indonesia. (Known by its Indonesian initials ICMI, the society is an Indonesian government sponsored think-tank which is attempting, like Anwar, to reconcile Islam with the needs of a modern, high-technology society.) Nowhere was the need for a generational leadership change more acutely felt than Indonesia, where the seventy-six-year-old Suharto had ruled for three decades and left his people guessing about who would succeed him. 'The main political factor in this country is Suharto,' said Sasono shortly before Suharto's overthrow. 'He represents the old value of power, authority. Well, the society is changing rapidly, so after Suharto the political situation will change quite radically.'[56]

The imminent handover of power from one generation to another at the top of south-east Asia's governments, along with the continued growth of the middle class, will have profound implications in every country in the region. It is true that the young idealists waiting in the wings are bound to have their enthusiasm blunted by the realities of government. As one eminent proponent of Asian values said of Anwar: 'His book is a collection of motherhood statements that no one can disagree with . . . You've got to judge a man by his deeds, so you wait and see. I would expect that when he takes over he will govern Malaysia as Dr Mahathir does.'[57] But official attitudes to politics, social norms, business practices and environmental policies are likely to change, as popular attitudes already have. The results – albeit with many stops and starts – will be a gradual loosening of central government control over politics and the media, a slow unravelling of the webs of corrupt connections between politicians and business-men, and the imposition of stricter environmental controls. To this one could add a more relaxed official approach to personal and social matters such as leisure, homosexuality and pre-marital sex, although in Indonesia, Malaysia and Brunei liberalization could be delayed or even temporarily reversed by the strong Islamic lobby. The probable effect – already visible in some cities such as Jakarta – would be an increase in the number of people living double lives. As in the Gulf states, many wealthier Moslems would publicly obey the strict religious tenets decreed by the authorities while privately drinking alcohol and visiting prostitutes when abroad.

'Asian values', meanwhile, are likely to fade from view. Several years ago, a group of south-east Asian academics, bankers and former ministers produced a document called *Towards a New Asia*; it advocated democracy within the rule of law and, while paying tribute to the importance of economic growth, suggested that Asia should 'move to higher ground' and 'become a greater contributor to the advancement of human civilization'.[58] These sentiments reflect one of the great ironies of the debate: south-east Asia's leaders are often attacked by their fiercest critics not for being too 'Asian' but for importing the worst aspects of western societies – consumerism, materialism, pollution – and labelling them 'Asian values'. As one Malaysian artist said of Mahathir: 'Everything he's doing is western – the assembling of cars, privatization, the "multimedia corridor", everything. This drive for market-driven development is a very western concept.'[59] Sondhi Limthongkul, a Thai businessman who tried to build an Asian media empire, is equally scathing. 'The problem of most emerging nations in Asia-Pacific is always the absolute worship of economic growth rather than the quality of life,' he told a conference in Hawaii. 'It's very unfortunate that we have learned and inherited so well from the West.'[60]

If they are interested in formulating any 'Asian values' at all, south-east Asia's next generation of leaders will want to do so by injecting ideas they see as genuinely Asian into a body of beliefs they accept as universal and which seem inevitably to permeate any society that has undergone an industrial revolution. 'The Asian world and Asian civilization cited so often of late have their origins not deep in the past but in modernization this century in an Asia in contact with the

West,' wrote playwright and professor Masakazu Yamazaki. Moderniz-ation, he said, had affected the entire fabric of Asian societies, lead-ing to the rise of industry, the formation of nation states under legitimate institutions and the secularization of ethics and mores. 'Members of the Association of South East Asian Nations have nearly reached consensus on such fundamentals as the separation of politics from religion, one-man – one-vote representation, and public trial. When it comes to social welfare, women's liberation, freedom of conscience, access to modern healthcare, and other social policies, almost all the countries of the region now speak the same language as the West.'[61] Kim Dae-jung, the Korean politician who has fiercely opposed 'Asian values' and the suggestion that Asians are by nature undemocratic, once noted that 'moral breakdown is attributable not to inherent shortcomings of Western cultures but those of industrial societies; a similar phenomenon is now spreading through Asia's newly industrializing societies'.[62] A dissident who spent his life oppos-ing authoritarian rule in his own country, Kim was elected President of South Korea in December 1997, vowing to promote democracy and transparency and bring an end to the collusion between govern-ment and big business.

Even the supporters of 'Asian values' accept that their countries will be more democratic and less authoritarian in the future, although they differ on the form democracy should take and on how long it will be before their people are 'ready' for the rough and tumble of genuine democratic debate. To speak of unambiguous 'Asian values' appears increasingly eccentric as the new millennium approaches. There was something bizarre, for instance, about the sight of Edward Heath, the former British prime minister, arguing on television with Martin Lee, the Hong Kong pro-democracy cam-paigner, about the political implications of the passing of the Chinese leader Deng Xiaoping on the day his death was announced. There was the westerner Heath espousing 'Asian values' and insisting that Chinese and Asians did not need democracy as understood in the West ('The Asiatic countries have a very different view'); and Lee, the Asian, saying that Deng himself had accepted the inevitability of political reform and arguing that Asians wanted democracy as much as anybody else ('I do not agree that there is such a thing as Asian values').[63]

The heyday of 'Asian values' seems to have passed. In Singapore, opposition politicians say Lee Kuan Yew talks less about Asian values and Confucianism than he used to. Mahbubani has toned down his comments as well, declaring in 1997 that Asians want good governance, open societies and the rule of law.[64] In Malaysia, Mahathir still denigrates the West from time to time. But he is as likely to mention the threats and opportunities of globalization – a more inclusive view of change – as to declare the superiority of the 'Asian Way'. Societies and cultures are changing so fast in south-east Asia that it hardly makes sense to attribute fixed values to them and try to preserve them intact from an imaginary western enemy. The argument that modernization leads to inevitable changes that are both good and bad is accepted throughout the region. Western governments may have learned something too. They can no longer lecture Asia about human rights and morality without having their own embarrassing failings – crime being the most obvious example – thrown back in their faces by their well-educated and well-travelled Asian interlocutors. In south-east Asia, however, the battles over social change and political reform are only just beginning. The campaign for 'Asian values' will come to be seen in the years ahead as a pragmatic interlude, during which Asian leaders briefly sought to justify authoritarian rule before losing power to the middle class they themselves had helped to create by managing their economies for so long with such success.

TWO

The new democrats

You'll be left behind. Then in twenty, thirty years' time, the whole of Singapore will be bustling away and your estate, through your own choice, will be left behind. They'll become slums. That's my message.

> – Singapore prime minister Goh Chok Tong, warning voters before the January 1997 election that their housing estates would be denied government renovation funds if they elected opposition members of parliament. The ruling People's Action Party won 81 of the 83 seats available.[1]

Golkar [the Indonesian ruling party] officials calculated as far back as last year that they would win precisely 70.02 per cent of the vote on polling day.

> – *Financial Times*, 24 May 1997. Golkar went on to win 74 per cent of the vote.[2]

In Singapore you have a one-party system. You have several parties, but it's all artificial.

> – Somsanouk Mixay, editor of the *Vientiane Times*, a state-controlled newspaper in communist Laos, discussing south-east Asian politics.[3]

The fact that the political parties are not functioning does not mean that people are not politicking. People do not stop breathing just because you shut the windows.

> – Dewi Fortuna Anwar, Indonesian political analyst.[4]

Elections in Singapore and Indonesia are very different affairs, but for decades they had the same outcome: the government won.

The 1997 election across Indonesia's sprawling archipelago was both colourful and violent. President Suharto's children joined the election campaign, officially labelled a 'festival of democracy' complete with parades and musical entertainment, on the side of the ruling Golkar party. His son Bambang Trihatmodjo, a wealthy businessman, appeared on stage with a popular singer who belted out catchy numbers such as 'Golkar, my sweetheart'. Throughout the country, the rival parties dressed up lampposts, vehicles and supporters in their party colours; in the remote eastern territory of Irian Jaya, tribesmen were persuaded to swap their traditional brown penis sheaths for new ones in bright, Golkar yellow.

Political competition, however, was a sham. There were three parties decreed by the government. Golkar was the one that was destined to win, as it had done for the previous quarter of a century. The United Development Party, known as the PPP from its Indonesian initials, was supposed to represent Islamic opposition and used the colour green. And the Indonesian Democratic Party (PDI) – red – brought together opponents of the left. These last two had the task of creating a semblance of democracy by disagreeing with the government without causing it serious embarrassment: they were in effect licensed opposition parties. In the 1997 election, though, it all went wrong. Megawati Sukarnoputri, daughter of the charismatic late President Sukarno, became leader of the PDI and seemed likely to win too many votes from Golkar. Even worse, the government feared she would break an unwritten understanding about the sanctity of President Suharto and stand against him in the forthcoming presidential election. In a move which provoked riots in the Indonesian capital Jakarta and elsewhere, she was removed by the government – which blatantly interfered in the running of the PDI – and replaced with a more compliant leader. Many of her supporters deliberately spoiled their ballot papers or stayed away from the polls in the subsequent general election and the PDI vote collapsed to a humiliating 3 per cent of the total from the previous 15 per cent. The PPP's Moslem supporters were not happy either, although their party increased its share of the vote to 23 per cent. They accused the government and Golkar of cheating. During political protests in Borneo rioters set fire to a shopping mall, killing 130 people who happened to be trapped inside, and destroyed dozens of other buildings. To add to the government's chagrin, some PPP voters carried banners in support of Megawati; she had nothing to do with the Islamic party but had come to be seen as a generalized symbol of opposition to the government. The conclusion was obvious: Indonesia's carefully structured but patronizing electoral system was no longer an adequate channel for the political aspirations of an increasingly sophisticated population. It was in fact falling apart, as subsequent events demonstrated. Instead of a picture of democracy that included a confident Golkar and tame minor parties, there was a beleaguered ruling party facing a strident Islamic opposition; and outside the official framework were a growing number of extra-parliamentary pressure groups which rejected the whole notion of state-sponsored pseudo-democracy. In 1998, as Indonesians felt the pain of the south-east Asian financial crisis and protested in the streets against the corruption of their leaders, Suharto himself was ignominiously forced to resign as president, leaving his hand-picked successor B. J. Habibie, his relatives and political allies to an uncertain future.

Elections are much more peaceful in the prosperous city state of Singapore. In the campaigning before the poll in January 1997, there were some noisy opposition rallies at which Singaporeans cheered every attack on the humourless and ruthlessly efficient People's Action Party which has run the country since independence. But the overall winner of the election was never in doubt, because the opposition parties left enough seats uncontested to ensure a parliamentary majority for the PAP. In doing so, they hoped to encourage cautious Singaporeans to vote for the opposition as a protest against the PAP while remaining secure in the knowledge that the PAP would continue to run the country.

Worried by the prospect of a reduced majority, Goh Chok Tong, the prime minister, and other PAP leaders pulled out all the stops in an attempt to crush their opponents. Goh famously threatened to deprive areas which voted against the PAP of state-financed housing upgrades; most Singaporeans buy apartments in government-built housing estates and can therefore benefit financially from such renovation schemes as well as enjoying the improved amenities.[5]

Nor was that all. Goh, Lee Kuan Yew and others deluged their opponents with lawsuits before and after the election, a practice they had employed before but rarely with such ferocity. In the most prominent case, the popular lawyer Tang Liang Hong, who had joined forces with J. B. Jeyaretnam of the Workers Party in a hotly contested, five-seat constituency, was sued by a dozen leaders of the PAP – including Goh and Lee – for calling them liars. In the statement that prompted this flurry of legal activity, Tang was responding to their accusations that he was a 'Chinese chauvinist' who opposed English-speakers and Christians. He pointed out that he spoke Malay, had a Christian daughter and was standing for election with an Indian Christian. This declaration of the facts was not enough to save him: Tang fled the country shortly after the election, saying the PAP was trying to bankrupt him, and was eventually ordered by a Singapore court to pay the equivalent of S$8.08 million (the equivalent of more than US$5 million) in damages to PAP leaders, although the amount was reduced to S$4.53 million (US$3 million) on appeal. Jeyaretnam was ordered to pay much smaller damages in a related defamation case brought by ten PAP members. The Tang case was notable for causing a serious diplomatic row between Singapore and neighbouring Malaysia. (In an affidavit, Lee Kuan Yew had expressed astonishment that Tang should have fled for safety to the Malaysian city of Johor, 'notorious for shootings, muggings and car-jackings'; Lee, lambasted by the Malaysian government and by government-sponsored demonstrators who gleefully insulted him as 'stupid' and 'senile', was forced to apologize.)[6] Singaporean ministers also became the object of international ridicule for pursuing opposition politicians through the courts for expressing thoughts that elsewhere would be part of the normal cut and thrust of democratic debate. The justice system was criticized too. But PAP leaders expressed no regrets, insisting repeatedly that they had to protect their reputations. They also won the election, halving the number of their elected opponents from four to two and leaving the opposition weaker and considerably poorer than before.

The most important feature that the 1997 elections in Singapore and Indonesia had in common was the absolute determination of governments to stay in power. 'Asian values' were receding into the background as a philosophical underpinning for authoritarian rule, but the authoritarian governments in south-east Asia were not about to yield willingly to their liberal opponents. In the continuing debate about the future of Asian politics, one side argues that economic growth leads to the education and empowerment of a middle class that demands, and achieves, democracy; the other insists that economic growth provides legitimacy for those in power and therefore prevents democratization. Both of these conflicting tendencies are visible in south-east Asia. But the evidence already shows that Asian countries, including those in south-east Asia, are either becoming more democratic or are under pressure from their citizens to become so. Taiwan and South Korea have progressed from authoritarian rule to democracy. A popular uprising in the Philippines in 1986 restored democracy there by overthrowing the dictator Ferdinand Marcos. Thais took to the streets of Bangkok in 1992 and 1997 to oppose the involvement of the armed forces and of old-fashioned, 'God-father-style' politicians in their parliament. Of course there have been numerous setbacks for the supporters of democracy, such as the failure of the Burmese military junta to recognize the 1990 election of Aung San Suu Kyi. Additionally, in Cambodia nearly 90 per cent of those eligible went to the polls in 1993 in a UN-organized election after years of civil war; but four years later, after a period of uneasy coalition government, the former Khmer Rouge commander Hun Sen ousted his co-prime minister Prince Norodom Ranariddh in a coup d'état, even though Ranariddh's party had won the most seats in the election.

In spite of such attempts to hold back democracy, the arrival of peace in south-east Asia and the region's rising prosperity have been accompanied by an increasing public awareness of political issues, much greater openness to international influences and a steady erosion of the authority of governments. As José Almonte, head of the Philippine National Security Council under President Ramos, has remarked, the contrast between the south-east Asia of today and of three or four decades ago could hardly be more striking. Vietnam, Laos and Cambodia were then becoming embroiled in the Indochina conflict, in which communists would triumph over the Americans and their allies. General Suharto had manoeuvred Sukarno out of power in Indonesia after the massacres of hundreds of thousands of people, including communists and ethnic Chinese. 'In this country [the Philippines] Senator Ferdinand Marcos had just been over-whelmingly elected President – an ironic beginning to the Filipino descent into authoritarian rule. In Thailand the military rule of Marshal Sarit Thanarat was passing to his closest associate, General Thanom Kittikachorn. And General Ne Win was just closing down Burma in what would be a hermetic isolation lasting thirty years.'[7]

The new democrats

The south-east Asia of today is clearly very different, although at first glance it seems as hard to make generalizations about the region's politics now as it was in the 1960s. What conclusions can be drawn about ten countries that include a military dictatorship in Burma, an Islamic Sultanate in Brunei, a noisy, American-style democracy in the Philippines, a one-party, communist system in Vietnam and Laos and a variety of democratic or quasi-democratic systems among the rest? Yet they do have more in common with each other than mere geography. First, they all acknowledge the importance of foreign investment and global trade and are committed – in word if not in deed – to modern market economics. Second, they are all embroiled in conflicts between old-fashioned authoritarians (who are usually in power), and younger, more liberal politicians (who are mostly confined so far to the opposition, or to the fringes of the ruling parties).

In both the Philippines and Thailand, voters can and do change their governments by means of elections. But truly representative democracy is only just beginning. In each country politicians tend to come from a small elite of landed gentry or business families – or the military. In 1997, the then president of the Philippines (Fidel Ramos) and one of the Thai prime ministers of that year (Chavalit Yongchaiyudh) were both former generals. Politics in Thailand has long been influenced, too, by powerful local businessmen – often gangsters involved in everything from drug-smuggling and illegal logging to gambling and property speculation – who sell their ability to deliver their local votes to a bewildering array of 'national' parties. Vote-buying (a vote can be bought for the equivalent of a few dollars) is so rampant in the poorer parts of the countryside that it is taken for granted even by the liberal media. 'The parties work for the private gain of their sponsors rather than for the good of the society at large or even for the people who elect the party candidates,' wrote two Thai academics in a survey of corruption in Thailand in 1994. 'None of the existing political parties have started from grass roots support. Rather, they originated as interest groups of influential people and businessmen.'[8] Only now are more idealistic politicians, supported by the more sophisticated voters of the Bangkok metropolis, starting to break into politics and trying to build political parties with some kind of ideological content. Liberals and others who want to modernize the country's politics are more optimistic

61

than they have ever been, although they acknowledge that it is only in Bangkok that people vote for parties without necessarily knowing the name of their member of parliament, as often happens in the West; in the Thai provinces, the opposite remains true – people know the name and reputation of their MP but are unlikely to know to which party he belongs this year. Ammar Siamwalla, the Thai political scientist and commentator, says that for the last half a century Thais have concentrated on their headlong lunge for economic development and largely ignored the need to modernize their politics while the armed forces and cliques of businessmen fought it out in a series of elections and coups d'état. Now that is changing. Public protests led to the formation of a constitutional panel; the constitution it produced in 1997 (Thailand's sixteenth since the abolition of the absolute monarchy in 1932) was aimed largely at ending what south-east Asians call 'money politics'. As Ammar says: 'To me that's a great step forward. We are engaged in political debates. We are trying to solve problems. It is very Bangkok-centred, but people are beginning to learn how to govern themselves.'[9] The old-style politicians are not giving up easily – both Chavalit and his predecessor as prime minister Banharn Silpa-archa fall into this category – but Thais are no longer tolerating their leaders' inability to manage a modern economy that faces global competition and needs to be run through solid institutions rather than backroom deals. (It was perhaps significant that the man who formed a new coalition government after the Thai economic crisis erupted was Chuan Leekpai of the Democrat Party. He is a mild-mannered man who likes to do things methodically and legally, although some of the politicians he was obliged to draw into his coalition were members of the old-fashioned and corrupt political class.) Both the rural poor and the urban elite have regularly demonstrated in the streets to air their grievances. 'In the last few years we have been very good at throwing the rascals out,' says Ammar. 'Of course we have been getting the rascals in too. The first step is to throw the rascals out without having the tanks running around the streets. The next step is to stop the rascals coming in.'[10]

Throughout south-east Asia, names and personalities are often as important as policies. The children of the region's leaders seem to be drawn inexorably towards power. In Burma, Suu Kyi took the unusual step of prefixing her name with her father's – Aung San, who brought the country to the brink of independence before he was assassinated – to announce her origins in a country where family names are not normally used. In Singapore, Lee Kuan Yew's son Lee Hsien Loong, known as BG Lee because of his military rank of Brigadier-General, is deputy prime minister. Before he was forced to step down, President Suharto had groomed his children – who had previously been more interested in business – to play a political role in Indonesia, while Megawati Sukarnoputri in opposition drew on the memory of her father Sukarno. In the Philippines, Corazon Aquino became President in 1986 largely because she was the widow of Benigno Aquino, the assassinated opponent of Marcos. And the winner of the Philippine presidential election in 1998 was a swash-buckling B-movie film star named Joseph 'Erap' Estrada; his vice-president is Gloria Macapagal-Arroyo, daughter of a respected former president. 'We have no idea of power in the abstract,' says Alex Magno, one of the leading political commentators in the Philippines. 'The ordinary Filipino does not talk about the presidency. He talks about Cory [Corazon Aquino] or Ramos.' Magno, who writes in both English and Tagalog, the local *lingua franca*, says his readers in Tagalog complained that he was inventing words when he thought up a word for 'presidency' – '*pangulohan*', derived from '*pangulo*' (president). According to Magno, Asian politics is about personalities and pragmatism. He is regularly asked to teach a course on Asian political theory, but says he cannot because there is none.[11]

But the focus on personalities is not a particular Asian phenom-enon. Similar tendencies can be found in Latin America or Africa. The Philippines has a peculiar political system closely modelled on the US, where film stars – Ronald Reagan is the best-known example – are also influential. More importantly for south-east Asia, the atten-tion given to individuals instead of their policies is a characteristic not just of developing Asia but of many pre-modern, pre-industrial political systems. And the situation is changing. South-east Asian countries have become richer and their inhabitants more educated and demanding, a transformation underlined by the criticisms of younger observers such as Magno himself. As President, Ramos came across as a forceful figure who liked to be seen chomping a big cigar, but he and his supporters repeatedly emphasized the success of his policies rather than his personality. His nickname, dull by Filipino standards, was 'Steady Eddie'. He compared his own achievements in restoring the Philippine economy, reviving its industrial competitiveness and attracting foreign investors to the failures of his predecessors: the nice Cory Aquino, who represented the restoration of democracy but allowed the economy to languish; and Ferdinand Marcos, who espoused a 'crony capitalism' in which corruption was rife and local industries were protected from foreign competition.

The democracies of the Philippines and Thailand are gradually moving towards a more modern form of democracy where policies count as much as personalities. At the other end of the political spectrum, the military junta in Burma and the communist regimes in Vietnam and Laos are also under pressure to modernize their political systems. From the inside, there are demands from middle-class citizens and students who want more representation. From the outside (particularly in the case of Vietnam, with its large exile community in the US), there is additional pressure for change as governments seek to encourage foreign investment and open their economies to the outside world.

Inevitably, political progress is slow. The middle class in these three countries remains small and weak; the average per capita income in Vietnam, Laos and Burma is less than a tenth of the figure in Thailand, whose inhabitants are themselves less than one fifth as rich as those of the United States. Furthermore, the Burmese generals and the communist rulers of Vietnam and Laos are no different from any other totalitarians: serious dissent is crushed, quickly and brutally. But political change is coming and the three governments know it. In Burma, the generals have tried to engineer a constitution which will allow them to continue controlling the country while they withdraw into the background behind a 'democratic' façade, but they have so far been stymied by an almost total lack of popular support.

In Vietnam, the statue of Lenin still stands tall in the centre of the capital Hanoi, with its broad avenues and crumbling French villas. The apparatus of communism remains intact. But since the government has embraced capitalism, the ideological basis for the party's rule has disappeared. This has put party leaders in a quandary. A few years ago they allowed the idea to be floated that the communist party might transform itself into a broad-based nationalist front and even permit the formation of opposition parties. Phan Dinh

Dieu, a mathematician and former member of the National Assembly, became a sort of licensed dissident who was permitted to spell out the contradictions of the Vietnamese system. 'When the Communist party declared its acceptance of the free market economy, it meant that the party is not truly a communist party. They have dropped the communist system,' he said in the presence of one of the government interpreters and 'minders' who routinely arrange government interviews for foreign journalists. 'The result is that the party is transformed from a communist party into a party of power.'[12] By 1997 the government seemed to regret its brief period of openness and Dieu's views were no longer welcome. Vietnamese officials seek to justify their continued control of the country by talking of socialism leavened with the 'thoughts of Ho Chi Minh', just as the Chinese speak of socialism 'with Chinese characteristics'. But the contradictions between a communist power structure ideologically committed to destroying bourgeois capitalism and an increasingly free-market economy have not gone away. The confusion is bad for the economy, because bureaucrats still favour poorly run state companies at the expense of private enterprise; and bad for politics, because the debate needed to resolve Vietnam's numerous problems is stifled. For the time being, Vietnam's leaders have settled for some uneasy compromises, mounting campaigns against corruption in high places, allowing increasingly outspoken criticism of government ministers in the National Assembly and increasing the number of non-communist (but still vetted) candidates for elections to the Assembly. 'The goal is socialism. But what is socialism?' asks one dissident in Hanoi. 'According to the authorities, it is so that people can be richer, the country stronger and society just and civilized – that's very vague. I don't understand the leaders of Vietnam. They are tangled up in contradictions and they can't get out, or they don't want to. On the one hand they have their beliefs, on the other hand they have the material profits. Maybe that's why they don't want to get out.'

So much for the democracies and the old-fashioned dictatorships. What of those in between? Political systems in Asia have been neatly placed in three categories: 'elite democracies' such as the Philippines; 'market Stalinism', as in Vietnam; and the 'veiled authoritarianism' of Singapore, Indonesia and Malaysia.[13] This last group is of particular significance. It includes two countries – Malaysia and Singapore – that have combined outstanding economic success with political stability under broadly unchanged governments for most of the last three decades. And it is to the 'veiled authoritarians', also known as 'soft authoritarians', that the leaders of newly developing countries such as Vietnam and Burma are looking for a political model that will allow them to retain power while still promoting economic growth. Even in the Philippines and Thailand, there are people who yearn for the apparent stability of strong government in place of the political bickering that plagues their democracies.

These 'soft authoritarian' governments are the political embodiment of 'Asian values'. They argue that the government of a developing country cannot afford to tolerate the confusion and disruption resulting from free speech and liberal politics as understood in the West. This is especially true in the early years of nationhood and of economic growth, when people are less educated, less conscious of their national identity and more liable to be drawn into violent ethnic conflicts by unscrupulous politicians. Central to the thinking of Mahathir, for example, are the riots of 1969 in which Malays rioted and killed scores of their ethnic Chinese fellow-citizens after an election. For Mahathir, there are more dangers in what he calls 'democratic extremism' than in authoritarianism.[14]

Rather than attempting to justify their rule, the authoritarians believe their best tactic is to denigrate democracies and point out their obvious weaknesses. They often compare India, Bangladesh, the Philippines and now Cambodia to stronger Asian economies and blame democracy for their relatively poor economic performance. Even under the reforming Fidel Ramos, the Philippine administration and the country's businesses have had to fight to implement the simplest economic decisions in the face of the country's US-style political system. The Supreme Court and a Congress beholden to numerous lobbies and to fickle public opinion repeatedly intervened to block decisions that would go unchallenged elsewhere in southeast Asia. In 1997, for example, the Supreme Court cancelled a government contract to privatize the Manila Hotel after years of negotiations on the grounds that the winning consortium was led by a foreign company and the hotel was part of the national patrimony. And as in the US, it is extremely difficult for a government to raise fuel taxes or allow fuel prices to rise – however compelling the fiscal or environmental arguments for doing so – without anger-ing the public and so losing public support. In the Philippines, the Supreme Court even intervened to prevent oil companies raising their prices to reflect the higher cost of oil imports after the mid-1997 south-east Asian financial crisis and sharp devaluation of the peso; it did so in spite of the fact that the local oil sector had been deregulated earlier in the year.

But perhaps the most common comparison made by the authori-tarians is between Russia and China, an illustration particularly relev-ant for the communist states of Vietnam and Laos but frequently applied to other authoritarian states in the region as well. The argu-ment is that Russia (or the Soviet Union as it was under Mikhail Gorbachev) liberalized its politics first and its economy later, causing poverty, chaos and a precipitate decline in gross domestic product; while China, under the late Deng Xiaoping, liberalized its economy but maintained firm political control, to the extent of shooting pro-democracy demonstrators after the occupation of Beijing's Tianan-men Square by protesters in 1989 – with the result that the Chinese economy has enjoyed double-digit economic growth along with social order and greater prosperity for most of its people. The counter-argument is that China has merely delayed the inevitable. 'Deng was widely congratulated not long ago for having avoided the Soviet "mistake" of putting political ahead of economic reform,' wrote one commentator. 'Now this is becoming a matter of reproach: the absence of democracy is assigned central responsibility for the dark side of the economic miracle.'[15] That dark side includes civil-rights abuses at home and an aggressive foreign policy. Nevertheless the Russia-as-failure and China-as-success argument is among the most commonly used ammunition in the arsenal of south-east Asia's authoritarians. In the same vein, they leap at the chance to blame democratization for any sign of political instability or economic difficulty in South Korea or Taiwan, while attributing the economic success of those countries to their authoritarian heritage.

An important feature of Asian 'soft authoritarian' governments such as those of Singapore and Malaysia is that they use one-person, one-vote political systems similar in form (but not in substance) to those in the West. This is partly because they inherited these systems from the colonial powers, and the leaders who used them to come to power would find it embarrassing openly to undermine them.

'Our most precious inheritance in Singapore is the fact that we have kept going British institutions of great value to us,' says the government's George Yeo, mentioning parliament, the judicial system and the English language. The combination of strong government and a democratic façade was justified in the 1960s, 1970s and 1980s by the need to oppose Asian communism; it was this search for a bulwark against communism that brought together the founders of Asean in 1967. The appearance of democracy remains valuable in the 1990s to satisfy domestic public opinion and to defuse any international criticism.

But there is no question of the opposition being allowed to win power in a national election. Witness the violent events in Indonesia surrounding Megawati's challenge to Suharto and Goh's threats to voters in Singapore. ('Do you think we could have done even half of what was achieved in the last thirty years if we had a multiparty system and a revolving-door government?' Goh once asked. 'Do you think we could have done just as well if we had a government that was constantly being held in check by ten to twenty opposition members?'[16]) Then there have been Mahathir's furious campaigns in Malaysia to bring errant states to heel – including the withholding of federal financial support – when they elect opposition parties. Just before the 1990 elections in Malaysia, Joseph Pairin Kitingan, chief minister of the somewhat disaffected state of Sabah in Borneo, withdrew his PBS party from the Barisan Nasional, the ruling national coalition led by Mahathir's Umno (the United Malays National Organization), and went on to win in Sabah. As the writer Rehman Rashid recounts, those who were with Mahathir at the time of the PBS pullout had never seen the prime minister so angry: 'The squeeze began,' writes Rashid. 'Sabah's timber export quota was lowered, decimating the state's principal source of revenue. Tourism was tacitly discouraged; domestic air fares were raised. (For [neighbouring] Sarawak, however, there were affordable package deals.) Domestic investment was redirected; foreign investment put on hold. (Sabah was "politically unstable".) The borders grew even more porous to illegal immigration from the Philippines and Indonesia. The local television station was abandoned. Sabah was denied permission to have on its territory a branch of a Malaysian university, as Sarawak did. Pairin was charged with three counts of corruption. Kota Kinabalu became a funereal town.'[17] The point about immigration was that most of the newcomers were Moslems, rather than the Christian Kadazans who formed the bedrock of PBS support, and they could therefore be drawn into Umno. The central government demonstrated it would do almost anything to bring Sabah into the fold again. In 1994 the state was back in central government hands after four years of opposition.

For years, people have struggled to define and analyse these kinds of authoritarian governments and explain their success. On the face of it, they are not one-party states, so the term 'dominant party politics' has come to be used. One of the best definitions to describe the combination of elections and unchallenged rule by a government party is Samuel Huntington's 'democracy without turnover'. Another analyst notes that the democratic system and the law are regarded by such governments as resources to exploit rather than restrictive frameworks within which they must operate; it is the people who are accountable to the government – in the sense that they must lose investments or bus routes or housing upgrades if they vote for the opposition – rather than the government which is accountable to the people.[18]

Yet neither Singapore, nor Malaysia, nor Indonesia can comfortably be labelled totalitarian. They are not usually brutal in governing their own people (Indonesia's war of conquest in East Timor in the mid-1970s is the obvious exception), which is why they have come to be known as 'soft' authoritarians. They allow their opponents to speak and to organize, albeit within certain limits. Although they use the security provisions inherited from their former colonial masters to detain or otherwise restrict opponents without trial, they do not normally use them to an extreme extent. The authoritarian policy of permitting limited dissent – while forbidding opposition parties to become too strong, let alone win – is rarely admitted in explicit terms, but is no secret. Asked why south-east Asian leaders bothered with the trappings of democracy when they believed so fervently in the importance of strong government, Juwono Sudarsono of Indonesia's National Defence Institute, one of Indonesia's foremost political analysts and a minister in the dying days of Suharto's rule, accepts that there is a level of 'tolerable dissent'. 'You devise systems which allow some degree of dissent,' he says. 'All south-east Asian countries do that, simply because it's practical.'

Opposition parties and other groups critical of the government are seen as sparring partners. 'Sparring partners are not supposed to win.'[19]

Coercion – sometimes outright force – remains a vital part of government tactics throughout south-east Asia. In its crudest manifestations, this means arresting and torturing government opponents; more subtly, it can mean that opposition leaders will mysteriously find it impossible to get work in government institutions (if they are teachers or doctors, for example) or to win government contracts (if they are in business). Even before Hun Sen overtly seized control of Cambodia in his 1997 coup d'état, members of parliament were all too aware of the dangers of speaking freely about the rampant corruption in their government. 'We are limited in our activities,' said Ahmed Yahya, an MP for the royalist Funcinpec party and a member of Cambodia's Cham Moslem minority. 'If I dare to speak up, I will feel lonely and a lot of people will hate me and I will get a bullet in my chest or my head or my hand, so I have to keep quiet.'[20] Shortly after he said this, fifteen people were killed when grenades were thrown at opposition leader Sam Rainsy, a pro-democracy campaigner and former finance minister. Hun Sen's followers were strongly suspected of being the perpetrators. Both Rainsy and Yahya subsequently went into temporary exile overseas.

There are other, less obviously violent methods by which governments maintain control. One is to restrict the rights of industrial workers and to ban free trade unions. (Sam Rainsy was particularly unpopular with the government and Asian investors because he championed the rights of Cambodian textile factory workers being paid as little as US$30 a month.) Vigorous and independent trade unions are the exception rather than the norm in south-east Asia, in spite of the universal tendency of workers to organize themselves as a country industrializes. In Malaysia, trade unions have been banned in the electronics industry, which is vital to Malaysian export growth. In Indonesia, the Suharto government harassed and arrested leaders of the free trade union SBSI and promoted a pro-government union called the SPSI. In Singapore and Vietnam, unions are closely linked to the government. Even in democratic Thailand, unions are weak and face various legal restrictions, some harking back to the struggle between the authorities and their communist opponents in the 1960s and 1970s. However, such restrictions are not always as controversial in south-east Asia itself as they appear to international labour rights campaigners. Many factories and workshops do have grim health and safety records and industrial employees do work long hours with fewer benefits than in the West. There are frequent worker protests at factories in the poorer countries such as Vietnam and Indonesia. But conditions in modern factories, particularly those owned by foreign multinationals with international images to maintain, are usually nothing like as appalling as they were in the textile mills of the English industrial revolution. Wages have been rising sharply, too. One of the biggest headaches for employers in the Malaysian electronics sector is not worker activism but job-hopping for higher pay. In Thailand, it was notable that when a left-wing British magazine sought to expose conditions in the troubled textile industry in Bangkok, it illustrated the article with a photograph of a happily smiling Thai seamstress. Wages were low and hours long, the article said. But it added: 'The most surprising feature of Bangkok is the absence of conflict between workers and owners. There is nothing of the smouldering hatreds of Jakarta, or the concealment of Dhaka. Neither side appears to see the relationship as exploitative.'[21] In the more developed southeast Asian economies, the combination of globalization, fast-growing economies and rising wages has helped to defuse the employer–worker conflict that has hitherto been an inevitable part of industrial revolution.

But the suppression of trade unions is only one aspect of authoritarianism in practice in south-east Asia. Much more sinister are the decline of the rule of law, the erosion of the independence of the judiciary and the increasingly explicit role of the police and security forces as agents of those in power rather than defenders of law and order. Some countries – Burma and Cambodia, for example – have been under authoritarian rule for so long that the young have no experience at all of a justice system in which courts and judges function independently of the regime's wishes. In other countries, there has been a gradual decline in the professionalism of the legal system and an increase in government interference since independence. Courts in most of south-east Asia routinely support the government in political cases, labour disputes and environmental challenges to government-backed projects; when they do not, both sides in the case are usually surprised – and such decisions are over-turned on appeal. The issue of the rule of law, vital for honest business executives and humble peasants alike, comes up again and again in interviews across the region. People usually regard the right to be treated fairly as more important even than the right to vote. The concept and practice of the rule of law existed long before the European Enlightenment and continue to exist in non-western societies.[22] Even if one can label liberal democracy as a 'western' demand, the same is not true of the rule of law.

For the Malaysian journalist Rehman Rashid, the government's decapitation of the Supreme Court in the 1980s was the last straw that drove him into voluntary exile. Mahathir had sharply criticized the judiciary after a number of cases in which judges had upheld freedom of speech and challenged a controversial government road contract. After the Lord President of the Supreme Court had protested about the government interference, he and two other Supreme Court judges were dismissed. 'Malaysia's judiciary was decimated,' wrote Rashid. 'Great gaping holes had been blown on the highest bench, and they would be filled by the premature promotions of the definitively inexperienced. Moreover, these jurists would know they owed their elevation to political forces, and their consciences would never command the respect of Malaysia's legal fraternity. To peer over the bench and see nothing but contempt at the Bar – how would that impact upon the discharge of their duties? The Malaysian judiciary would be a beleaguered and fearful shadow of what it had been.'[23] At first the concern was focused on political matters. But by the 1990s there were fears that large, well-connected Malaysian companies were using the courts for purely commercial advantage. 'Complaints are rife that certain highly placed personalities in Malaysia, including those in the business and corporate sectors, are manipulating the Malaysian system of justice,' said Mr Param Curaswamy, a lawyer and special rapporteur on the independence of judges and lawyers for the UN Commission on Human Rights.[24]

Other countries have similar problems. In Indonesia, the independence of the judiciary was undermined by the fact that most senior posts in the Justice Ministry and the High Court were filled by graduates of the military law academy.[25] Thailand's justice system is affected by bribes paid to prosecutors, judges and the police.[26] Philippine courts are subject to corruption too. By one estimate, only about seven in every fifty judges were honest. 'Certainly the crooked judges live lives way beyond the means of their income,' said Senator Gloria Macapagal-Arroyo, who went on to become vice-president.[27]

It has become increasingly difficult to discuss such matters openly in south-east Asia. Critics fear they will be found in contempt of court by the very courts they are criticizing. This is what happened to Lingle, the American professor working at the National University of Singapore. In 1994, he wrote an article in the *International Herald Tribune* responding to an earlier commentary, critical of the West, written by Kishore Mahbubani of the Singapore foreign ministry. Without mentioning any particular country, Lingle said some Asian governments relied on a 'compliant judiciary to bankrupt opposition politicians'. The prosecutor in Singapore asserted that this must be a reference to Singapore, where Lee Kuan Yew and his PAP colleagues indeed had a record of suing opposition politicians for defamation. Lingle (who had fled the country), and the editor, publisher, printer and distributor of the newspaper (which has one of its printing sites in Singapore) were ordered to pay enormous fines and costs for contempt of the Singapore judiciary. The offence was not to say that the government bankrupted its opponents, but to call the courts 'compliant'. Lingle vividly described the unusual experience – for a mild-mannered university professor – of suddenly finding himself being interrogated by the police for expressing unremarkable opinions. He ran away – fearful until his plane was airborne that he would be arrested – leaving behind his job and most of his possessions. He has since become one of the most cogent critics of Singapore, comparing it unfavourably to South Africa in the apartheid era, when he says he openly denounced the regime without fear of repression. Subsequently, Singapore's leaders continued to sue their opponents – notably Tang and Jeyaretnam in 1997.[28] The fact that both men are lawyers is a reflection of the traditions of independence that the judiciary once boasted of: the law was one of the few professions where people felt far enough removed from government patronage and influence to practise opposition politics. That no longer seems to be so. Tang, like other opposition figures before him, fled overseas.

Singapore's ministers are adamant that they must defend the reputation of the country and its leaders. They deny that they have become absurdly litigious (a habit which Asians frequently mock as an American disease) and believe that courts in the West are too liberal in allowing apparently defamatory attacks on important people. 'I don't think Singapore can exist if ministers and national leaders are placed on the same level as second-hand-car dealers,' says George Yeo. 'It would be a disaster. How can we run the place like that?' Some Singaporeans insist that whereas westerners – out of respect for individual rights – say it would be better for a guilty person to go free than to convict an innocent one, Asians prefer the innocent person to be convicted if that will help the common good.[29] But there is an unresolved contradiction in the attitudes of south-east Asian authoritarians. They defend their right to have a different, non-liberal, non-western system of justice, but at the same time governments can insist – on pain of legal action – that they have not in any way undermined the independence of their judiciaries.

Some authoritarian governments in south-east Asia deploy soldiers to break up demonstrations. They sometimes suppress labour movements and sometimes manipulate the courts. For the region's more sophisticated authoritarians, however, coercion alone is not a satisfactory method either of developing the country or of keeping power indefinitely. The repeated use of force alienates the population, antagonizes foreign governments and makes overseas investors uneasy; it is, in short, politically destabilizing. A much more effective solution is to co-opt the government's potential opponents, leaving coercion as a last resort to bring into line the few intransigents who refuse to be brought into the fold. Why crudely censor the media, for example, when you can persuade editors and journalists to censor themselves? Singapore's Lee Hsien Loong, deputy prime minister and son of Lee Kuan Yew, acknowledges the role played by co-option in south-east Asian politics. For him and his government colleagues, it is essential that the government should be allowed to govern while planning and legislating for the future without being pulled this way and that by various pressure groups. 'If people continually make such suggestions which make sense we will soon have him in our system, rather than keep him outside and throwing stones at us or criticizing us, because if he's making sense we will bring him in and use him,' says Lee. 'We don't believe that it is a good thing to encourage lots of little pressure groups, each one pushing its own direction and the outcome being a kind of Ouija board result rather than a considered national approach.'[30]

South-east Asian governments devote much time and effort to this task of co-opting their citizens and forging a sense of national purpose – a purpose for which only the government or the ruling party, it is understood, are qualified to succeed. It is not only the region's communist states that run Orwellian propaganda campaigns. The Burmese authorities organize crude pro-government rallies which usually end, according to the official media, with 'tumultuous chanting of slogans'.[31] Suharto's Indonesia practised a form of guided democracy based on the vague ideology of '*pancasila*', the five principles of belief in one God; humanism; nationalism; popular sovereignty; and social justice. Suharto was called the 'Father of Development'. Singapore is famous for its government campaigns. An agency once called the 'psychological defence unit' of the information ministry and now renamed the 'publicity department' has promoted patriotism through singing, starting with the early hit song 'Stand up for Singapore' in the mid-1980s. Other campaigns have urged Singaporeans to have more or fewer babies, depending on the population growth rate and demand for labour; to defend their country; to flush the toilet; to turn up at weddings on time; and not to be too greedy at hotel buffet lunches. Richard Tan Kok Tong, a former head of the Psychological Defence Unit – and one of those Singaporeans who met his wife through the official match-making service of the Social Development Unit – says people respond to such campaigns partly because they feel vulnerable in a small, multiracial city state surrounded by the large Moslem populations of Indonesia and Malaysia. 'We have a background where the people are told you're here as migrants and we either pull together or we get hanged together,' he said. 'It's against this sort of precondition that people can accept this sort of propaganda.'[32]

Such propaganda, however, is not enough to ensure the support of the more sophisticated members of society. In most of south-east Asia, patronage – the conferring of favours in exchange for loyalty – is also an essential part of the political system. It is of course true that neither political patronage nor corruption are confined to Asia, or to authoritarian governments. In Thailand, Banharn became a member of parliament and then prime minister largely because he was adept at directing the government's budget to the projects he favoured. His constituency of Suphanburi became famous for its excellent roads and facilities – and was nicknamed 'Banharn-buri'.

In the Philippines, senators and members of the House of Representatives are expected to dispense largesse by sponsoring weddings, buying trophies for village athletics competitions and writing letters of recommendation to possible employers for people they have never met. Such patronage is typical of old-fashioned political systems in which personal loyalties are prized and institutions are weak; it can also be risky for both sides, because shifting political alliances and regular elections mean that those who are powerful today will not necessarily have influence tomorrow.

But in an authoritarian state, the existing government is the only reliable source of patronage; and it usually intends to remain so. The result in countries such as Indonesia and Malaysia has been an exceptionally close relationship between government and big business. Selected companies benefit from large infrastructure projects initiated or funded by the state – roads, power stations and so on – and from government licences to exploit natural resources such as timber. In return, businesses are expected to be politically loyal and to provide financial support – sometimes for government purposes and sometimes for individuals. In Indonesia, the involvement of President Suharto's children and a handful of his longstanding ethnic Chinese associates in big industrial and infrastructural projects and in trading monopolies was notorious. In Malaysia, where the government has had an explicit policy of favouring Malays over the Chinese who previously dominated business, the web of connections between corporations and the ruling Umno party has been extensively documented.[33]

In Cambodia, there has been an open exchange of favours and cash between Hun Sen's government and the coarse but powerful businessman Theng Bunma. One of the more bizarre manifestations of Cambodian patronage has been the building of hundreds of 'Hun Sen schools' around the country; the businessmen pay and Hun Sen supposedly wins the admiration of an education-starved populace. Meanwhile the education ministry can barely pay its teachers, let alone build schools, because it is starved of funds by the Hun Sen government – which neglects the collection of formal taxes from big businesses. One senior member of Hun Sen's Cambodian People's Party explained the country's patronage system by saying that if a businessman wanting a concession offered money to Hun Sen in the 'Asian way', Hun Sen would say, 'Build me a school'; if offered flowers, he would say, 'I don't want flowers. Give me food and fish and noodles for the army.'[34] In few countries are the ties between politicians and businessmen as unsubtle as in Cambodia, but the symbiosis of the two is common throughout the region. The extent to which companies rely on governments for their profits has obvious economic and commercial implications which are discussed in chapter 4. Politically, it simply means that big businessmen tend to identify closely with governments and publicly support their aims.

In the 1980s and early 1990s, the south-east Asian model of authoritarian politics seemed remarkably successful. Economies grew at 6 per cent, 8 per cent, 9 per cent, even 12 per cent a year. Businesses were expanding at breakneck speed. The poor got less poor. The rich got richer. Ethnic differences were apparently buried. Governments and their business allies began to boast of the success of 'Asian values' and to formulate theories that justified their authoritarianism and rejected 'western' democracy. There was little sign that the newly enriched elites wanted to rock the boat by opposing their governments just when they were starting to lead comfortable, even luxurious, lives. They enjoyed working for banks, stockbrokers or industrial conglomerates in Jakarta or Bangkok, shopping for brand-name clothes and travelling overseas just like their counterparts in London or New York. Privately, they mocked the simplistic slogans of their governments, but few took part in any serious opposition movements. As Malaysian businessman David Chew puts it: 'More and more people now are stakeholders in the country; and if you're stakeholders you'll want to preserve what you have ... Maybe this is the better brand of democracy. Of course, it's a little bit more autocratic.'[35]

As confidence grew, so too did talk of exporting successful authoritarian political models to newly developing countries in south-east Asia. Indonesia was regarded as a particularly useful model for Burma and Vietnam because it had developed a quasi-democratic system of government in which the armed forces are given explicit political privileges (by being allocated seats in the national assembly, for example), and in which they play an even more influential role behind the scenes. In all three countries the soldiers believe they have a right to a role in national politics because of their involvement in the struggle for independence from foreign powers, and – in the cases of Indonesia and Burma – in maintaining order and keeping fractious ethnic minorities in the national fold after independence. The idea of exporting this model – known in Indonesia as *dwifungsi* (dual function) because it grants the armed forces a sort of guardian role in politics and society in addition to their normal security function – is not without difficulties. Indonesia's generals are anxious not to be associated too openly with Burma's military junta for fear of discrediting the whole *dwifungsi* concept. They fear that Burmese soldiers might again commit some internationally-condemned atrocity against their own people, and they are uneasy about the seeming inability of the Burmese generals to relinquish control and retire elegantly behind the scenes. Whereas in Indonesia the management of the economy was successfully delegated to the western-educated economists known as the Berkeley mafia, the generals in Burma tried to run the economy themselves – with predictably disastrous results.

Another difficulty for authoritarians is that the legitimacy that a government or an army earns from an independence war or a fight to restore domestic order is soon diminished by generational change; most Vietnamese today were born after the end of the Vietnam war in 1975. 'In our time of rising popular expectations,' said José Almonte, who was national security adviser to former Philippine president Fidel Ramos, 'authoritarian governments are essentially fragile – no matter how commanding they may appear to be. Because they rule without popular consent, their claim to legitimacy depends on their ability to restore stability and to develop the economy. And, once civil order is restored, authoritarian governments in developing countries are undermined by both their economic failure and their economic success.' Economic failure obviously makes them unpopular, while 'economic growth unavoidably generates social change that multiplies people's demands for political participation and respect from their rulers.'[36]

Aristides Katoppo, a senior Indonesian journalist and head of the Sinar Harapan publishing company, predicted before Suharto was forced to resign that a more demanding electorate would eventually oblige the Indonesian government to modify its authoritarian stance. 'I think they [the people] don't mind a strong executive government, but it must be more just and less arrogant. Rule of law is the issue.' He acknowledged that the reduction of military influence in government and the erosion of the power of the authorities would take time, but he had no doubt about the way things were going. 'The direction,' he said, 'is very clear.'[37] South-east Asian liberals are beginning to make their voices heard. They affirm the need for justice, whatever a country's political system. They reject the idea that democracy is 'un-Asian', pointing to various democratic – or at least consultative – village traditions. And they have begun to pick holes in some of the favourite arguments of the authoritarians.

One of the most compelling justifications for authoritarian rule is the idea that democrats cannot run an economy properly, particularly in the early stages of a country's development, because they are buffeted this way and that by powerful interest groups. Democrats are prone to corruption and endless bickering. They allocate capital inefficiently, on the basis of bribes rather than the national interest. It is much better, the argument goes, to have a sensible if rather authoritarian government running the show. Thailand and the Philippines, the two most democratic states in south-east Asia, are certainly riddled with corruption. The Thai police force, for example, operates an almost formal system of corruption and protection rackets; money extorted from citizens and businesses such as brothels is passed up from policemen on the street to their senior officers. Meanwhile, Thai gangster-businessmen known as *jao pho* ('godfathers') fight each other for influence over provincial territories – usually with guns, but on one memorable occasion with a rocket launcher used to blow up one of the godfathers in his car – and then move on to exert control over national politicians.[38] Vote-buying is still a common practice in Thai elections: several recent prime ministers have taken office not because they were admired for their policies or leadership capabilities, but because of the number and power of their political allies. Corruption is a problem in the Philippines as well, to the extent that policemen have been implicated in the kidnappings of ethnic Chinese businessmen.

Although such corruption is clearly damaging for the countries concerned, it is not necessarily true that the cause of the trouble is democracy or that they are any worse than their more authoritarian rivals. Several points need to be borne in mind. First, corruption also affected Britain and the United States during their industrial revolutions in the eighteenth and nineteenth centuries. As in Asia, businessmen of often dubious reputation, made wealthy by the economic boom, were able to buy respectability and transform their families into pillars of society. Corruption is easy and effective at a time when old-fashioned traditions of patronage survive alongside new – and weak – political institutions.

Second, corruption appears to have passed its peak in Thailand and the Philippines as increasingly sophisticated citizens lose their tolerance for gangsterism and incompetence. Thai and Filipino politicians have tried to expose corruption by asking how their enemies became 'unusually wealthy'.[39] This is the policy recommended by Gloria Macapagal-Arroyo, Philippine vice-president, for dealing with gangsters and corrupt politicians and judges. 'It's the Al Capone solution. They didn't catch him on murder. They got him on tax evasion,' she said.[40]

Finally, Thailand and the Philippines are much more open societies than their south-east Asian neighbours. Journalists and academic researchers are able to investigate corruption and publish their findings without intimidation. More is known about corruption because of this openness, rather than because they are necessarily more corrupt. Indonesia has long been notorious among business people for its nepotism and corrupt practices, but it is difficult to pin down the details of suspicious deals. The same is true of Burma. In Malaysia and communist Vietnam, corruption often comes to light because the government announces a crackdown, not as a result of an independent investigation. Sometimes financial transactions are exposed by accident. Muhammad Muhammad Taib, the chief minister of the prosperous Malaysian state of Selangor and a vice-president of Umno, was stopped and charged in Australia for failing to declare the equivalent of more than 1.3 million Australian dollars in cash he was carrying as he left on a flight from Brisbane in 1996. He resigned his chief minister's job. He was acquitted by an Australian court on the grounds that he had not intended to break the law by failing to declare the money, but in mid-1998 was still the subject of anti-corruption investigations in Malaysia. Only Singapore has avoided the worst excesses of financial corruption, by paying its civil servants and government ministers high salaries and by efficiently policing the island's three million people.

The argument that authoritarian states manage their economies more efficiently because they are not subject to lobbying by powerful interest groups does not withstand close inspection. In Indonesia,

Malaysia, Vietnam, Burma and Cambodia, powerful businessmen –
with the right family ties, military connections or party affiliations –
can win contracts, ignore regulations, set up industrial projects of
doubtful value and receive favourable tax treatment because of who
they are rather than because they are offering the best deal. Entrepreneurs
sweeten their sponsors and contacts in the government by
offering them shares in companies as they are floated on local stock
exchanges (where the shares have traditionally soared after flotation).
Army generals and entrepreneurs enrich themselves by selling
their country's natural resources – usually timber – before
retiring to luxurious villas. There is not much more economic efficiency
here than there was in the Philippines under Marcos and his
'crony capitalists'. Negotiations in a democracy may be painfully
slow, but they have the advantage of being more transparent. 'We
will be predictable because it's basically the rule of law, versus the
whim of some autocrats,' argues Roberto Romulo in defence of
democracy. Romulo, the former Philippine foreign minister and now
head of the PLDT telephone company, believes economic liberalization
has a better chance of enduring if it arises from debate and
legislation, however laborious, rather than from executive fiat.[41]

According to the proponents of 'Asian values', people should
respect their governments, however authoritarian, and governments
in turn should be wise and far-sighted in the interests of their people.
It rarely turns out like that in south-east Asia. Asians give credit to
their governments for the economic achievements of the 1970s and
1980s, but they mock the corruption and wastefulness of their
leaders and boorish hangers-on, and are sometimes willing to risk
their careers – even their lives – in defence of what they regard as
their rights. In the past few years, people have died for democracy
on the streets of Burma, Thailand and Indonesia. Democratic feelings
have never been stronger.

The democracy restored to the Philippines in 1986, in which
businessmen and the army finally turned against a corrupt and inefficient
dictator, is still intact more than a decade later. In Thailand,
pro-democracy demonstrations in the 1970s were led by left-wing
students. Nowadays they include businessmen, doctors, lawyers and
office workers. 'Big business used to be a strong ally of the military,
say, twenty years ago, but as the economy becomes liberalized and
deregulated the competitive environment demands a different set

of roles in politics,' says Abhisit Vejjajiva, a Democrat Party member of parliament in Bangkok. 'There is great awareness that we need to have a more open, cleaner, more effective political system . . . It's not keeping up with the social and economic needs of the country.'[42]

In Malaysia, a new generation of politicians is openly expressing its weariness with old-fashioned 'money politics'. Abdul-Rahman Adnan, whose think-tank promotes the agenda of former deputy prime minister Anwar Ibrahim, rejects the suggestion that corruption is an acceptable part of Asian politics. 'You may say this is the way things are done in Asia. But we don't buy that,' he says. Adnan also refuses to accept that Malaysians should live in an authoritarian society where the media is controlled. 'I feel that we are a bit too un-free at the moment,' he says. 'They [the press] will write about corruption but they won't really ask the tough questions. For instance, one MP gets caught with two million dollars cash overseas. What do you do about it? What do the papers say about it? Here they will try to find out what's really happening, but it won't get published . . . The problem is that all our newspapers are owned by the political masters.' Adnan concludes: 'I think people don't want to be made fools of. They expect the government to be more accountable.'[43]

In Vietnam, senior members of the Communist Party continue quietly to discuss how to reform their highly authoritarian system of government. Some favour a transition to a 'soft authoritarian' model; others appear to lean more towards western-style, multi-party democracy; many, needless to say, maintain that any relaxation of Communist Party control will lead to chaos. Unfortunately for these opponents of reform, the Party has little appeal for young Vietnamese and is already starting to lose its grip. Le Hong Ha, a former Communist Party official and an advocate of democracy, spent two years in jail in the mid-1990s for revealing 'state secrets'; his crime was to have publicized a letter to the politburo from Vo Van Kiet, then the prime minister, in which Kiet recommended political reform and an end to favoured status for state companies. Ha was subsequently released in August 1997, four months early. 'Now even in the politburo there are people who take the side of the dissidents,' said one Vietnamese supporter of democratization.[44]

To understand the strength of the movement for political reform in south-east Asia, it is worth looking at the extraordinary impact on the region of recent events in South Korea – particularly the 1996 trial of two former presidents and several corporate chairmen on corruption charges. In what was known in Seoul as 'the trial of the century', Chun Doo-hwan was sentenced to death and his successor Roh Tae-woo was sentenced to twenty-two years in jail for their actions when they ruled South Korea between 1980 and 1993. They were found guilty of amassing US$1 billion in slush funds and of ordering the army to suppress a pro-democracy demonstration in 1980 in which more than 200 people were killed. Although there was an air of political theatre about the trial (they were later pardoned), the effect on the public of the news and pictures showing the former strongmen humbled and dressed in prison fatigues to hear their fate in the courtroom was electrifying. Pro-democracy campaigners were delighted. In countries with a free press, such as Thailand, cartoonists and columnists had a field day pointing out the obvious lessons for old-fashioned authoritarians and corrupt politicians. In Indonesia, it was enough for newspapers to print the photograph of the two men humbled before their accusers on the front page with an explanatory caption; readers knew what it meant, and eagerly discussed it on the buses of Jakarta. In Malaysia, a caller to a live phone-in television programme on an entirely different subject used the opportunity to mention the Korean trial, to criticize Mahathir, the prime minister, and to remind him of Chun's fate. Burmese opponents of the military government in Rangoon could hardly contain their glee. The Burmese generals, one teacher said, 'are very afraid of what is happening in Korea'.[45] For the democrats there was an important snag: Chun and Roh had eventually ushered in democratic rule – and if they were to be so severely punished, what incentive would there be for other Asian autocrats to loosen their grip on power? Yet the power of the trial lay in its symbolism. The two men were pardoned anyway, and for Asian democrats the trial heralded a new era: those in power could eventually be brought to book for whatever cruel and corrupt acts they had perpetrated while ruling their countries without the people's consent.

The Korean trial had an impact on south-east Asian countries half a continent away for another, entirely different reason. It demonstrated how difficult it had become for governments to control the dissemination of information in an increasingly interconnected world. Central government control of news and ideas is undermined by the sheer number of methods – some old-fashioned and some the product of high technology – that are now available to transmit information. They include terrestrial, satellite and cable television, mobile telephones, fax machines, domestic and foreign radio stations, and, of course, the Internet. Add to these the very rapid growth in travel to south-east Asia by foreigners, and by south-east Asians to destinations overseas, and the enormous task facing any government bent on censorship becomes clear.

This is not to say that governments in south-east Asia have stopped trying to control what people know. Burma has some of the most extreme controls. James Nichols, honorary consul in Burma for Denmark and several other European countries and a supporter of Aung San Suu Kyi, died in prison – allegedly after being deprived of sleep to force him to confess his links to the opposition – after being jailed and kept in isolation in a small cell: his crime was to use a fax machine without permission. The maximum sentence for unauthorized use of a computer with a modem (the device that enables it to communicate with the outside world via a telephone line) is fifteen years in prison. Burmese are supposed to get their news from *The New Light of Myanmar*, the official newspaper previously known as *The Working People's Daily*. But the absence of real domestic news in the paper, the plethora of irrelevant foreign stories taken from news agencies and the empty formulas used to describe the meetings of government ministers have the Orwellian flavour of the press in a Soviet satellite state in the 1970s. Rangoon, Burma's dishevelled capital, is dotted with huge red and white billboards bearing bizarre official slogans in praise of the army. At the corner of the leafy University Avenue, where Suu Kyi lives in semi-confinement in a part of the street that is behind government roadblocks, was one that read: 'People's Desire – Oppose those relying on external elements, acting as stooges, holding negative views. Oppose those trying to jeopardize stability of the state and progress of the nation. Oppose foreign nations interfering in internal affairs of the state. Crush all internal and external destructive elements as the common enemy.'

The billboard was opposite an advertisement for Foster's lager. Given the government's total control of the media, it is no surprise that the Burmese secretly listen to the Burmese language radio services of the BBC and the Voice of America to find out what is happening in the world and in their own country.

South-east Asia's 'soft authoritarians' are more subtle. Singapore and Malaysia ban privately-owned satellite television dishes and exercise firm control over the mainstream local media: television, radio and the main newspapers. Singapore 'punishes' foreign publications – *The Economist* and the *Far Eastern Economic Review* have been among the many victims – by restricting their circulation. Singaporean officials openly admit that their aim is to 'filter' information before it reaches the general public. But high-tech Singapore believes its economic future depends on information technology, so it has embraced the Internet while trying to limit its potentially adverse effects on society and government. Internet users are required to route their requests for access through 'proxy servers', computers which screen out blacklisted sites regarded as objectionable by the government. Internet service providers, 'cybercafés' where people can use a computer to 'surf' the Internet, and those injecting locally produced pages for the Internet's World Wide Web on political or religious matters, must all register with the Singapore Broadcasting Authority. Restricted material includes not only pornography but statements 'which tend to bring the Government into hatred or contempt, or which excite disaffection against the Government' and 'which undermine the public confidence in the administration of justice'. These are extraordinarily broad provisions, but then Lee Kuan Yew has said that only the 'top 3 to 5 per cent of a society' can handle the chaotic free-for-all of ideas and information available on the Internet.[46]

Indonesia has a much more lively media than Singapore, and a tradition of sophisticated, independently-owned newspapers and magazines to serve its immense population. Suharto's government tarnished this reputation in the mid-1990s by closing down publications deemed too critical of the authorities, including the news magazine *Tempo* – the Indonesian equivalent of the US magazine *Time*. But there are no restrictions on the Internet or on satellite television. This allows those who can afford it to watch CNN or BBC World Service Television and to download news onto their computers. The government's calculation seemed to be that there was no harm in informing the tiny elite who understand English: the bulk of the population would continue to receive their news either directly from the government or from independent news services wary of offending the government.

Political censorship, overt or covert, is not aimed solely at news providers in the region. It also affects films, books and the arts. The appearance of any mildly risqué satire or comedy in Singapore is invariably greeted by hopeful liberals as a flowering of artistic freedom, but the government always ensures that the satire does not bite too deep. Theatrical scripts have to be submitted for approval before a performance. 'They [the goverment] are worried that artists will link up and through their influence reduce the authority of the PAP,' says one Singaporean artist.[47] As for books, Singapore's shops have an unrivalled selection of works about Asia, but few of the best-known books on Singapore itself. The official – and probably accurate – explanation for this is that the distributors will not handle such books because they fear libel actions from Lee Kuan Yew and other PAP leaders. Pro-democracy activists in Singapore and Malaysia now worry that self-censorship, always practised by the local media, is spreading to foreign newspapers and magazines nervous about the cost of libel cases and the possibility of being deprived of circulation in one of the most prosperous English-speaking Asian markets.[48]

A much more severe blow for political liberals would be a drive by south-east Asian governments to co-operate in restricting the free flow of information throughout the region. Several Asean governments have already banned, broken up or restricted meetings by non-governmental organizations on the Indonesian occupation of East Timor; the idea is to avoid offending the government of Indonesia, the largest and most powerful member of Asean. Likewise, Singaporean officials were reported to have persuaded the local Foreign Correspondents' Association to retract an invitation to Megawati Sukarnoputri, the Indonesian opposition leader who challenged Suharto, to speak at one of their meetings.[49] An Asean-wide ban on information that might be offensive to any of the nine member governments, however, is probably too ambitious a plan. Thais and Filipinos cherish freedom of information too much to make it practical. The Malaysians delight in selling books about neighbouring Singapore which are not on sale in Singapore itself. Singapore, meanwhile, is trying to become a regional centre for the arts; at a recent film festival it allowed the showing of a documentary, admittedly before an audience of only a few dozen, about the Indonesian writer Pramoedya Ananta Toer, whose writings are acclaimed overseas but were banned by the Suharto government.[50] And some events, such as the smog caused by the burning of forests in Indonesia that blanketed south-east Asia in 1997, are too obvious and too appalling for news of them to be suppressed.

Whatever Asian governments may say about wanting to control pornography and 'western decadence', their efforts at censorship are usually directed not at cultural imports but at their political opponents. That is why it is easy to see Hollywood films and ludicrous American television programmes such as *Baywatch*, and difficult to get copies of the serious works of the region's own novelists. But the governments, like their authoritarian counterparts in the Middle East, know they are fighting a losing battle to stem the tide of information and ideas. One reason is the advance of hardware: every year, the devices capable of receiving information get cheaper and smaller, and therefore easier to hide; it will be harder to enforce bans on satellite dishes when they are the size of a salad-plate than it is today, when their large frames loom conspicuously over people's houses. As for the Internet, any Singaporean wishing to evade his government's controls simply has to ring a service provider in a neighbouring country. 'The engineers have defeated the politicians,' says Adi Sasono of Indonesia. 'So who can control the infotronic revolution?'[51] Even the Singaporeans, masters of media control, acknowledge that their power to control pornography or political commentary is limited. 'If one is technically savvy, no amount of restriction is going to stop him [the Internet user],' says William Hioe, director of corporate plans at Singapore's National Computer Board. 'It's like a spider's web. There are a number of ways to get to the same path . . . so the government is trying to spread the message, to educate the people to do self-censorship, especially the parents.' Hioe accepts that the Internet has produced new challenges for commerce, for the protection of intellectual property rights – and for censorship. 'I guess it's an impossible task, and the government recognizes it – short of censoring every e-mail message that goes out,' he says. 'The Internet has thrown up a lot of challenges for us. The problem is growing and we don't have any answers.'[52]

Singapore's government ministers insist that even a limited amount of control is better than none, if only to send signals to people about what is acceptable and what is not, and to keep undesirable influences out of the mainstream of society. But the challenges faced by authoritarian governments are not just technological. East

Asia's educated and increasingly worldly middle-class citizens are thirsty for information and ideas; the technology merely makes the material available. The appetite for commentary and analysis on everything from sexual habits and popular music to politics and the environment seems insatiable, especially in countries where debate on such topics has been long restricted by tradition, by government decree, or (in Cambodia, for instance) by the absence of modern media such as television and colour magazines. Dozens of publications on fashion, music, society and politics have sprung up in south-east Asia in recent years, even in tightly controlled countries such as Vietnam. Kean Wong, editor of the Malaysian magazine *Men's Review*, once described it as 'a mix of "babe of the month" and serious political stuff' – political stuff that pro-government newspapers do not give space to.[53]

Radio phone-ins and television talk shows are increasingly popular too. In Thailand, the armed forces still control several television channels and radio stations, but their influence has been diluted by new channels on cable and satellite. Malaysian television has been liberalized as well, with the introduction of live discussion programmes, although these are confined, for the moment at least, to domestically uncontroversial topics: Afghanistan, Chechnya, French nuclear testing, traffic jams and price inflation are all okay, while East Timor, Burma or corruption in Malaysia would usually be considered too sensitive for the expression of uncontrolled opinions.

One paradox of this restrictive political culture is that governments find themselves fighting their own achievements: economic growth, education and modernization. Further development, according to social commentators such as Chandra Muzaffar, a Malaysian politics professor and human-rights campaigner, depends on the growth of ideas. 'The cultural and intellectual empowerment of people has not matched the economic dynamism that the region has displayed.'[54] Such is the popular demand for intelligent debate that the print media and radio and television channels – even when they are owned by a government or its supporters – often feel obliged to supply a measure of genuine discussion for fear of losing their audience, and thereby market share. Many Indonesians, for example, were pleasantly surprised by the relatively frank debates and interviews broadcast on TV stations owned by Bambang Trihatmodjo, President Suharto's son.

South-east Asian governments and their supporters have inevitably been drawn into the global forum of the Internet, responding to critics and correcting what they see as misinformation – implicitly accepting, in short, the benefits of open discussion. A search for Web sites on Burma or Indonesia reveals government pages as well as those posted by the government's opponents in exile, not to mention free-for-all bulletin boards where opinions vary from the serious to the absurd, from the dull to the highly inflammatory. 'Nearly all states in the region [East Asia] are facing major challenges simply because they are modernizing so quickly,' wrote the political analyst Gerald Segal in an article on the impact of modern media. 'When their leaders become so agitated about retaining their values, one suspects that they know they are losing control. Acute criticism by those leaders of Western intellectuals and the media is a sign that the information revolution is overwhelming their defences.'[55]

Educated people in south-east Asia regard their governments' efforts to control what they see and hear with a mixture of amusement and frustration: amusement, because the censorship does not work – if a businessman wants to read an article on his country that appeared in a banned foreign magazine, he simply gets it faxed to him or reads it over the Internet – and frustration, because the censorship suggests their leaders are unable to comprehend the commercial, social and political value of freely available information. 'They don't want citizens to think for themselves,' says one Indonesian businessman critical of the government. 'Lobotomy is very dangerous.'[56]

Authoritarian governments have been forced by technological change and public demand to yield ground on the information front. But they still seek to monopolize political power. This requires political skill at the best of times, and is made much more difficult when the people that a government wants to control are daily exposed to information and ideas that may be hostile to the government in question. In a democracy, popular opposition to a government is usually channelled into formal opposition parties that have a chance of winning an election. In an authoritarian state, opposition parties are not supposed to win (assuming they are allowed to exist at all). The danger for governments is that their opponents will therefore feel obliged to divert their energy into activities outside the official political system. This is exactly what has happened in south-east Asia.

Perhaps the most obvious outlet for informal opposition – and the most sinister for governments – is religion and religious extremism. The social implications of the fall and rise of religiosity in the region are discussed further in chapter 3. Politically, religion is a headache for governments because they usually want to be seen to be devout themselves while defeating their religious opponents. The multiplicity of religions and ethnic groups in south-east Asia also means that political grievances frequently find expression in attacks on religious or ethnic enemies. In Indonesia, the burning down of Christian churches by Moslems became a regular occurrence in the 1990s. But the Suharto government's efforts to co-opt and appease its religious opponents did not succeed. It bowed to Islamic opposition to gambling and banned a lottery. Suharto went on the Haj – the pilgrimage to Mecca – and was given the honorary first name Mohammed. A government-sponsored organization called ICMI – the Moslem Intellectuals Society of Indonesia – was established to try to reconcile Islam and modernization. Yet religious leaders continued to criticize the government, and outbreaks of violence continued. 'There has been a lot of religious and ethnic violence in Indonesia,' says one Indonesian diplomat. 'We thought that was in the past. But there are enough issues out there that will inflame ethnic and religious sensitivities.'[57] In Malaysia, the Islamic party (Parti Islam se-Malaysia) has been in power in Kelantan running the only opposition-held state in the federation, administering strict Islamic laws and infuriating Mahathir, who wants a modern Islam that will fit in with his plans for economic and social development. Malaysia and its neighbours have already banned al-Arqam, a fundamentalist Islamic sect which was growing in popularity in the early 1990s. Buddhist monks have sometimes been at the forefront of anti-government protests in Burma and Vietnam.

Another south-east Asian political phenomenon of recent years has been the rise in the number of non-government organizations (NGOs). As their name implies, these are independent groups. Although they exist in other regions, they are particularly prominent in south-east Asia, both in democratic countries such as Thailand

and in 'soft authoritarian' ones such as Indonesia. Funded by foreign and local donors, NGO workers tend to be liberal or left-wing and usually campaign for causes which they believe are neglected by the political establishment: environmental protection, poverty allevi-ation, human rights, women's rights and so on. Authoritarian govern-ments therefore try to suppress them – for example by denying them the right to receive funds from overseas to finance their activities – or to imitate them, by setting up 'pro-government' NGOs – a contradiction in terms known in Britain as a Quango (quasi-autonomous non-government organization). Yet the independent NGOs receive plenty of publicity in the local media; they are often the only source of alternative views to those of the government or its tame opposition parties.

Independent and quasi-governmental 'think-tanks' have also sprung up in almost every south-east Asian country to analyse econ-omic policy, political developments and regional security. Their members can be outspoken or timid – depending on the oppres-siveness of the country in which they operate – but even the most slavish think-tanks are forced by academic discipline to acknowledge the rich variety of political ideas circulating in Asia and the rest of the world. In Indonesia several powerful politicians and organiza-tions have set up their own think-tanks to compete in this new arena of domestic politics. This, along with the liberalization of the media, is part of what the Indonesian political scientist Dewi Fortuna Anwar calls 'the creeping development of civil society'. Although it might not be the intention of the government, the growth of civil society is the inevitable result of modernization. 'If you start to educate people you have to take into account the fact that they will become more independent,'[58] she says.

The proposition that Asians are culturally inclined to shun indi-vidualism and to reject liberal democracy is looking increasingly shaky. As south-east Asia continues to industrialize, as its peoples move from rural to urban lives, and as they become integrated in the world economy and its global information networks, there is every sign that they are subject to the same political pressures that affected the industrializing nations of the West in the eighteenth, nineteenth and twentieth centuries. Only if democracy is portrayed as an alien 'western' import can a credible case be made for the durability of authoritarian rule. If, on the other hand, democracy is seen as an accompaniment to industrialization and the rise of a modern middle class, it is probable that more representative forms of government will appear in the future. This is what happened in England after the world's first industrial revolution in the eighteenth century; by the first quarter of the nineteenth century, people had started using the term 'middle class', public opinion had become an important factor in politics, the monarchy's influence was declining and the House of Commons had graduated from a talking shop to a place of business.[59] Francis Fukuyama has noted that Spain, Portugal and the countries of Latin America were – like Asia – once also consigned by political scientists to perpetual authoritarianism for cultural reasons. Now they are almost all democratic. 'The argument was once made that there was a distinct Iberian tradition that was "authoritarian, patrimonial, Catholic, stratified, corporate and semi-feudal to the core",' wrote Fukuyama. 'To hold Spain, Portugal, or the countries of Latin America to the standards of the liberal democracy of Western Europe or the United States was to be guilty of "ethnocentrism". Yet those universal standards of rights were those to which people in the Iberian tradition held *themselves*.'[60]

Evidence is mounting that Asians too want individual rights and democracy, not because they see such rights as 'western' but simply because they want their own views on how their societies should be managed to be heard and to be acted upon. 'To me the trend is irreversible,' says William Klausner, a consultant to the Ford Foundation's office in Bangkok and a veteran researcher into changing Asian societies: 'The question is going to be whether these countries cope with this change, how they adapt to it. The direction is towards egalitarianism, the breakdown of hierarchy, the breakdown of patriarchy, the breakdown of consensus.'[61]

There is already an almost palpable political tension in several southeast Asian countries over the issue of who will inherit power from the elderly generation of post-independence leaders. One of the great advantages of established democracy is that it allows the peaceful and honourable transfer of power from one group of people to another. Political successions in authoritarian states are more complicated, and sometimes violent. Singapore and Vietnam appear to have resolved the matter for the time being by choosing successors from within the ruling party. Lee Kuan Yew of Singapore has already given way to Goh Chok Tong as prime minister, although early suggestions that Goh would be more relaxed and liberal than his predecessor have not, so far, been backed up by events. In Malaysia, Mahathir's nominated successor was Anwar Ibrahim, whose public pronouncements suggested he would be less authoritarian, although Mahathir later felt threatened by his deputy and fired him. But there is confusion in Burma and Indonesia. In both countries the armed forces want to maintain control behind a democratic façade.

To argue that south-east Asian politics will remain illiberal and that future generations of leaders will be as attached to anti-democratic 'Asian values' as their predecessors is to ignore the evidence of the present. There is no doubt that democratization will take time. Even the Philippines and Thailand are imperfect democracies, plagued by corrupt politicians and the naïveté of rural voters. And even liberals argue that a gradual transition to democracy may be safer than a sudden change. As in nineteenth-century England, there are fears among the ruling elites that the demands of the 'mob' could undermine economic progress. But there is a gradual growth of support for political parties or movements that have some ideological purpose, that are not interested purely in seizing power or promoting a particular ethnic group or gang of landowners. And there is more support for liberal politicians who challenge the established order – people such as the Philippine senator Juan Flavier; Megawati Sukarnoputri in Indonesia; and the young Democrat Party MPs in Bangkok. International financial institutions which are full of praise for the economic achievements of East Asian authoritarians now accept that political change is unavoidable. 'Not all the challenges facing Asian governments come from outside,' said the Asian Development Bank in a recent report that focused on the political, social and environmental consequences of economic growth. 'Increasingly complex economies demand more sophisticated forms of government. Asia's people are themselves demanding more and different things from their governments. Rising political participation and democratization are bringing new opportunities, but also new demands.'[62]

A strong indication that the ideological battle is being won by the liberals comes from the authoritarians themselves. Increasingly they are agreeing that democracy is the ultimate aim, and justifying their continued rule not on the basis of eternal 'Asian values' but on the grounds that south-east Asia is in a transitional period that requires firm government. Burma has been under military rule for more than thirty years; the present junta has been in power since 1988. But its spokesman Major Hla Min says: 'We always say we are a transitional government.' Asked about the rise of liberal democracy, R. J. Pillay, Singapore's ambassador in London, responded that Asian leaders saw it as gradual but inevitable. 'I don't think any Asian leader says it will not happen,' he says. 'There is a hankering for more liberal democracy.'[63] As the millennium approaches, the liberals see their chance. For Abdurrahman Wahid, the Indonesian liberal whose Nahdlatul Ulama organization represents millions of Moslems, democracy means the rule of law, an independent judiciary and the accountability of the government to the people. He is fed up with being brushed off by authoritarians arguing that democracy cannot be achieved overnight. 'If you don't begin at *any* point,' he says, 'it will be hopeless.'[64]

THREE

Sex, drugs and religion: Social upheaval in the 1990s

It changed the lives of men beyond recognition. Or, to be more exact, in its initial stages it destroyed their old ways of living and left them free to discover or make for themselves new ones, if they could and knew how. But it rarely told them how to set about it.

> – E. J. Hobsbawm on the human results of the British industrial revolution between 1750 and 1850.[1]

To be modern is to find ourselves in an environment that promises us adventure, power, joy, growth, transformation of ourselves and the world – and at the same time threatens to destroy everything we have, everything we know, everything we are. Modern environments and experiences cut across all boundaries of geography and ethnicity, of class and nationality, of religion and ideology: in this sense, modernity can be said to unite all mankind.

> – Marshall Berman.[2]

So many hundred Hands in this Mill; so many hundred horse Steam Power. It is known, to the force of a single pound weight, what the engine will do; but not all the calculators of the National Debt can tell me the capacity for good or evil, for love or hatred, for patriotism or discontent, for the decomposition of virtue into vice, or the reverse, at any single moment in the soul of one of these its quiet servants, with the composed faces and the regulated actions.

> – Charles Dickens in *Hard Times* (1854) on the industrial revolution in England.[3]

Abdul-Aziz Nordin's mother died when he was nine years old. His father was a local official in the southern Malaysian state of Johor. Abdul-Aziz was an ordinary teenager who didn't like his stepmother.

95

By the age of fourteen he was smoking marijuana. Two years later, when no one could find any marijuana for a few days, he tried heroin. That first experience, he says, was 'very wonderful'. But life went downhill from then on. He moved from Johor at the age of nineteen to stay with his elder brother, who was working at a bank in Kuala Lumpur. The heroin addiction got worse, in spite of a two-month pause after his father took him to a *bomoh*, a spirit medium. Within a few years, he had started to break into houses to finance his drug habit; he committed more crimes and was in and out of jail; eventually his father rejected him. 'My life after that was – what do they call it? – a living hell,' he said. 'I suffered a lot – many tears – I used to pick out food from the garbage. People used to hit me and spit at my face. I had to find shelter from the rain.' From 1990 he spent two years in a government rehabilitation centre, but he was soon back on the streets. 'This time it was really rock bottom, and in early '93 I was in a coma, and hallucinating for fourteen days. They sent me to a general hospital in KL. My lip was swollen, my arm was paralysed. I spoke to the doctor. I cried and asked him if I could stay. But no. I went back to the street and I bought two tubes of heroin. I wanted to commit suicide, but I didn't feel anything. That's when I realized I had to do something about my life.'[4]

Nordin was one of the lucky ones. He went to a halfway house funded by Australians and Malaysians and weaned himself off heroin. He worked for an American consultancy firm studying AIDS and HIV, the virus that causes it – HIV is common among drug users who share needles – and these days is helping drug users at the Ikhlas drop-in centre. Now forty, he looks fit and well and was relieved to find he did not have HIV. He has been off drugs for more than four years.

Ikhlas, however, is not short of customers from each of Malaysia's main ethnic groups: Malays, Chinese and Indians. The drop-in centre in the Kuala Lumpur district of Chow Kit, a warren of busy streets and lanes lined with concrete shophouses and frequented by gangsters, drug addicts and prostitutes, was set up by a gay charity called Pink Triangle whose workers used to find homeless addicts living on the streets with maggots crawling out of abscesses on their bodies. The centre has a simple clinic, showers, a kitchen and dining area and a sleeping room. Upstairs is a similar refuge for prostitutes and transsexuals. It provides the services that the Malaysian government – which frowns on homosexuality and confines drug abusers in its twenty-eight drug rehabilitation centres around the country – does not. Addicts sprawl on mattresses on the floor in the middle of the day. 'Many of them have been away from their homes for ten, fifteen or twenty years,' says Palaniappan Narayanan, the Ikhlas project manager. 'We don't want them to die like dogs on the street – which has happened quite a few times.'

Malaysia's drug addicts are the losers in the country's high-speed industrial revolution, rarely noticed by those who admire its modern shopping malls and electronics factories. And there are plenty of addicts: officially 180,000 at the last count, with some estimates more than double that figure – alarming in a country with a population of twenty-one million, especially when many of the addicts are so young. 'We've had this crisis for over a decade now. The problem is that the rehabilitation services have not been very successful,' said Narayanan. 'In two years [the term inmates spend in the rehabilitation centres] Malaysia changes so rapidly. When they come out they don't have a job, they don't have families, they don't have money and they go back to their friends on the street.' Addicts come from all levels of Malaysian society. The bored rich can get their kicks from easily obtainable Ecstasy, heroin and now cocaine, while the poor more often than not turn to drugs out of despair, having often migrated from small country farms or agricultural estates to make their fortunes in the capital. 'In here we've got clients from very rich families to very poor families. People come out of kampongs [villages] and estates where their parents and grandparents have been living and come to the city and industry and they want to make money. So when they come to KL there are many who *don't* get jobs, who lose out in the race.'

Even prosperous young Moslem Malaysians are confused, torn between consumerism and traditional values of family and religion. 'Our Malaysian generation today are people who are weak at dealing with their own feelings or their lack of skill in life,' said Haji Mohammed Yunus, a former addict who heads the independent Pengasih ('caring') halfway house, where addicts are treated in a group of buildings next to a motorway in Kuala Lumpur. 'Our youngsters have no one to turn to. Urban values are very materialistic.

People go for prestige. Drugs are available.' Neither political nor Islamic leaders are much help. 'The youth leaders fail because they are not youths – they are old,' says Yunus. 'The ulema are failing to attract the young. They are always explaining the rigidity of religion. You cannot be rigid. Malays are confused about what is religion and what is culture.'

Jaafar Daud, the HIV/AIDS co-ordinator for the Pengasih association who is himself an HIV-positive former addict, explains the typical progression of a fifteen-year-old Malay from ordinary teenager to hopeless heroin addict: he starts with alcohol and cigarettes and moves on to marijuana and any pills he can find; his father is hypocritical, telling him to pray but not praying himself, telling him to be honest but being dishonest himself; the teenager lives in a crowded apartment with four or five brothers and sisters, and both parents go out to work. 'There is only limited space, so where else can they go except the shopping complex to be with their friends and laugh,' says Daud. 'And at the shopping complex anything can happen – there is smoking, they can take cough mixture, tablets and sell their body freely . . . There is sex addiction – as well as drugs.'

Malaysian heroin addicts see the dark side of south-east Asia's glittering industrial revolution. Economic growth has improved the quality of life of tens of millions of people in the region. They eat better, they live longer, they are better educated and they are richer. But industrialization, which has only just begun to transform the region's political systems, has already caused immense social upheaval – an upheaval on the same scale as in nineteenth-century Europe but more drastic because of its greater speed. In less than a generation, the lives of many families have been completely changed. Men and women have migrated in their millions from villages to larger and larger cities, coming into close contact for the first time with technological marvels such as cars, telephones, televisions, refrigerators and elevators, as well as with urban slums and industrial pollution. Women who would once have toiled in the paddy fields have found jobs as factory production line workers, office cleaners or secretaries, while the men have secured posts as government bureaucrats, messengers, parking attendants or bus drivers. As in previous industrial revolutions, some people have become immensely rich, particularly ethnic Chinese business families. The gap between the wealthy few and the mass of less fortunate people, both urban and rural, has become a burning issue in several south-east Asian countries.

Habits, morals, language and culture in south-east Asia have all changed at great speed. The new urbanites of Hanoi, Bangkok, Rangoon and Jakarta use modern ceramic toilets. They sometimes eat hamburgers instead of noodles. They enjoy hours of leisure which bring them into contact with other cultures; they watch soap operas or soccer on television; they wander around shopping malls on Saturday afternoons; they travel within their own countries and sometimes outside them. Other changes are not so superficial. Women, better educated than before, are earning money and starting to exercise their new-found power. Pre-marital sex is more common, as is open homosexuality. Small, urban, nuclear families of mother, father and children are appearing where once the extended family of cousins, aunts, uncles, grandparents and grandchildren was the norm. And these nuclear families are in turn under pressure from rising divorce rates – single-parent families are no longer a rarity in south-east Asia.

Youth culture – or rather a collection of youth cultures – is emerging as teenagers flush with new-found spending power and independence start to rebel against what they see as the hypocrisy of their elders, while the older generation frets about 'social ills' and 'westernization' or waxes nostalgic about the rural past. Fan Yew Teng, a former MP and a critic of the present Malaysian administration, believes that the government, by identifying teenage rebels and drug addicts as the cause of 'social ills', is missing the point. 'Every day for the past month, they have been talking about social ills. But one would have thought that one of the greatest ills is corruption itself. But they are not talking about that. They are talking about teenagers. It looks to me like a diversion from the bigger social ills of the adults.' He sees people going to the mosque on Fridays but pursuing their materialistic interests for the rest of the week: 'We are becoming a nation of hypocrites.'[5] According to Abhisit Vejjajiva, a young, English-educated member of parliament in the Thai capital Bangkok, 'a lot of people complain about westernization, in the sense of losing our national identity . . . The fact is that people now use English words and phrases when they are speaking Thai. There is rap music in Thai, and game shows.'[6] Entertainment, says Victor Chin, a Malaysian artist who regrets the greed of modern Kuala Lumpur and the decline of rural life, is an unstoppable growth industry. 'Fashion, music, drugs. It's a way of life, it's international. What's happening in New York or London is happening here the following day.'[7] At its most harmless, teenage rebellion means loud music or pink hair. At its worst, it means heroin addiction. Alcoholism, drug abuse and crime are growing problems, belying the image of a region immune to modern ills because of the strength of 'Asian values'.

Disillusioned with their politicians and uncertain about their place in a fast-changing society, some south-east Asians have turned against their inherited religions in disgust; others have swung to the other extreme and sought refuge in the apparent certainties of religious extremism. Some have found solace in old-fashioned superstition, while others have become fundamentalist Moslems, Christians or Buddhists. 'The family spirit is dissolving,' says Huu Ngoc, an elderly Vietnamese writer, 'like many other aspects of traditional life, like respect for the elders and love of children – so that now there is a moral, ethical battle, especially as concerns the young.'[8] In the space of a few decades, the peoples of south-east Asia have become much wealthier, more sophisticated – and bewildered.

One reason for their bewilderment is that growing numbers of people are leaving behind their small, self-contained village communities, where life was lived at a steady pace and to a familiar rhythm, to migrate, sometimes seasonally and sometimes permanently, to the big cities. These are dirty, noisy, dangerous, ill-planned and crowded, but hungry for workers to staff the new factories and to cater for the needs of the new middle class. As in all industrial revolutions, the growth of the cities seems unstoppable because their attractions are irresistible. Greater Bangkok, with its tower blocks, factories and suburban housing estates spreading across the Chao Phraya valley, has only a tenth of Thailand's population but accounts for an estimated 40 per cent of the country's gross domestic product; the figures for Manila are similar, and average annual incomes there of US\$2,650 are more than double the Philippine national average of US\$1,140.[9] South-east Asia will see exceptionally high rates of urbanization in the next decade, according to the Asian Development Bank, and the process will continue well into the twenty-first century. Some of the less developed countries are expected to double the proportion of their citizens living in cities over the next thirty years; in the more developed ones the urban population will rise from half to as much as three quarters of the total. In Cambodia, the level of urbanization is forecast to rise from 20.7 per cent in 1995 to 43.5 per cent in 2025; in Malaysia the figure is expected to rise from 53.7 per cent to 72.7 per cent. South-east Asia will also have the dubious distinction of having four of Asia's twenty 'megacities' – the name given to cities of more than ten million people – by the year 2025: Jakarta, Manila, Bangkok and Rangoon.[10]

Living in such cities is not easy. Jimmy and Emily Traya are in their thirties and live in a tiny, bare, one-room concrete apartment in a government housing project in Quezon City, part of the sprawling Manila metropolis. The place would be small for the two of them, but they have seven children aged between one and thirteen, and Emily is pregnant again. Each day, she and the children make a dozen cheap baskets at home out of plastic strips and sell them to local wholesalers or in the market. Jimmy drives a jeepney – one of the colourful, locally made vans that ply the roads of the Philippines picking up paying passengers – which he is buying on hire purchase. Emily is from Quezon province and came to Manila to work as a bus conductor. Her husband was from the island of Negros and had moved to Manila to work as a bus driver. They met on the buses and married and lived in the huge squatter area known as NGC. (The initials stand for National Government Centre, an area set aside for government offices that were never built.) However grim the conditions in the new apartment, they prefer it to squatting in shanty towns with tens of thousands of other people. 'It's better, it's safe,' she says. 'We have a gate and a playground here.' Their neighbour Johnny Quiap was a teacher from the southern island of Mindanao. He too used to live as a squatter before moving into the apartment building with his mother and two sisters. He moved to Manila because he got bored of working as a teacher in a remote rural area; now he survives by running a small beauty salon.

Back in the squatter zone, the smiling Epifania Piadoche sits outside her house of breezeblocks and corrugated iron on 'Steve St', so called because one of the first squatters in the 1960s was named Esteban (Stephen). There are no sewage pipes, and black, stinking waste water flows down the side of the dusty lane where she lives. Theft is a problem. But she has no intention of moving, and like most residents is fighting the authorities for the title to the plot where she has lived for the last sixteen years. Piadoche's story is not unusual. She migrated to Manila from the desperately poor sugar-growing island of Negros with her family in 1981, because her father had found a job as a security guard. She married and has three children, but separated from her husband four years ago. Her eldest daughter is studying computer science; her sister married a German agricultural engineer and lives in Germany. Piadoche herself earns her living as a freelance tailor and dressmaker. 'Sometimes I earn 300 pesos [about twelve dollars] in a day, sometimes 150. There's no fixed income,' says the thirty-nine-year-old Piadoche, dressed in jeans, a T-shirt and flip-flops, the new uniform of southeast Asia's urban poor. She has electricity and television in the house. 'I prefer it here in Manila. It's easier to earn money.'

In common with many NGC residents, Piadoche wants the authorities to provide essential services. In Metro-Manila only about 17 per cent of houses are connected to sewage pipes. But at the same time she opposes the government's redevelopment plans for NGC, which would involve the destruction of people's homes and the building of hundreds of 'medium-rise' buildings – such as those inhabited by the Trayas and the Quiaps – and a shopping centre. One problem is that residents of the new buildings would have to pay rent for the first time; another is that big companies would set up shops and drive small stall-holders out of business. At the moment the main road in the area, Commonwealth Avenue, is a mass of small stores, pawnshops, videoke parlours, dental clinics, garages and shacks.

Life on the fringes of Manila – acres of grey, grimy concrete buildings and ramshackle sheds – is tolerable for some and nightmarish for others. There are some 600 informal 'squatter' settlements in and around the capital which are home to about 2.5 million people, nearly a third of the city's population.[11] Rape, child abuse and incest are rife, exacerbated by overcrowding and – in the case of incest – by the fact that many mothers work as domestic servants overseas, often in Hong Kong or the Gulf; according to Bernadette Madrid, head of the child protection unit at the Philippine General Hospital, a daughter with an absent mother – looking after her father and her siblings – can become the mother of the household 'in more ways than one'. She estimates that there are 75,000 children living on the streets in Metro-Manila alone, where they fall prey to hunger, pimps, drugs, crime and pollution-related diseases such as asthma.[12]

There are also uncounted thousands of street-children in countries such as Indonesia, Thailand, Cambodia and Vietnam, shining shoes, begging, selling newspapers – and selling themselves to paedophiles from Asia and the West. The similarities to the Victorian London of Charles Dickens are obvious, but the magnitude of the problem after such a rapid period of industrialization and urban migration poses a formidable challenge to the governments of south-east Asia. 'Some things are quite new,' says Le Do Ngoc, of the Vietnam Committee for the Protection and Care of Children, who puts the number of Vietnamese street-children at around 50,000. 'For example, child drug addiction and sexually abused children and child labour. Street-children we had before but not in such great numbers.' The lure of the big city can be irresistible. A shoeshine boy in central Hanoi might make the equivalent of two dollars a day, far more than his mother and father growing rice in desperate poverty in the country-side. 'He can save half of the earnings for the family,' says Ngoc. 'He can earn much more than his father working.' As for prosti-tution, says Ngoc, parents are sometimes willing to sell their children to pay off their gambling debts, and Taiwanese businessmen believe they will be more successful if they have sex with virgins. 'There's so much demand, there's bound to be supply,' he says.[13]

The rich – those who have benefited the most from Asia's econ-omic boom – are usually spared the unsavoury experience of seeing the living conditions of the urban poor. In Manila, many of the rich live in fortified 'villages', where security guards control access to tree-lined avenues of comfortable houses; only the beggars scratch-ing at the windows of their cars when they leave the compounds provide them with an uncomfortable reminder of the world outside. A wealthy resident of Jakarta is likely to live in a big house with several servants, usually people who have migrated from the Javanese countryside in search of work: a driver, two maids, a security guard or two and someone to clean the swimming pool.

For years, the received wisdom has been that east Asian economic growth was historically remarkable for having been achieved without increases in income disparity. World Bank figures comparing the progress of the richest fifth of the population with the poorest fifth supported this argument. But doubts have begun to emerge. In Thailand, for example, a Japanese economist who studied different population segments – the top tenth and the bottom tenth – found that income disparities more than doubled between 1981 and 1992, by which time the richest had thirty-eight times as much share of national income as the poorest.[14] Inequality in Thailand is probably worse than among its south-east Asian neighbours, but the gap between rich and poor is an increasingly urgent political issue throughout the region; this is so in spite of the fact that even the poorest are, on average, better off than they were ten or twenty years ago. 'People feel they are not enjoying the fruits of economic development,' says Sofjan Wanandi, an ethnic Chinese businessman in Jakarta. Chinese businessmen and women are frequently the targets of Indonesian rioters, as they were at the time of the demonstrations that led to the resignation of President Suharto in 1998, and he is acutely aware of the dangers of an angry, unsatisfied mob. 'Through television, they easily see all the malls, but even if they go and enjoy the air conditioning, they cannot buy anything.'[15] Rizal Sukma, a researcher at the Centre for Strategic and International Studies in Jakarta, says that people who were satisfied with their lot in rural Java inevitably become more acquisitive in a large town. 'In big cities it's different,' he says. 'People can always compare things, and this is one of the sources of social resentment. The feeling that they are being sidelined by the whole process of economic development grows. The peasants are better off now than they were twenty or thirty years ago, but in the cities the gap is very wide between rich and poor. In my view, that's more dangerous than the gap between rural and urban areas.'[16]

For nearly three decades, south-east Asia has been notable for a lack of militancy among factory workers and the poor in general. Many political protests have originated among students or middle-class professionals. Labour strikes and outbreaks of Luddism have been uncommon, possibly because economies have grown so fast that the demand for industrial labour has often outstripped supply and wages have risen rapidly. But it is doubtful that the passivity will last much longer, especially if south-east Asian economies remain mired in economic recession. Already there are signs of unrest, both in cities and in the countryside. In Vietnam, factory workers have protested on several occasions against the heavy-handed methods of

South Korean managers; peasants in a commune near Hanoi threw rocks and petrol bombs at police when Daewoo, the South Korean conglomerate, started on a project to turn their fields into a $177m. golf course; and rice-farmers in Thai Binh province south of Hanoi staged a big demonstration over taxation and government corruption in 1997, although the number of casualties and other details are unclear because the news was suppressed by the communist government.[17] In Indonesia, there were frequent outbreaks of rioting in the mid-1990s. Before Suharto was obliged to resign, his government sought to crush an independent trade union by arresting its leaders and sponsoring a tame surrogate. (Mukhtar Pakpahan, the union leader, was one of the first political prisoners to be freed after Suharto stepped down.) So sensitive was the poverty issue that President Suharto sharply criticized Indonesia's social scientists in 1997 for attributing so many of the country's troubles to the gap between rich and poor.

Neither poverty, nor a sense of rebelliousness, nor the anonymity of urban life, nor the breakdown of families can be blamed singly for the rise of drug abuse in south-east Asia, but the combination of all four has certainly contributed to a drug problem that is close to being a crisis in several countries. In recent years it has become alarmingly clear that drug abuse is not a purely western phenomenon, and that drug-taking in Asia is not confined to a few hill-tribesmen peacefully smoking opium pipes for the benefit of tourists. Frequent reports of police raids on bars and discotheques, rising seizures of drugs from traffickers and increasing numbers of official anti-drug campaigns show how seriously governments are taking an ominous trend which they regard as a threat to future economic growth and prosperity. In Thailand, the health department is struggling with a lack of accurate data on the problem and can only estimate that there are between 100,000 and 600,000 heroin and opium addicts in the country. But it is sure of three facts: heroin is widely available and widely used; the average age of drug abusers has been falling; and heroin is by no means the only dangerous drug on offer.[18] In 1997, the head of the Thai general education department recommended that all schools should regularly conduct urine tests on students because of the abuse of various drugs, including amphetamines and solvents.[19] Amphetamines are particularly widespread in Thailand, where truck drivers use them to stay awake

– a practice which helps to explain Thailand's exceptionally grim record of road accidents. According to the UN International Drug Control Programme, more than half of Thai truck drivers take drugs.[20] Thailand is estimated to have 260,000 amphetamine abusers, and had a total drug addict population of 1.27 million in 1993.[21] Malaysian statistics are equally alarming. A survey of young people between the ages of thirteen and twenty-one by the Youth and Sports Ministry showed that 14 per cent took hard drugs.[22]

South-east Asia has the misfortune to be the source of most of the world's opium, the substance from which heroin is synthesized. Opium poppies are harvested in and around the notorious 'golden triangle', where Thailand, Laos and Burma meet near the borders of south-western China. Heroin is then exported to the outside world, usually via south-east Asia; and some of it is sold on the way through. 'Along trafficking routes there's always some leakage because syndicates pay their couriers in kind,' says Vincent McClean, director of the UNDCP's regional centre in Bangkok. 'Traffickers are businessmen and if they can develop a local market as well as an international market, they will.'[23] Vietnam's heroin problem is worsening partly because the country has recently become a favoured export route for drug-smugglers. In other countries – including Thailand – some drug-dealers have switched to amphetamines in the face of international efforts to restrict the opium and heroin trade. It is easy and profitable for a chemist to make amphetamines under cover in a garage, close to the target market, whereas growing opium on a Burmese hillside is a slow, highly visible and sometimes dangerous business. The decline of the ethnic guerrilla groups which have traditionally dominated opium growing and the spread of roads and other communication links to previously remote country villages have made it easier for governments to curb the heroin trade. The realization is dawning on these governments that drugs are threatening their achievements of the last three decades. 'Whereas some years ago governments in east Asia regarded drug abuse as a problem affecting western societies,' says McClean, 'they now perceive it as a threat to the economy and social fabric in their own countries.'[24]

South-east Asia's attempts to curb drug use, including the death penalty for trafficking in several countries, are nevertheless undermined by the involvement of corrupt politicians and policemen in the very activity they are supposed to be suppressing – a particular weakness in Burma, Thailand, Cambodia, Vietnam and Indonesia. In one Bangkok school, a policeman's son was said to be re-selling to his fellow pupils drugs that had been previously seized by his father's colleagues; in another Thai school, pupils were taking amphetamines sold to them with the connivance of a local official, who was himself a close associate of a local MP. Vietnam has similar difficulties. 'The pushers are in the schools,' says one opponent of the Vietnamese government in Hanoi. 'It's getting much worse. The ideal for everyone is to become rich, and it doesn't matter how. It's even the police – even the anti-drug police – who sell drugs because they have the power to do so.'[25]

It is hard for ordinary citizens to take official anti-drug campaigns seriously when the children of the new elite – the sons and daughters of politicians and tycoons – are spending their money freely on drugs at house parties and discotheques. Ecstasy tablets, already popular in Britain, spread rapidly throughout south-east Asia in the mid-1990s and have been especially favoured by urban yuppies – young stockbrokers, bankers and entrepreneurs. In predominantly Moslem countries such as Malaysia and Indonesia, Ecstasy has an added attraction: when young people return from a party to their parents' homes, they do not smell of alcohol. 'In London or New York, people take Ecstasy once a week,' says one American-educated businessman in Jakarta. 'But here it's every other day, because it's new. It's quite rampant.'[26] The sheer quantity of Ecstasy in circulation aroused suspicion that there was high-level involvement in the trade from the beginning. 'There was enough Ecstasy in Jakarta to feed an enormous and overnight demand. There was massive availability,' says one disc-jockey in an Indonesian bar. The motive for Ecstasy dealing was surely financial rather than political, but he added an afterthought: 'It's the perfect drug for an oppressed population. It's an emotional manipulator. It makes you feel happy. It doesn't make people think or turn them into subversives . . . they pop it here like mad, and the typical clubbers aged between sixteen and thirty have no information about the negative effects.' Indeed, Ecstasy has been so popular and widespread that it seems to have lost its 'cool' status in Indonesia, and may have passed its peak. Cocaine is taken by the wealthy, and heroin is back in vogue as well.

The sharing of needles by intravenous drug users has contributed to the spread of another scourge whose seriousness most south-east

Asian governments are only now beginning to appreciate: AIDS. More than 2 per cent of adults in Cambodia, Burma and Thailand are infected, and the number of cases is rising fast in Indonesia, Malaysia and Vietnam. The constant migration of workers in the region, widespread use of prostitutes and the rise of other sexually-transmitted diseases which increase the chances of HIV infection have all worsened the epidemic. 'Asian policymakers are generally unprepared for the spread of AIDS,' said the Asian Development Bank in an unusually frank warning. 'The large number of projected AIDS cases, the relatively high cost of caring for people with HIV and AIDS, and the concentration of the disease among individuals in their prime productive years all suggest that the social and economic impacts of the epidemic are potentially staggering.'[27] The first case of AIDS in Thailand was reported only in 1984, but by the year 2000, nearly one million children will have at least one parent with HIV. Villagers in some regions of Thailand and Burma, like their counterparts in east and central Africa, have endured a series of deaths and funerals and witnessed the gradual depopulation of their communities.

Thailand is often used to illustrate the AIDS crisis in Asia not just because it has a large number of cases but also because it has been relatively open about the disease, and has taken steps to educate its people about the dangers. Thailand's neighbours, more reluctant to confront the epidemic head-on, have produced statistics which are regarded as serious underestimates of the real number of HIV/AIDS infections. In Burma, for example, official figures in 1996 suggested that fewer than 15,000 Burmese had HIV or AIDS, while other estimates put the real number at more than half a million and it was reckoned that between 60 and 70 per cent of intravenous drug users in the country were infected with HIV.[28]

Malaysia has reported 18,000 HIV cases, mostly among drug users, but the lack of anonymous blood-testing for the virus nationwide means that there is no clear picture of the disease's prevalence in the general population. AIDS researchers in Malaysia were disappointed when it was decided to hush up the fact that a pop star had died of AIDS a few years ago, because they felt his death could have been used to educate people about the dangers of the disease. Even the activism of Marina Mahathir, the prime minister's daughter, in the cause of AIDS education has yet to produce a coherent government campaign to tackle the spread of HIV. Ignorance is widespread, as is the common prejudice that AIDS is a 'foreign' problem. A small survey of transsexual prostitutes in Malaysia found that more than half agreed with the statement: 'I can't get HIV/AIDS as long as I don't fuck with male foreigners.'[29] Heterosexuals, comforted by early reports linking AIDS to drug use and homosexuality, are equally ill-informed about the dangers of unprotected sex. 'The general population have not personalized the disease. They say, "it's not our problem",' says one Malaysian researcher. 'Increasingly we are getting older men in their forties and fifties coming in in the later stages [of AIDS], and women too ... What's hampering our AIDS education effort here is a lack of political will and commitment. I think our government has been very preoccupied with the idea of development, going high-tech and so on. So HIV was never seen as a top-priority issue.'[30]

Drug abuse has contributed not only to the spread of AIDS but also to the growth of crime in south-east Asian cities. Fast-growing cities during any industrial revolution provide opportunities and incentives for crime: opportunities, because a crowded city provides a shield of anonymity and a pool of potential victims that a small village cannot; and incentives, because the need for money to survive and the desire for alcohol, drugs and luxuries to make life bearable is that much greater. Although violent crime is probably lower than in the West – Singapore certainly feels one of the safest cities in the world after dark – few countries produce reliable statistics about overall crime rates, partly because the police and other officials are frequently involved in crime themselves. In Manila, there were more than 600 kidnappings between 1992 and 1995, with most of the victims being members of ethnic Chinese business families. Policemen and senior military officers have long been suspected of protecting the kidnappers in exchange for money, and even of carrying out the kidnapping themselves. 'They are even accepting cheques these days,' said Teresita Ang See, who has campaigned to stop the kidnaps and been the target of several attempts herself. 'These groups are highly organized.' It is not surprising that Filipino executives believe crime and corruption are among the most serious obstacles faced by the private business sector in the Philippines.[31]

Manila, however, is not the only town in the region with a crime problem. Take Medan, the largest city on the Indonesian island of

Sumatra and home to more than two million people. Busy and polluted, with an uneasy mix of Dutch colonial architecture, Chinese shophouses and new shopping malls of concrete and glass, Medan looks like a typical product of Asia's rapid industrial revolution. There is nothing unusual about the illegal brothels, the fights in bars, or the policemen who stop cars outside the town, accept 500-rupiah bribes (about twenty-five US cents) and wave the cars on without even a pretence of looking at the drivers' documents. But residents say Medan is something of a 'cowboy town'. Two large, rival gangs – each thought to have hundreds of members and unofficially licensed by factions in the army – compete for control of the city. Their bread-and-butter business is protection – threatening violence against a business or person and taking money in exchange for not carrying out the threat. Officials appear to tolerate and even encourage the practice, which is seen by the locals as a sort of informal taxation of the rich ethnic Chinese minority. One gang, Ikatan Pemuda Karya (Association of Working Youth), was set up in the 1980s as a counterweight to the other, Pemuda Pancasila (Pancasila Youth), which officials feared was becoming too powerful. 'Pemuda Pancasila is a nationwide organization,' said one Medan resident, 'but in northern Sumatra it has long had a history of doing dirty work for the military in return for being given a free hand in illegal activities such as gambling and prostitution.'[32]

These are some of the grimmer aspects of the industrial revolution. But it would be wrong to conclude that modernization has brought only drug abuse, disease, urban squalor and crime to south-east Asia. Although romantics mourn the loss of peaceful village life – as they do in Europe – ordinary people are usually delighted to exchange a life of rural toil and boredom for urban jobs that earn them spare time for leisure and cash to pay for entertainment.

A visit to the Plaza Blok M shopping mall in Jakarta on a Saturday afternoon shows how rapidly Indonesians are able to adapt to modern urban lifestyles once thought typical of the West. Families and groups of friends can be seen window-shopping, eating fast foods, or going to the multiple-screen cinema at the top of the mall. At a cybercafé called X.Trac, teenagers wearing jeans, T-shirts and baseball caps sit drinking Pepsi under a ceiling gaudily decorated with purple neon, while their ears are assaulted by loud rock music. For a few dollars they can use the café's computers to surf the World Wide Web. Or they can watch the sixteen television screens showing MTV, the music television channel that runs almost continuous rock videos. Behind the café is a large electronic and video game parlour where people are reeling in giant tuna (a lifelike fishing rod responds to the supposed thrashings of the fish), racing motorcycles on the Isle of Man (you sit astride a model of a motorcycle and swerve and lean your way around the track), grappling 3D martial arts champions on a big screen (the game is Virtua Fighter 3 and the machine is called Megalo 410), or flying an advanced fighter-bomber (Xevious 3D/G). The faces and the speech of the customers are Indonesian, but otherwise the scene is identical to those being played out on Saturdays in malls from London to Los Angeles. Other south-east Asian cities have also succumbed to mall culture. Just as Canadians go to a mall for warmth and entertainment in the winter, so Asians go 'malling' to enjoy themselves and cool off in the air conditioning. There is even a mall in Bangkok with a slope of artificially-made snow, allowing Thais to frolic in a substance most have never seen in nature.

It might be argued that such developments are superficial because they concern only the rich. Only the reasonably affluent, for instance, can afford to pay nearly a dollar per session for the sophisticated video games in Jakarta's Plaza Blok M. But the artefacts and services of modern industrial society have already spread to all but the remotest areas of Indonesia, Burma, Laos and Vietnam. Villagers in north-eastern Thailand may not play video games every day, but almost all families have access to a television and a motorcycle. Changed eating habits also affect both rich and poor. The imported McDonald's hamburger bars, the Pizza Huts, the Kentucky Fried Chicken outlets, the Irish pubs in Hanoi, the Starbucks cafés and croissant-shops of Singapore, and the wine sections of the region's supermarkets are frequented either by Asia's new middle class or by foreign visitors. But the overall variety and quality of food, along with food production, distribution, storage, refrigeration and retailing, has greatly improved for almost everyone. The average Asian has increased the intake of calories by 35 per cent in the last twenty years. Processed food is spreading rapidly, and by 1995 some 90 per cent of urban Malaysians had refrigerators.[33] In south-east Asia, the mass production of chicken, the marketing of milk, the creation of the instant noodle, and the ubiquity of the plastic bag have made it easier than ever, and sometimes cheaper, for the poor to nourish their families; and many people now take it for granted that they can afford small luxuries such as soft drinks, ice cream and beer. While malnutrition persists in remote rural areas – hundreds of people were reported to have starved as a result of drought in 1997 in Irian Jaya, Indonesia's eastern outpost – some of the urban rich are even starting to suffer from previously 'western' complaints, including obesity and alcoholism.

Better nutrition is in any case making Asians taller and larger, as the manufacturers of trousers, skirts, shirts and brassieres can attest. But that is not the only concern of textile and clothing companies. They also have to accommodate a revolution in dress codes. For everyday use, businessmen and government bureaucrats have generally adopted the western business suit, which is wholly unsuitable for tropical climates but bearable in the air-conditioned cars and offices where most of them now work. Young, urban men and women tend to wear jeans and shirt or T-shirt for casual use, and miniskirts are popular with smart ethnic Chinese women in Singapore, Malaysia and Indonesia. The wealthy and the fashion-conscious buy branded clothes and accessories from Gucci and Calvin Klein. Brash clothes have even come to the conservative and somewhat sleepy society of Laos, where a young woman was spotted recently wearing a cut-off top that untraditionally exposed her stomach and the ring through the side of her belly button. Sales of modern disposable baby nappies have been surging in the Philippines, Thailand and Malaysia.[34] In most of south-east Asia, traditional clothes generally survive among the poor, the old, in rural areas and for use on formal or religious occasions; at such times Filipino men wear the *barong Tagalog* and Indonesian men the *batik* shirt, both loose garments that hang over the top of the trousers, while Vietnamese women wear the close-fitting *ao dai*. Civil servants of the nationalist Burmese military government and most ordinary Burmese in Rangoon still wear the *longgyi*, the traditional Burmese sarong for men and women.

It is not just tastes in food, drink and clothing that are converging with those of the rest of the world. People drive the same cars – from Mercedes-Benzes to Toyota pick-ups – and fly in the same Airbuses and Boeings. They are persuaded to make their purchases by the same kind of advertising on television and in magazines (the advertising industry expanded rapidly in the 1980s and early 1990s as successive waves of south-east Asians reach new levels of disposable income). If they have the money, they want the same kind of private healthcare and private education. Even homes are starting to look similar, at least for some of the new middle class. Growing numbers of urban south-east Asians live not in traditional wooden houses (although a few remain) but in modern apartment blocks or housing estates indistinguishable from those in the West – and they aspire to suburban two-storey houses with a lawn.

Leisure activities have changed too. Traditional sports survive in south-east Asia, and some – such as badminton – are more popular than they are in the West. But Lycra-clad Indonesians, like Americans, can be seen on mountain-biking expeditions on Sunday mornings. For the less energetic elite, there are Harley-Davidson motorcycle fan clubs in Jakarta and Bangkok. Golf is the game of choice for politicians and businessmen. Soccer is almost universally popular, although, as in Europe, many more people watch it than play it. None of these material changes necessarily implies that the people of south-east Asia are becoming culturally 'western', any more than the lambada music played by a Hanoi bus as a warning when its reverse gear is engaged means that the Vietnamese are becoming Latin Americans. But they are all signs of the emergence of a global urban culture so pervasive that city-dwellers in one continent easily feel at home when transplanted to a city in another.

The direct impact of western entertainment on Asians is often overstated, particularly by governments seeking a scapegoat that can be blamed for what they call 'social ills'. Hollywood movies dubbed into local languages and foreign pop stars are certainly popular and – as far as governments are concerned – politically and culturally suspect; when the American band Hootie and the Blowfish played at the Hard Rock Café in Jakarta, the lead singer waved a bottle of Jim Beam and toasted the city in bourbon whiskey to roars of applause from the mixed middle-class crowd of Moslems, ethnic Chinese and foreign residents. But audience surveys show that viewers and listeners overwhelmingly favour entertainment in their own language rather than English.[35] South-east Asia's producers of television programmes, films, popular music and art shows have typically adopted the structures of entertainment already popular in the West – the TV soap opera, the radio chat show or the three and a half minute pop song – but ensured that the content is either local or sufficiently adapted to make it seem so.

Such soap operas are remarkable for providing the confused inhabitants of a fast-changing society with an almost instant replay of both the fun and the anguish of modernization, a digital-age version of the serialized stories of Charles Dickens in Victorian England. In Indonesia, there was a big following in the late 1980s for the TV serial *Losmen*, which revolved around a hotel in Yogyakarta and confronted such dilemmas as marital infidelity and whether the daughter of the family should become a singer.[36] In Thailand, historical dramas and soap operas are hugely popular too. Some are about the dangers of losing your soul when you become rich; others deal with the growing independence of women. 'In *Nuan nang khang khiang* (the pork vendor's daughter), a market-vendor family follows the traditional route of investing all its savings in the education of the son,' wrote Pasuk Phongpaichit and Chris Baker in *Thailand's Boom!*, their socio-political study of Thailand. 'But the daughter defies tradition both by becoming the family's breadwinner, and by choosing her own career and lifestyle.'[37]

Some cinema films made by local directors address social and political issues much more directly. In Singapore, for example, the young director Eric Khoo made a film called *12 Storeys* about the sexual and social travails of three households in one of the island's government-built apartment blocks. Thai director Supachai Surongsain made a film in 1997 about young girls from northern Thailand heading south to work in the sex trade, where they can earn the money to buy consumer goods for their families. 'Electricity has become part of their lives so now everybody must have a refrigerator, a TV and a radio,' Supachai was quoted as saying. 'Buffaloes have now been replaced by motorized ploughs which require gas and oil. All these things require money of course ... The film states that materialism has had a detrimental effect on the old way of life – but that these changes were inevitable.'[38] Another Thai director made a film called *Sia Dia 1* ('What a Pity! 1') about five girls who turn to drugs to try to forget their sufferings.[39] Cambodian playwright and director Dy Sethy, who wrote a play about a young woman working as a beer waitress and prostitute in a restaurant, said he wanted to 'understand the tears behind the smile and the grim reality of modern-day Cambodia as well as its humour and charm'.[40] Watching such serious films and plays, however, remains a minority pursuit of intellectuals in south-east Asia, where most audiences, like those in the West, prefer action dramas from Hollywood or Hong Kong or local studios.

The comforting certainties of what once seemed to be the solid cultural identities of each country are rapidly disappearing. For many years, it was an academic cliché to declare that Thailand had succeeded where its neighbours had failed in creating a national culture that was a source of social stability; even the ethnic Chinese had been thoroughly absorbed and become thoroughly Thai. Yet in the past few years academics have started talking of Thailand as a 'multicultural' society that includes Mon, Khmer, Lao and various Chinese groups. 'Suddenly Chineseness has become rather chic,' said Chanwit Kasetsiri, head of the history department at Thammasat University. 'You want to show that you are part of it. It would have been unthinkable twenty years ago or thirty years ago.' The ethnic Lao of north-eastern Thailand, a poor, densely populated rural area known as Isarn and absorbed by the Thais when the French were distracted during the Second World War, have long had their differences with the urban Thais for whom they work as servants, prostitutes and labourers. Chanwit recalled seeing car stickers declaring 'I'm glad the car behind is Lao as well', and suggested there was a move towards what Americans, with their designations of African-Americans and Irish-Americans, call hyphenation. 'You can have your identity and be Thai at the same time,' he said.[41]

Such 're-tribalizing' can be both unsettling and exciting for those in search of a cultural identity. But it is only one of several conflicting trends in modern south-east Asia. Many people are being 'detribalized' by global or foreign cultural influences, and by rapid urbanization. 'I don't speak my tribal language any more,' says Indonesian political commentator Marsillam Simandjuntak, who is from a family of Bataks from northern Sumatra but was born in central Java. 'I understand it, but my children don't understand a word.'[42] Scattered and previously isolated ethnic groups are brought together by better communications and by the 'melting-pot' effect of crowded cities. Governments seeking to promote national unity have reinforced this tendency with the imposition of 'national' languages – Pilipino (essentially a simplified Tagalog, the principal language of the island of Luzon) in the Philippines, and the closely related Bahasa Malaysia and Bahasa Indonesia in Malaysia and Indonesia –

together with the use of English as a *lingua franca* for the elite. English, incidentally, has taken on a life of its own in various Asian countries, the most famous example being 'Singlish', the Singaporean version in which English is peppered with Malay and Chinese words and unusual exclamations and grammatical forms: 'Come on, lah. You siow or what? I tell you hah, I cannot tahan anymore!' ('Come on, are you crazy? I tell you I can't tolerate it any more').[43] Many south-east Asians are therefore bilingual or trilingual (an educated Indonesian might speak Javanese, Bahasa and English), but dialects are lost and certain subtleties of speech in traditional languages start to disappear, even if they are eventually replaced by idiosyncrasies in the new national tongue. There are big differences between the classical Tagalog of some parts of Luzon, and the Manila Tagalog that is the basis for Pilipino. Foreign words are borrowed freely in Manila. A jobless man who hangs around and drinks beer is known as an *istambay* ('standby' in English), while a zipper is called a 'zipper' and a straw is 'straw'; in more traditional areas, a zipper is *paparoo 't paparito* ('goes here and goes there') and a straw is *panulayan ng tubig* ('bridge for liquid'). 'Tagalog is very precise on levels of sentiment, anger or love,' says the Philippine newspaper columnist Alex Magno. 'There are several gradations of joy.' His children, he laments, will never understand such gradations because Pilipino is not a literary language – they are likely to read in English instead – but a tool for simple conversations. 'It's a language of the television age.'[44]

Linguistic changes in south-east Asia also show how traditional social hierarchies are being eroded. Languages are becoming more egalitarian, because they are being used in more egalitarian societies. The political and social corollaries are obvious: people no longer automatically respect their elders, or the social superiors who were once their rulers. Much the same process has been taking place over many years in Europe, where the polite forms of 'you' in the singular (*vous* in French and *usted* in Spanish) are used with decreasing frequency. On the Indonesian island of Java, modernization has started to blur the neat social stratifications previously accepted by high and low alike; there is confusion over correct use of *kromo* or the 'high speech level' previously used to address superiors, and it is now usually used between strangers – if they are not already using the national *lingua franca* Bahasa.[45] Thailand also has a tradition of hierarchical language. In the Thai language, there are separate vocabularies for use by and with monks and members of the royal family, and the Thai spoken by ordinary people, especially the personal pronouns representing the English 'I' and 'you', can be used to display complex gradations of respect for superiors and condescension for inferiors. But the language is changing fast, partly as a result of the young challenging the old hierarchies, and one result is a fluid collection of new and often informal personal pronouns. 'The younger generation finds itself uncomfortable with the formality of the power-laden language of the past, particularly when speaking among themselves,' wrote William Klausner in an essay on the changing Thai language. 'This verbal revolt is part of a social rebellion that takes many different forms.'[46]

Perhaps the most significant social changes concern the family. One of the foundations of the 'Asian values' thesis is the belief that Asians are uniquely loyal to their families, their communities and their leaders, whereas westerners are more individualistic. But the belief is based on a misunderstanding. Most Asians (and Africans for that matter) do at present show great respect for their families and extended families, but that is not because they are Asian or African; it is because their habits are rooted in pre-industrial and pre-urban societies that are only now beginning to change as people migrate to big cities and families fragment. Even in England, two centuries after the start of the industrial revolution, the extended family is not quite extinct, although its influence has evidently declined. Just as Horatio Nelson needed a well-placed relative in the Admiralty to ensure his early advancement in the Royal Navy at the time of the Napoleonic wars (it was called having 'interest' at the Admiralty), so an Indonesian today – whether he or she is the child of the president or a distant cousin of a minor official – expects his relatives to help him when they can. 'In Indonesia you look after your family first,' says one Indonesian official. Sometimes that means a small service in the village, and sometimes something more. 'If I became a regional governor, my first instinct is to give projects and so on to my family.'[47] In Laos, where industrialization has only recently begun, good family connections are equally important. Business executives visiting the capital Vientiane are struck by how often they come across the same family names when they do the rounds of ministries and companies. 'The large families have people spread throughout the government,' says one Vientiane businessman.[48]

It can be startling for a European stockbroker or American professor in Bangkok to discover that his thirty-five-year-old Thai colleague is still living with his parents in a compound of houses or apartments that accommodates various grandparents, uncles and cousins. Relations between siblings tend to be closer than they are today in the West. The pattern, however, is changing. In densely populated zones such as the Indonesian island of Java and in all the region's big cities, nuclear families (mother, father and children) are gradually becoming an accepted social unit. As one Indonesian put it: 'My in-laws in West Sumatra have seven children and they are not going to live with any of them.' Intermarriage between racial groups – made possible largely by urbanization – has further undermined the extended family with a common language and cultural heritage. The loss of the financial and psychological support provided by the extended family network is often liberating *and* frightening. For Surin Pitsuwan, a Thai MP who studied political philosophy at Harvard, an individual's independence from his extended family is the biggest social change of recent years. 'Now you feel liberated in a sense,' he says. 'The negative side is that you feel disconnected with the social structure to which you were once required to belong . . . In a way you're on your own. You've got to survive. You've left the security of the home, of the extended family.'[49] The younger the individuals, the less likely they are to feel traumatized by the transition from a past that they never knew anyway; like young Europeans, young Indonesians do not automatically yearn to be part of a large network of relatives. 'All these young Indonesian yuppies don't have the time to meet their grandfathers any more,' says the Indonesian Juwono Sudarsono. He is talking in a Hilton hotel coffee shop teeming with Indonesian and foreign business executives clutching mobile telephones. 'Young people are busy working even on Sundays, with their Internet and their mobile phones, to compete with Japan and Taiwan. They don't care about meeting the extended family.'[50]

The second important trend in south-east Asian family life is that the recently established nuclear family is itself declining in size. This is not, of course, a peculiarly Asian phenomenon; the more prosperous, educated and urban parents become, the less likely they are to think they need numerous children to work on the farm or support them in their old age; in modern cities, a surfeit of children who need to be educated and cared for becomes an expensive luxury. Family sizes have fallen sharply as south-east Asian economies have expanded and as men and women with salaried jobs have begun to marry later in life. Governments have also promoted family planning in an attempt to keep their populations at manageable sizes. Thailand, Indonesia and Singapore have had particularly successful programmes. In Thailand, the average household size fell from 5.7 in 1970 to 4.4 in 1990.[51] Efforts to control population size in the Philippines, however, have been hobbled by the anti-contraception policies of the influential Roman Catholic church, and the government has been unable to meet popular demand for easily available birth control methods.

The third change – again familiar to westerners – is that tensions within the east Asian nuclear family have started to increase as modernization gathers pace. The respect traditionally shown by children to their parents is diminishing, and divorce rates are rising. That is not to say that the old ways have altogether disappeared. In Cambodia, for example, parents often expect to choose or at least approve their children's spouses. In scenes reminiscent of eighteenth-century England, one middle-class Phnom Penh family threatened to cut off their son without a penny if he married his sweetheart, a provincial girl from Kompong Cham with little education; they introduced him to six or seven suitable girls, and pointed out that according to Cambodian tradition his younger sister could not be married until he was. He was faced with a choice as old as history between love and duty. He chose the latter. But the combination of paid labour (which gives young men and women a measure of financial independence), the social freedoms afforded by city life and by exposure to new ideas on television and video, and the poor marriage choices made by parents, has left rebellious thoughts in the minds of Cambodia's youth. Young Cambodians have noticed the inability of their elders to keep up with the country's fast-changing society in their search for ideal marriage partners: in the late 1970s, after the Vietnamese invasion, middle-class parents wanted to marry off their daughters to soldiers because they had guns to protect families and businesses; then, as poverty began to bite, they favoured customs officers because of their high earnings from corruption in the customs department; by the mid-1980s doctors and other professionals trained in the East Bloc countries and skilled in smuggling were the preferred choice as future sons-in law; in the early 1990s, attention switched to Khmers living in the US or France, but some of them sullied their reputation by abandoning their wives or even selling them as virgins to pimps elsewhere in Asia; by the late 1990s, the long-suffering parents of Cambodian girls wanted them to marry businessmen, who seemed to be taking full advantage of the liberalization of the economy.[52]

Family values in south-east Asia are changing fast. Although divorce rates have yet to reach the very high levels seen in the West, the claim that Asians are immune to the social changes that accompany industrialization elsewhere looks increasingly untenable. The divorce rate across Asia in the early 1990s was almost triple what it was in the 1950s. In Singapore it was forecast to increase a further two and a half times from the current level to reach about 2.6 per 1,000 people per year, about the same as Canada now;[53] in Thailand, one research institute found that divorce rates in towns and cities were two and a half times higher than in rural areas.[54] Part of the increase can be attributed to the greater assertiveness of women. East and south-east Asia have been particularly successful compared with other developing regions at educating women and incorporating them into the labour force, although customs and laws in most countries still discriminate against them. By 1993, women accounted for 37 per cent of the south-east Asian labour force, a percentage of the same order as those found in advanced industrialized countries.[55] Many such women will no longer tolerate male behaviour – including frequent visits to prostitutes and the keeping of a mistress known in Thailand as a *mia noi* ('minor wife') – which was once an accepted tradition. Each country has different moral and religious codes, but attitudes are changing throughout Asia, especially among the urban middle class. Corazon Aquino, the devoutly Catholic former Philippine President, was shocked when her unmarried, twenty-four-year-old daughter Kris, an actress, had a son by a forty-seven-year-old divorcee. So shocked, in fact, that she faxed a prayer for Kris to Philippine newspapers which they duly printed on their front pages. Aquino asked God to give Kris 'the grace to be humble and to admit the emptiness of her life without Your divine guidance'. She later told an interviewer: 'It's so difficult to know how to deal with your children.'[56]

Doubts have even emerged about whether children will willingly support their ageing parents in the future – an issue with economic as well as humanitarian implications because of the boast of Asian governments that they can run their countries with only minimal welfare provision. Singapore, apparently concerned that its citizens might shirk their filial duties, felt obliged to pass the Maintenance of Parents Act in 1995 to compel children to help their parents if they were unable to support themselves. The issue is particularly important for countries such as Singapore which have curbed population growth and therefore found themselves with a rising proportion of elderly people who have to be supported by fewer people of working age. 'Asian society will therefore have to cope with relatively more old people in an environment of eroding family commitment to support them,' the Asian Development Bank said in 1997. 'The Asian family is unlikely to provide the social safety net that it used to.' Governments, the ADB said, would be called on to provide everything from day care for children and welfare for single mothers to pensions for the old and compensation for the unemployed and disabled. 'Although Asia need not follow the path of other advanced industrial economies directly, such social problems as crime, drug abuse, broken homes, and neglected children that are common in Western society, will probably rise in Asia too.'[57]

Listen to some Asian politicians condemning the decadent ways of the West and you might start to think that south-east Asia was a haven of morality and sexual fidelity. This is no more true than it was of Victorian England. Nor is decadence limited to the notorious go-go bars of Patpong in Bangkok or Metro-Manila. Supposedly squeaky-clean Singapore, having successfully persuaded its people to have fewer children, is now trying to make them have more with syrupy advertisements promoting the three-child nuclear family. As the government advertising poster puts it: *So much fun/So much laughter/So much love/For ever after/Why wait?/With a family/Life's great.* . . The reality is not always like that. Anyone walking at night along Desker Road on the fringes of Little India, Singapore's Indian quarter, can see transvestite prostitutes plying their trade. In the sordid alleyway behind, bored women sit outside under pink lights waiting to take customers into their tiny rooms. At the end of the alley, a vendor in jeans and a T-shirt is selling hard-core pornographic videos, including one called 'Ass openers etc.' depicting buggery of women. 'You want Russian, Japanese, Thai, Hong Kong Chinese, Negro American?' he asks. 'We have everything. Young girls, see, from Japan.'[58]

In south-east Asian countries, as in so many other cultures, men have long granted themselves the right to a sexual freedom outside wedlock which they deny to women. Women have (usually) been expected to be virginal before marriage and faithful afterwards, while men commonly visit prostitutes; one book on the sex trade in Singapore made a rough estimate that nearly half of the sexually experienced men in the country had had sex with a prostitute.[59] The view that unmarried women must either be prostitutes or virgins persists throughout much of the region. But pre-marital sex between consenting young men and women is becoming more common, for the same reasons that traditional family values are changing: anonymous city life and paid labour have made young women and men more independent of their families, contraception is available and increasingly assertive women no longer feel so tightly bound by tradition.[60] Pre-marital sex, in fact, is gradually becoming ordinary, not only in tolerant Buddhist countries such as Thailand but also in predominantly Moslem societies such as Indonesia. People meet each other at parties or through 'lonely hearts' advertisements. The magazine *Men's Review* in Malaysia – admittedly racy by south-east Asian standards – discusses such weighty matters as penis size, how to have sex on your first date and fears about contracting the virus that causes AIDS. As one female columnist put it (none too delicately): 'It's simply not easy to pick up potential shags anymore, either because you're too scared of The Disease Which Name We Shall Not Mention, or the other party is.' This was particularly regrettable because the period of Christmas holiday parties was fast approaching and ''Tis the season to be shagging'.[61]

Homosexuality is gaining acceptance too, in spite of the antipathy of politicians such as Mahathir in Malaysia and Thailand's Sukhavich Rangsitpol, who as Thai education minister attempted to ban gay teachers on the grounds that homosexuals were 'no different to drug addicts who need treatment' and were bad role models for children.[62] Recent developments in Thailand are particularly interesting. The country has a very long tradition of accepting the *katoey*, the 'female-oriented' and often transvestite homosexual male. Even in remote parts of the country, restaurant 'waitresses' often turn out to be men, an occurrence so common that it is barely noticed, and comic theatrical performances by *katoeys* are a popular form of entertainment. But the public assertion of an overtly male homosexual identity is an entirely new and – to many Thais – shocking phenomenon. A decade ago, there were no homosexual publications, and now there are more than a dozen.[63] Homosexuality has become a big topic of discussion in neighbouring Cambodia, too, with newspapers and radio stations interviewing gays and carrying prominent reports of a same-sex wedding.[64] Across south-east Asia, there are now gay bars and gay pressure groups. In Malaysia, there are an estimated 10,000 transsexuals – usually men who have identified themselves as women – most of whom end up working in the sex industry because they are rarely accepted in other jobs.[65]

Prostitution and pornography have long been part of the fabric of life in several south-east Asian countries. Thailand's notorious and highly visible sex bars for foreigners account for only a fraction of a quiet, efficient industry that is directed mainly at local customers – from the truckstop brothels for lorry drivers to the fashionable 'member clubs' where businessmen go after work to drink overpriced whisky and cavort with expensive prostitutes from Thailand, China and, more recently, Russia. Less well researched than the trade catering for men is the nascent gigolo business for prosperous local women and Japanese visitors: Bali and Bangkok – the south-east Asian equivalents of the Tunisian and Gambian resorts that satisfy the sexual needs of north European women – are two favourite destinations for bored Japanese women looking for sex.

Even in countries with a tradition of sexual tolerance, however, people are worried about what seems to be a collapse of conventional morality. One concern is the explosion of brothels in the recently liberalized economies of Vietnam and Cambodia, which has contributed to the rapid spread of HIV and AIDS. The main red-light district of Phnom Penh, centred on a potholed road on the outskirts of the city where girls dripping with make-up wait for their customers on benches outside wooden shacks, has grown fast in the 1990s: the road seethes with thousands of prostitutes and customers, while new clusters of brothels (identifiable by their pink neon striplights) have sprung up in other parts of the capital as well. Another worry is the tendency of young women who do not see themselves as prostitutes to sell sex to older men so that they can buy expensive clothes and fashion accessories – a problem first commented on in Japan and recently noticed as far afield as Singapore, Indonesia and the Philippines. Materialism, it seems, is the order of the day. 'Sex-for-sale,' wrote the author of a study on Singapore's sex trade, 'is just another commodity, one among many, in today's lucky-draw, free-gift, door-gift, table-gift, what-prize, what-price, got-discount, want-want-want, me-first, me-only, me-now, money-mad, materialistic Singapore.'[66]

Most sinister is the rise of paedophilia. It is hard to tell how much of the increased publicity about sex with children is because of a worsening problem and how much is simply the result of greater awareness and more effective campaigns to stop the practice. But the ease with which it is now possible to travel to the region and within it, and the gap between the wealthy potential customers and the desperately poor potential victims, do seem to have contributed to rising child prostitution involving girls and boys. Some social workers reckon there are as many as a million child prostitutes in Asia.[67] Hundreds of children, for example, have been 'bought' from their parents in poor Vietnamese villages by middlemen who promise to secure them jobs in restaurants but send them instead to brothels in Cambodia; there they are hired by paedophiles from Cambodia itself or Taiwan, Hong Kong, Japan, America, Europe or Australia.[68] Thailand and the Philippines are also much visited by 'sex tourists' seeking young girls and boys. The Philippines government has attempted to crack down on the practice by arresting and prosecuting suspects, and although offenders have skipped bail in the past, they will find it more difficult to escape court appearances in the future because Australia and some European countries have introduced legislation allowing their nationals to be prosecuted at home for child sex offences committed overseas.[69] Child abuse, however, is not something that involves only foreigners or concerns only the formal sex industry. In Vietnam, reported rapes of children under sixteen rose to 327 in 1996, up by 59 per cent from the previous year, and in Thailand, a child psychiatrist recently noted that hundreds of children were being abused every year, some of them so badly that they had to be admitted to hospital.[70]

Both the Malaysian and Vietnamese governments have mounted vigorous campaigns against the 'social ills' afflicting their youth. Malaysians were horrified by the results of a 1995 survey of young people aged between thirteen and twenty-one showing that 71 per cent smoked, 40 per cent watched pornographic videos, 28 per cent gambled and 14 per cent took hard drugs.[71] 'There's been a moral panic about how we must address these "social ills" – juvenile delinquency, drug addiction, pre-marital sex, homosexuality, the spectre of the rise of HIV/AIDS,' says Kean Wong, editor of *Men's Review*. 'These kids have a totally different reality from their elders. They have left the life of paddy fields, kampongs and fishing villages behind.'[72] In short, urban teenage Asians appear to have the same preoccupations as their peers in America, Europe, Australia or New Zealand, even if their cultural pursuits – music being the most obvious example – are tinged with a local flavour. Indonesians have been known to go to heavy metal rock concerts and smash up expensive cars afterwards, or engage in British-style hooliganism while watching football matches. When worried Lao émigré parents in the US send their offspring back to sleepy Vientiane in an attempt to imbue them with some traditional morality, the children often behave just as badly there as they did in California, sniffing glue, getting drunk and vomiting in the toilets of late-night bars. Bored Vietnamese and Thai youths defy the police by racing motorcycles along the streets of central Hanoi and Bangkok. A generation gap is evident throughout south-east Asia, especially in Vietnam, where most of the population were born after the end of the war in 1975 and are therefore unimpressed by their elders' talk of the sacrifices and the socialism that defeated the Americans. For many of them, the dead American film star James Dean is as much of a hero as General Vo Nguyen Giap.[73]

Then, of course, there is the music. *Dangdut*, the onomatopoeically named crossbreed of western rock and Asian and Middle Eastern rhythms, has long been popular in Indonesia and Malaysia.[74] In Thailand, one band of young women called The Angies who made it big in 1997 shamelessly trace their origins and their style to Britain's Spice Girls. British and American bands such as Michael Jackson and UB40 regularly tour south-east Asia to satisfy their fast-growing numbers of fans. Far from rejecting western influence, Asian teenagers revel in it. And, rebellious as ever, they do so particularly in countries where their governments are telling them not to. The popularity of mixed-race music stars, actresses and models appears to be part of this desire to identify with the West. 'Amongst the singers, models, and actors/actresses who became the role models of this youth culture, the mixed-race look became massively fashionable,' wrote Pasuk Phongpaichit and Chris Baker in one of their books on Thailand. 'To be successful, such models usually had to have the black hair and eyes that marked them as distinctly Asian. Ideally the Western genes added only secondary features – fair skin, height, Caucasian nose. The look said: I am Asian but I have borrowed from the West.'[75]

Malaysian fans of Michael Jackson were disgusted at the hypocrisy of the government officials who tried to stop him from performing in Selangor on the grounds that he was a bad influence on the young, particularly when these same sanctimonious officials were known to be involved in what is euphemistically referred to in Malaysia as 'money politics'. But in general, they could not care less about being too-western or not-western-enough. 'The anxiety among thirtysomethings I know doesn't run terribly deep,' wrote Kean Wong in one of his editorials for *Men's Review*, 'and much of this has to do with the fact that so many of the Malaysian middle class are now plugged directly into this all-encompassing global economy.'[76] Like the generation that preceded them, today's south-east Asian teenagers will doubtless find their way to a culture that combines the local and the modern.

The religions at the heart of most societies have not escaped the traumatic process of modernization unscathed. Religious beliefs are changing rapidly, albeit in unpredictable and contradictory ways, and governments are struggling to understand and benefit from the shifts to avoid being destroyed by them. Some people, especially young, materialistic, rationalist city-dwellers, have rejected or are ignoring the religions of their parents; others continue to go through the motions of religious practice to avoid giving offence. Many are undergoing a loss of religious belief which runs parallel to the experience of people in industrialized Europe. Others, however, are clinging to their religions more fervently than ever, rejoicing in the comfort of religious certainty when everything else – family, community, country – seems to be swirling in a maelstrom of shifting values; included in this last category are those who find in religion a framework for opposing authoritarian governments – Buddhist dissidents in Vietnam, Roman Catholics in East Timor, Moslems seeking autonomy for southern Mindanao from the Philippines, or

Islamic fundamentalist separatists trying to prise Aceh in northern Sumatra out of the grip of Indonesia.

In strictly numerical terms, Islam is the predominant religion of south-east Asia. As in the Middle East, Islam in Asia is also the religion that appears to have the most difficulty in dealing with the worldwide relaxation of traditional moral codes. Disputes over the role of Islam therefore look set to play an ever more important role in the region's politics, an already noticeable trend discussed in greater detail later in this chapter. But other creeds are also being transformed by rationalism, cynicism and other manifestations of modern, urban societies. Animism and various sorts of superstition (the word with which we dismiss beliefs which fall outside the major religions) persist throughout the region, largely but not exclusively in rural areas and often intermingled with conventional Buddhism, Christianity or Islam. Thus Cambodians saw in the comet Hale-Bopp in 1997 a portent of political violence (they were unfortunately right), and Indonesians suggested that the earthquake in west Java in the same year was a similar warning of political upheaval (they were right too); thus the Akha hill-tribe people will sacrifice a dog in an attempt to make a sick person recover, Thais continue to worship at an old phallus shrine in the garden of Bangkok's Hilton hotel, and a Bangkok businessman will ensure that the shape, structure and orientation of his new office building conforms to the rules of *feng shui*, or Chinese geomancy. Such beliefs, although much stronger than in the long-industrialized West and particularly vigorous at times of crisis, are a gradually weakening force in a modern south-east Asia where educated people are more likely to be in thrall to a big religion or inclined to agnosticism.

Established religions, however, are not having an easy time of it. The traditional Thai *sangha*, the monkhood, has been racked by repeated sexual and financial scandals, and (like the Church of England) is being dismissed either as too old-fashioned or too new-fangled by large numbers of its potential followers. 'We have seen the decay of the Buddhist order because there have been so many misbehaving monks that they have reduced the trust and respect of the people,' says Paiboon Wattanasiritham, a senator and former commercial banker who now concentrates on social work. 'Moral standards and spiritual development have gone on the downside. There are some good monks, but not enough. The system is in decay.'[77] In one particularly well-publicized scandal, the charismatic monk Phra Yantra Amarobhikkhu was disrobed after multiple accusations of sexual harassment. He was alleged to have made love to a Cambodian nun on the deck of a Scandinavian ferry and to have seduced a Danish harpist in the back of a van in Austria, although one senior Buddhist insisted that it would be impossible to get an erection outside in Scandinavia because of the cold.[78] Many Thais have started to consult fortune-tellers or to adhere to charismatic, quasi-Buddhist cults – often featuring a monk attributed with exceptional spiritual powers – that appear to offer solace in times of trouble, prompting one philosopher to warn of the risk that 'an all-encompassing religion could be replaced by religious offshoots or cults that meet specific demands. In marketing terms, I would call it greater segmentation.'[79] One such cult involved the late king Rama V – King Chulalongkorn – the 'modernizing' ruler who introduced economic, administrative and legal reforms at the end of the nineteenth century; by the mid 1990s hundreds of devotees were gathering around an equestrian statue of the king in downtown Bangkok in the evenings to offer him flowers, food and even Scotch whisky.[80]

Traditional Christian churches are in difficulties too, although Christianity itself appears to be thriving in those countries where it has taken root. In the Philippines, hundreds of thousands of people have switched allegiance from the dominant Roman Catholics to the evangelical movement Iglesia ni Kristo (the Church of Christ). In Singapore, charismatic and fundamentalist Christian sects have grown rapidly since the 1970s, alarming a government which regards the obedience of citizens to the secular state as all-important. By the 1990s, a fifth of the island's population were Christians – roughly double the number of a decade earlier – and the religion seemed to be continuing to spread among the young. Baptists and gospel fringe churches took over several old cinemas to accommodate their growing congregations, and even Anglican bishops were offering to cure the sick. Most Singaporean Christians are from the Chinese community, apparently because the Chinese practice of ancestor-worship has a looser hold on its adherents than Islam has on Malays, or Hinduism on Indians. The spread of Christianity in Singapore – which has a parallel in South Korea – is regarded by some Christians as a reaction to the materialism of present-day Asian societies. But non-believers in Singapore link the rise of charismatic

Christianity, which encourages the idea of direct communication between God and the individual, to the soullessness of a country where overt individualism and freedom of expression are frowned on by the government. A charismatic church service – in this case an Anglican one in the Victoria Concert Hall – is certainly the only forum in this disciplined city in which one can see a middle-aged Chinese woman lying on her back in a public place, moaning and twitching and saying: 'It was wonderful. I saw many bright lights.' Such behaviour among the Chinese is disturbing enough for the government. But Singaporean officials are particularly wary of evangelism involving other races, because they do not want to upset Singaporean Moslems or provoke an outcry from their much larger and predominantly Moslem neighbours, Indonesia and Malaysia.[81]

The development of Islam, and the way it affects the politics and the economies of Asia's Moslem societies, are of critical importance for the future of the region. 'The religion of Asean is predominantly Moslem,' says Dewi Fortuna Anwar, the Indonesian scholar. She is one of the many people who have charted the Moslem revival of recent years, although opinions are divided about its causes and possible consequences. Renewed religiosity among mainstream Moslems, she believes, is partly a result of greater affluence, which has allowed more people to perform such Moslem duties as giving alms and going on the Haj, the pilgrimage to Mecca; new wealth has also funded the establishment of expensive private schools for Moslems, whereas private education was previously dominated by Christians. Other residents of Jakarta say more middle-class people attend Friday prayers these days, and they comment on the number of Mercedes-Benzes and BMWs parked outside the city's mosques. Goenawan Mohammed, who edited the news magazine *Tempo* before it was closed by the government, has noticed a 'Moslemization' of the middle class: property developments, complete with homes and mosques, are marketed as Moslem suburbs; more women wear the headscarves and other modest garb regarded as acceptable in Islam: and more young Indonesians, uncertain of their place in a confused urban community, have started to pray. 'In the old days the rich looked down on devout Moslems,' he says. 'Now they are more Moslem themselves ... In Ramadan [the holy month of fasting, feasting and prayer] you see children in the middle-class houses gathered together and praying. I never saw this before.'[82]

It has long been argued that south-east Asian Islam, especially the mystical and unorthodox version espoused by many Javanese, is 'milder' than the various Islamic beliefs and practices of the Middle East, and that there is therefore little likelihood of an upsurge of Islamic fundamentalism. Islam was brought to Indonesia by traders from Arabia and Persia from around the fourteenth century, and orthodox Moslems, known as *santri*, are numerous on the coasts of Sumatra, Sulawesi and Kalimantan. In Java, however, many of the poor are classed as *abangan*, Moslems whose beliefs are mingled with pre-Islamic Javanese mysticism as well as Hinduism and Buddhism. 'Increased spiritualism doesn't mean increased fundamentalism,' says Dewi Anwar. However true that may be, others are less sanguine about the dangers of religious puritanism, exclusivity and even armed fundamentalism. South-east Asia's 200 million Moslems are as diverse in their beliefs as Moslems are in the Arab world or Christians are in the West. They include the mystics of Java, the Cham fisherfolk of Cambodia and the Libyan-backed Moro Islamic Liberation Front guerrillas of the southern Philippines. In Indonesia, there have been frequent incidents in which Moslems have burnt down Christian churches. In Malaysia, the Parti Islam se-Malaysia (PAS), the Islamic party which was running the northern Malaysian state of Kelantan in the 1990s – the only opposition-held state in the federation – has infuriated the central government by introducing *sharia* law, and is also suspected of supporting separatist guerrillas in the Moslem part of southern Thailand across the border. Islamic puritans have won several less well-publicized victories. Islamic banks, which theoretically avoid the use of interest payments or receipts in their transactions, have been set up in Indonesia and Malaysia alongside the long-established commercial banks; a national lottery in Indonesia was abandoned after weeks of demonstrations and protests from students and religious leaders who opposed the whole notion of gambling and the way the lottery was managed; young people of Moslem parentage drink less alcohol than they used to; and dress codes and standards of entertainment have been tightened. In the Malaysian state of Sarawak on Borneo, the religious affairs department banned Moslems from body-building contests because (male) competitors were exposing too much flesh, and in Selangor, again in Malaysia, three Malay women were arrested for taking part in a beauty contest.[83]

The Jakarta car stickers announcing 'Right – we're Moslems' – a sort of Islamic counterpoint to the 'Honk for Jesus' message seen on the highways of America – seem jovial and harmless. But Malaysian and Indonesian liberals fear their societies are gradually becoming less tolerant of non-Moslems, and more inclined to restrict recently acquired women's rights. Sisters in Islam, a small group of Malaysian women formed to fight for equal rights within Islam, is frustrated by the contradictions in a society which wants women to participate fully in the economy but at the same time confers on them what they see as an inferior legal and social status – especially with regard to marriage and divorce. 'The majority of Malays want a more progressive Islam, but they don't speak out,' says Zaina Anwar, one of the group's members. 'The government has campaigns saying be good to your neighbours, but in these marriage courses they say women shouldn't visit their neighbours, or leave the house without permission!'[84] Marina Mahathir, the prime minister's daughter, has been equally outspoken, using her column in *The Star* to accuse Malaysian men of wanting to oppress women and force them to stay at home 'having babies endlessly and covered head to toe'. She added: 'Compared to incest, child abuse, wife battering, drug abuse and corruption, whether you're dressed right or wrong according to someone's arbitrary values should rank pretty low in the scale of concerns of our times.'[85] Malaysian liberals are appalled by the stricter application of Islamic rules, including those forbidding close contact between unmarried Moslems of the opposite sex. This is reminiscent of the excesses of the religious police in Saudi Arabia (in one Malaysian state the religious department said it had hired spies in hotels to report on the behaviour of bad Moslems with their girlfriends). It is also doubly controversial when a large minority of the population is not Moslem and is therefore not bound by restrictions on dress, alcohol or kissing. A person's religion has become more important in Indonesian society as well. One young Indonesian businessman said it was now much more difficult for couples of different religions to maintain their relationship without one or the other agreeing to convert. 'I've just split up with my girlfriend and people say, I'll introduce you to some girls – you want a Moslem or a Christian girl? That question wouldn't have been relevant ten years ago.' He said he had noticed a curious combination of greater decadence (in the form of drug-taking, corruption and consumerism) and greater religious observance among the urban rich. 'The same people could do both of these at once without feeling hypocritical at all.' Religion, he thought, was regarded as a comfort in a turbulent society. 'In confusing times, religion is supposed to be a sure thing,' he concluded. 'I think this society will become much less tolerant.'[86]

Political leaders have been taken aback by the rise of Islamic religiosity, and they are unsure how to react. They have sought to crush their most dangerous Islamist opponents with brute force: so the Indonesian army has tried to stamp out Islamic separatism in Aceh – according to Amnesty International, the human-rights group, Indonesian troops have summarily killed about 2,000 civilians there. In 1994, the Malaysian government banned the al-Arqam sect, which was gaining a following in the region, and arrested some of its supporters. Mahathir despises many Islamic leaders as obscurantists whose views will damage his efforts to modernize Malaysia, and is prepared to use every political tactic to bring them to heel. But he and Suharto – who ruled Indonesia for three decades – balked at cracking down too hard on their more conventional Islamic opponents for fear of damaging their political standing among Moslems. They neither adopted the secular approach to modernization of a Moslem state pioneered by Ataturk in Turkey, nor yielded as much ground to the Islamic fundamentalists as the Gulf states in the Middle East. Instead, they have trod an uncomfortable middle path as they attempt to build countries that are both Moslem and modern. Both have established Moslem organizations to promote Islam as something compatible with the technological, social and economic development they are pursuing.

Yet neither the Indonesian nor Malaysian governments appear to have been particularly successful at co-opting puritan Moslems; indeed it is the middle-class liberals who unexpectedly find themselves looking to their authoritarian governments to protect them from the puritans. The problem for the governments and their liberal opponents – and the opportunity presented to fundamentalists – is that political repression has left religion as almost the only outlet available for those who want to express their opposition to the authorities. Suharto deliberately emasculated political Islam after the overthrow of Sukarno in 1965, forcing all Moslem parties into the new United Development Party (PPP) and framing the non-confessional official ideology of '*pancasila*'. In the 1990s, his government began to discourage Indonesians from studying in countries such as Saudi Arabia to prevent them absorbing extremist Islamic ideas. But Islam became a powerful banner for poor Moslems seeking to remedy what they saw as the unjust enrichment of Suharto's friends and relatives, and of the Chinese business community, many of whom happen to be Christian. Abdurrahman Wahid, the elderly leader of the country's largest Moslem organization, the Nahdlatul Ulama, which is credited with some thirty million supporters, is a firm believer in democracy and is a moderate Moslem leader who finds himself under constant pressure from some of his followers to take a more radical stance. 'When we have a widening gap between the rich and the poor, the real trouble lies there – but the form it [the trouble] takes is religion,' he says. Wahid spends much of his time preaching religious tolerance to big audiences across Indonesia in an attempt to counteract the xenophobic sermons given by some Moslem clerics who insist that non-Moslems are plotting to 'Christianize' Indonesia.[87] 'I was surprised one day when my eight-year-old daughter said she was on the same bench as a Christian girl at school,' he once said. 'Eight years old and already talking about things in religious terms! It's not healthy for Indonesia ... Ten years ago there was no word of "Christianization" in the mosques: now there's plenty.' Wahid was unusual among Moslem leaders for defending Salman Rushdie's right to free speech after Ayatollah Khomeini of Iran had condemned the British writer to death for alleged blasphemy in his novel *The Satanic Verses*. He remains convinced that Indonesians can be Moslem, democratic and tolerant. 'I saw the hanging of Jews in Baghdad in 1969 – fourteen of them. That's when I decided to go for democracy,' he said with disgust. 'As long as we're given the right to explain the human side of Islam, then I'm convinced that Indonesians will always be moderate Moslems.'[88] But what NU leaders preach and what its followers do are not always the same thing; supporters of the government say the NU's members are as likely to go on the rampage as anyone else. And the NU faces competition from other 'mass organizations', including the Muhammadiyah, and new groups such as Masyumi, which takes its acronym from a Moslem party, Majelis Suryo Muslimin Indonesia, which was banned in 1960 for involvement in an armed rebellion. 'Political awareness among the people is increasing,' said Rudini, a retired general and former army chief of staff and home minister. 'Middle-class and intellectual groups feel [existing] political structures cannot tackle people's aspirations.'[89]

Islam is equally bound up with politics in Malaysia, partly because the ruling Umno party has felt obliged to take a more Islamic stance in an effort to counter the popularity of the fundamentalist PAS. Liberals are worried that Mahathir will fail in his attempts to build a society that accommodates devout Moslems but is also tolerant of non-Moslems and is economically successful. Film-maker Hishamuddin Rais, a fellow activist who fled the country when Anwar, Mahathir's ousted heir apparent, was first detained in 1974, says the problem for Malaysian politicians is that even if they have secular ideas they must use religion to win votes when campaigning in the countryside. 'So there's always this schizo attitude,' he says. 'Turkey is facing the same thing as Malaysia now. Have we decided where we are heading – a secular Malaysian state – or what? . . . A big section of the Malay middle class is worried about what is coming next. A lot of them have gone underground in the sense that their lifestyle is less visible. When I came back [after twenty years] I was shocked by how few of my buddies drink.'[90] There is more talk of Islam in the newspapers and on television, but the cultural identity of the Malays who make up half the country's population is still in flux. In Rais's home state of Negeri Sembilan, families are matrilineal and people have drunk home-brewed rice alcohol known as *tapi* since time immemorial. 'Some religious sects said we should abandon it as un-Islamic,' says Rais. 'Are we Malay first and then Moslem, or Moslem first and then Malay?' Mahathir's problem, as liberals see it, is that he wants a multiracial, economically successful society but cannot or will not insist on the impartial, non-religious rule of law that would make such a society possible.

For some Asians, especially Moslems, this is precisely why Asia has the chance to do a better job of industrialization and modernization than the West: whereas supposedly rational post-Enlightenment Europeans flounder in decadence without a moral compass, Asians could be both economically successful and devout followers of religious and family values. Chandra Muzaffar, a professor at the University of Malaya and a well-known social commentator, says that industrializing Asia has not experienced the intellectual revolt against established religion seen in western societies. 'The mosques get fuller and fuller,' he says. 'In Malaysia people are very concerned about restaurants and whether the food is halal. Concerns like this are much more prominent than fifteen years ago . . . The religious revival is taking place within the same time frame as the industrial revolution.' He adds: 'I don't see Islam coming into conflict with most aspects of modernization.'[91] Others are not so confident, and Muzaffar himself acknowledges that Asian leaders need to allow greater freedom of expression and to resolve the contradiction between public religiosity and private corruption and greed.

The unanswered question about south-east Asia's increased religiosity is whether it is a passing phase – a brief period of solace for those left behind or simply confused by the industrial revolution – or something which will survive into the next generation. If it is temporary, the region could eventually start to feel more like Europe, where religion is an accepted part of private life and public tradition but virtually a spent force in political and social systems now run by secular laws. If, on the other hand, religion (especially Islam) plays an ever greater role in government and in the setting of social norms, then there are likely to be conflicts with non-Moslems and with liberals demanding the implementation of impartial laws for all.

For the time being the people of south-east Asia are engaged in a desperate hunt for moral, religious or political antidotes to the extreme materialism that has been probably the most noticeable social effect of the world's fastest industrial revolutions. Big businessmen blithely chop down forests and knock down city landmarks, leaving devastation in the countryside and architectural wastelands in the cities. Students want to study business, not so that they can be educated but so that they can be rich. Teachers and doctors employed by the state demand money to teach people or treat people privately after hours in order to supplement their meagre incomes. Civil servants want bribes. Balinese who once danced for free in local ceremonies now want to be paid. Women in Vietnam and Thailand sell their children into prostitution so that they can buy televisions; and the result of watching them is that they jealously measure their prosperity not against the wealth of their parents thirty years ago but against the unattainable standards of soap-opera characters. What Sulak Sivaraksa, a nostalgic defender of traditional Thai culture and religion calls 'demonic consumerism' has spread across the region.[92] People buy cars and clothes they can barely afford not because they are practical but because they are emblems of high status. 'This is the nouveau riche phenomenon which you find all over south-east Asia – crass display of wealth and big cars, flashy suits and so on,' says Singapore minister George Yeo. 'We'll get past this phase. It's temporary.' Yeo believes it will take time for south-east Asians to add a sense of the public good, of 'civic responsibility', to their existing loyalties to themselves and their families. But it can be done, he says, just as parents can teach their children the difference between right and wrong. 'A society has got to be organized, a society has got to be held together by culture, by common values. How can you run a society based on the market alone?'[93] The economic recession in south-east Asia may give everyone time to think about this question. Headlong economic growth has papered over social issues that desperately needed to be addressed: the gap between the rich and the poor; corruption and materialism; drug abuse and crime; the sacrifice of artistic endeavour and intellectual debate on the altar of authoritarianism; and the conflict between religion and secularism. In south-east Asia, these battles are only just beginning.

FOUR

The day of the robber barons

Massive and rapid growth is a wonderful buffer. Like a river
in flood, it hides the rocks on the river bed.

– Mahathir Mohamad, Malaysian prime minister, on the virtues
of Asian economic growth.[1]

We lived under an illusion of wealth and this is the price we
are paying for it.

– Suthee Audsarat, chairman of one of the fifty-six Thai finance
companies shut down during the 1997 financial crisis.[2]

We have a free market like the time of the robber barons in
the US or the industrial revolution in the UK. There are no
restraints put on these big businesses.

– Dewi Fortuna Anwar, Indonesian political scientist.[3]

Doing business in south-east Asia at the height of the economic
boom was sometimes exceptionally lucrative, but it could also be
exceptionally risky. North American investors in Bre-X, a small Canadian mining company, could hardly believe their luck when news
broke in February 1996 that Bre-X had made one of the biggest
gold discoveries in history at its remote Busang site in Borneo. A
year later, the company's geologists confirmed that the deposit contained at least seventy-one million ounces of gold and might contain
more than 200 million ounces. 'One would have to go back to the
Klondike or the discovery of the Witwatersrand in South Africa a
century ago to find anything that compares to the apparent size of
Busang,' declared one stockbroker's report. The value of Bre-X's
Canadian-listed shares increased more than tenfold, and the company was valued at nearly US$5 billion. But Bre-X directors had not

bargained for the corporate feeding frenzy that would be provoked by a gold deposit of such richness. Having failed to finalize a binding contract with the Indonesian government, they found themselves confronted with an array of big mining companies in various alliances with President Suharto's children and associates, and with the sons of cabinet ministers. Their aim was to take as much of Busang's wealth as possible from Bre-X for themselves.[4]

It was an unedifying spectacle. One of the competitors was the big Canadian company Barrick Gold, whose board included former US President George Bush and former Canadian prime minister Brian Mulroney. These eminent men used their influence to lobby the Indonesians on behalf of Barrick, and the company formed an alliance with Siti Hardijanti Rukmana, Suharto's eldest daughter, in a plan to take three quarters of Busang. That would have left 25 per cent for Bre-X, although both parties were then supposed to offer 10 per cent of their stake to the Indonesian government. Bre-X, meanwhile, sought influence of its own; it offered a company associated with Sigit Harjojudanto, Suharto's eldest son, a 10 per cent stake and a consultancy fee of US$1 million a month for forty months. At first it seemed that Barrick was winning. But Suharto's political opponents had seized on the negotiations over the gold as an opportunity to criticize the increasingly controversial business dealings of the ruling family, and the saga was far from over. Mohammad 'Bob' Hasan, the timber tycoon who was one of Suharto's closest confidants, became involved in the scrabble for Busang, apparently appointed by Suharto to mediate between the siblings and defuse the political attacks. Placer Dome, another Canadian company, was also reported to be interested in the future gold mine. But it was Freeport-McMoRan Copper and Gold, the US company which operates the large Grasberg copper and gold mine in the remote eastern Indonesian territory of Irian Jaya, which won out in the deal finally brokered by Hasan. Bre-X was to retain 45 per cent, 30 per cent was to go to Indonesian companies linked to Hasan and the Suharto family, 15 per cent to Freeport and 10 per cent to the Indonesian government. Bre-X shareholders could breathe a sigh of relief; at least they had a substantial stake. 'They're still being mugged, but not quite as bad,' said one mining executive. 'I think Suharto did a good job making it look like a market deal.'

Busang, however, was soon to turn into a bizarre moral fable. The enormous gold deposit which had attracted the world's mining companies and Indonesia's most influential people did not in fact exist. The whole 'discovery' was a fraud. Freeport announced that it had found 'insignificant' amounts of gold at the site. Bre-X shares collapsed. Meanwhile Michael de Guzman, a Filipino who was one of the two Bre-X geologists who 'found' the gold, disappeared, and was said to have committed suicide by jumping from a helicopter in Borneo; a body was later found in the jungle, although there were doubts as to whether it was his: it was reportedly unrecognizable and disembowelled by wild pigs. His Canadian colleague John Felderhof, who like de Guzman made millions of dollars by selling Bre-X shares when they were still worth something, went to the Cayman Islands and applied for permanent residency there. Bre-X announced that for three years de Guzman and his fellow workers had 'salted' rock samples from Busang with gold from elsewhere to give the impression of a huge gold find. Investors in North America were furious. Hasan was philosophical, perhaps because the fraud was uncovered before the Indonesian side parted with any money to pay for its share of the project. 'It's all business,' he said. 'Sometimes you make money, sometimes you don't.' But there was little doubt that the fiasco had embarrassed Suharto. As one Jakarta business consultant put it: 'We cannot measure [its] effect only from a material angle. It is also about loss of face. The Busang saga was a manifestation of the extent of the first family's greed.'

Mining has always been a ruthless business, but the kind of political pressure brought to bear in the Busang affair did not inspire confidence in Indonesia among foreign investors. Nor would bona fide investors have been particularly impresssed even if the gold deposits had turned out to be real. Indonesia's lack of concern for contracts, fair play and the rule of law was even less appropriate for more sophisticated industries in manufacturing and services, such as car production and banking. But in these sectors too it was seen as foolish – if not impossible – to become involved in Indonesia in the 1990s without high-level connections. The same business ethos existed across much of south-east Asia. Corruption was rife, particularly in big infrastructure projects where it was governments that awarded the contracts. But opportunities were plentiful and there were few complaints from big companies. Business magnates, the 'robber barons' of the late twentieth century, were the new heroes of the age. To ordinary people, they were more glamorous than those worthy politicians or soldiers who had fought for independence from the colonial powers. With their Mercedes-Benzes, mobile phones, deal-making in luxury hotels and generous tipping, they epitomized the region's economic success; they were as much to be admired as envied. To government ministers, the new entrepreneurs were a source not just of personal enrichment but of political power; it was businesses, after all, which had driven south-east Asia's rapid economic growth, giving the region's leaders the right to boast about 'Asian values' and the coming 'Pacific Century'.

Of course there were forces other than local business acumen at work as south-east Asian economies advanced. Japan, facing high employment costs at home, had invested heavily in the region to make everything from cars to televisions; the US and Japanese markets were open to many Asian exports after the Second World War; ethnic Chinese family businesses – some were to become multi-billion-dollar conglomerates – traded and invested on a grand scale; and technocrats in central banks and finance ministries won praise for ensuring a stable macro-economic climate in which local and foreign enterprises could prosper. Savings were high and taxes were low. People worked hard. Asean countries such as Singapore, Malaysia and Thailand were envied by less successful developing nations in Africa and Latin America and praised by the World Bank for their remarkable economic achievements.[5] Like their European and American predecessors of a century or more ago, Asian tycoons were sometimes criticized for destroying the environment or exploiting their workers (nearly 200 women were killed in one notorious fire at a Bangkok toy factory in 1993) but they were more often praised for their entrepreneurial flair. They were beneficiaries of the industrial revolution, but they were also contributors to its glorious successes. They had even started to buy companies in the US and Europe, proving that their countries were now sufficiently developed to initiate foreign investment as well as absorb it. At about the same time that the Busang fraud was being exposed, however, the economies of south-east Asia were about to be plunged into a financial calamity. After 1997, the tycoons would never again be regarded with such uncritical admiration.

*　　*　　*

For years, a handful of analysts had pointed out the weaknesses of south-east Asian economies and of the region's business methods,[6] but by the 1990s their voices were mostly drowned by the enthusiastic chorus of gurus who saw nothing ahead but a long-running Asian boom that would eclipse the US and European economies in the first quarter of the next century. One of the most prominent sceptics was Paul Krugman, economics professor at Stanford University, who declared in 1994 that there was no Asian 'miracle'. High economic growth, he said, was the result of high economic inputs which could not be repeated. In Singapore, for example, women were brought into the workforce and the share of the population in employment surged from 27 per cent to 51 per cent between 1966 and 1990. In the same period, government spending on education dramatically improved the skills of the workforce, while investment as a share of total economic output nearly quadrupled to 40 per cent. It was simply impossible to repeat such increases. 'From the perspective of the year 2010, current projections of Asian supremacy extrapolated from recent trends may well look almost as silly as 1960s-vintage forecasts of Soviet industrial supremacy did from the perspective of the Brezhnev years,' he wrote. 'The newly industrializing countries of the Pacific Rim have received a reward for their extraordinary mobilization of resources that is no more than what the most boringly conventional economic theory would lead us to expect.'[7] Krugman's comparison of Singapore with the Soviet Union enraged some of the island's officials – it was certainly obvious that Singapore in the 1990s was far more efficient than Moscow thirty years earlier – but his assertion that Asian economic growth was bound to slow because investments there would yield diminishing returns looks much less extraordinary at the end of the decade than it did to his detractors in 1994.

There were signs of unease among other economists about south-east Asia as early as 1996, when it became apparent that corporate profits would be undermined by a surplus of expensive manufacturing capacity in the electronics industry (especially computer chips), that export growth was starting to slow, and that newly built homes and offices in many big cities were overvalued and under-occupied. China had emerged as a formidable competitor for attracting foreign capital to finance industrial expansion. Many companies, especially property companies, had borrowed too much (and banks had lent them too much) in local and foreign currencies. Wages were rising fast, sometimes faster than productivity, which meant that south-east Asia – partly as a result of its own success – was losing its advantage as a 'low-wage' location to do business. In the year to the end of June 1996, container traffic through US west-coast ports – the trade links with Asia across the Pacific Ocean – declined for the first time in the twenty-four years that records had been kept.[8] South-east Asian exports, which had risen 22.8 per cent in dollar terms in 1995, increased only 5.6 per cent the following year.[9] In Thailand, there was no export growth at all in 1996, and it was in Thailand that the crisis first erupted into full public view.

The downturn in Thailand which had become evident in 1996 gradually gathered momentum in 1997. The property bubble burst, and real estate companies had difficulties paying their debts. Finance houses, which had lent heavily to property developers and had earned much of the rest of their income from trading on a stock market that was now stagnant, began to totter. One of the most severe shocks came in March when Finance One announced it was seeking to merge with a local bank to save itself (a deal which later fell through). Finance One had been the country's biggest finance company and a favourite with foreign and local investors; it was led by one of the new breed of aggressive entrepreneurs, the forty-six-year-old Pin Chakkaphak. If even Pin could not extricate himself from the financial morass without seeking a rescue, what hope was there for the rest? Eventually fifty-eight of Thailand's ninety-one finance houses had their operations suspended by the government in the clean-up that followed, and fifty-six were closed. Stockbrokers in Bangkok wrote a humorous epitaph for Finance One and Thailand's boom years in the manner of the popular Elton John song, 'Candle in the Wind':

> *Goodbye Finance One,*
> *I wish I'd never known you at all,*
> *You brought me to ruin,*
> *And I've lost my Benz and all.*
> *Maybe I was greedy,*
> *But I thought I just couldn't lose,*
> *And Pin was so convincing,*
> *Though it clearly was a ruse.*

Goodbye Finance One.
Why have you given me such pain?
My Gucci shoes were never made
For chasing buses in the rain.
Goodbye Finance One,
I wish I'd never heard your name,
So I curse the wretched farang [westerner]
'Cause there's no one else to blame.

And it seems to me I must live my life
Eating noodles like before . . . [10]

By May 1997, as more Thai companies ran into difficulties, there was intense speculation against the Thai currency, the baht. The currency had been pegged within a narrow band to the US dollar, a system that had benefited company planning during the years of economic growth by ensuring that exchange rates were reasonably predictable. Unfortunately companies and individuals had also borrowed heavily in US dollars (for which interest rates were low) to invest in Thailand (where baht interest rates, and returns on investments, were relatively high). They had assumed that they could repay their US dollar debts at roughly the same exchange rate at which they had borrowed; in the early 1990s there was even talk that the baht was undervalued and might be allowed to appreciate. What actually happened on July 2 was that the central bank, after vainly spending billions of dollars and exhausting its reserves to prop up the baht, was forced to allow the currency to float, whereupon it sank. This made it much more expensive in baht terms for Thai companies to repay their dollar debts, which in turn exacerbated the economic crisis; only Thai exporters with little debt could reap immediate benefits from the baht's fall.

In a stark demonstration of how interconnected the world economy has become, the crash of the Thai currency and stock markets in mid-1997 had knock-on effects around the globe: first in the south-east Asian markets of Malaysia, Indonesia and the Philippines; then in Hong Kong, South Korea and the developing economies of Latin America; and finally in Japan, the US and Europe (although the initial falls in western markets were seen at the time as harmless corrections to the price of overvalued shares). One problem often led to another. In Malaysia, the fall in prices on the Kuala Lumpur stock exchange meant that banks (themselves sometimes in difficult straits) were threatening to call in loans to companies and wealthy individuals backed by collateral in shares, because the collateral had fallen sharply in value. But in order to raise the money to repay the loans, the borrowers would have to sell shares, which would depress the stock market further, thus prompting another round of loan recalls, and so on.[11] The region-wide problem was that economic policymakers and business executives had become accustomed to high economic growth. They had, after all, known nothing else. Even the so-called 'recession' of the mid-1980s was nothing of the sort; it was merely a temporary slowdown which south-east Asians called a recession because 4 per cent annual growth seemed so much worse than the 8 per cent or 10 per cent they were used to. Most of the big south-east Asian economies had been expanding for a generation, and business decisions – like political decisions – were usually taken on the understanding that growth would continue indefinitely and swamp any minor mistakes with a flood of rising production and increasing exports.

South-east Asia was thus ill-prepared either in policy terms or psychologically for the crisis that accompanied the Thai crash. Currencies such as the Indonesian rupiah, forced out of the narrow bands in which they had traded against the US dollar, plunged to as little as a sixth of their former value. Stock markets fell too. Companies, commercial banks, central banks and rich individuals suddenly found themselves short of cash. The incipient 'tiger' economies of south-east Asia – which only months earlier had been the envy of their rivals in the developing world – were obliged to turn to the International Monetary Fund for assistance. The IMF co-ordinated a US$17.2 billion rescue package for Thailand, in return for which the Thai authorities would have to reform the country's ailing financial sector, restore a budget surplus and keep both inflation and the current account deficit – the gap between imports and exports of goods and services – within tight limits.[12] With Thailand in political confusion following two administrations run by old-fashioned politicians more interested in patronage than macro-economic orthodoxy, there were doubts about whether the money would be enough and about the government's determination to push through the required austerity measures. Indonesia, meanwhile, needed its own bail-out programme. The IMF and the World

Bank put together a US$37 billion rescue plan, the biggest such package since the $50 billion for Mexico in 1995. In return, Indonesia also had to reform its financial sector and implement various policy changes, including the liberalization of foreign investment, the acceleration of privatization, the removal of non-tariff barriers to trade (such as monopolies in the distribution of foods, including soya beans and wheat) and an end to special tax exemptions. The idea of these reforms was to reduce the opportunities for corruption and the longstanding collusion between the Suharto family and big businessmen. The Indonesian government quickly closed down sixteen of the country's 240 banks. Mar'ie Muhammad, the finance minister, said the affected banks were 'insolvent to the point of endangering business continuity and disturbing the whole banking system'. Significantly, Suharto's relatives had large stakes in three of the banks closed, and they protested loudly. Bambang Trihatmodjo, Suharto's second son, who was regarded by western bankers as a more competent businessman than most other members of the family, filed a lawsuit against the finance minister and the central bank governor over the closure of his Bank Andromeda. He was persuaded to withdraw it, although he soon re-created his bank under the name Bank Alfa. Probosutedjo, Suharto's half-brother and owner of the closed Bank Jakarta, complained that travel restrictions imposed on stakeholders in the targeted banks to stop them fleeing the country were a breach of human rights. As one commentator noted, there was something comic about such complaints coming from such people, but 'being losers is a new experience for them'.[13]

Explanations for the depth of the crisis in south-east Asia were not long in coming. One problem was that the technocrats at the Thai finance ministry and central bank were not quite as brilliant as their admirers had thought. They had failed to curb rash lending by banks and finance houses. In 1996, they had belatedly moved in to rescue the Bangkok Bank of Commerce, which had been used by unscrupulous Thai politicians, its own managers and a Middle Eastern arms dealer as a source of funds and had racked up the equivalent of US$3 billion of bad and doubtful loans.[14] Jeff Sachs, director of the Harvard Institute for International Development, compared Thailand's trauma to Mexico's two years earlier. 'Thailand's 1997 crisis has the same hallmarks: overvaluation of the real exchange rate, coupled with booming bank lending, heavily directed at real estate.'[15] Another similarity to Mexico, and another problem for south-east Asia, was the size of some of the region's current account deficits, especially in Thailand and Malaysia. This simply meant that countries were importing a greater value of goods and services than they were exporting. This in turn might put downward pressure on the local currency but is not in itself necessarily bad or unusual for a fast-developing economy, particularly if the deficit is accounted for by imports of heavy equipment – factory machinery, say – which can be used to create future exports. In south-east Asia, however, it turned out that investments had not been as productive or efficient as first thought; much money was in fact being spent on 'prestige' infrastructure projects which seemed likely to consume more foreign exchange than they could hope to generate. This was particularly true of Malaysia. Growth there had been very high, but not as high as it should have been given the level of investment. 'There is a concern that capital has not been used very efficiently,' said Professor Mohammed Ariff, executive director of the Malaysian Institute of Economic Research. 'For our level of investment, we should have been having double-digit gross domestic product growth.'[16] Indifferent investment decisions would have gone almost unnoticed had the region's economies continued to grow at their familiar cracking pace. But the crash soon exposed weak companies and poor investments with exceptional clarity.

At first, there was a tendency to blame foreign speculators for the region's problems rather than to examine matters closer to home. Mahathir, the Malaysian prime minister, further undermined confidence in the Malaysian financial system by threatening to impose curbs on currency and stock trading and by lashing out at foreigners. He became involved in a slanging match with the currency trader George Soros. He called him 'a moron', while Soros described Mahathir as 'a menace to his own country'. Mahathir, whose country had benefited so much from foreign investment and the growth of world trade, hinted at a conspiracy by jealous westerners to undermine Malaysia's successful economy; noting that Soros was Jewish, he even spoke of a Jewish 'agenda' against Malaysia.[17] In fact, of course, foreign investors were as disturbed as south-east Asians themselves by what was happening. Multi-billion-dollar infrastructure projects, including Malaysia's Bakun dam in Borneo and the US$3.7 billion

road and rail mass transit project being built by Hong Kong's Hope-
well Holdings in Bangkok, were cancelled or suspended. As economic growth forecasts were repeatedly lowered in the aftermath of
the crisis, the building of more power stations and other projects to
cater for rising demand that might not now materialize for several
years were also thrown into doubt. South-east Asian companies,
strapped for cash, delayed repayments on loans and bonds denomi-
nated in dollars. There were opportunities as well. Some Asian or
foreign companies with money to spare swooped on distressed companies, their path smoothed by government decisions to ease protectionist restrictions on foreign ownership of certain kinds of
businesses.[18]

The new rich and the new middle class found that they could no
longer afford luxuries they had started to take for granted: overseas
holidays, expensive cars (which were often paid for in instalments),
mobile telephones and expensive clothes with foreign brand names.
In Thailand, the Japanese car-maker Toyota, which has a third of
the local market, suspended production from November 1997 for
several weeks to try to clear a backlog of unsold cars.[19] Bangkok
entrepreneurs tried to unload everything from Rolex watches to golf
clubs to pay their bills. One man who wanted to sell a light aircraft
for 4.75 million baht (about $100,000) threw in two Mercedes cars
for nothing to sweeten the deal.[20] Casinos in London, such as
Maxims, reported a drop in the number of customers from south-east
Asia.[21]

In the short term, governments were torn between keeping interest rates high to defend their currencies and keeping them low to
help struggling businesses; healthy manufacturing companies complained that hard-pressed banks were depriving them of working
capital that would have allowed them to take advantage of falling
Asian currencies by increasing exports. Looking into the future,
Asian governments acknowledged the need for economic austerity
measures as prescribed by the IMF, including tight domestic budgets
and curbs on their current account deficits. But there was also worldwide criticism of the IMF's prescriptions and of the comparisons
made between south-east Asia's problems and the former travails of
Latin America. Too much austerity, it was said, would make it hard
for south-east Asian companies to repay their debts and increased
the danger of mass loan defaults. South-east Asia was not afflicted

so much by high government debt or poor macro-economic policies (which would have justified IMF-style austerity). The biggest problems were lax control of financial markets and bad management in companies which had borrowed too much money abroad and made unsuitable investments.

There was a dawning realization that the way people did business in most of south-east Asia would have to be fundamentally changed. The deal-making between governments, army generals, ruling families, bankers and unscrupulous tycoons was often corrupt and usually bad for the long-term future of the country concerned. The best that could be said was that the collusion between government and business was inefficient and unsuitable for the modern era of global competition, however easily it may have been accepted in the early years of the industrial revolution. Decades of fast economic growth had not only disguised the need for political and social reforms but also delayed the urgent task of overhauling south-east Asia's management and business practices.

One of the abiding myths about south-east Asia's successful economies was that they operated unbridled free market capitalism and free trade. Those who abhorred the destruction of the environment, the use of child labour and other negative results of industrialization even identified untrammelled 'free enterprise' as the cause. While it was true that influential businessmen often seemed to be able to do as they pleased, this was not because they were operating in a free market regulated by impartial laws. Rather the opposite was the case: south-east Asian economies have long been protected from competition both by formal laws and by the informal influence of these same businessmen. Generally, what south-east Asian countries have done is create an attractive business environment for *exporters*, whether they be foreign companies or local ones. 'The growth of manufactured exports in East and Southeast Asia during the past three decades cannot be reasonably portrayed as the product of generalized free and open markets throughout the region,' said the Asian Development Bank. 'While average import tariff rates were lower than in most other parts of the developing world, they were still far from zero, and governments regularly used tariffs and quotas to protect favoured industries. Nonetheless, one common pattern exists across the region: the most successful Asian economies all established free and flexible markets for exporters.'[22]

South-east Asia's domestic markets, on the other hand, have long been quite restrictive. In Singapore, for example, there are tight controls on the markets for information and labour; the media and the trade unions, in other words, operate on government sufferance. Several of the region's governments have promoted national champions – including Malaysia's Proton national car project and Indonesia's IPTN shipbuilding and aircraft company – and protected them from foreign competition, at least until they are seen to be strong enough to fend for themselves. Foreign investors have typically been limited to a fixed percentage of joint ventures, although regulations vary according to country, industrial sector and the perceived need to encourage or discourage foreign businesses. Such strategies are not original. Nor are the hypocritical declarations of support for 'free markets'. As James Fallows and others have pointed out, England 'strong-armed its way to prosperity' in the eighteenth and nineteenth centuries 'by violating every rule of free trade' – before loudly declaring its free trade doctrine. 'America's economic history follows the same pattern,' wrote Fallows. 'While American industry was developing, the country had no time for laissez-faire. After it had grown strong, the United States began preaching laissez-faire to the rest of the world – and began to kid itself about its own history, believing its slogans about laissez-faire as the secret of its success.'[23]

Although the initial shock of the financial crisis of 1997 tempted some regional leaders to consider tightening their protectionist rules further to insulate their economies from global competition, most policymakers realized that the time had come to liberalize and expose their national businesses to foreign rivals. In theory, this would encourage them to be more efficient. Asian countries had been facing increasingly strident demands from the US to open their domestic markets in world trade negotiations, and in any case there was an urgent need for capital which only foreign investors could provide. Governments eased several protectionist regulations, focusing on the two hardest hit economic sectors – property and financial services. Malaysia abolished a M$100,000 levy applied to foreigners buying property worth more than M$250,000, although quotas limiting foreign purchases in new housing developments were maintained. Thailand also proposed relaxing restrictions on foreign ownership of land, although it too kept many protectionist measures in place. (Only Thais, for instance, can legally work as architects or hairdressers.)[24] In the financial sector, Thailand eased a 25 per cent ceiling on foreign ownership of commercial banks and finance companies, allowing foreigners a 49 per cent stake – and even 100 per cent ownership for at least ten years. Indonesia, the Philippines, Singapore and South Korea also announced they were relaxing curbs on foreign involvement in their domestic financial sectors.

But protectionism and the absence of a free market in goods and services are not simply a matter of legal restrictions on foreigners or the inability of Bangkok bus operators to raise fares without permission from the transport ministry. Informal, hidden barriers to free trade are just as important as explicit rules and regulations. Monopolies, duopolies and cartels run by powerful local businessmen thrive in sectors from transport and timber to brewing and construction. As the Busang gold saga demonstrated, doing business in south-east Asia is not for the faint-hearted, and even the boldest require powerful partners; in a recent A–Z guide to doing business in Thailand, the A stands for assassination. Take the example of Carlsberg in Thailand. When the Danish brewing company decided it wanted to break into the potentially lucrative Thai beer market (as people became richer, they were switching to beer from cheaper, rum-type drinks known as 'whisky') it realized it faced the formidable quasi-monopoly of the Boon Rawd Brewery and its well-known Singha brand. In 1993 Carlsberg teamed up with Charoen Sirivadhanabhakdi, an ethnic Chinese businessman who produces and distributes Mekong, the most popular Thai whisky. Charoen's price was high – he and his local partners demanded a deal which gave them 90 per cent ownership of the joint venture and reserved the right to make their own brand of beer as well – but his distribution network was vital in the fight against Boon Rawd. As one Carlsberg manager pointed out, the rivalry between Carlsberg and Singha agents selling beer on the backstreets of Bangkok and other towns was 'fairly violent'.[25]

Outright corruption, and collusion between governments and private sector tycoons, have also severely distorted south-east Asia's markets, wasting public money and nurturing inefficient conglomerates in the process. Senior military officers – usually with no economic or commercial experience – are also deeply involved in business in several countries, with predictably harmful results for the com-

panies concerned. In Cambodia, it is often simply a matter of breaking the law, cutting down trees in 'protected' forests and selling
them. Thailand moved on from that stage, and different military
services were granted different fiefdoms in big business. Thus the
air force was allowed to dominate the national carrier Thai Airways,
with the result that the airline ended up with a hugely expensive
plethora of aircraft and engine types from different manufacturers
because senior officers had negotiated their own deals – and com-
missions – with suppliers. Air force officers also controlled the Communications Authority of Thailand (responsible for international
telecommunications), while the army had the Telephone Organization of Thailand (domestic telecommunications); unlike the
civilian-run Electricity Generating Authority of Thailand, these two
bodies failed dismally to keep up with the fast-rising demand generated by economic growth. Although Thai civilian governments
started to ease military men out of state enterprises in the 1990s, it
was a slow process. No one was surprised when the air force – confronted with a request to move out of Bangkok's main airport at
Don Muang so that it could be expanded for civilian use – demanded
shares in the airport's business and a 'moving allowance' from the
government worth more than two billion dollars. 'I'm thinking,
"they are civil servants – you shouldn't even be negotiating!",' said
Korn Chatikavanij, a leading stockbroker. 'But most people don't
question it.'[26]

Dubious business practices were particularly rife in big south-east
Asian infrastructure projects, partly because of their mouthwatering
size and partly because the contract is usually awarded by the government or a state corporation with no outspoken shareholders to
answer to. By way of explanation, Asian tycoons used to argue that
there was a flexible, pragmatic 'Asian way' of doing business which
westerners could not hope to understand. But Asian companies were
just as likely to be the victims. In Bangkok, foreign and local investors
were outraged when the Thai government decided to renege on the
terms of a US$1 billion contract to build a toll-road in the city just
as construction was completed in 1993 by a consortium led by Japan's
Kumagai Gumi. The dispute was eventually resolved, but not before
Thailand had been accused by foreign financiers of effectively
nationalizing the project because it suddenly seemed to be very

profitable. After five years of work, Kumagai Gumi was obliged to sell its stake to a consortium led by Ch. Karnchang, a construction company with close links to the Thai armed forces.[27]

Such disputes were not confined to Thailand, or to those with military connections. As in freewheeling, post-Soviet Russia, there was close collaboration between businessmen and government politicians in the Philippines, Malaysia and Indonesia. Under Ferdinand Marcos in the 1970s and 1980s, the Philippines was renowned for its 'crony capitalism', whereby associates of the president were granted monopolies and protected from foreign competition in exchange for their support of the regime. The result was that the country's south-east Asian neighbours raced ahead of the Philippines and left its export industries fifteen years behind. Malaysia did better, but by the time the financial crisis erupted in 1997 there was mounting concern about the unhealthily close relations between big business and the ruling coalition led by Umno – the United Malays National Organization. In September of that year, S. Samy Vellu, the public works minister, suggested the introduction of open, competitive tendering for government projects. The existing system of 'negotiated tender', whereby the government chose a group to execute a project and then negotiated the price, was obviously more expensive for the taxpayers than one which would award contracts to the lowest bidders – but it meant that the chosen businesses owed Mahathir and the government a debt of loyalty.[28]

It was the huge economy of Indonesia, however, that dominated the thoughts of those concerned about corruption and inefficiency in south-east Asia. There were two big forces in domestic Indonesian business: Suharto's family, and Suharto's ethnic Chinese business associates. His children and grandchildren took interests in a wide range of industries, often in lucrative concessions – broadcasting, telecommunications and toll-roads, for instance – which were in the gift of the government. Bimantara, the group controlled by Suharto's second son Bambang, was given a licence allowing it to operate international telephone services. Bimantara then asked international telecommunication companies to bid for a stake in the new company, Satelindo. The point about Bimantara, after all, was not that it knew anything about telecoms: it didn't. What it offered was political connections. One investment banker recalled that when the bids were opened 'Bambang was as excited as a child at Christmas'. The winner was Deutsche Telekom, which paid nearly US$600 million for a quarter of Satelindo, a company based on nothing more than a licence. But the real winner was Bambang: Satelindo was suddenly worth almost US$2.4 billion.[29] Still more extraordinary was the tale of Indonesia's 'national car'. Suharto's youngest son Hutomo Mandala Putra, better known as 'Tommy', was granted special tariff concessions to build a car called the Timor. He had no experience of car manufacturing, but arranged a co-operation agreement with South Korea's Kia Motors. (Bambang was meanwhile building his own cars with Hyundai, another South Korean company, and was furious not to be granted the 'national car' concessions himself.) Particularly galling for Indonesia's existing car-makers, mostly Japanese-run joint ventures, was the decision to grant Tommy the right to import 45,000 Sephia saloons from Kia in South Korea duty-free and call them Timors; this was because his factory had not been built yet. Sixteen Indonesian banks, including four state-owned ones, agreed to lend Tommy's company PT Timor Putra Nasional US$690 million to construct an assembly plant near Jakarta. There were howls of protest from the US, Japan and Europe, which accused Indonesia of blatant protectionism and of violation of its obligations as a member of the World Trade Organization. (The WTO eventually upheld the complaint.) Imported Timors, meanwhile, were not selling well in spite of being much cheaper than their heavily taxed rivals.[30]

But the most effective sanction against the Timor – and against every dubious deal of the Suharto children – was the dramatic impact in Indonesia of the financial crisis that began in 1997. As the rupiah plunged and prices rose, Indonesians took to the streets to demand the removal of their president. After hundreds of demonstrators had been killed in riots, he was forced to step down in May 1998. Almost immediately, Indonesians sought to recover some of the vast wealth that had found its way into the hands of Suharto's friends and relatives over the previous three decades and to detach some of his companies from their previously secure sources of revenue. This was no easy task. Michael Backman, a consultant who has studied Asian business networks, identified 1,247 separate companies in which the Suharto family had significant stakes. Pertamina, the state oil company, said it wanted to end corruption and announced that at least 120 of its suppliers and contractors were owned by Suharto's relatives and associates.[31]

International investors, such as Thames Water of the UK which had an alliance with Suharto's eldest son, were appalled. For years foreign businesses had assumed that it was vital to fix a deal with one of Suharto's children to ensure the success of a major joint venture. After Suharto was ousted, such connections with the former first family were worse than embarrassing. Nor was it only Suharto's relatives who had been placed above the normal rules of the marketplace. B. J. Habibie, the former research and technology minister and vice-president who succeeded Suharto as president, had pushed through controversial – and expensive – projects to build aircraft and ships with government money. Ethnic Chinese tycoons also prospered on the basis of their friendships with Suharto. One such is Liem Sioe Liong, head of the Salim group. In the 1950s he was a businessman selling supplies to the Indonesian army in Semarang in central Java, where the commander was one Lieutenant-Colonel Suharto. By 1990, after Suharto's rise to power, the Salim conglomerate included more than 300 companies, employed 135,000 Indonesians, had annual revenues of about US$8 billion, and accounted for 5 per cent of Indonesia's gross domestic product. In flour, cement, steel, sugar, rice and more besides he benefited from state protection or cheap finance.[32] Another was 'Bob' Hasan, to whom Suharto turned to resolve the dispute between his children over the non-existent Busang gold deposit. Hasan too had started on the path to becoming a billionaire by selling provisions to the army, although he differed from most of his fellow Chinese traders in converting to Islam and accompanying Suharto on a pilgrimage to Mecca. (His Chinese name was The Kian Seng.) By the 1990s, he played golf with Suharto twice a week. With huge forestry concessions in the Indonesian side of Borneo, his main business was timber and plywood.[33]

So great were the business opportunities in the world's fourth most populous country that even companies that did not enjoy government favouritism were able to prosper as the economy grew, provided they trod carefully. 'We can't compete with the [ruling] family,' said one ethnic Chinese businessman during the Suharto era. 'We don't get involved in anything that needs a government licence.'[34] Sofjan Wanandi, whose Gemala group followed a similar strategy and focused instead on service industries and pharmaceutical joint ventures, pointed out that Indonesia could still be a very profitable market in spite of the cost of corruption. 'This is a high-cost economy, but why is the investment still coming? Profitability in Indonesia is quite high too,' he said. 'We can pay this and that but still calculate that we are making a profit. This is the beauty of Indonesian business in a way.'[35] But the problem was that the Indonesian economy, although growing steadily, was not expanding as quickly as it could have or should have given the amount of money being invested. And although millions of Indonesians had been lifted out of poverty, there was an all too visible chasm between the rich and the poor. As Indonesia developed more sophisticated industries and steadily integrated itself into the competitive global economy, the corruption and inefficiency became ever more glaring. Conglomerates which had set up their own banks rather than seeking funds on the open market were criticized by foreign investors for opaque accounting practices and impenetrable webs of cross-ownership between their component companies. Trading monopolies, which had once been defended on the grounds of national security, were condemned by ordinary Indonesians because they had raised prices for consumers and merely acted as cash cows for favoured tycoons. These and other failings were highlighted and partially corrected at the time of the IMF rescue package.

Suharto – although he wavered repeatedly in his application of the IMF medicine – was probably persuaded to swallow it partly because he realized Indonesians were losing their tolerance for the abuses perpetrated by wealthy businessmen. There was an outcry when Eddy Tansil – an ethnic Chinese businessman sentenced to twenty years in jail in 1994 for defrauding the state bank Bapindo of some US$450 million – 'escaped' from prison in 1996. It soon emerged that Tansil, like other wealthy, non-political prisoners, had lived a comfortable life in prison and may even have been allowed out from time to time to do business or play golf. According to the Justice Minister, when Tansil 'escaped' he was escorted to a waiting minivan by prison officials.[36] Indonesians were further outraged by the uses to which the government put a multi-billion dollar 'reforestation fund' financed by levies on logging companies. Among the known transfers was a US$200 million injection for the state aircraft company managed by Habibie, and a US$100 million loan to a paper pulp company controlled by 'Bob' Hasan.[37]

By the time of the IMF rescue, Indonesians recognized that the much-trumpeted 'liberalization' of their economy was going wrong. The private sector was being given a larger slice of the economy to manage, but there was no rule of law, let alone effective regulatory institutions, to ensure that there was fair competition between companies and that non-business interests (the environment, for example) were protected. Political analyst Dewi Fortuna Anwar lamented the fact that there was a free market only in the sense that big companies could act inside Indonesia almost as they pleased – but without being exposed to international competition. 'We have a free market like the time of the robber barons in the US or the industrial revolution in the UK,' she said. 'There are no restraints put on these big businesses and they do harm to smaller businesses without allowing the market to mature. These conglomerates are not really educating themselves to be competitive internationally.'[38]

In varying degrees, other south-east Asian countries were starting to suffer from the same lack of competitiveness caused by the same cosy relationships between politicians and businessmen. Probably the least affected was Singapore, which as a result was initially less hard hit than its neighbours by the financial crisis because there was no obvious need for urgent reform. Although the Singapore government plays an important guiding role in the economy, both through state companies and through official advice and encouragement to private companies to ensure they follow government policy, the city state prides itself on the incorruptibility of its ministers and officials. It is also obsessed about the importance of remaining internationally competitive, and has for years created a favourable business climate for foreign multinationals.

By the end of 1997 it was clear that reforming the economies of south-east Asia would be slow and painful. It was not just a matter of governments cutting expenditure and implementing other austerity measures for a few years and then watching their economies boom again. The way in which many big local companies did business was hopelessly old-fashioned and would have to change. Robber barons, in short, were obsolete: their secretive, unscrupulous and sometimes thuggish ways might be suitable for monopolistic commodity trading, road-building, or the exploitation of plentiful natural resources in the early stages of a country's development, but not for complex manufacturing industries where they had no relevant business or technical skills to offer. It is not surprising that it is in the raw, undeveloped economy of Cambodia that one of the most colourful and boorish entrepreneurs has thrived. Theng Bunma, head of the Cambodian Chamber of Commerce, once shot at the tyre of a Boeing 737 airliner at Phnom Penh's Pochentong airport with one of his bodyguards' pistols because he was annoyed about losing his luggage. 'If it wasn't dark, I would have shot out all the tyres,' said the unrepentant Bunma, who was not punished for the shooting. He has been banned from entering the US because of suspected drug-trafficking, which he denies. But he makes no bones about his close alliance with Hun Sen, the Cambodian leader, and boasted that he financed Hun Sen's July 1997 coup d'état to the tune of US$1 million. 'He asked me if I had the money in Cambodia,' Bunma told an Australian television station. 'I said no, but I would send a hundred kilograms of gold in a plane into Cambodia.' While other factories, offices and homes were looted, Bunma's property was well protected by Hun Sen's troops during the coup.[39]

Most big businesses in south-east Asia are run by ethnic Chinese. Others belong to government-supported groups such as the *bumiputra* ('sons of the soil', mainly Malays) in Malaysia, the Indonesian equivalents known as the *pribumi*, or members of the armed forces. In the early years of development, one of the main advantages enjoyed by these businesses was their access to capital for investment. But in more developed economies, when eager foreign companies are banging at the door offering direct investment (in factories) and portfolio investment (through the stock market), this advantage becomes less important. The political connections of tycoons and big companies are useful for winning franchises (in telecommunications, say, or oil distribution) and big projects; but they do not mean that the companies concerned are any better than their competitors at running the franchise or fulfilling the contract once they have it. Such tycoons often made their first fortunes from property speculation, profiting from the fast-rising urban land prices that usually accompany industrial revolutions, and they may know nothing about the business in hand. The only reason they are involved at all is because they are well-connected nationals in the country concerned. As in the Gulf states, they are obliged to hire a foreign partner with the relevant technical skills in telecommunications, power generation or whatever industry or service is involved.

There is nothing particularly surprising about all this. But unbroken years of economic growth convinced many south-east Asian entrepreneurs – and over-enthusiastic foreigners who invested in some of their businesses – that they were invincible. They became over-extended, borrowing heavily and moving into unfamiliar lines of business as their conglomerates expanded. By the time of the 1997 financial crisis, tales of fraud, incompetence and simple over-ambition were multiplying. In Vietnam, a late starter in the economic race, the cycle from high-flying stardom to failure or arrest (or both) was completed in a matter of years for several of the entrepreneurs who came to prominence in the early 1990s. The companies affected included Minh Phung, a big clothing and construction group; the trading company Tamexco; Lam Son Lacquerware; and the private businesses of Nguyen Trung Truc, head of the Vietnam operations of Hong Kong's Peregrine group, who collected classic cars and was hailed as one of the country's most successful businessmen before being jailed on suspicion of tax evasion (though he was later released).[40] The fate of Peregrine itself was a salutary lesson. The Hong Kong-based investment bank, founded in 1988 with the help of ethnic Chinese investors, boasted of its deal-making prowess in Asia's emerging markets. Philip Tose, the chairman and co-founder, was scornful of Asian democracies such as the Philippines, advocated authoritarianism and was convinced of Asia's economic supremacy over Europe.[41] But Peregrine collapsed ten years after it was established, buried under millions of dollars of unpayable debt owed by Indonesian companies.

In Thailand, Sondhi Limthongkul, who had started with a successful Thai business magazine and went on at breakneck speed to try to build an Asian media empire embracing English-language publications and satellite broadcasting, was forced by financial difficulties to suspend publication of *Asia Times* and radically slim down his other assets. Alphatec, a semiconductor manufacturer and one of the most high-tech companies in Thailand, was floated on the Thai stock exchange in 1993, and only four years later was unable to pay its debts on time; worse, an independent audit found that the company had overstated its profits by at least $164 million from 1994 onwards.[42] The new entrepreneurs were rapidly falling from grace. Sheryll Stothard, a Malaysian who owns a publishing consultancy in Kuala Lumpur, wrote a scathing attack in the *Far Eastern Economic*

Review on the new breed of greedy Malaysian entrepreneurs. They were guilty, she wrote, of 'crude opportunism' and were ill-placed to do business overseas because they were used to being bailed out by their government at home and doing business based on 'know-who' rather than knowhow. 'It has been all too easy for just about anyone to hook up with the right connections and achieve short-term success,' she wrote. 'In this go-go, fast-food style entrepreneurship, Malaysian businessmen display little or no regard for long-term strategies, a scary naïveté about global market forces and a contemptuous disrespect for sheer hard work.'[43]

For businessmen to rely too much on their government connections was an obvious weakness, particularly at a time of political instability. But there was also a realization that the whole informal style of doing business in south-east Asia was unsuitable for complicated commercial operations. Pin Chakkaphak, the head of the soon-to-expire Finance One, had told Goldman Sachs stock analysts in 1996: 'We have no defined structure. Touch and go, play it by ear, that has always been the way we operate.'[44] All over the region, ethnic Chinese businessmen had operated in much the same way for decades. They favour instant decisions over the cumbersome boardroom rituals of the West. They emphasize pragmatism and calculated risks rather than strict legality, cash flow rather than profits. The big bosses, the *taipans*, are autocratic and usually reluctant to delegate. Such methods worked well in the past, allowing their practitioners to seize opportunities and exploit their connections with local politicians and with other Chinese businessmen (particularly those of the same clan) elsewhere in Asia.[45] This is how Thailand's Charoen Pokphand group, starting as a vegetable-seed store in Bangkok in the 1920s, grew to be a multinational conglomerate which is probably the largest investor in China. By its own, deliberately vague estimates CP has more than 200 companies, employs more than 50,000 people and has an annual turnover of over US $5 billion. With operations from animal feed to telecommunications, and petrol stations to motorcycle manufacturing, CP is Thailand's largest company. But it is also secretive, and the links between its publicly listed companies and the Chearavanont family's private interests have long frustrated stock market analysts. CP boss Dhanin Chearavanont, asked if he simply made money by using his influence to direct foreign technology into difficult markets and taking a cut, gave a typically elliptical response. 'CP is a project manager and not a middleman,' he said. 'We are also an investor. As a project manager you have to seek people or companies with the right technology.'[46] CP did not escape Asia's financial turmoil. In 1998 it decided to sell its Chinese motorcycle manufacturing operation, and Dhanin found himself talking about consolidation and the need to raise new capital. In April of that year, CP Pokphand, its Hong Kong subsidiary, asked lenders to await payment on nearly US$100 million of loan notes while it reviewed its financial position.[47]

Many other Asian conglomerates were in much deeper trouble. 'These companies don't have strategies. They do deals,' said Michael Porter, a Harvard Business School management guru who was preaching the need for Asian businesses to reform themselves and become more focused while others were singing their praises. 'They are widely diversified because their opportunistic mode of operation drives them . . . We're already starting to see competitive forces starting to make these past ways of competing less and less effective and less profitable.'[48] Trevor MacMurray of McKinsey, the consultancy, put it slightly differently, arguing that many overseas Chinese groups were 'structurers' rather than 'builders': they chased franchises rather than trying to create internationally competitive products or services, and as the lucrative franchises were eroded by deregulation and competition, their weaknesses as 'builders' would be exposed.[49]

For Bradley Babson, a south-east Asian expert at the World Bank, another way of analysing the development of business is to say that the old-fashioned pre-industrial 'language of relationships' is fighting a rearguard action against the modern 'language of contracts'.[50] Both languages are spoken in south-east Asia today, but the new generation of entrepreneurs is more likely to use the latter than the former. That is partly because many of the *taipans* used their wealth to educate their children overseas before they handed over the family company, an education that often included a spell at a business school in the US or Europe, which imbued the Asian executives of the future with relatively modern ideas of management. Typical of the new generation was Thailand's Richard Han. Like his father, he is an entrepreneur to the core. When he was studying for his MBA at City University in London, the man who went on to become chief executive of Hana Microelectronics had a sideline importing Thai silk flowers and selling them to shops such as Harrods; later he assembled cheap digital watches at home and once sold one million watches to Texaco for a UK petrol station promotion. But when he returned to Thailand in his early thirties, he faced the daunting task of turning around the family business. His father Swie Yam Han had realized early on that microelectronics was the business to be in. The company developed a profitable business making light-emitting diode and liquid crystal display modules for watches, before moving on to circuitry for analogue quartz watches and branching out into integrated circuits, creating Hana Semiconductor in 1984. But the company had two related problems: the new businesses were short of money for investment, and the traditional management structure was such that nobody dared to tell his father – the revered, paternal-istic, all-powerful boss – what was going wrong. Losses on the semi-conductor side almost matched the watch profits and the watch market was maturing and becoming increasingly competitive.

'No manager ever told my father he was wrong,' said Han. 'In Thailand, because of this respect for one's elders, initiative in middle management is lacking. My father would never be questioned so he could never get feedback or decision-making from middle manage-ment. The company had grown and it was still very much a top-down management structure.' His father's mistake, said Han, lay partly in creating a financial framework for the capital-intensive semiconduc-tor business that was almost identical to the successful formula adopted for its more labour-intensive forerunners. 'The capital was enough to buy half of one of those wirebonding machines,' Han said, gesturing towards the floor where attendants supervise the soph-isticated equipment for making electronic circuitry. 'Now we've got fifty of them.' Although his father urged him to sell the semiconduc-tor business, he set about applying what he had learned at business school. He raised money and built a new factory to introduce the economies of scale he believed were necessary; Han realized that international customers wanted to be sure that Hana could produce large runs of good quality components for their products at a reason-able price. He sold some of the company to outside investors, who diluted the absolute power of the family and were able to offer advice on financial strategy in the boardroom. He took the company public and by the mid-1990s it was growing fast (while other Thai elec-tronics companies were struggling), employed 3,700 people, and counted Kodak among its customers (it was making small circuit boards for Kodak cameras). Han gave his father credit for spending time in Hong Kong and letting him tackle the restructuring. 'It depends if the father is willing to release the reins,' he said. 'There are companies where the father still retains a stranglehold over the whole operation.'[51] In mid-1998, Hana Microelectronics was one of the few south-east Asian companies to be reporting sharply higher profits.

Two other weaknesses of south-east Asian business identified both by these young entrepreneurs and by their governments were a shortage of skilled workers and a lack of technical innovation. The last point should not be overemphasized: it would be unrealistic to expect the region's fledgling corporations and universities to match the research and development records of their well-funded American and Japanese counterparts, and there is plenty of money to be made by applying imported technology. (Much money has also been made from outright piracy. South-east Asia has attracted stiff criticism from the US and Europe for violating 'intellectual property rights' by copying everything from music and computer software to Rolex watches and Yves Saint Laurent handbags.) But as wages have risen closer to the levels of industrialized countries, fears have been expressed by Asian and western economists that Asian companies will lose their competitive edge unless they can develop valuable innovations and 'intellectual property' of their own – especially as the world economy becomes more biased towards high technology and service industries. It is significant that south-east Asian stock markets are dominated by companies that are either in low technology industries or sectors that are protected from foreign competition (property, banking, telecommunications, construction and agricultural trading). In 1996, one consultant pointed out that high-tech stocks accounted for only about 0.5 per cent of stock market capitalization in south-east Asia, compared with 5 per cent in Japan and 9 per cent in the US.[52]

Asian governments prided themselves on their respect for education – indeed, they rightly regarded good schools as one of the pillars of their economic success – but in the 1990s there were lively debates about the quality and relevance of the region's various educational systems. One complaint – familiar to Britons and other westerners – was that too many students were taking 'wishy-washy' liberal arts subjects such as English literature and not enough were studying science. Another was that Asian students – even at university – tended to learn by rote and were therefore ill-prepared for any sort of creative thinking in the workplace; visiting foreign professors, however gratified they may have been by the deference shown to them by pupils, were often horrified by the students' reluctance to ask questions or challenge orthodox views. Governments and big companies did take measures to try to improve education. In Thailand, where less than half of school pupils finish secondary education, successive governments have sought to introduce secondary education for all.[53] Government agencies and the Alphatec company also jointly established a Microelectronics Research and Development Centre only months before Thailand and its neighbours (and Alphatec itself) were engulfed in the financial crisis of 1997. One Alphatec executive spoke of creating 'the next Silicon Valley' and Charn Uswachoke, the company's chief executive, said: 'In past years, Thailand has only been an importer of technology. The setting up of the MRDC will not only help us to develop our own technology and to develop our people, but will also enable us to create more IC [integrated circuit] business in Thailand, which is a high value-added business. It will also step up other related industries such as the computer and communications industries which in the end will benefit our country's economic position.'[54]

In Singapore, the most advanced economy in south-east Asia, the debate about education and creativity is particularly intense. Singaporean officials have noticed that although their education system produces people who are generally much better at reading and writing and mathematics than America's, it does not produce large numbers of graduates who are 'really creative'. 'The American system does allow this to happen,' says Goon Kok Loon, a senior executive of the Port of Singapore Authority, one of the high-tech state businesses which has helped make Singapore an Asian trade and services hub. Was this lack of creativity a cultural phenomenon – the downside of the discipline and respect for hierarchy that Singapore boasted about as 'Asian values'? Or was it simply the fault of the education system, a structural flaw that could be repaired with the help of new policies? The answer is much disputed, but many Singaporeans believe that the Asian traditions demanding nothing of pupils except to sit there, absorb facts from the teacher and pass examinations with flying colours will have to be changed. 'I think it can no longer be the case for south-east Asia,' says Goon. 'This is a big debate going on in Singapore.'[55] In 1997, the Singapore government decided to spend S\$1.5 billion on promoting innovative thought in schools, and invited Edward de Bono, the pioneer of 'lateral thinking' to a conference on thinking to be held in 1998.[56] Lee Hsien Loong, the deputy prime minister and son of elder statesman Lee Kuan Yew, is not so sure that it is either possible or desirable to make classrooms more lively in order to pursue the worthy goals of innovation and creativity. 'We are trying to [encourage creativity]. I'm not sure how far you can go,' he said. 'If you look at the Japanese who have talked about this for years and years – and nothing has really happened – it's very difficult. You understand that there's a problem but you can't change your society and your ethos in the classroom. If you take an Asian classroom – almost anywhere in Asia except the Philippines – and an American classroom and you compare, in the American classroom everybody's dying to stand up and say something; the teacher asks and everybody puts his hand up. In an Asian classroom everybody waits his turn to be called, and you can say that you would like to change and move some way towards the American direction, but you can't really do that unless you change the whole of society, which is not possible and probably a high-risk operation.'[57]

Lee may not want to 'change the whole of society' for the sake of innovation, but he and other Singaporean leaders are obsessed by the need for their economy to remain competitive in the twenty-first century. 'The population, having seen thirty years of growth and been told that all is well in the region, don't always know all the things which keep us awake at night, and that is a problem,' he says. 'We worry about competitiveness, we worry about security, we worry about whether some change in technology may render [Singapore's] position no longer key, and then we suddenly will become a backwater, which can easily happen.'[58] The risks are even greater for the south-east Asian countries less technologically advanced than Singapore. This, then, is one of the biggest challenges facing the region's business leaders and economic planners: how to adapt fast enough to stay abreast of the latest developments in technology and commerce at the same time as promoting the high growth in the overall economy needed to bring millions more people out of poverty and illiteracy. The increased speed of each successive industrial revolution, and the growth of world trade (and therefore global competition), make this a more daunting task than ever. Engineers who developed steam technology and factory machinery were essential contributors to the first industrial revolution in Britain, but – since that was the beginning of the industrial age – they faced negligible external competition. However frenzied it may have seemed at the time, by the standards of today, industrialization proceeded at a leisurely pace. Nowadays an industrializing country in south-east Asia has to make a difficult combination of choices: it can train engineers or computer software experts at home or abroad (slow, expensive but ultimately effective as long as the trainees do not emigrate in large numbers); it can import the engineers; or it can import the relevant finished products and try to capitalize on some other advantage – cheap, unskilled labour perhaps, or a suitable climate for tourism. But the global demand for skilled labour (relative to unskilled) has been increasing steadily as a result of factory automation and computerization in the office, which has made many assembly line workers and clerks redundant. 'Countries with large shares of unskilled labour ignore these changes at their peril,' warned the Asian Development Bank in 1997. 'The need to upgrade skills and technology is paramount. Without such upgrading, countries will find that they can compete in world markets only through a continuous decline in the price of their export goods. The result will be a steady loss of real incomes . . . Some Asian countries should aspire to become sources of innovation and technical advances, rather than merely imitators.'[59]

South-east Asia's post-war economic record is undoubtedly remarkable, but the complacency of the early 1990s is fading rapidly as Asians realize that the success was based partly on cheap labour (a fast-eroding advantage) and partly on the 'catch-up' factor: it is easy to catch up with existing industrial powers by applying cheap labour to their technologies, but not so easy to overtake them by inventing one's own technologies as labour costs rise. In the quarter-century between 1970 and 1995, for example, Thailand's fast-growing economy raised per capita income in the country from 11 per cent of the US level to 28 per cent. Other countries boasted of similar achievements, but economic growth rates tend to slow as income rises. 'What is striking about the region [east Asia],' wrote one financial columnist, 'is how many countries have managed to seize available opportunities to import modern technology and managerial skills and converge on the incomes enjoyed by advanced countries ... This is neither a miracle nor the fruit of uniquely Asian virtues: Chile has already demonstrated that it is possible to learn from east Asian countries, despite being an ocean away.'[60] Asia, furthermore, was simply regaining weight in the world economy after a period of relative decline. 'The IMF has estimated that Asia's economies will be half as large again by 2000 as they were in 1993 and that they will by then account for about 30 per cent of world output,' wrote Chris Patten, the last British governor of Hong Kong who handed over the territory to China. 'In 1900, their share was 32 per cent. Asia is unlikely to recover its position of a century ago before 2010.'[61] In place of the talk about Asian 'miracles' and the weaknesses of western societies, analysts in the 1990s began to make more sober assessments of the merits and failings of the economic systems and business methods of East and West. Europeans and Americans, burdened by their expensive welfare systems, looked to Asia (especially Singapore) for guidance on low taxation and how to manage and finance social security. Asians looked to Europe for an understanding of 'quality of life', a concept which embraced more than raw economic growth and rising incomes, and to the US for its high-technology leadership and its business dynamism: the US was praised in particular for its culture of accepting business failure as a necessary evil in cases where Japan and other Asian governments would have been tempted to bail out the unfortunate and the incompetent – with damaging long-term consequences for the economy.[62]

The recession in south-east Asia which began in Thailand in July 1997 turned out to be more severe than almost anyone had anticipated. A year later several countries, burdened with unpayable amounts of short-term foreign debt, faced the prospect of shrinking economies and rising unemployment. Many banks and other companies were either actually or effectively bankrupt. To make matters worse the sharp devaluation of the region's currencies did not immediately boost exports as expected, probably because nervous banks were depriving manufacturing companies of the working capital they needed to operate effectively. The impact was felt around the world. Other developing countries in Latin America and Africa, tainted with the 'emerging markets' label, sometimes found themselves shunned by wary American and European investors. International companies which had supplied everything from luxury cars and diamonds to business degrees and holidays to wealthy Asians found that many of their customers could no longer afford the expensive items they once took for granted. Economists took the view that fickle western bankers and investors were partly to blame for the severity of the economic downturn, because they had first poured too much money into south-east Asia and then panicked and pulled too much out. According to the Institute for International Finance in Washington, net flows of private money to Indonesia, South Korea, Malaysia, the Philippines and Thailand jumped from US$48 billion in 1994 to US$93 billion in 1996, and then plunged to minus US$12 billion in 1997.[63] But there were lessons for south-east Asia too. Indonesia, the most corrupt country in the region, underwent a political revolution in 1998 as a result of the financial crisis and was expected to suffer the most severe economic decline in the region. Early indications were that the two most democratic countries in south-east Asia (Thailand and the Philippines) and the most conservatively run economy (Singapore) were coping better than their neighbours with the economic turmoil. Lee Kuan Yew, Singapore's elder statesman, insisted that 'Asian values' had not been discredited, but he did acknowledge that some Asian governments had run their economies badly. 'Not enough checks and balances, too much cronyism or *guanxi* [use of connections], which aggravated misallocation of resources,' he said.[64] As financial empires tottered, companies collapsed, debts went unpaid and unsavoury dealings were exposed in Malaysia, Thailand, the Philippines and especially Indonesia, it became clear that many of the region's entrepreneurs were still robber barons from another age.

FIVE

Nature in retreat: South-east Asia's environmental disaster

It was a town of machinery and tall chimneys, out of which interminable serpents of smoke trailed themselves for ever and ever, and never got uncoiled. It had a black canal in it, and a river that ran purple with ill-smelling dye, and vast piles of buildings full of windows where there was a rattling and a trembling all day long, and where the piston of the steam-engine worked monotonously up and down, like the head of an elephant in a state of melancholy madness . . . Down upon the river that was black and thick with dye, some Coketown boys who were at large – a rare sight there – rowed a crazy boat, which made a spumous track upon the water as it jogged along, while every dip of an oar stirred up vile smells.

– Charles Dickens in *Hard Times* on the fictional industrial city of Coketown.[1]

Through the heart of this sore afflicted town flows the Sungei Segget, a river by only the most extravagant leap of the imagination. To say it 'flows' is to do hideous injustice to the word; the Sungei Segget is a rank, black, stagnant, noisome ditch, filling the town centre of Johor Baru with the aroma of raw sewage and rotting carcasses. At the first sight and smell of the Sungei Segget, it is no longer difficult to imagine the river that must flow through Hell.

– Rehman Rashid on the pollution in the southern Malaysian town of Johor Baru.[2]

The Indonesian fires are one of the biggest environmental and conservation disasters of all time.

– World Wide Fund for Nature.[3]

Like the waterways of Britain's industrial Midlands or London's River Thames at the height of the industrial revolution in the nineteenth century, many of the canals and rivers of south-east Asia have been so polluted that they are black and biologically dead. Anyone who has witnessed the crowded wooden speedboats ferrying commuters along Bangkok's canals will know what Dickens meant by 'vile smells' and 'a spumous track upon the water'. It is not only the region's waterways that reek of sewage and industrial filth. Factories and power stations pollute air, land and sea with toxic waste delivered by chimneys, dump trucks and outfall pipes. City-dwellers choke on a poisonous cocktail of vehicle exhaust fumes, industrial pollutants and dust from construction sites, where Victorian edifices or wooden residences are torn down by property developers to make way for more profitable towers of concrete and glass. Out in the countryside, gangs with chainsaws race through the remaining natural forest, chopping down trees and turning them into plywood for export to Japan and the West. Farmers burn and level the land for rice paddies, while the surviving wild animals retreat to ever smaller enclaves in the hills; even there they are hunted so that their bones and antlers and glands can be turned into Chinese medicines and aphrodisiacs. These may be tiger economies, but they have precious few real tigers left to boast about. Even the sea is not safe from pollution and over-exploitation. Fish are blown up with dynamite, poisoned with cyanide or trawled out of the ocean in vast nets. The places where fish once bred are dying, the mangroves uprooted for prawn farms and hotels, the coral reefs smothered with sediment and sewage. Like their counterparts in the industrialized world, the fishermen say the fish are fewer and smaller with every passing year.

During the decades of economic growth after 1960, south-east Asia's politicians and tycoons barely gave the environment a thought. At first they dismissed it as a 'western' concern. Later, the horrors that confronted them every day obliged them to admit that there was a problem, but they said it was not a priority. There were two strands to the argument. First, environmental protection was an expensive luxury that only rich countries could afford; therefore the best strategy was to get rich, regardless of the environmental damage, and then use the new-found wealth to clear up the mess. Second, their forerunners on the road to industrialization – Europe, the US, Japan – had done much the same sort of damage to their natural surroundings and were therefore guilty of hypocrisy in criticizing Asia's environmentally destructive economic development. They had in fact adopted the same 'damage first, get rich and repair later' philosophy as Asia. If anything, they were much worse offenders than the still-modest economies of south-east Asia because their rich industrial and consumer societies were using much more energy, producing more pollutants and emitting more of the 'greenhouse gases' that contributed to global warming. Furthermore – as Malaysia's Mahathir often asserted – the West was guilty of trying to impose its own social and environmental standards on Asia in order to make Asian economies less competitive internationally.[4]

Debate was heated. Western environmentalists agreed that the industrialized world had an abysmal environmental record, but they drew the opposite conclusion from Mahathir about what action to take, urging south-east Asian governments not to repeat the mistakes made in the West, in Japan and in Taiwan. They produced studies showing that it was possible to combine rapid economic growth with environmental protection, and that it was more expensive to repair environmental damage after the event than never to have done the harm in the first place. Often they joined forces with newly established local pressure groups which were trying to help the victims of the region's careless industrialization: villagers displaced by dams for hydroelectricity and irrigation; factory workers poisoned by industrial pollutants; small fishermen deprived of their livelihood by falling fish stocks; and the urban middle class appalled by the filth and congestion of the cities in which they had to live. But irreparable damage had already been done, damage that would affect not only the south-east Asians of today but also their unborn children and grandchildren. 'In 1965 South-East Asia was still a land-, forest- and resource-rich region. This is no longer the case, and many of its nation states have wasted their major environmental assets, either for short-term gain or simply through poor and corrupt government,' wrote geographers Jonathan Rigg and Philip Stott. 'The consequences of all this mismanagement are now being experienced, and a "greening" of South-East Asia is occurring, but perhaps too slowly and too late.'[5]

It is bad enough for south-east Asia's 500 million people that they face environmental problems – including both chronic damage and sudden disasters such as landslides or mass poisonings – as severe as those of the West. Still more depressing is the possibility that their problems will be much *worse* than those of the industrial states that preceded them. Having begun their industrial revolutions relatively late, they could have enjoyed significant advantages. Much more is known today, for example, about the causes and effects of pollution, whether it be the destruction of trees by acid rain, the damage to children's intelligence caused by too much lead from car exhausts or the carcinogenic effects of microscopic dust particles. More is known, too, about how such problems can be remedied, or at least contained, through 'clean' technology and environmental legislation. But unfortunately much of this knowledge was wilfully ignored by businesses and governments in the race for profits and growth. There are other reasons to be pessimistic about the future of the region's environment. First, the sheer speed at which the industrial revolution is taking place has made it much harder for governments to limit environmental damage. Technology often threatens rather than protects. Take the hotly contested issue of deforestation. In Britain, the destruction of woodland for human settlements, agriculture and industry took place over hundreds of years, partly because it had to be done by hand. In modern south-east Asia, logging companies with bulldozers and chainsaws can lay waste to vast tracts of forest in a matter of months. Another concern is that so much damage has been done in the early stages of industrialization, leaving scope for further devastation as the developing Asian countries continue to close the gap between themselves and the most industrialized nations. A third worry is that the pressure of expanding populations in south-east Asia, although it differs from country to country, is generally much greater than in previous industrial revolutions and will therefore put more strain on the region's – and the world's – already overstretched natural resources. England had only about seven million inhabitants at the beginning of the first industrial revolution in the eighteenth century. Today south-east Asia is home to hundreds of millions, and Asia to thousands of millions; the population of Asia as a whole is expected to increase by 50 per cent in the next three decades to reach nearly 5 billion.[6]

None of south-east Asia's environmental challenges is insuperable, but together they will test the skills of politicians and the tolerance of the region's inhabitants to the limit. It is they who will have to live in the potentially nightmarish 'megacities' of the future or in a countryside that risks being denuded of trees and impoverished by soil erosion and drought. In the 1990s, more and more Asians have started to consider the costs as well as the benefits of the economic boom. They do not want to put the industrial revolution into reverse, although, like westerners, some are nostalgic about the simple rural idyll they believe they have lost. But what of culture, natural heritage, and that indefinable aim, 'quality of life'? As Thais, Filipinos and Malaysians sat in giant traffic jams on the way to work in the 1990s and watched their children breathing the fumes engendered by their economic success, many of them reflected that there was more to life than money and a rise in gross domestic product. 'At the moment we just go with the trend of materialism, consumerism, competitiveness, and that leads to higher and higher destruction of resources,' said Paiboon Wattanasiritham, a banker who turned his back on commerce and became a rural development activist in Thailand. 'Our growth has clearly been at the expense of natural resources. It has been expensive, this economic growth.'[7] In 1997, a disaster occurred which affected the lives of millions of south-east Asians, brutally bringing home to them the fragility of their natural environment. It coincided with a severe financial crisis. But unlike with the gyrations of stock and currency markets, there was no way governments could blame this disaster on western speculators. The fault lay squarely in south-east Asia.

Hundreds of thousands of hectares of Indonesian forest were ablaze. The fires – mostly lit by companies clearing land for oil palm plantations in Borneo and Sumatra and exacerbated by drought – sent up a pall of smoke and haze that was more than 3,000 kilometres from east to west, covered all or part of six countries over an area nearly as large as western Europe and affected about seventy million people.[8] The impact on health, transport, business – and on neighbourly relations within Asean – was dramatic. In the capitals of Singapore and Kuala Lumpur, visibility was sharply reduced. Malaysians adopted the 'Petronas Towers test' – counting the number of floors in the world's tallest buildings that were visible from the ground – to measure the thickness of the smoke. People found it unpleasant to breathe outside and their eyes watered. In Kuching, the capital of the Malaysian state of Sarawak in Borneo, the situation was much worse. According to Malaysia's air pollutant index, a reading between zero and fifty points indicates that air quality is good, fifty-one to one hundred is moderate, 101 to 200 is unhealthy, 201 to 300 is very unhealthy and 301 to 500 is hazardous. In September, Kuala Lumpur had a measurement of 302, while Penang, the island which is the home of many of Malaysia's high-technology industries, showed 371. Kuching's reading of 839 was off the scale.[9] And the haze was not a one-day disaster: it endured, with varying degrees of intensity, for more than three months. Tens of thousands of Indonesians and Malaysians suffered from serious respiratory problems, and the problem was apparently worsened because the woodsmoke helped to trap the other pollutants pumped out by cars and factories closer to the ground. Some foreign embassies and companies evacuated members of their staff and families. For those who remained, the long-term effects of being forced to smoke the equivalent of several packets of cigarettes a day were incalculable. The poor visibility was also blamed for contributing to the crash of an Indonesian airliner attempting to land in Sumatra, in which 234 people were killed, and to collisions between ships in the Strait of Malacca between Sumatra and the Malayan peninsula: twenty-eight crewmen of a cargo ship that sank after a collision with a tanker were missing, presumed dead. Schools, offices and factories were affected too. Airports in the worst hit areas had to be closed, and Malaysian and Indonesian airlines were forced to cancel numerous flights. Businesses, such as mines in remote areas, faced delays in receiving equipment sent by air. Even if they could still fly in, tourists and business travellers shied away from destinations shrouded in smoke, leaving some hotels almost empty and further eroding the profits of the region's airlines. So thick was the haze that there were fears that the shortage of sunlight would affect agriculture, reducing food crops and the production of commodities such as palm oil.[10] The effects on wildlife were hard to quantify, but the World Wide Fund for Nature, calling the fires one of the worst environmental disasters in history, said small groups of endangered rhinoceroses were at risk and hundreds of rare orangutans had probably been killed.[11]

More damaging still was the blow to south-east Asia's reputation, already battered by a financial crisis that was now spreading to South Korea and Japan. Who would want to invest in a high-tech business in Malaysia's proposed 'Multimedia Corridor' if it meant subjecting your employees, and your sensitive equipment, to such pollution? Malaysia dispatched hundreds of firefighters to help the Indonesians douse the fires. Japan and other foreign governments sent equipment and advice. But it was a hopeless task. The fires were enormous, and in some places the peaty ground itself was ablaze. All that the Indonesians could do was wait for the rains. The forests and the peat had been burning since July; the rains finally arrived in November. It was time for a reckoning.

When it comes to forest fires, the usual scapegoats for south-east Asian governments are the small numbers of traditional 'slash-and-burn' subsistence farming communities which still survive in the region. They clear an area of forest, harvest a couple of crops of cassava or corn and move on to fresh land when the soil is exhausted, returning to the first plot only after several years, if at all. Indonesian officials and logging and plantation companies did make half-hearted efforts to blame these small farmers for the fires in 1997, but they put more emphasis on drought caused by the global weather phenomenon known as El Niño.[12] It was true that there was a lack of rainfall that year, probably exacerbated by El Niño, but the government had been aware for months of the risks of drought. Satellite photos showed that the fires were raging in areas of forest being cleared for big new commercial plantations, mainly of oil palms, rubber and quick-growing trees used to make pulp for the manufacture of paper. Some of these areas had already been logged by Indonesian timber companies, and the remaining scrub put to the torch to clear the land. The fires spread. Embarrassingly for the Malaysian government, many of the companies establishing the plantations were Malaysian-Indonesian joint ventures; land and labour are cheaper in Indonesia, and the Malaysians were taking advantage of Indonesia's determination to overtake Malaysia as the world's largest producer of palm oil. Indonesia banned the burning of forest to clear land in 1995 after previous fires got out of control, but big companies were as cavalier about this rule as they were about other environmental legislation. 'If you do land-clearing in pioneer areas, where no roads are established, the only practical way to get rid of the debris is to burn it,' A. F. S. Budiman, executive director of the Rubber Association of Indonesia, was quoted as saying with remarkable frankness in the *Far Eastern Economic Review.* But what if a local official tried to enforce the ban on burning? 'You just bribe him,' Budiman said. 'At the most, you promise to give him some shares. Then he'll just wash his hands of the matter. Who will know? It's such a big area.'[13]

So serious was the smoke in 1997 that finally the Indonesian government was forced to act. It revoked 151 licences of twenty-nine companies suspected of using fire for land-clearing and threatened to withdraw more, including some granted to companies owned by President Suharto's relatives and friends.[14] More important for regional diplomacy was the fact that Suharto – who saw himself as the senior figure in Asean – felt obliged to make a rare apology to his neighbours for the damage caused by the fire. He did so in a speech to Asean environment ministers in September – their meeting had to be moved to Jakarta from the planned venue at a resort because of the smog – and apologized again three weeks later.[15] The extraordinary truth about the fires of 1997 was they were not a new phenomenon at all. There had been huge Indonesian forest fires in 1982, 1983, 1991 and in 1994 – and there were to be more in 1998. In 1991, the smoke over Kuala Lumpur was so bad that it caused a sharp increase in respiratory ailments and eye complaints and delegates noticed it at a meeting of Commonwealth ministers.[16] The fires in Borneo in the early 1980s were estimated to have affected three million hectares of lowland tropical rain forest, swamp forest and peat forest and were also exacerbated by El Niño. They were described as 'one of the most spectacular ecological events witnessed in recent times'.[17]

Asean's much vaunted 'Asian Way' of diplomacy, which preferred 'consensus', public harmony and 'non-interference' in the affairs of other countries to disagreement and confrontation, had proved disastrous for the health and well-being of thousands, perhaps millions, of south-east Asians. Instead of tackling the problem of the fires with urgency and determination, Asean ministers sought to avoid embarrassing Indonesia, talked little about the problem and did almost nothing. They saw the environment as an issue used by westerners to try and restrict their exports of timber and other products, not as something which directly affected their own countries. In 1995, Asean environment ministers reacted to the previous year's haze by ordering the Asean Institute of Forest Management to draw up an action plan to prevent a recurrence. The plan, involving joint monitoring and firefighting strategies, was unveiled in 1996 in Kuala Lumpur. Canada, generous as ever with its foreign aid, agreed to provide US$1.5 million of funding for the programme as long as Asean matched the offer. Asean chose not to. Instead, Asean environment ministers met in the Thai resort island of Phuket in January 1997 and merely released a statement which 'expressed their appreciation [for] Indonesia's efforts on the issue of trans-boundary haze pollution'. The appreciation was misplaced, for Phuket, like Kuala Lumpur, was subsequently shrouded by smoke.[18] It did not take long for Asean's gentle diplomacy to be exposed as inadequate. Criticism of Indonesia in the Thai press, which had long taken an interest in environmental matters and was largely free from government interference, was predictably vociferous; one English-language newspaper called Indonesian loggers and plantation companies environmental terrorists and contrasted the Jakarta government's quick clampdowns on political dissidents with the slowness of its efforts to punish the perpetrators of the smoke.[19] Even *The Straits Times* of Singapore, normally restrained in its comments on sensitive issues, was outspoken in rejecting Indonesian explanations for the smoke and demanding immediate action. 'The patience of Singaporeans and Malaysians is wearing thin,' it said. 'The cost of the haze is getting unacceptably high and it will get higher if not enough Indonesian officials act urgently, decisively.'[20] In Malaysia, there was only a small public demonstration to protest against the government's failure to do anything about the smog, but there was much discussion in the media and in private about the crisis. The Malaysian government's reaction to the media coverage was characteristic: it decided to stop academics from painting a gloomy picture of the smog disaster. Najib Tun Razak, the education minister, announced that any academic research relating to the problem would have to be submitted to 'higher authorities' for approval; this was to prevent academics being manipulated by the foreign media to blacken Malaysia's image, he said. It was as if Malaysians were worried about their health and foreign visitors were shunning Malaysia not because of the smog itself, but because there were news reports about the smog. If the news reports disappeared, the smog would simply pass unnoticed. To people who had been breathing in the smoke for weeks, this was absurd. 'This is absolutely ridiculous,' said Fan Yew Teng, a former member of parliament and critic of Mahathir, the prime minister. 'They talk so much about wanting a free media because of the "multimedia super corridor" and yet they suppress this.'[21] In 1998, as the Indonesian fires broke out again and the smoke returned, the Malaysian government – anxious about the country's image because it was hosting the Commonwealth Games – told TV stations their licences would be revoked if they used the word 'haze'.[22]

Except perhaps to the Malaysian government, the lessons of the great smog of 1997 were unambiguous. The ideal of 'non-interference' in the affairs of other states had turned out to be impossible to maintain in the face of Indonesia's unwillingness to enforce its own environmental laws without pressure from its outraged neighbours; 'non-interference' was in any case a myth in such an interdependent world, since south-east Asian countries were continually 'interfering' with each other through trade, investment and support for a government here or a rebel group there. The crisis had also shown that if a problem arose, there was no substitute for dealing with it quickly and firmly, whatever the sensitivities of the country or countries concerned. This was not 'western': it was merely common sense. It had taken a particularly disastrous series of fires to jolt south-east Asian governments into admitting there was a problem at all, but those affected by the smoke hoped that at least the crisis of 1997 might prompt Indonesia and Asean to tackle it seriously as they had failed to do after the earlier outbreaks. These lessons do not just apply to the environment (by the mid-1990s Asean's members were discovering the need to talk firmly to China about its territorial ambitions in the South China Sea, a problem examined in chapter 6), but environmental issues do have a habit of ignoring international frontiers: apart from dealing with the smoke, in future Asean will need to make decisions about several regional concerns including marine pollution and overfishing.

Within individual countries as well as across the region, the need for stricter environmental controls is becoming more obvious every year, not because sentimental westerners demand them but because locals want them and governments are starting to understand that their economic future depends on them. The Indonesian forest fires that culminated in the smoke cloud over south-east Asia followed what has now become a familiar pattern for the region's environmental disasters. First, there is the greed. Big companies see an easy way to make money – especially easy if it involves the exploitation of natural resources that can be had for free or bought very cheaply. Then there is the collusion of the government. Corrupt officials win a share of the profits for turning a blind eye to infringements of any environmental rules, and central governments as a matter of policy are inclined to support any activity that seems to feed their obsession for economic growth. This is followed by the disaster: forest fires perhaps, or a drastic depletion of fish stocks, or the poisoning of an entire river by a factory. Then comes denial. If it can be, the disaster is blamed on foreigners or on the uncontrollable forces of nature. Finally, there may be a belated recognition that this is a home-grown disaster which needs to be tackled at home.

It is difficult to overemphasize the scale of the environmental problems confronting south-east Asia, or the speed at which they are developing. In terms of wildlife, Indonesia is one of the richest countries in the world. The archipelago has only 1.3 per cent of the earth's land surface, but it hosts 10 per cent of its flowering plant species, 12 per cent of its mammals, 16 per cent of its reptiles and amphibians, 17 per cent of its birds and more than 35 per cent of its fish species. Indonesians use an astonishing 7,000 different kinds of fish as sources of protein. In other words, the country is staggeringly rich in 'biodiversity'.[23] The concept has been dismissed by some critics as a western fad of little consequence to ordinary people in developing countries. But it is not merely the survival of a few obscure species of beetle that is at stake as the logging companies raze the last few tracts of virgin forest with their bulldozers. Deforestation, careless farming and the pressures of a growing population are eroding and impoverishing millions of hectares of Indonesia's soil. In some areas official figures define 20 to 30 per cent of the land as degraded. Fish stocks in some places – off the coast of north Java, for example – are severely depleted by overfishing, pollution and the destruction of fish breeding grounds. Inland, rivers have been rendered filthy by industrial effluents. In Jakarta, the air is heavily polluted, and the excessive extraction of fresh water from the ground has allowed salt water from the nearby sea to intrude below the city, contaminating the fresh water and threatening the foundations of buildings with corrosion.[24] Most of the other countries of south-east Asia suffer from similar urban and rural environmental problems. The economically advanced city state of Singapore is different, partly because it strictly enforces environmental laws to control vehicle and industrial pollution and partly because it has – like other industrialized nations – largely completed the process of converting as much of its territory as it wants into places for humans to live, work and play. Its record, however, is not unblemished. Most of its mangrove forests have been cleared for industrial and housing developments, leaving only 0.5 per cent of the original area of mangroves, mostly in protected zones. 'The absence of a significant economic rationale for conserving mangroves, coupled with the land needs of a rapidly growing and industrializing country, mean that probably only token mangrove areas will be conserved for aesthetic and educational purposes in the future,' said one report on Asean's marine fisheries. Singapore's seagrass beds, also important as fish nurseries, have been drastically reduced by land reclamation, dredging and pollution, while its coral reefs have been badly damaged and are now 'among the most stressed in Asia'.[25] Commercial fishing barely exists in Singapore's waters; the country concentrates on the development of its port, the world's busiest.

Appeals for the protection of biodiversity, perhaps understandably, leave most Asian governments cold, however much excitement the discovery of new species of wild cattle in the remote hills of Vietnam generates among western biologists.[26] Environmentalists have therefore taken to pointing out the economic costs of destroying the environment and the benefits of protecting it. Some calculations are straightforward. Tourists are less likely to want to visit cities notorious for traffic congestion, or to swim at beaches where the sea is mixed with garbage and raw sewage, as Bangkok and the sleazy resort of Pattaya in Thailand have discovered. Other costs and benefits are harder to quantify, although economists have tried. One method is to work out an economic growth rate that measures not the absolute growth but the rate at which the economy would have grown if the statistics also accounted for the destruction or use of natural resources such as oil and timber. The idea is to show that present nominal growth rates may be unsustainable and to emphasize the importance of conserving resources, especially those that are renewable – trees and fish, for instance – if carefully managed. Thus in Indonesia, according to one estimate, the economic growth rate of 6.7 per cent in 1991 was a mere 2.5 to 3 per cent if the depletion of natural resources was accounted for.[27] A longer-term estimate, for the years between 1971 and 1984, was that Indonesia's annual 'resource-adjusted' growth rate was 4 per cent, compared to the official rise in gross domestic product of 7.1 per cent a year.[28] Another method of measuring the effect of environmental destruction is simply to attempt to add up the costs of the damage: healthcare for the victims, lost productivity and so on. Studies quoted by the Asian Development Bank examined the costs of particulates (dust and other small particles in the air) and lead emissions in Jakarta; the particulates cause premature death and the lead reduces children's mental abilities. The damage from those two pollutants alone was estimated to cost more than $2 billion a year.[29] The trouble with these statistics is that they are – as even the people who calculate them usually admit – particularly prone to error, because some components of the sums are little more than guesswork. They are too vague to impress either the governments or the citizens of south-east Asia. What *is* beginning to impress them is the filth, chaos and discomfort they experience in their daily lives. These difficulties are particularly noticeable in cities such as Kuala Lumpur, Jakarta and Manila. But it was Bangkok in the 1990s that became a byword for Asia's urban nightmare.

It is Monday, 6.30 p.m., on Sukhumvit Road in Bangkok in the rainy season. A European businessman in a pinstripe suit with rolled-up trousers wades through eighteen inches of rainwater and raw sewage, briefcase in one hand, shoes in the other, heading for home. In another flooded road nearby, a pair of Thai schoolgirls are trapped with the family chauffeur in their BMW. The engine is still running in spite of the water, but the traffic ahead is stationary. They left school three and a half hours ago and are only halfway home. A secretary who left work at 5 p.m. is standing in a crowded, motionless bus. She will not reach her home in the suburbs until 11 p.m. An Englishman is forced to abandon a business trip to southern Thailand after missing his flight; it took him more than three hours to reach the airport, normally a forty-minute trip. His pregnant wife has just spent six hours in a taxi trying, and failing, to keep an appointment. Back in their apartment, she vents her frustration by methodically ripping to shreds a novel set in Thailand entitled *A Haunting Smile*.[30]

Bangkok's notorious traffic congestion has made a lasting impact on the city's eight million inhabitants; it affects their physical and mental health, their wealth, their social life and their family relationships. Cars have become second homes for many middle-class Thais. They sleep, read books, watch television, make telephone calls and do their homework in the Volvo. Mothers rise before dawn, drag their children out of bed and into the car to beat the rush hour and feed them breakfast at the school gates. On one notorious night in July 1992, traffic jams were so bad that some children were not collected from school by their parents until 11 p.m. At one school the last pupil left at 2 a.m. the next morning. In 1993, a Thai author won a literary prize for a novella called *A Family on the Road.* In it, an urban family lives entirely in the car; the book ends with the wife becoming pregnant.

Thai commuters quickly adopted survival tactics to deal with the ordeal of spending six hours a day in their cars. In 1993, Esso garages in Bangkok began selling the 'Comfort 100', a five-dollar portable toilet, which looks like a plastic petrol container with a funnel. Another model was the 'Easi Pee', a plastic bag containing a liquid-absorbing gel. For defecation as well as urination, there was the all-purpose 'Combi', a bag in a cardboard box. For those in a hurry to get around the city, gangs of motorcycle taxi-drivers wearing coloured overshirts (for which they have to pay protection money to the police) are clustered at various street corners. They weave skilfully – some might say recklessly – with their pillion passengers in and out of immobile lines of cars. Then there are the mobile offices. Narongchai Akrasanee, once head of the General Finance group of companies and later a government minister, used a modi-fied Volkswagen Transporter van fitted with swivel chairs, a tele-phone, a facsimile machine, a television, video and compact disc players and a refrigerator. 'It's mad,' Narongchai said of the traffic as he demonstrated his vehicle. 'It's the major suffering of the people here.' His company estimated that traffic congestion cost the city's inhabitants nearly $2 billion a year in wasted fuel and time. But it is more than a matter of inconvenience and money. Each day people are poisoned by the carbon monoxide, lead and toluene spewing from thousands of exhaust pipes. A United Nations agency which studied Asian urbanization concluded that living in a large Asian city was a risky affair. Rates of lung cancer, tuberculosis and bron-chitis were high. In Bangkok, average levels of lead in the blood were four times the US standard and there was evidence that lead poisoning had caused permanent brain damage in children.[31] Another report from the US Agency for International Development described airborne particulates in Bangkok's air as a 'serious threat to public health' that could lead to 1,400 deaths a year. Yet another report – this time from a Thai university – found that the often manic behaviour of Bangkok bus drivers at the wheel could be explained by their breathing exhaust gases 'powerful enough to devastate the central nervous system, brain functions and consciousness'.[32] A fifth of the city's traffic policemen have hearing problems, and many have lung disorders as well.

The causes of Bangkok's urban catastrophe are fairly well understood. Successive governments, corrupt or inept and sometimes both, failed to plan the city's development or provide any form of urban public transport other than buses and taxis. Property developers built high-rise blocks on narrow lanes too small for the traffic the buildings were bound to generate, and they flouted such zoning regulations as there were with well-placed bribes, while only 9 per cent of Bangkok's surface area was given over to roads (compared with the 25 per cent typical of the world's other big cities). Thais were becoming more prosperous and buying cars. Each day an extra 450 new cars jostled on to the city's crowded streets, making Thailand a bigger market for cars than Australia and putting the country on its way to becoming Toyota's biggest foreign market outside the US.

Bangkok's traffic congestion may eventually be eased by the completion of several big public transport projects, including an elevated light railway, that have been delayed for decades. More immediate relief came with the sudden recession of 1997; hundreds of Bangkok drivers could no longer keep up the hire purchase payments on their cars, which were then repossessed by the leasing companies. But Bangkok's residents, like the inhabitants of Los Angeles or London, will not easily give up the cult of the motor car. The same is true of the rest of south-east Asia, where vehicle use (rather like the size of the economy) was doubling every seven years before 1997. Even the relatively small city of Kuala Lumpur suffers from severe traffic jams and outbreaks of 'road rage', in which frustrated motorists lash out at their fellow victims. Only Singapore has effectively limited the use of cars. It invests heavily in public transport, slaps burdensome taxes on new cars, charges fees for entry to the city centre at peak hours and has introduced an electronic road-pricing scheme.

* * *

Yet traffic congestion and its associated pollution is only one of several environmental problems that make life difficult. Like consumer societies in the industrialized world, south-east Asian cities have started to produce vast amounts of garbage which has to be collected and then dumped somewhere. Although the garbage crisis is not as severe as in the more advanced economy of Taiwan – where riot police have had to escort garbage trucks to fend off angry villagers near the dumps and allow the vehicles to discharge their loads – there have been protests, and it may yet come to batons and water cannon.[33] Then there is the matter of fresh water supplies, and the treatment of the sewage and industrial effluents that have turned canals and rivers black. In southern and eastern Bangkok, the over-exploitation of groundwater – pumped out for industrial use – causes the city to sink by five to ten centimetres a year.[34] Only 2 per cent of the city's inhabitants are connected to sewage treatment plants – most of the rest of the waste flows straight into the Chao Phraya river – and it was only in the mid-1990s that the authorities began the costly process of installing sewage facilities.

It is not just a matter of physical health. Thais remember Bangkok in the 1960s as a pleasant place to live; now it is an ordeal, as those responsible for trying to keep the city clean readily admit. Pornchai Taranatham, deputy director-general of Thailand's Pollution Control Department, remembers the boyhood pleasures of catching fish from the Chao Phraya. 'Thirty years ago it was easy,' he says. 'When I was in high school we could walk along the river and get shrimp and big fish. Not any more.' The river is heavily polluted and levels of life-sustaining oxygen in the water have fallen steadily. Dissolved oxygen levels near the Bangkok port of Klong Toey are consistently close to zero, and species of fish found a decade ago have disappeared from the lower reaches of the river.[35] There is a similar wistfulness in Indonesia. 'I used to drink straight from the well in the middle of Jakarta when I was a kid, and now I don't even try,' says Sarwono Kusumaatmadja, the former environment minister. 'I used to play in the numerous creeks in west Java and you could find fish and crayfish. The simple joys of life are gone now.'[36]

South-east Asian cities are not only dirty. They are ugly. The problem is not the scarred landscape of uprooted trees, flattened hills and bare red earth that can be seen from the air where construction companies are building new industrial estates, housing complexes and motorways: even if the process is more rushed in Asia than it ever has been before, that is the price that all societies seem to pay for industrialization and the inevitable urbanization that accompanies it. The objections are that most of the new concrete buildings are dull, cheap and utilitarian, a triumph of accountancy over architecture; that historic and considerably more elegant buildings are routinely demolished by brash property developers and brash governments; and that there are not enough parks and green spaces set aside for the hard-pressed inhabitants who crave them. As Kwaak Young Hoon, who was chief planner for the 1988 Olympic Games in Seoul, said recently, the main problem with Asian cities is that they are becoming homogeneous and characterless. Speaking at a conference on the future of Asian cities held in Jakarta, he said the development of the Indonesian capital had been driven by economic rather than social considerations. 'What is wrong with Jakarta is that it could be Bangkok, Seoul or anywhere,' he said.[37] The region's cities are typically ringed with slums and middle-class housing estates, while city centres consist of random clumps of high-rise office buildings interspersed with empty lots and the occasional surviving house. Old hotels and mansions and lively streets of Chinese shophouses are swept aside to make way for more profitable real estate. 'The historic cores of Asia's cities are doomed,' declared Khoo Salma Nasution, secretary of Malaysia's Penang Heritage Trust, in a recent polemic. 'Rapid economic growth has unleashed forces that have little regard for the tangible past. Heritage buildings are being demolished faster than the region's nascent conservation movement can tally them up.'[38] Singapore, which has a tourism industry to promote, has belatedly tried to conserve some of its old buildings and re-create others, and for its pains has been accused by purists of trying to construct ersatz heritage sites without the vigorous communities that once gave them life. The latest battleground between developers and conservationists is the Vietnamese capital Hanoi. Ironically it is poverty and war that have preserved the broad, tree-lined avenues and dilapidated colonial villas from the days of the French. As the economy grows, the city needs modern homes and offices, but some residents want to preserve its charm for themselves and in order to attract international tourists. With the first high-rise buildings already sprouting in the city, the battle is just beginning.

Although industrialization in south-east Asia has been concentrated – and in some cases over-concentrated – in capital cities, secondary towns are starting to feel the same environmental pressures. Chiang Mai, Thailand's northern capital and second city, was described in the sixteenth century by Ralph Fitch, a visiting merchant from London, as a 'very faire and great town with faire houses of stone'.[39] But in the late 1980s and early 1990s Chiang Mai became a boomtown, and instead of building 'faire houses' property developers furiously threw up concrete shophouses, condominiums and petrol stations, filling the town with dust and noise. At 200,000 or so, Chiang Mai's population is a fraction of Bangkok's, but it began to duplicate in miniature the problems which afflicted the capital: traffic jams and pollution compounded by a lack of urban planning. An environmental report from the municipal authorities contained a catalogue of woes, including inadequate rubbish collection and encroachment by property developers on public land. The filthy main canals in the city were called 'a disgrace'. And in the new Lamphun industrial estate, waste disposal was a haphazard affair, with electronics companies burying toxic waste in drums or burning it in their yards on Saturday nights because of the complexity of the paperwork needed to send it out of the export processing zone. Visitors and migrants who sought relief in the cool climate and calm surroundings of Chiang Mai were disillusioned. 'Fifteen years ago I left Bangkok and thought I'd made the right decision,' said Chayant Pholpoke, a travel agent and environmental activist. 'Now I'm not so sure. It's another Bangkok. I'm afraid, partly because people like myself [from Bangkok] are here.' Tanet Charoenmuang, director of the local government studies project at Chiang Mai university, was scathing about the way Chiang Mai had failed to learn anything from the disastrous development of Bangkok. 'They are both hells,' he said. 'Chiang Mai is following Bangkok very closely.'

As people become richer, they are freed from spending all their waking hours earning a living to the exclusion of other interests and pursuits. They can look around them and see the need to make their towns and cities more habitable. In previous industrial revolutions, the pace of development was slow enough for public transport networks to be established, old buildings to be rescued and land set aside for public parks; the tragedy for Asians today is that development is so fast that by the time people have actually expressed the desire for clean air, green spaces, or the preservation of a monument, it is almost too late to act. Victor Chin, a Malaysian graphic artist, described his disappointment when only about two dozen members of the Malaysian Nature Society came to a 'last picnic' he helped to organize in the smallest of Kuala Lumpur's three remaining parks. 'They are destroying this park,' he said. 'It's not a big park but it's as old as Malaysia. They are going to knock it down and build a huge development of mixed office, entertainment and commercial development . . . Progress is good, development is good, but there is too much of a good thing.'[40] A little too late, the urban inhabitants of south-east Asia are beginning to wonder what sort of homes they have made for themselves and their children. It was significant that in 1996 the residents of Bangkok elected a mayor, Pichit Rattakul, on an explicitly environmentalist platform. He set about limiting the dust from the capital's building sites, prosecuting litterbugs, and promised to clean the filthy canals. 'We won't give up,' he said. 'We really want to make Bangkok clean.'[41] It was not clear how far he could take his campaign without support from the national government, but he had made a start on a job that would take decades. It has taken a long time to clean up the River Thames in London after Britain's industrial revolution, and it will probably be years before Thais like Pornchai Taranatham can go fishing again on the lower reaches of the Chao Phraya.

But most of the region's inhabitants still live in the countryside and their complaints are less audible than those of their urban fellow-citizens. Their communities are smaller and more scattered, but they too are suffering the environmental consequences of rapid modernization. It is not that they are sentimental about their disappearing wildlife. On the contrary, they are no more enthusiastic about the tigers and elephants that eat their animals and destroy their crops than Europeans were about bears and wolves. Like Europeans, they clear forests to make fields; and like the Europeans of the past they traditionally see the forests as dark, wild and frightening. The British geographer Philip Stott has noted the distinction drawn in Thailand between the *pa thu 'an* – the barbaric, forested lands filled with spirits, wild animals and foreign peoples – and the *mu 'ang* – the civilized heart of the country where the king rules and nature is controlled and benign.[42] Still more telling are the words used in Malaysia by rural people who have long struggled with the forest to grow their crops; the expression meaning that things are going from bad to worse is *belukar menjadi rimba* – 'scrubland is reverting to forest'.[43] Little wonder that rural people poach game in south-east Asia's poorly patrolled wildlife sanctuaries; shrug when they see soldiers with chainsaws cutting down trees in a Cambodian nature reserve; and express no surprise that businessmen should take over a Thai national park and turn it into commercial prawn farms.[44] On the banks of a tributary of the Rejang river in the forests of Sarawak in Malaysian Borneo, an elderly woman who is the oldest inhabitant of one of the tribal 'longhouses' – wooden villages on stilts – explains through an interpreter how life has improved in recent decades. Television has made it less boring, and outboard motors have made it easier. Above all, the monkeys and other animals that used to eat the villagers' crops have mostly been exterminated. Many of the men have jobs with the logging companies. But even this unsentimental soul has noticed that not all is well: there are fewer fish in the river nowadays, possibly because the human population has grown or because the water, filled with mud by soil erosion from the logging areas upstream, has become murky.[45]

For rural Asians, environmental issues can be separated into four broad areas: competition for resources with cities and modern industry; population growth and migration which put pressure on food supplies; the controversial business of forestry; and damage to the marine environment. The relationship with the cities is complicated. Many rural people migrate, permanently or temporarily, to the region's fast-growing towns, and the cities buy their rice and other foodstuffs from the countryside. Sometimes, however, there is a direct conflict of interests. In Thailand, for example, poorly managed cement factories coat nearby fields with dust. Golf courses needing constant irrigation in the hot climate deprive villagers of their usual water supply. Factories and mines sometimes spill toxic waste into rivers, killing all the fish. Other conflicts are more ambiguous. Tourist resorts and mining projects may bring environmental problems, but they also bring jobs. Dams have been particularly controversial in south-east Asia. Villagers moved off their land to make way for dam reservoirs often complain of inadequate compensation; the dams also obstruct freshwater fish migration and so reduce their supply. Yet the dams generate electricity for cities and villages, and may also be used to irrigate farmland for rural people. Thai villagers, allied with local and foreign environmentalists, mounted several successful anti-dam protests in the 1980s.[46] In the 1990s, the two most bitterly contested projects were in Malaysian Borneo and in Laos. Deep in the forests of Sarawak, Malaysia planned to build a US$6 billion dam nearly twice the height of the Aswan dam in Egypt, flooding an area bigger than Singapore and displacing nearly 10,000 tribespeople. It would generate 2,000 megawatts of electricity to be transmitted to peninsular Malaysia via 1,800 kilometres of cable, 650 kilometres of it under the sea.[47] The affected tribespeople took the government to court to stop the dam, pointing out that they had not been consulted as required by environmental regulations. They won the case, but work continued and the decision was later overturned on appeal. It was only the difficulty of raising funds for the huge project, particularly after Malaysia was hit by the regional financial crisis of mid-1997, that caused work on the dam to be suspended. The proposed US$1.2 billion Nam Theun-2 dam in Laos, from which the Lao government hoped to sell electricity to neighbouring Thailand, was also embroiled in arguments between supporters and opponents. Western environmentalists argued that building it would force thousands of people from their homes and flood an irreplaceable habitat for wildlife, including rare animals such as tigers. The pro-dam lobby insisted the area was already degraded by logging and farming and almost devoid of wildlife; more important, Laos desperately needed the income from the dam to help it catch up with its fast-growing neighbours. Such disputes were typical of the hard choices facing the generation of south-east Asians born at the start of their hectic industrial revolution. Governments such as those of Malaysia and Indonesia, which have tended to blame interfering foreigners for all environmental protests, were seen as 'anti-environment' and appeared to favour development at almost any cost. Local environmentalists in turn were characterized as sentimental 'anti-development' activists who preferred saving trees and animals to improving the welfare of their fellow-citizens. In the Philippines, for example, vocal non-government organizations have opposed almost every sort of electricity generation at one time or another: coal power stations were dirty and affected neighbouring villages; nuclear power was unacceptably dangerous; and dams and geothermal energy stations (drawing on heat below ground) intruded on nature reserves and tribal areas. The Philippine NGOs also repeatedly opposed raising the price of the imported oil products, which accounted for much of Manila's pollution, on the grounds that higher fuel prices would harm poor Filipinos.

The second set of rural environmental problems derives from the pressures of growing populations. With Malthusian predictions of disastrous population explosions now widely discredited,[48] some analysts have gone to the opposite extreme and denied that there is any problem at all. Even if they are right in saying that it will be physically possible to feed the extra mouths and house the extra bodies, they are answering the wrong question. It may be possible. But is it desirable? Some governments – Indonesia and Thailand, for example – have introduced effective birth control programmes to limit population growth, but the leaders of more thinly populated countries such as Malaysia believe greater numbers of inhabitants will enhance their power in the region. In densely populated Vietnam, lowlanders short of space have been moving into the hills, forcing the hill-people higher up the slopes. The same has happened in the Philippines and Thailand, leading to the cultivation of steeper and steeper slopes and more erosion of the topsoil.

Like the salt contamination of fields caused by farmers' poor irrigation practices, erosion has none of the international popular appeal of issues such as wildlife preservation or global warming, but it is a serious threat to south-east Asian agriculture. The Asian Development Bank calls soil erosion Asia's most widespread natural resource problem. In Thailand, where it is common to see water red with mud scouring its way down a bare slope on a hillside farm, the mean rate of soil erosion is an annual thirty-four tonnes per hectare, compared with a 'tolerance level' for tropical soil of thirteen tonnes per hectare per year.[49] Population pressures on the land are particularly severe in the Philippines, partly because of the influence of the Roman Catholic church, which opposes artificial methods of birth control. Like Italians, most Filipinos – however devout – would willingly ignore the church's strictures on family planning, but the church concentrates its lobbying on the central government, which in turn restricts the nationwide provision of family planning services. This has led to a colourful war of words between Cardinal Jaime Sin, Archbishop of Manila, and Juan Flavier, a medical doctor, senator and former Health Secretary. Cardinal Sin equates contraception to abortion and has accused a 'global dictatorship' of swamping the

Philippines with a 'deluge of contraceptive drugs and instruments'.[50] Flavier is philosophical. 'He hates my guts ... Every *barrio* [district] he went to he found condoms and pills,' he says of his time in charge of health. Flavier believes that unrestricted population growth not only damages the health and wealth of parents and children, but depletes the country's already overstretched natural resources. 'Our mountains are denuded, devastated,' he says. 'We have erosion. Our rivers are getting polluted, our seas are getting polluted and now our watersheds are being damaged.'[51]

The island of Palawan is the new front line in the environmental battle in the Philippines. In sharp contrast to the rest of the archipelago, half the island's forest cover and many of its coral reefs remain intact. Salvador Socrates, the island's governor, and Edward Hagedorn, mayor of the capital Puerto Princesa, have revoked all commercial timber concessions, clamped down on illegal logging, prohibited commercial fishing within fifteen kilometres of the island, banned the export of wildlife and campaigned against litter. They have also opposed mass tourism, allowing only a small number of exclusive resorts for high-paying customers who – rightly or wrongly – are considered less likely to damage the environment. The idea is to avoid the chaotic industrialization and modernization which has left other Philippine islands, and other parts of south-east Asia, devoid of natural forest, short of fish and heavily polluted. In Palawan, the local authorities seek to encourage 'sustainable development' and 'eco-tourism'. 'Palawan is really the final bastion of Philippine ecology,' says Socrates, the governor. 'We know how easy it would be to develop the island into a Bali or a Phuket but what would be destroyed in the process? Our principle is that the integrity of the environment is non-negotiable.' But Palawan's ecological future is by no means secure. It depends on the determination of a few men. They can be voted out of office, or they might simply lose the battle against corrupt entrepreneurs who want to sell the trees, export wildlife, and catch the fish with cyanide and dynamite regardless of the consequences for the future. A more insidious danger is population growth. The island's population has doubled to about 650,000 in the past decade, and the very fact that Palawan's environment is relatively undamaged makes it a favoured destination for land-hungry migrants from other parts of the Philippines. The quiet and previously unremarkable town of Puerto Princesa is starting to smell of diesel smoke and motorcycle fumes; big corporations want to invest in cement and steel plants; mining companies and gold prospectors are accused of polluting the rivers; and illegal deforestation continues.[52]

Forestry – the third broad environmental issue that affects the countryside – is at first sight a rather peculiar subject for dispute. After all, few people deny the need for humans to clear land for their settlements, farms and factories. Agriculture and industry in the West were built on deforestation. Many people feel a twinge of sympathy for Mahathir when he disputes suggestions that tropical forests are part of the world's common heritage, complains about western environmental 'imperialism' and mocks those who want to keep primitive forest tribes 'eating monkeys and suffering from all kinds of tropical diseases' instead of making them conform to modern habits.[53] Malaysia has good reason to be defensive about the timber trade; in the early 1990s, it accounted for nearly half the world's recorded exports of tropical timber, compared to 26.7 per cent for Indonesia and a mere 2.4 per cent for Brazil.[54] But logging in most of south-east Asia is not a matter of timber companies managing forests so that they can export now and in the future, or of a few farmers clearing land for their fields. It is controversial because greedy businessmen, often in league with government officials or military officers, are engaged in a frenzied fire-sale of natural resources. Even officially massaged government figures usually show that logging at present rates is completely unsustainable. The damage in terms of soil erosion, siltation of waterways and flooding – sometimes resulting in loss of life – is incalculable. And the long-term economic benefits for the region's inhabitants are doubtful, since much of the money goes into the pockets of a few well-connected individuals and never finds its way into government coffers.

Corruption and incompetence are particularly flagrant in Cambodia, where – following the opening of the Cambodian economy in the early 1990s – logging companies from Malaysia, Thailand, Indonesia and elsewhere are stripping out valuable trees at breakneck speed. Cambodian forest cover has halved since the 1970s from 74 per cent to about 30 per cent in 1997, and the figure continues to drop with every month that passes. Logging concessions, sometimes overlapping, have been granted for almost all Cambodia's remaining forests, and illegal tree-felling in newly designated national parks and reserves is rampant.[55] Officials who try to enforce the law are threatened and sometimes killed by government soldiers. Chhan Sarun, chief of the forestry department in the Ministry of Agriculture, explained how difficult it was to stop the illegal export of timber to Thailand by sea by Thai and Cambodian gangsters. 'My ministry and I are trying to crack down on the problem, but the sea is full of men with guns,' he said.[56] Asked how business was done in Cambodia, Yu Zhongling, export manager of China Everbright (a company linked to the Chinese government and involved in Cambodian logging), explained that it was fairly simple. 'We pay little brown packets under the table like everyone else. If it's a big problem, we pay big money. If it's a small problem, we pay small money.'[57] The appalling management of Cambodia's forests is a direct threat to the country's economic progress. Unlike its larger and more sophisticated neighbours, Cambodia lacks modern industry. Economic growth is therefore likely to depend heavily on tourism (which in turn relies partly on the country's natural beauty) and on the sale of natural resources. Yet those resources are being wasted. 'People say we have water, forests, oil and fish,' says Lao Mong Hay, executive director of the Khmer Institute for Democracy in Phnom Penh. 'But there are no big fish in the market now. As for forests, some parts are like my head' – he points at his bald pate – 'so we'll depend for a long time on international assistance.'[58]

Thailand banned logging on its soil after a series of floods, but illegal cutting continues and the forest is already sorely depleted. Thai timber companies have partly compensated for this with operations in, and imports from, Cambodia, Burma and Laos. In 1960, more than half of Thailand – a country the size of France – was forest, but by 1990 that figure had fallen to between 10 and 14 per cent. For years, official Thai figures have shown that 30 per cent of the country remains forested, but the figure refers to areas legally defined as 'forest land'. The fact that some of it contains hardly any trees is conveniently overlooked.[59] Indonesia's record is equally grim, although the exploitation is at an earlier stage; the country still has big tracts of forest and exports about $4 billion of timber a year, mostly as plywood. Bizarrely, the government admits that the present rate of logging is unsustainable and promises to move towards a sustainable rate in the future, apparently ignoring the obvious point that the longer it waits the smaller the sustainable yield will be. 'Wood is not being harvested, it's being mined,' was the verdict of one foreign aid official in Jakarta. In a damning report on the industry, Walhi, Indonesia's leading environmental group, explained how logging companies routinely flout regulations, bribing forestry inspectors to encourage them to under-report the amount of timber extracted from concessions. It quoted a forestry department report from 1990 which pointed out that only twenty-two out of 578 concessionaires had actually followed regulations on selective cutting and replanting, and cited another official report which disclosed that only 30 per cent of log production in East Kalimantan on Borneo was reported to the government as required. Walhi also observed that Japanese figures for the import of wood products from Indonesia were far higher than the Indonesian figures for exports to Japan. The organization concluded that the state captured only 17 per cent of the economic rent from timber in taxes and fees, compared with 85 per cent for the much more technologically sophisticated oil industry. Precise figures on logging company malpractice are by their nature impossible to obtain, but the World Bank reckoned in 1996 that more than forty million cubic metres of Indonesian wood were being felled annually, compared to the official rate of thirty million cubic metres and the sustainable rate of about twenty-two million cubic metres. Because of the waste and corruption, timber product exports are expected to fall sharply in the coming decade. Unlike the situation in the Philippines or Vietnam, Indonesia's forests are not subject to severe pressures from a growing population; the pressure comes from the logging companies. According to the Asian Development Bank, the Indonesian government could probably increase its annual timber earnings by about $1 billion, while actually halving the area logged each year, by awarding timber concessions for longer periods and introducing competitive bidding.[60]

Most of Malaysia's exported timber now comes from Sarawak, where the World Bank calculates that wood has been extracted at no less than four times the sustainable rate. Logging companies seeking the valuable tree species are working in increasingly remote areas as supplies close to the coast become scarce. The anecdotal evidence is as compelling as the figures. Fifteen or twenty years ago, according to locals in the building trade, it was common to use a soft, decorative wood known as ramin for ornate ceilings. Nowadays it is almost unobtainable, and a substitute called bindang – which is more grainy and less consistent in colour – is used instead. But even this substitute is becoming harder to find.[61] As for the Philippines, deforestation there began early. It is estimated that 92 per cent of the land was forested in 1575, at the start of the Spanish colonial period – but then the total population was less than a million, compared with more than seventy million today. Between the 1920s and the 1960s the Philippines was Asia's largest timber exporter, and by the 1990s there was little virgin forest left; in the meantime Philippine logging companies helped to launch the Indonesian timber business in the 1970s, buying concessions in untouched Indonesian territory as their own exports inexorably declined. At home it was deforestation of the watershed around Ormoc, on the Philippine island of Leyte, that was blamed for the great flood there on November 5, 1991; the fields that had replaced the forest were unable to absorb heavy rainfall and a torrent tore through the town. Four thousand people were killed, and hundreds more disappeared.[62]

The early rise and fall of the Philippine logging industry was a lesson for the rest of south-east Asia. It was a lesson that was largely ignored. In almost every country in the region, the desire for a quick profit was overwhelming. Occasionally the timber companies established plantations of fast-growing eucalyptus or of oil palm on the land they had harvested for their plywood factories and their pulp and paper mills. But these 'monoculture' plantations were almost empty of wildlife and therefore of scant comfort for villagers who had relied on the forest since time immemorial to supplement their food supplies by hunting animals and gathering plants, especially in difficult years when the rice harvest failed. The logging tycoons enriched themselves at the expense of their fellow-citizens and of the future of their own industry; and when they began to exhaust the natural resources in their own countries, they expanded their logging operations abroad, first to other countries in Asia and the south Pacific, and then to South America.

As if the depredations on land were not enough, rural south-east Asians also suffer from the increasing abuse of the marine environment. In common with other seas and oceans around the world, the waters of the region are overfished, although the extent of the damage varies widely: the Gulf of Thailand is particularly bad, while the coastal waters off some of the less inhabited Indonesian islands are still rich in marine life. The Malaysian writer Rehman Rashid tells a surreal story about his time as a civil servant at the Fisheries Research Institute in Penang, Malaysia, which illustrates both the problem and the foolish attempts to hide it. One day the Minister of Agriculture decided to visit Penang and go fishing at one of the artificial reefs planted in the sea by the institute to try to replenish depleted fish stocks. Unfortunately, most of the reefs were barren because there were no surviving natural reefs nearby to seed them, and Penang's waters, Rehman recalls, were 'nearly dead, opaque with effluent and sewage'. He could hardly believe his ears when the director called him into his office and instructed him to buy a live grouper from a fish farm, don his scuba gear and attach it to the minister's fishing hook. When he pointed out the difficulty of keeping hold of a live fish underwater, the director suggested a dead fish. ' "A *dead* fish, sir?" I said. "What will the Minister say when he sees he's hooked a dead fish?" "Don't worry about that," said the Director. "We can always say it died on the way up." ' In the event the plan was scrapped, and the day saved by a passing fisherman who had a big red snapper in his *sampan.* 'The Minister was duly photographed pointing proudly at this fish while its captor held it aloft. The Director was pleased as punch.'[63]

The history of the exploitation of the sea mirrors the story on land. Fish catches grew rapidly – Thailand's annual landings rose from 200,000 tonnes in 1960 to 1.4 million tonnes a decade later to help make the country one of the world's largest exporters of seafood – but the harvest turned out to be unsustainable and so declined in most areas, with the proportion of low-value 'trash fish' in the catch rising year by year. The reasons for declining fish stocks in south-east Asia vary from place to place but they include the rapid growth in the number of trawlers since the 1960s; the introduction of other destructive and wasteful fishing methods, including cyanide poisoning and dynamiting; rising human populations; the destruction of breeding grounds, principally coral reefs, seagrass and mangrove forests (often uprooted to make way for prawn farms); and pollution from sewage, industrial effluents and oil spillages. The big Thai fishing companies – like the logging companies – began to hunt for supplies further afield after exhausting their own resources. There were battles at sea, sometimes involving naval patrol boats, as these areas too began to suffer from overfishing. Armed Thai fishing vessels financed by gangster businessmen routinely raid foreign waters from Burma to Vietnam. Between 1990 and 1995, Malaysia's Fisheries Department reported the detention of 785 foreign fishing vessels, most of them Thai. Several people have been killed and Thai fishermen are often jailed. 'Sometimes there were agreements with other countries under the table,' says Suraphol Sudara, of the Department of Marine Science at Chulalongkorn University in Bangkok. 'But one company might sign the agreement and then find its fleet imitated by other illegal fishing boats. They would paint their boats the same and you might find ten boats with the same number.'

The solution, he says, is to reduce the fishing 'effort' by cutting down the number of boats, but this is as controversial in Asia as it is in Europe, and politicians eager to win votes are reluctant to advocate such a course.[64] 'Our fishing fleet is so big, there is no control or monitoring system and we have run out of fish,' says Surin Pitsuwan, a Thai MP from a southern fishing constituency.[65] For south-east Asia's rural poor, the shortage of fish has been doubly damaging. First, what was once a cheap source of protein is now much more expensive. Even fish once eaten all over Thailand such as *pla tu*, a type of mackerel, are rarer and costlier; the same has happened in Malaysia.[66] One of the few compensations is that the overfishing of predators has led to an explosion of the squid population, while the shortage of fish at sea has also led to an expansion of the fish-farming industry. Second, coastal fishermen have lost their livelihoods. Some villages have fought to defend their fish stocks by building artificial reefs to snag the nets of trawlers fishing illegally close to the shore, but the future of south-east Asia's marine resources ultimately depends on the determination of governments to control their fishermen and protect their coastlines from pollution and other damage.[67]

For rural people, then, environmental issues usually revolve around competition for resources.[68] For middle-class townspeople, the battles are often about 'quality of life'. In fact south-east Asian middle-class attitudes to the environment are converging with the attitudes of westerners as each country proceeds further down the road to industrialization. Property advertisements showing neat, self-contained houses in leafy estates with children playing happily by a lake or stream suggest a common dream of suburban life. Like westerners, people complain about traffic congestion and pollution, and they wax nostalgic about an idealized rural past; like westerners they also suffer from 'nimby-ism' – that is, they want conveniences such as motorways, sewage plants and power stations but 'not in my back yard'. Interest in environmental issues is growing throughout south-east Asia, although inevitably there is at first more lamentation than action. Television and newspapers have begun to give more time and space to environmental battles, and people have formed numerous pressure groups. Some of them are dedicated to defending the interests of the rural poor, while others specialize in primarily urban matters such as air pollution or the preservation of historic buildings; in Thailand, Buddhist monks have been drawn into the fray and have been known to 'ordain' trees, wrapping them with orange sashes, to protect forests from the ubiquitous loggers armed with chain saws. Although some of these NGOs receive financial support from overseas, Asian environmentalists have rejected suggestions by governments and their business allies that attempts to protect the environment are all foreign-inspired and based either on sentimentality or on conspiracies to undermine Asia's economies. Instead, they point out the potentially disastrous economic consequences of allowing environmental degradation to go too far and emphasize the region's own traditions of environmentalism. Tommy Koh, the Singapore diplomat who chaired the preparatory committee at the UN's 'earth summit' in Rio de Janeiro, once wrote that he was confident Asia would meet its environmental challenge, 'not because of external pressures but because Asians are demanding the right to live in a clean and healthy environment as well as the right to development'.[69] Or, as Rehman Rashid put it when he commented on the opposition to a 'Disneyland-style theme park' on Penang Hill: 'Environmental activists were not "anti-development"; they were merely house-proud.'[70]

Reluctantly and rather slowly, south-east Asian governments have started to respond. They had to. There is ten times more industry in east Asia than there was in 1965. Cities are expanding at frightening speed. Pollution and over-exploitation affect the land, air, rivers and seas. Governments have enacted environmental laws, insisted on 'environmental impact assessments' (EIAs) for big projects, established environment ministries, set up national parks, tried to protect watersheds, and started monitoring pollution. But most of them still cling to the idea that they can damage the environment first and think about repairing it later, when they have caught up with the economies of industrialized countries. They have therefore been lax about enforcing their new regulations. EIAs, for example, are often treated in Malaysia more as a formality than as a serious attempt to analyse and avert possible damage. And in Thailand, property developers frequently build hotels and resorts in environmentally sensitive areas where they are expressly forbidden. They know that Thai governments usually shrug and accept the *fait accompli*. Throughout the region, environment ministers may have big offices, but they cannot match the power of their colleagues responsible for investment, industry and the sale of natural resources. 'If someone says, we've got an air pollution problem in Manila or wherever, tell the Ministry of Environment to handle it – that's a great way to make sure nothing happens,' says Bindu Lohani, Manager of the Asian Development Bank's Environment Division.[71] If they wanted, south-east Asian governments could begin saving their battered environment and save billions of dollars in the long term by investing now in environmental protection. That is the message from the ADB, the World Bank, the UN and countless environmental groups. But it is hard to get the message across to politicians who are interested in short-term gains and convinced that they are doing exactly what other industrializing powers did in their scramble to get rich. Even during the pause in economic growth prompted by the 1997 financial crisis, it was not certain that they would find time to listen to the ADB's grim warning in the same year:

> During the past thirty years, Asia has lost half its forest cover, and with it countless unique animal and plant species. A third of its agricultural land has been degraded. Fish stocks have fallen by 50 per cent. No other region has as many heavily polluted cities, and its rivers and lakes are among the world's most polluted. In short, Asia's environment has been under attack . . . In contemplating the choice between action today and action tomorrow, Asian policymakers should note that time is not on their side. Every day more children are poisoned by lead, more money is lost to traffic jams in megacities, more tons of productive soil are eroded, and more unique environmental assets are lost. The economic and welfare costs of environmental damage are already staggeringly high.[72]

SIX

*Enemies outside and in:
The 'Balkans of the Orient'
and the great powers*

Even a playboy can become a good husband after his marriage, with the family's help. That's the Asian way.
– Thai Foreign Minister Prachuab Chaiyasarn, explaining why
Asean could accept Burma as a member despite the notoriety of
the Burmese regime.[1]

The main reason Southeast Asia – the Balkans of Asia – has
held together is through . . . consensus-building.
– Kishore Mahbubani of Singapore's foreign ministry.[2]

Nowhere has the myth of special 'Asian values' been more persistent
than in the foreign policy arena. While demands for democracy and
justice have gradually undermined the legitimacy of the authoritarian 'Asian Way' in domestic politics, south-east Asian governments
have been able to point to the apparent success of the 'Asian Way'
of diplomacy. This type of diplomacy – sometimes also called the
'Asean Way' after the Association of South East Asian Nations –
concentrates on building a consensus among leaders behind closed
doors, is non-confrontational, and emphasizes flexibility and informality rather than contractual agreements. The absence of major
conflict within Asean since it was established in 1967 is taken
as proof of the method's success. But the reality is that south-east
Asian diplomacy is as much in need of modernization as the
region's political systems and business practices. A vague consensus
about economic and political aims was adequate while the region's

economies were all growing fast, foreign markets were open to its still small volume of exports, the US provided a security umbrella across the whole Asia-Pacific region, and there were no issues on which Asean members had dangerous disagreements. In the face of a real threat from outside (from China, for example) or a serious internal dispute (over fishing rights, say, or smog from forest fires), there is no substitute for a realistic assessment of why the situation has arisen, an honest appraisal of the danger, and a robust response. Until recently, Asean has not just been skilful; it has also been lucky.

After the end of the Cold War – which divided south-east Asia along an ideological frontier between the communist Indochina of Vietnam, Cambodia and Laos and the anti-communist founder members of Asean – China has emerged as by far the biggest external threat to south-east Asian security. China's maritime trade in the region and the extraction of tribute from the states on its periphery pre-dates the arrival of ships from Europe and the colonial era by hundreds of years. Millions of ethnic Chinese – many of them traders – have settled in south-east Asia. China largely turned in on itself during the Cultural Revolution, but since then it has liberalized its economy and begun a more conventional revolution of the industrial kind, becoming richer and more assertive in the process. South-east Asian leaders have sought to accommodate China, whether the Chinese authorities were killing pro-democracy protesters in Tiananmen Square in 1989 or threatening Taiwan – which China regards as a renegade province – in March 1996. Asean, in spite of its close commercial ties with Taiwan, was characteristically silent when Beijing was making belligerent noises in the Taiwan Strait, and it was left to the US to send aircraft carriers to the area and issue stern warnings about the need for restraint. But now a resurgent China is encroaching on Asean's own backyard, loudly reaffirming its claims to the whole of the South China Sea (China lies to the north of the sea and Asean countries encircle it to the west, south and east), arguing with Vietnam and the Philippines over the disputed atolls of the Spratly Islands, and befriending the Burmese and Cambodian governments with weapons supplies and diplomatic support in a manner that their neighbours, including India, regard as ominous. 'China today wields more influence in Southeast, South and Central Asia than at any time since the height of the Qing power in the eighteenth century,' said Commodore Uday Bhaskar of India's Institute for Defence Studies and Analysis.[3]

In recent years, tensions have run high in several parts of south-east Asia. The record of modern disputes with Vietnam, a traditional enemy of China, is particularly long. China seized the Paracel islands in 1974 from the South Vietnamese, who were then preoccupied with their imminent defeat by the communist North. In 1979, China briefly invaded the north of the now united Vietnam, apparently in retaliation for the Vietnamese occupation of Cambodia, where China had been supporting the Khmers Rouges. In 1988, China won a naval skirmish with Vietnam in the South China Sea and secured control of six of the Spratly Islands. And in the 1990s, there was a series of disputes over maritime boundaries: the typical pattern was that Chinese ships, sometimes in a joint venture with an American company, would prospect for oil or gas in an area claimed by Vietnam; Vietnam would protest and the two sides would agree to talk, but China would not yield.[4] This was important to Asean for two reasons. First, Vietnam joined the organization in 1995 and saw that one of the main benefits of membership was support from other Asean members in any confrontation with China. (Vietnam was also desperate to improve relations with its former enemy the United States.)[5] Second, Asean realized that China's expansionism was part of a pattern that affected not just Vietnam but several other member states as well.

To the east, the Philippines had a confrontation with China – both sides deployed naval ships – after the Chinese sent 'fishermen' to occupy Mischief Reef, one of the uninhabited parts of the Spratly Islands claimed by Manila, in 1995. Two years later, China sent a group of amateur radio enthusiasts to Scarborough Shoal, a tiny rock which the Philippines says is inside its exclusive economic zone, prompting protests from Manila and a subsequent landing on the islet by two Philippine congressmen affirming their country's sovereignty. By this time, Indonesia had become concerned as well, because China's claims appeared to extend to a huge South China Sea gas field that Indonesia was thinking of developing near Natuna Island. Some senior Indonesian military officers still held to the view that China was dangerous because it exported communism, but others were beginning to realize that the real danger lay in a resurgent Chinese nationalism, given muscle by successive years of high economic growth and increased military spending.[6] A security agreement between Indonesia and Australia reached in 1995 was widely interpreted as the beginnings of a joint Indonesian-Australian strategy to deal with the 'threat from the north'. There are five Asean states directly concerned by Chinese activities in the South China Sea, because Malaysia and Brunei also claim some of the Spratlys. But as an organization Asean was forced to sit up and take notice of the disputes in the South China Sea only in 1992, when China issued a 'Law on the Territorial Waters and Their Contiguous Areas' which claimed 80 per cent of the Sea,[7] and when it signed an agreement with a small US oil company to explore for oil between Vietnam and Malaysia. At a meeting of Asean foreign ministers in July 1992, Malaysia said it was watching events with 'grave concern', the Philippines spoke of the need to avoid 'perilous developments' and Indonesia mentioned the danger of 'mutually destructive confrontation'.[8] Since then these contested waters have been a regular topic for Asean discussions, and José Almonte, national security adviser to President Ramos of the Philippines, once suggested half-seriously that they should more accurately be called the 'Southeast Asian Sea'.[9]

The difficulty was knowing how to deal with China, whose diplomats appeared to be more skilful practitioners of the subtle arts of the 'Asian Way' than their south-east Asian interlocutors. By the 1990s, China rarely used overt shows of force to stake its claims, insisting that smart-looking buildings on Mischief Reef complete with satellite dishes were 'shelters for fishermen' rather than the symbolic assertions of sovereignty that they obviously were, claiming that its exploratory forays off Vietnam were normal oil and gas prospecting operations and pointing to the innocent radio hams at Scarborough Shoal (even though their ship was cheered by nationalist crowds as it left for the Shoal from Guangzhou and the expedition was led by a former Chinese army radio operator).[10] China was unfailingly polite and usually agreed to discuss the matter in the future with whoever was protesting, but then quietly carried on with whatever it had been doing to provoke the other side. 'China has a pattern of acting unilaterally and then agreeing to resolve the matter peacefully through negotiation,' said Mark Valencia, a South China Sea expert at the East-West centre in Hawaii.[11] Gerald Segal of the International Institute for Strategic Studies in London has noted 'a clear pattern of creeping Chinese assertiveness'. He wrote: 'China will take tiny steps forward, create new facts, and wait patiently for an opportunity to move further. China never gives up territory.'[12] Asean has tried and failed for years to persuade China to accept its 1992 'Manila Declaration' calling for a peaceful resolution of the disputes over the Spratly Islands, and after the Mischief Reef incident in 1995 its patience snapped. In talks with China, Asean bluntly condemned China and told it to stop. Asean had discovered the weakness of the polite diplomacy of 'consensus': it only works if everyone agrees already, or if one of the parties is prepared to compromise.

Asean also had to be realistic about the other great military power in the region: the US. Washington had been defeated in South Vietnam by the communists from the North, and the Southeast Asian Treaty Organisation (Seato) was abolished in the 1970s. But the US retained close ties to countries such as Thailand, the Philippines and Singapore and remains to this day the region's pre-eminent maritime power, while the global collapse of communism from the late 1980s extinguished the Cold War challenge of the Soviet Union. Asean countries, with their fast-growing economies, could boast that they were transforming themselves from dominoes (liable to fall to communism) into dynamos. They were more self-confident, and they were increasingly able to afford new military equipment, but they still relied on the US as the ultimate guarantor of Asia-Pacific security. Typically, they were reluctant to say so publicly. Only Singapore, a small island vulnerable to its neighbours as well as to the super-powers, routinely pays tribute in public to the importance of the US presence. Other governments have been ambivalent, privately welcoming American warships but anxious not to offend nationalist sensitivities at home. The US, reluctant to pay the high financial price demanded by Filipino nationalists and dismayed by the damage from the volcanic eruption of Mt Pinatubo, withdrew its forces from the Clark air base in 1991 and from the Subic Bay naval base in the Philippines the following year. Singapore agreed in January 1998 to allow US aircraft carriers, submarines and other warships to use a planned naval base from the year 2000. But Thailand refused a request to let the US keep ship-borne arms depots off its shores for rapid deployment in Asia or the Gulf to the west.[13] This did not seem wholly unreasonable at the time. The Cold War was over, Asean was confident, the US was promising not to weaken its overall military commitments to Asia and the focus of attention was in north-east, not south-east Asia – Taiwan and North Korea, in other words, were the likely trouble spots. Most of the 100,000 US troops in the region are in South Korea and Japan.

But with the US distracted by events in north-east Asia – and anyway reluctant to become embroiled in territorial disputes over the reefs and atolls in the South China Sea except to insist on the sanctity of international sea lanes – who was going to look after the security of south-east Asia in the face of an assertive China? Other outside powers were of only limited value. There was support for the modest 1995 security agreement between Indonesia and Australia, while Malaysia and Singapore already had loose military ties with Britain, Australia and New Zealand through the Five Power Defence Arrangement; there was also talk of a 'grouping of middle powers', justified by the belief that Australia, New Zealand and the ten countries of south-east Asia 'can deploy economic and political weight comparable with any of the great powers', as José Almonte of the Philippines put it. (Note that he did not say military weight.)[14] South-east Asia saw the European Union as a potentially useful political and economic counterweight to the regional dominance of Japan, China and the US, but the Europeans seemed uninterested, had no desire for military involvement and strongly disagreed with south-east Asian governments on issues such as human rights and the way to deal with the military junta in Burma. Russia was seen as a spent force by the end of the Cold War, in spite of its traditional links to Vietnam, but re-emerged in the late 1990s as a supplier of military aircraft and other weapons and was, after all, a power in the Pacific as well as Europe. Lastly, there was Japan, whose invasion of Asia during the Second World War and subsequent defeat had left it without a regional security role except as sleeping partner of the Americans; many of Japan's fellow Asians, particularly China, the Chinese populations of south-east Asia, and the Philippines, still regarded any Japanese interest in a more active role with suspicion. Successive Japanese prime ministers had sought to make their mark on Asia by laying out new foreign policy doctrines, but these were usually dismissed either as inconsequential or menacing; when Ryutaro Hashimoto suggested the 'Hashimoto Principle' in 1997 – basically a proposal to strengthen ties with south-east Asia with regular summit meetings to discuss security as well as commerce – his ideas were coolly received, partly because Asean members did not want to antagonize China by being seen to have specially close ties to its old enemy Japan.[15] Although Japan has gradually taken on more security responsibilities – its troops participated in a small way in the UN mission to rebuild Cambodia in the early 1990s in their first overseas foray since the Second World War – south-east Asians continued to look to it principally as a provider of investment. Since the 1960s Japan had characterized its regional economic role as the leader of a formation of flying geese, a considerably more modest vision than the East Asia Co-Prosperity Sphere of 1938. But even this new role had sometimes been the subject of nationalist protests in south-east Asian countries such as Indonesia and Thailand, albeit with decreasing frequency.

The hostility, weakness or lack of concern of the big powers has driven Asean to look to its own members to ensure the stability and security of south-east Asia. This may seem obvious now, but such a development has only been possible since the end of the Cold War, during which south-east Asian countries lined up openly or tacitly on one side or the other of the communist–capitalist divide and sought the protection of the appropriate superpower. Asean is by no means a multilateral security organization. One of its main functions now is to promote free trade (through the planned Asean Free Trade Area) and investment within the region. But it has been concerned with security and regional co-operation among its members since its foundation in Bangkok at the height of the Cold War in 1967,[16] and Asean today wants to expand that role to fill the gap left by the collapse of the Soviet Union and the diminished interest of the US. Until 1997, its task was made easier by the growth of the regional economy and the resulting increase in confidence – some might say overconfidence[17] – of its members in negotiating with foreign powers. Asean members decided, however, that they needed to take two important steps in order to enhance the influence of south-east Asia and the security of the countries in the region. They would have to bring all ten countries into Asean; and they would set up the 'Asean Regional Forum' to discuss Asia-Pacific security with the big powers, including the US, China, Japan and Russia.

The drive for the 'Asean 10', the completion of the Asean project, became intense in the mid-1990s. South-east Asia's disparate countries had been brought together for a few years by Japanese occupation in the Second World War, and then vaguely lumped together afterwards by the victorious allies, but fifty years later they were developing the beginnings of a common identity. 'South-East Asia has evolved from a category of convenience employed by a military command for dispossessing Japan of its wartime gains into a distinctive region with a growing sense of coherence and self-confidence,' wrote Michael Leifer, Professor of International Relations at the London School of Economics and Political Science.[18] Asean began with five countries in 1967, taking in Brunei at its independence in 1984 to make six. South-east Asia had previously been called the 'Balkans of the Orient'. Singapore, dominated by ethnic Chinese, had been forced out of Malaysia in 1965; and there are secessionist struggles in East Timor, Aceh and Irian Jaya (against Indonesian rule), and by Moslems in southern Thailand and the southern Philippines. But Asean members were confident that it was time to expand. Vietnam became a member in 1995, with Laos and Burma following in 1997. Only Cambodia remained outside, its entry delayed at the last minute by Hun Sen's seizure of power in a coup d'état in July of that year.

Everyone knew it would be difficult for Asean to absorb the newcomers, not least because of the enormous economic disparities between them and the richer countries, a particularly difficult issue in view of the planned free trade area and the absence of any European Union-type mechanism for subsidizing poorer members. Fears of a 'two-tier' Asean were exacerbated by the extra time conceded to the new members to lower their trade tariffs. Even the basic logistics of membership were difficult for a country like Laos, which was desperately short of English-speakers (English is the group's official language) to attend the scores of meetings held by Asean each year. But the sacrifice was considered worthwhile because Asean would have what Lee Hsien Loong of Singapore called 'a louder voice, a more significant voice' and 'a bit more mass'.[19] In some ways the debate was similar to the one in Europe over whether it was wise to 'widen' the EU and accept new members without 'deepening' the commitments of existing members. 'Within Asean we will live with them,' said Lee of the new recruits. 'They will slow us down in our economic development. It will take us longer to reach consensus even on political issues, but it's a problem which even the EU faces when you bring in new members.' A less publicized but equally important reason for enlarging Asean was to counter the influence of China in Laos, Cambodia and especially Burma. Ostracized by much of the rest of the world, Burma's military junta has strengthened military and commercial ties with China, which in turn is delighted to have helped the Burmese navy set up electronic military signals intelligence outposts along its coast and on Coco Island in the Andaman Sea, and to have secured new trade routes to link south-western China to the sea.[20] 'All of us [in Asean] are very worried about it,' commented George Yeo, another Singapore minister, on China's growing influence in Burma.[21]

Asean, however, is paying a high price in lost credibility at home and abroad for its decision to accept Burma's military junta into its ranks. Western governments which had happily dealt with 'soft authoritarian' governments such as those of Malaysia and Singapore were much less willing to negotiate politely with a military junta that had gunned down hundreds of pro-democracy protesters, showed no serious intention of giving up power to civilians or reforming its badly run economy, and continued to keep Aung San Suu Kyi, the pro-democracy campaigner and Nobel Peace Prize winner, under virtual house arrest. Even those who believed that Asean was already a cynical organization devoted to preserving the legitimacy of authoritarian governments think it may have problems absorbing a regime as ruthless and nasty as Burma's. 'The basis of the [non-interference] principle is to ensure the survival of regimes,' said Mak Jun Nam, Director of Research at the Maritime Institute of Malaysia, shortly before Burma was admitted. But he added: 'Burma is seen as a tremendous legitimacy problem. We want to make Asean accepted as an international act. If we get a pariah state like Burma in, what does that do to our own standing?'[22] By embracing Burma, with its brutal rulers and primitive economy, Asean implies that it has no minimum political or economic standards that members are obliged to meet; the inevitable conclusion is that Asean has no common values and little coherence. What then *does* Asean stand for?

Some Asean governments, such as those of the Philippines and Thailand, are painfully aware of the risks of being tied too closely to Burma and initially opposed the country's entry into the organization. It was significant, too, that Cambodia's entry was delayed, even if Asean had hardly any choice. The fact that Hun Sen had staged his coup d'état only weeks before Cambodia was due to join would have made the occasion acutely embarrassing: Indonesia and Asean had played a crucial role in brokering the 1991 peace agreements that led to Cambodia's all-too-brief period of democracy after 1993. To cap it all, Hun Sen had rudely rebuffed Asean attempts to mediate after the coup, telling them not to interfere in Cambodia's domestic affairs. This was ironic, because 'non-interference in the internal affairs of others' has long been one of Asean's key principles. But the delay to Cambodian entry – leaving Asean with only nine members instead of the expected full complement of ten at the Asean meeting in Kuala Lumpur in July 1997 – exposed 'non-interference' as a fiction and hinted that Asean did in fact have some common principles, although nobody could explain exactly what they were. It was intriguing that a Singaporean official, Kishore Mahbubani of the Foreign Ministry, later wrote that 'Asean's decision not to accept co-Prime Minister Hun Sen's seizure of power by force in Cambodia in July [1997] showed that minimum standards of good governance are being established'.[23] In Kuala Lumpur, Asean announced a new policy of 'preventive diplomacy', and Asean officials said the organization might have to intervene publicly in regional politics in certain circumstances. One of the guidelines suggested was that 'the change of a government through the use of force is unacceptable'.[24]

For an organization that prided itself on 'pragmatism' and many of whose members scoffed at what they saw as the misguided liberalism and idealism of the West, this would have been a revolutionary change – and there was no immediate public shift in official policy. But there were already stirrings of reform within Asean among the bureaucrats in the white-tiled Asean headquarters in Jakarta and among politicians and academics in some of the member states. In the three decades since Asean's foundation, it must be recalled, south-east Asians had become richer, more educated and less tolerant of authoritarian leadership. 'There is an emerging school of thought among the younger diplomats that it [Asean] should not just be a venue to discuss inter-state problems, but that Asean has now reached a stage where it should adopt some *standards,* both in inter-state relations and the conduct of national affairs,' said one Asean official of the younger generation who asked to remain anonymous.[25] Various drafts of possible south-east Asian codes of conduct have been circulated internally, including some that deal with human rights, hitherto a 'western' subject that Asean has shied away from whenever possible. At a 1996 meeting of south-east Asian 'citizens' in Manila – in other words, a meeting outside the formal confines of Asean – a group of intellectuals and politicians adopted a document called 'Towards a southeast Asian community: a human agenda', which contained a number of broadly liberal clauses. They called for 'freedom of movement of goods and services, capital and labour, information and technology, across the political boundaries within the region and between the region and the outside world'; they wanted 'people empowerment', 'more just, equal, tolerant and caring societies'; and they advocated 'ecologically sustainable development strategies'.[26] In a speech in China in the same year about the future of Asean, José Almonte, the Philippine national security adviser, explicitly suggested a minimum standard for civil liberties in Asean: 'The Asean collective sense will want to see a minimum adherence to the rule of law and a measure of respect for human rights.'[27]

Of course, he was Filipino, and that did make a difference: there had long been disagreements within Asean – which was, as everyone accepted, a very heterogeneous organization – between the more democratically inclined countries, such as the Philippines and Thailand, and the more authoritarian ones, such as Indonesia. Until now the authoritarians have been the dominant group, and this was usually reflected in the types of 'consensus' that tended to be reached at Asean meetings. Security for Asean members was very broadly defined, so that threats were perceived not just in a military context but also in political and cultural terms.[28] So it was that Asean came to be seen by Asian democrats as a brotherhood of authoritarian states ranged against liberalism, and that it welcomed Burma into the club. 'This anti-democratic realpolitik is working,' wrote one Bangkok-based academic. 'Isolated, weak-kneed, and almost ashamed of their democratic credentials, the Thai and Philippine governments have, predictably, allowed themselves to be pushed into endorsing the majority position on Burma.'[29]

But there is no reason why the balance of power should not eventually change, particularly if Indonesia – the largest and most powerful member of Asean – one day adopts a genuinely democratic political system following the popular uprising which forced President Suharto to step down in 1998. Thais, Filipinos and others have begun to worry that Asean has become too much of a club for the preservation of authoritarian regimes, rather than a group to promote security and co-operation between peoples with very different political outlooks. 'I think the Thai middle class are more assertive and more expectant than the Malay or Indonesian middle class for their participation, for their freedom and free expression because there's less restraint in the culture, in the tradition,' says Thai MP Surin Pitsuwan. 'We are used to more openness and I think in the long run this is the direction of Asean. We are ahead of it.'[30] According to Asean orthodoxy, criticism of, say, the Indonesian occupation of East Timor or human-rights abuses in Burma cannot be made publicly because that does not accord with the 'Asean way' or 'Asian traditions'. But liberals argue that this is the case only because authoritarian regimes are setting the Asean agenda: what of the Thai and Filipino respect for free speech, or the Confucian right to criticize unjust rule? Ammar Siamwalla, a Thai academic, recalling attempts in Thailand to silence protests about Indonesia and Burma, says he wants one day to see a situation where his government will stand up and declare that its democratic traditions do not allow it to suppress free speech.[31]

It was not just the Asean world view which was coming under attack. The hurried decision to admit Burma and the last-minute embarrassment over Cambodia in mid-1997 also raised questions about the way Asean conducted its business with a mixture of secret discussions and bland public statements. Asean members prided themselves on their informality. In Kuala Lumpur, even Madeleine Albright, the US Secretary of State, joined in the light-hearted singing session that has become a regular social event after Asean summits with 'Don't cry for me, Asean-ies,' sung to the famous tune about Argentina from the musical *Evita*. But the lack of formal negotiating procedures (ideal for lifetime authoritarian leaders who know each other well, perhaps, but less suitable for quick-changing democratic governments) seemed to encourage Asean leaders to skirt around the issues in order to reach consensus, instead of engaging in a vigorous debate. It appeared that neither the consequences of Burma's admission into Asean nor the need to ensure Burma's proper behaviour once it was a member had been thought through; tellingly, Shanmugam Jayakumar, the Singapore prime minister, criticized Europe for wanting Asean to have a 'pre-nuptial agreement' with Burma, whereas 'in Asia, we marry first, then expect the bride to adapt her behaviour after marriage'.[32] The Thai foreign minister of the time made a similar comment.

Asean's failure to deal with the repeated outbreaks of forest fires in Indonesia, which sent a particularly severe cloud of smoke across the region in 1997, is another example of the weakness of its procedures; here was a multilateral problem that Asean should have been able to tackle, but its members were reluctant to offend Indonesia. 'A tacit agreement prevails to avoid sensitive issues. This sometimes results in problems being hidden rather than resolved,' was one of the comments about Asean in a recent study of south-east Asian security.[33] It also made the point that most interaction between Asean states – including military exercises and other forms of security co-operation – took place at the bilateral level, not in the consensus-building multilateral negotiations leading to a unanimous (and often anodyne) Asean decision. Another analyst noted that Asean members did not share a common strategic outlook, since they differed in their assessment of threats to regional security; and that even after decades of independence problems such as border disputes and the challenge from fundamentalist Islam had been 'contained rather than solved'.[34] In the words of one Rangoon-based western diplomat (exasperated by Asean's drive for consensus), Asean politicians were keen to be respected and accepted by their fellow-leaders because they did not understand that 'diplomacy isn't about being liked. It's about pursuing your interests'.[35] Kavi Chongkittavorn, Executive Editor of the Nation Multimedia Group, worked at Asean headquarters in Jakarta for eighteen months. The organization's members remain jealous of their national sovereignty, he says, which is why it is difficult to take multilateral action even if a superficial consensus is achieved. 'Asean outside looks very strong, because they have a united voice,' he says. 'Asean inside is very weak because the structure of Asean is very weak and member countries want it that way.'[36]

Asean has not been entirely inactive on the security front, however, even if its bilateral disputes over territory or politics – such as the occasional exchange of insults between Malaysia and Singapore – continue to simmer outside Asean's ambit. In 1971, Asean members declared south-east Asia to be a 'Zone of Peace, Freedom and Neutrality' (ZOPFAN); under the 1976 Treaty of Amity and

Cooperation (TAC), Asean members are obliged to refrain from the threat or use of force to resolve disputes; and in 1995 all ten south-east Asian states agreed to the Treaty on the Southeast Asia Nuclear Weapon-Free Zone (SEANWFZ), which forbids them to test, acquire, or have control over nuclear weapons – although the nuclear superpowers were inevitably reluctant to endorse the Treaty if it meant restricting their ability to deploy their own nuclear arsenals. Perhaps Asean's biggest achievement was the way in which it overcame the legacy of confrontation left by the Cold War, accepting Vietnam and Laos as members and helping to negotiate the Cambodian peace agreements which led to a UN-organized election in 1993.

From the mid-1990s there was some international concern about a 'south-east Asian arms race' as Asean's increasingly wealthy members sought to modernize their military arsenals by buying weapons from overseas and establishing their own military industries. Malaysia, for instance, reportedly spent about US$3 billion on weapons under its 1991–95 defence plan, an increase of more than 200 per cent over the previous five years (its orders included British-made Hawk jets. US F-18s and Russian MiG-29s, and the government also wanted to buy offshore patrol vessels).[37] Between 1992 and 1996, Thailand, Indonesia, Malaysia, Burma and Singapore are believed to have spent more than US$8 billion on weapons;[38] and for the first time in 1996, east Asia as a whole imported more than the total international arms purchases of Nato and western Europe.[39] Some western defence analysts outlined alarming possible scenarios for conflict between east Asian rivals, based on Asia's ability to buy arms with its new wealth, the region's need to import more oil from the Gulf and more food from elsewhere, the presence of maritime 'choke points' where trade could be disrupted, and the increasing use of civilian nuclear power stations whose by-products could be used to make nuclear weapons. Most Asians are rather more sanguine about the arms build-up in south-east Asia which has in any case been curtailed by the economic downturn. It is normal, they say, for countries with the money to do so to establish credible military forces, particularly navies that can patrol the region's sensitive maritime boundaries and keep pirates and illegal foreign fishermen out of their waters. The Indonesian scholar Dewi Fortuna Anwar noted that in some countries in the region where the absolute level of defence spending had risen, it had actually fallen as a proportion of gross national product (because the economies were growing faster than defence spending), although Burma was a notable exception. 'Southeast Asia is now more at peace with itself than at any other time in its modern history,' she wrote.[40]

Yet it was not enough for south-east Asia merely to be at peace with itself if it was to survive in an unstable world. Asean's solution was to establish the Asean Regional Forum, an informal Asia-Pacific discussion group on security which could meet at the same time as Asean's so-called 'Post-Ministerial Meetings', the dialogues with various Asian and non-Asian trading partners held after Asean gatherings. The ARF seemed significant in the aftermath of the Cold War because it brought together the superpowers as well as Asean members, other Asian countries, Australia and New Zealand. (Founded in 1993, its members are Australia, Brunei, Burma, Cambodia, Canada, China, the European Union, India, Indonesia, Japan, South Korea, Laos, Malaysia, New Zealand, Papua New Guinea, the Philippines, Russia, Singapore, Thailand, the US and Vietnam.) Subsequent ARF meetings have espoused measures to improve transparency in security matters, including the voluntary exchange of information about each country's national defence programmes. But the ARF, like Asean itself, has been criticized by western diplomats for being so vague and informal as to be almost meaningless. Unconstrained by the need to keep their promises, Chinese officials can happily participate, smile at their polite interlocutors, agree that peace and security are good, and then go off and send their troops to occupy another atoll in the South China Sea. 'Asean at times confuses the passage of time and the appearance of harmony with genuine progress towards a resolution of disputes,' remarked *The Economist* tartly after an ARF meeting in 1996. 'The ARF's western members may be making the same mistake.'[41]

Asean and the ARF are very loose organizations. Most of their members are reluctant to admit that their potential military enemies are either their own neighbours or China. Asean, says Thai MP Surin Pitsuwan, is 'rather soft as an organization'. As for the ARF, 'it's not a solid mechanism. It's not a very precise mechanism like Nato. It's not like a regional security set-up in the traditional way. It's an open process, a clearing house, a forum for discussion, for the airing of concerns . . . The idea is to avoid open conflict because the organization itself is not set up to deal with it.'[42] Yet even if Asean and the ARF are not very effective, they have not – so far – proved disastrous either. China certainly remains a threat, and a conflict in Korea would be even more disturbing for south-east Asia than for the rest of the world. But south-east Asians have pressing problems at home. To achieve real security, they have to do more than increase their military strength. They need to manage political and social upheaval and prevent further environmental disasters. Overwhelmed by the speed of the changes wrought by decades of economic growth, they have been weak in the one area where they needed to be strong: in the management of the industrial revolution.

SEVEN

Ten troubled tigers:
The nations of south-east Asia

This book is about the modernization of south-east Asia, and about the profound political, social and economic changes that are affecting every country in the region. These trends – democratization, the rise of consumerism, the loosening of social mores, the adoption of new business methods, and the devastation of the environment – are discernible in each south-east Asian state to a greater or lesser degree.

But each country also has its own unique history and culture (or cultures); each therefore absorbs the forces of modernization in a different way and colours them according to its own habits and traditions. Although linked by geographical proximity, the ten countries form a heterogeneous region. It straddles the equator and extends from the Indian Ocean to the seas off Australia. Its various parts have been traded in, colonized and fought over at various times by Chinese, Arabs, Portuguese, Dutch, English, French, Spanish, Americans and Japanese – and by south-east Asians themselves. The region is home to countless ethnic groups, tribes and languages. Its inhabitants have a wide range of religious beliefs, including most of the world's great religions. Some of its political systems are communist, some are capitalist, and others are wholly or partly controlled by the armed forces. In per capita terms, its economies include some of the world's poorest (Vietnam, Cambodia, Laos and Burma), and one of the richest (Singapore).

As this book seeks to explain, the ten countries of south-east Asia are becoming more closely linked to each other and more integrated with the rest of the world, but each country is certain to be very different from its neighbours for decades to come. It is not possible here to give a detailed history of each south-east Asian state, a task which in any case is best left to the historians who have already produced studies of individual countries. What I have tried to do in the sections that follow is briefly to examine recent events in each country, from west to east, and explain how governments and peoples are coping – or failing to cope – with the wave of political and social modernization sweeping through south-east Asia.

BURMA
Democracy delayed

'Orwellian', that overused word, is rarely more apt than when applied to present-day Burma under military rule. Although it has been in power in various guises since 1962, the army, paranoid and isolationist, is constantly trying to mobilize its subjects against imaginary foreign plots. Such plots, the government says, are planned by 'destructionists' or the 'minions of neo-colonialists'. Even the country's official institutions are bizarrely named: the junta which has been in charge since 1988 was until recently called the State Law and Order Restoration Council, producing an English acronym – Slorc – which sounded like the sort of personification of evil that the novelist Ian Fleming might have dreamt up: Lt-Gen. Khin Nyunt, the army intelligence chief and one of the most powerful men in the junta, was given the Kafka-esque title 'Secretary-One'. As Burmese intellectuals joke, George Orwell wrote two books about Burma: one was called *Burmese Days*; the other was *Nineteen Eighty-Four*. Political jokes are as common in Burma as they were in the East Bloc countries before the collapse of Soviet communism, and for much the same reason – other avenues for political expression are blocked. A favourite recent joke suggests that the junta has actually reduced the number of enemies confronting the Burmese people. How so? According to one Burmese tradition, there are five enemies – fire, flood, storms, rulers and thieves; now there are only four, because the rulers and the thieves are one and the same.

Burma became independent from Britain in 1948, but failed dismally in the following five decades to emulate the economic success of its south-east Asian neighbours. Although the foreign-educated children of the junta's generals and a handful of entrepreneurs and drug barons are wealthy enough to frequent the new discotheques of Rangoon and Mandalay, the urban poor live in slums as muddy and miserable as those of Bangladesh or India. The education and justice systems have declined sharply since independence. Officially, 80 per cent of Burmese are literate, but independent estimates put the figure at 55 per cent or less.[1] It has been calculated that 16

BURMA (Myanmar)

Capital city:	Rangoon (Yangon)
Population (1995):	47 million
Government:	Military
Annual per capita GDP (1994/95 estimate):	US$250
Real economic growth 1994/95:	4.6 per cent
Real economic growth 1998 (estimate):	n/a
Main language:	Burmese
Main religion:	Buddhism
Date of independence:	1948
Former colonial power:	Britain

Sources: ADB; US Embassy Rangoon; author.

per cent of children are severely malnourished, with 43 per cent moderately or mildly malnourished. AIDS (acquired immune deficiency syndrome) has been spreading rapidly, as have malaria, tuberculosis and dengue (haemorrhagic fever).[2]

Burma's military rulers justify their continued grip on power by insisting that a strong central authority is required to keep the country united. Around the so-called 'Burman' heartland live numerous ethnic groups and hill-tribes who have often taken up arms against the central government, sometimes with the support or acquiescence of neighbouring countries. Certainly there was chaos after Burma's independence, and sporadic fighting continued until the mid-1990s, when the Burmese army succeeded in defeating or making peace deals with all of the main ethnic guerrilla armies which once fought for autonomy or independence.

However, none of this fully explains the army's reluctance to yield power to civilians and accept a more representative form of government. After General Ne Win seized power in 1962 and introduced a disastrous state takeover of the economy under the 'Burmese Way to Socialism', the Burmese people became increasingly impoverished and bitter. Pro-democracy protests culminated in mass demonstrations in the streets of Rangoon and other towns in 1988. Ne Win stepped aside but troops killed more than a thousand demonstrators, sometimes with machine guns, as violence swept through the country. The Slorc took over in what appears to have been a stage-managed military coup d'état, with Ne Win remaining active behind the scenes. Hundreds more were killed before the Slorc re-established military control. The junta, which prides itself on its nationalism, demanded that foreigners call the country Myanmar or Myanma (the Burmese name for Burma has always been Myanmar, so this was not a renaming of the country; it was akin to the Germans insisting that the British and French call their nation Deutschland instead of Germany or Allemagne). More importantly, the Slorc promised to hold the first free elections for three decades.

This seemed like Burma's chance to open up to the outside world and join the ranks of democratic states. Opponents of the government coalesced into the National League for Democracy (NLD). Aung San Suu Kyi, the Oxford-educated daughter of the Burmese hero Aung San – it was he who brought the country to the brink of independence in the 1940s before he was assassinated – had returned to Burma in April 1988 from England to look after her sick mother. She soon became the NLD's secretary-general and its popular figurehead. In spite of the Slorc's efforts to intimidate its opponents – among other actions it kept Suu Kyi under house arrest from 1989 until 1995 and prevented her standing in the election – the NLD won an overwhelming victory in the 1990 poll. It took 392 of the 485 contested seats, soundly defeating the pro-military party.

The Burmese generals, so out of touch with the mood of their own people that they had not contemplated the possibility of losing, were stunned. To this day the election remains an embarrassment to the junta and to its allies in Asean. In criticizing western interference and pressure for democracy in south-east Asia, Asean leaders like to say that it is not for outsiders but for the people of the region to decide for themselves what form of government they want. In this case, the Burmese people voted decisively in favour of democracy.

Democracy, however, is not what they got. The Slorc prevented the parliament from convening and played a stalling game, instituting a national convention in Rangoon to decide a new constitution. The convention has been a fiasco, dragging on for years and being subjected to the army's increasingly brutal demands for an Indonesian-style political system under the influence of the military: a quarter of the seats in parliament, for example, were to be reserved for the armed forces. The NLD has meanwhile been the victim of repeated rounds of repression, its members arrested and sometimes tortured. Suu Kyi, although theoretically released from house arrest, finds that her visitors, telephone calls and her own movements are controlled by the military. This author was one of several writers, diplomats and others who had made appointments with her in early 1997 to be turned back without explanation at a government roadblock at the end of her street. A plainclothes security officer, backed by armed police, demanded I produce 'written permission'. But permission from whom? I explained that Burmese government officials had assured me she was a free woman; and she had agreed to see me. Another officer ostentatiously took a photograph of me – a favourite form of intimidation in Burma – and I was frogmarched down the road to the nearest intersection after fifteen minutes of pointless argument. When I tried to telephone her to apologize for my non-appearance, the call was intercepted by the authorities and cut off. In 1991, Suu Kyi was awarded the Nobel Peace Prize and has since become a symbol of the fight for democracy and justice in south-east Asia and the rest of the world. Some of her former admirers in the diplomatic community and the Burmese opposition movement have started to criticize Suu Kyi and the NLD for the vagueness of their economic policies, but to her supporters this seems a bit like attacking Nelson Mandela while he was in jail for not having devised a clear strategy on tackling South African price inflation. It is difficult to formulate policy when party members risk jail or worse for attending meetings.

In their three decades in power, the armed forces have alternated between quiet repression and outright brutality. As the Slorc, they nurtured a civilian surrogate known as the Union Solidarity and Development Organisation, which claimed to have five million members, but its rallies were so obviously government-organized that it never seemed likely to win widespread popular support. The army stopped an upsurge of student unrest at the end of December 1996, partly by moving tanks into the centre of the capital Rangoon. But trouble keeps on erupting; a curfew was imposed in Mandalay in 1997 after Buddhist monks – angered by a botched official renovation of a local pagoda and the rape of a Buddhist girl by Moslems – went on an anti-Moslem rampage. At the end of that year, desperate to improve their image, the junta's leaders changed its name from the State Law and Order Restoration Council to the State Peace and Development Council, pensioned off fourteen of its twenty-one members and replaced military men with civilians in the ministries of finance and planning.[3] The new name was supposed to suggest a permanent development role for the armed forces, along the lines taken by the Indonesian military, rather than a temporary intervention 'to restore order'. But the regime's critics were unimpressed. 'They could call themselves the Warm and Fuzzy Council,' said one, 'but a junta by any other name would still be an international pariah and deeply unpopular with its own people.'[4] The army seems able to keep forcing the lid back on to the boiling cauldron of Burmese politics but is unwilling to enter serious negotiations about the country's future, apparently paralysed by fear of popular retribution if it loses control. As Suu Kyi once said: 'They are like a chess player who can only think one or two moves ahead.'[5] Her supporters are weary. 'After thirty-four years we're tired of this system of government,' said her elderly associate Kyi Maung. 'Before that we had civil liberties, even in colonial days. We had a very good press then. So we're completely fed up with them. Not even Indonesia had an experience like this. They [the Indonesian military] had sense enough to have some qualified people known as the Berkeley mafia [to run the economy]. But here our blockheads don't have anyone to rely on; they don't trust any civilians.'[6]

For decades Burma lacked what other south-east Asian authoritarians relied on for their legitimacy – a growing economy. Ne Win's 'Burmese Road to Socialism' and his habit of putting his superstitions into practice (amazingly, banknotes in the local currency, the kyat, were issued in denominations of ninety and forty-five because nine was his lucky number) made nonsense of economic policy. By the 1990s the economy finally began to grow, boosted by investment from Asian countries such as Singapore, increased foreign tourism, and border trade with China. New hotels sprang up in Rangoon and Mandalay. Burma's prospects were further improved by the discovery of natural gas offshore and the building of a gas pipeline to Thailand which was due to start operating in 1998. But the regime's ignorance of economics, its refusal to accept a formal devaluation of the kyat (which was worth as little as a fiftieth of its official value on the black market and in semi-official trading), its suspicion of private enterprise and international economic pressure continued to make life difficult for investors and for the Burmese people. Fearful of consumer boycotts in their home countries, several companies, including PepsiCo, Heineken and Carlsberg have pulled out of Burma, and in mid-1997 the Clinton administration banned new US investment. Most departing western investors were quickly replaced by companies from Singapore or elsewhere in Asia, but even Asian investors have found the business climate difficult. As in Vietnam, foreign companies are often pushed into joint ventures not with local private sector partners – who are in any case few and far between – but with companies owned by the government or the army, such as the military conglomerate Union of Myanmar Economic Holdings.

Much of Burma's financial mess can be traced to the junta's heavy defence spending. The regime has expanded the army from 185,000 men before 1988 to 300,000 today, imported weapons from China, and increased defence spending to half of the Burmese annual budget at the expense of health and education. Not that the budget figures reflect real revenues or expenditure. It is estimated that heroin and opium trafficking are worth at least as much as all official exports put together.[7] 'Business is very bad,' said one Burmese opponent of military rule who has spent many of the last thirty years in jail. 'The government has no money. Their main source of funds is through these drug warlords and laundering money.' He is resigned to further misery. 'We've always been ruled by despots. Our kings were first-class bastards.'[8]

Burma was welcomed into Asean in 1997 and was able to boast to its new allies that it had made peace on its borders, at least for the time being. A spokesman for the junta said Burma wanted to be a 'friendship bridge between south Asia, China and Asean' and even 'a Switzerland of Asia'.[9] Peace, however, remains fragile. Several truce agreements with guerrilla armies were reached by allowing ethnic groups such as the Wa to continue opium-trafficking. The fact that well-known drug barons were being given amnesties by the authorities and were openly investing their money in Rangoon and Mandalay infuriated the Americans.[10] It could also prove embarrassing for bona fide Asian investors: as in Cambodia, they risked finding that their co-investors in big property projects were drug warlords or their representatives. Just as significant is the lack of progress in Burma's domestic political negotiations. While other Asean members spoke of their special understanding of Burma and the need for 'constructive engagement' with the regime, the Burmese themselves continue to yearn for democracy, or at the very least for an end to crude military dictatorship. 'I am certain that our cause will prevail,' said Aung San Suu Kyi in a recent interview.[11] 'I am convinced that we will reach our goals. It may take a long time, but we will get there.'

THAILAND
The smile that faded

Thailand was portrayed for years as the quintessential south-east Asian success story, a nation that survived and thrived on the winds of change: like the proverbial reed, it was flexible, not rigid. Never colonized by a western power (it was sandwiched between British territories to the west and French ones to the east), Thailand absorbed Chinese immigrant traders, yielded to early western demands for commercial access, accepted Japanese occupation during the Second World War and allowed itself to become an American staging-post in the Vietnam War. Thereafter Thailand rapidly and peacefully entered the industrial age, enjoying decade after decade of economic expansion as its leaders concentrated first on exporting farm products such as rice and tapioca, then on clothing and shoes, and finally on electronics and service industries such as tourism.

This looked like a textbook example of progress and development. But it was remarkable in Asia for not being the work of a single, far-sighted leader, or even of a few, far-sighted governments. It was the product of a society so renowned for political instability and corruption that outsiders and educated urban Thais sometimes found it hard to take seriously. Politicians were – and still are – known for drug-dealing, bribe-taking and vote-buying. Although democracy was introduced after the abolition of the absolute power of the monarch in 1932, no elected government has survived for its full term without being either overthrown in a military coup d'état (there have been sixteen coups and coup attempts) or forced to dissolve parliament because of betrayals within the ruling coalition. Army generals and air force marshals with scant understanding of finance have routinely been appointed to the boards of big state and private companies.

The police force has been corrupted from top to bottom. In one of the more celebrated cases of recent years, a Thai worker in Saudi Arabia was accused of stealing US$20 million of jewellery from the palace of his employer, a Saudi prince. He was arrested after his return to Thailand and the recovered items proudly displayed by

THAILAND

Capital city:	Bangkok
Population (1995):	59 million
Government:	Democratically elected
Annual per capita GNP 1996:	US$2,960
Real economic growth 1995:	8.8 per cent
Real economic growth 1998 (estimate):	Minus 9 percent
Main language:	Thai
Main religion:	Buddhism
Date of independence:	n/a
Former colonial power:	Not colonized

Sources: ADB; *Far Eastern Economic Review,* author.

the police. But triumph quickly became farce when the cache was sent back to Saudi Arabia, where most of the returned jewels turned out to be fakes copied from the originals. A police general's wife was later seen – and photographed – wearing what appeared to be one of the stolen necklaces, although she and her husband later insisted this too was a fake. The frustrated Saudi chargé-d'affaires in Bangkok, whose mission was to solve the mystery and bring back the jewels, was pictured in the media comically brandishing a pistol for the cameras and vowing that justice would be done.[1] More sinister was the murder in Thailand of several people connected to the case, including the wife and child of a jeweller who was an important witness. They were bludgeoned to death, although the police forensic department initially announced – to cries of disbelief and derision – that they had died in a car accident. One of the best studies of materialism in Thailand summarized the saga thus: 'When the police arrested the thief, they promptly stole most of the jewels for themselves. Several gangs of policemen then fought to control the loot. As the scandal started to surface, they killed one another to cover their tracks. When the affair was concluded, they competed to put one another in jail.'[2]

Thailand's economic success is no more attributable to a strong set of ethics than to political stability. Even Buddhist institutions, supposedly the religious bedrock of Thai society, have been undermined by corruption, greed and depravity. Poor families from the north and north-east of the country routinely sell their female children into prostitution through brokers who tour the villages searching for the prettiest girls. Thailand has become notorious throughout the world for its highly-developed sex industry; the respectable English-language *Bangkok Post* has a weekly guide called 'Nite Owl' about the brothels and go-go bars catering for foreigners.[3]

But foreign sex tourism accounts for only a fraction of an enormous sex industry directed mainly at Thais, whether they are truck drivers or tycoons. A few years ago, the Thai press reported with relish how thirty government members of parliament had been at an end-of-term 'bachelor' party with prostitutes at Bangkok's Emerald Hotel: there was nothing particularly remarkable about the event – the MPs won prizes in the form of hotel room keys for their liaisons – except that it occurred during an official campaign against the sex trade. General Chavalit Yongchaiyudh, leader of the political party concerned, said the women were singers, not prostitutes, but he did not dispel the notion that it was normal for MPs to cavort in this way. 'Had they been prostitutes, the party would have been held secretly,' he said. There was no question of any of the MPs resigning, and Chavalit went on to become prime minister.[4] Such behaviour is often regarded as traditional in Thailand, but these are hardly the kind of family values that supporters of the 'Asian Way' have in mind when talking of Asia's supposed moral superiority over the West.

Until the 1990s, most Thais – and many foreign observers – believed that the corruption in politics, business and society as a whole was not an impediment to further economic growth. It seemed that Thailand would always muddle through, by being flexible, by negotiating politely and by making deals. This was the 'Thai Way', a version of the 'Asian Way' that rejected supposedly 'western' norms of political or social behaviour.

Eventually, however, the economic dream lost some of its magic. Most Thais were certainly richer. But uncontrolled industrialization had contaminated the land, the rivers and the sea. Bangkok, where property developers were unfettered by proper planning rules, became notorious for air pollution and traffic congestion: jams were lasting so long that car drivers started buying special plastic containers so that they could relieve themselves en route. Thailand, which had once dreamed of turning south-east Asia's 'battlefields into markets',[5] found its regional ambitions curtailed by neighbours resentful of its unscrupulous foreign policy – which usually involved the rape of other countries' forests with the help of whatever group, rebel or government, seemed most convenient at the time. There were problems at home, too. Education, the key to further economic advancement, was neglected. The rural poor felt left behind by the urban rich with their Mercedes-Benz cars and their mobile phones. The students and the educated middle class in Bangkok began to chafe at the corruption and inefficiency of the military men and old-fashioned gangster-politicians who ran the country. Demonstrators and the security forces clashed in 1973, 1976 and 1992, with bloody consequences. The 'Thai Way' was discredited: when troops killed fifty people on the streets of Bangkok in 1992, a Thai businessman turned to a foreigner in an office lift and said grimly: 'Welcome to the land of smiles – and bullets.'

The Thai economy itself, the engine of prosperity that by 1995 had brought eleven Thai business families into Forbes magazine's list of dollar billionaires, started to misfire in the mid-1990s as labour costs rose – with devastating consequences for much of south-east Asia. Thai economic growth owed much to Japanese post-war investment in everything from cars to computers, but at the end of 1996, factory workers angry at reduced year-end bonuses set fire to the Bangkok headquarters and warehouse of Sanyo, the Japanese electrical goods company. Thai exports had stagnated in 1996 after years of double-digit growth, and the overblown property market began to collapse, but successive Thai governments and the hitherto much-admired bureaucrats at the Bank of Thailand, the central bank, failed to do anything to stave off the impending crisis.

Confidence in the Thai economy suddenly evaporated in 1997. The Bank of Thailand spent billions of dollars trying to support the local currency, the baht, to no avail. Thai companies had taken out short-term foreign loans for long-term domestic investments, and began to default on loan repayments as the baht fell in value and the cost in baht of their dollar loans soared. Finance companies and banks that had lent heavily to property developers ran into trouble. The central bank began to run out of money. The baht and the Thai stock exchange plunged, and the nervousness about stocks and currencies spread to Malaysia, Indonesia, the Philippines, Vietnam and even further afield in Asia. Investors and speculators were suddenly as nervous about Asia as they had been over-confident before; perhaps, they thought, the Asian 'miracle economies' were not so miraculous after all. Thailand closed fifty-six of its ninety-one finance companies, and the International Monetary Fund was obliged to arrange a US$17.2 billion rescue programme to bail the country out.

Thailand's humiliation was complete. But there was no immediate agreement about the political and economic remedies that would have to be applied. The debate in south-east Asia revolved around one vital question: was Thailand in trouble because it was democratic and therefore chaotic, or because it was still run behind the scenes by undemocratic, authoritarian politicians? The answer was both, in the sense that the democratic system was being abused by the old-fashioned politicians. It was estimated that they spent the equivalent of US$800 million to buy votes during the 1996 election campaign – money that would have to be recouped by the politicians from corrupt business deals once they gained office.[6] Since its first election in 1933, Thailand has been neither an efficient democracy, where the views of voters are translated into policy designed to benefit the country as a whole, nor an efficient authoritarian state, in which a leader or group of leaders pushes through the policies that they think will best serve the national interest.

There is, perhaps, a cultural explanation for Thailand's predicament. Like many pre-industrial or recently industrial societies – but maybe to a greater degree – Thailand is hierarchical. Thais are great respecters of rank and status, a national trait reflected in language and in social etiquette. When Thais greet each other with a *wai*, the gesture in which the hands are held together in front of the face, the type of *wai* and the degree of deference shown by each person depend on their relative social standing. And when Thai leaders are known to have robbed their fellow-citizens, even when they have killed them, they are not punished. Many educated Indonesians and Burmese rejoiced at the punishment meted out in a South Korean court to two of the country's ex-presidents for corruption and repression; but many Thais – who live in a democracy and might therefore be expected to be tougher on political crimes – 'cringed with embarrassment' at this humiliation of such important people. 'I did,' said Korn Chatikavanij, who was then head of Jardine Fleming Thanakom, one of Thailand's leading stockbrokers. 'Thais are not used to seeing people who used to be in authority treated like dirt in that way. Coup leaders are at most ignored.'[7]

Yet Thailand is changing. Even the traditional respect for the monarchy – King Bhumibol, the world's longest-reigning monarch who came to the throne in 1946, is treated like a demi-god by his people – is fading before the onslaught of the sordid marriage break-ups and adulterous affairs of the royal children, an Asian version of the British royal soap opera. Voting patterns show that the educated elite of Bangkok are no longer prepared to tolerate the incompetent and corrupt politicians elected by rural voters whose support has been bought for a few dollars by a local 'godfather'. Rural people themselves are losing patience. About 10,000 peasant farmers and other country-dwellers camped for weeks outside parliament in Bangkok in 1997 to air their grievances, including inadequate compensation for land submerged by hydroelectric dams. Their world view is changing. 'People on the lower rungs of the ladder today are not so accepting,' said William Klausner, an expert on Thai culture at the Ford Foundation in Bangkok. 'The villagers traditionally believed in karma. That still exists, but more and more they are not blaming themselves [if something goes wrong]. They are saying perhaps it's due to corruption, abuse of power.'[8]

For the first time in 1992, Thais elected a prime minister who was known neither for corruption, nor for a military background, nor for high social standing. Chuan Leekpai, the son of a vegetable seller, was a mild-mannered lawyer in charge of the Democrat Party who expressed his concern about such matters as the rule of law and the need to control police corruption. His coalition did collapse, and he was succeeded by more traditional Thai prime ministers (one was a godfather known as the 'walking ATM' because of his cash hand-outs, and another was an ex-general),[9] but not before his government had lasted more than two and a half years – a record for an elected Thai government. And it was to Chuan that the country turned again in 1997 to lead Thailand out of its economic crisis at the head of yet another fragile coalition. In the same year, a new Thai consti-tution was prepared. (It was finally passed in 1998.) This in itself was not extraordinary, because it was the sixteenth in only sixty-six years, but it was the first constitution to emerge from a process of public consultation rather than because someone had seized power and torn up the old one. It also contained some revolutionary pro-visions: a system of proportional representation to reward broad-based national parties in elections; direct election of senators to the upper house; an independent electoral commission; a bill of rights guaranteeing equality to all citizens; and the establishment of special courts to hear complaints about abuse of power by officials and politicians.[10]

Thailand is still an Asian success story. It has developed a vibrant, entrepreneurial economy based on products ranging from prawns to computer disc drives and on a successful tourism industry. And it has done so while maintaining an open, easygoing atmosphere at odds with the glum authoritarianism of some of its neighbours. Thailand's political system, however, is old-fashioned, and it is only now starting to develop one as modern as its factories and shopping malls. Future democratic governments will spend more time manag-ing the economy and less time enriching individual politicians and their cronies, but even the most optimistic Thais believe it will be many years before corruption is conquered and the 'big people' in business and politics are held responsible for their failings. 'Never underestimate these negative forces, these evil forces,' warned Anand Panyarachun, a businessman and respected former prime minister who was one of those in charge of devising the new constitution. 'In many ways we still live in the dark ages in Thailand.'[11]

LAOS
No escape from modernity

If you wander into the imposing French colonial mansion that houses
the Lao Revolutionary Museum in the sleepy capital Vientiane, you
might find you are the only visitor looking at the busts of Lenin and
Ho Chi Minh, the personal belongings of former communist leader
Kaysone Phomvihane (including binoculars and bamboo bowl and
spoon) and a small collection of mangy stuffed animals. The nearby
State Bookshop offers cheap wooden curios, posters of Marx and
dusty boxes of unsold Russian books. A few streets away, the ex-Soviet
cultural centre vainly tries to interest passers-by in Russian tractors.
Outside, on the mud banks deposited by the Mekong River, men
are casting their nets for fish and children are playing football. Laos
is south-east Asia's sleepy backwater: a delight for tourists seeking
temples and hand-woven textiles, a source of frustration for foreign
investors, a land where communism has been and gone and no one
is quite sure what is supposed to take its place.

But even landlocked Laos, with its swathes of forest and an ethnically diverse population of just five million, cannot escape the wave
of industrialization and social change that has swept across its neighbours in Burma, southern China, Vietnam, Cambodia and Thailand.
Thai companies have built clothing factories on the outskirts of
Vientiane; Australia paid for a US$30 million bridge across the
Mekong that now links Laos to Thailand and the sea; highways are
being constructed that will make the country an Asian crossroads, a
truckstop between Singapore and China (Laos has already made
money by levying a US$1,300 transit fee on luxury cars on their way
to the tycoons of China's Yunnan province); logging companies are
penetrating remote parts of the country in search of timber; satellite
television dishes are sprouting from urban rooftops; and teenagers
are roaring around on motorcycles on Friday nights in Vientiane.
Spared the excesses (and the benefits) of modernization from the
time the communist Pathet Lao guerrillas took power in 1975 until
the decline of world communism in the late 1980s, Laos now finds
itself struggling against its more energetic neighbours in an attempt

LAOS

Capital city:	Vientiane
Population (1995):	5 million
Government:	Communist, one-party state
Annual per capita GNP (1996):	US$400
Real economic growth 1995:	7 per cent
Real economic growth 1998 (estimate):	n/a
Main language:	Lao
Main religion:	Buddhism
Date of independence:	1953
Former colonial power:	France

Sources: World Bank; ADB; author.

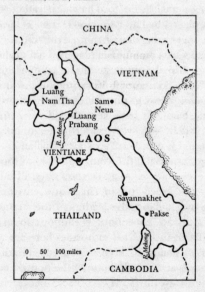

to maintain its cultural identity and its economic independence.

It is Thailand across the Mekong that looms largest in Lao minds. Thailand is the biggest foreign investor in Laos, but Lao businessmen complain that their own companies – dependent on Thai ports and roads – are held to ransom by Thai bureaucrats and an oligopoly of Thai trucking companies. The two countries are close culturally and linguistically, and Thailand has dominated Lao lands for so long that France is credited with having preserved Laos as an independent state by colonizing and uniting its various components – although the heavily populated and mainly Lao region known as Isarn was ceded to Thailand and is now that country's north-eastern corner. Laos and Thailand fought a border war in the late 1980s, but the conflict now is not on the battlefield. Instead, Lao intellectuals fear their easygoing country will be swamped by Thai companies, Thai materialism and Thai culture. The relationship has been likened to that between the US and Canada. Already many Lao watch Thai television soap operas, listen to Thai local radio (complete with advertisements placed by Lao companies), buy Thai popular music, and find their speech becoming more akin to Thai. Government campaigns to stop bars and hotels playing Thai and western music have been stymied by the shortage of Lao compact discs. 'Laos is a small country,' says Somsanouk Mixay, editor-in-chief of the state-controlled *Vientiane Times*, gazing out at the sunset over the Mekong from a riverside bar. 'We have kept this identity throughout centuries, surrounded by very, very powerful neighbours. Now we are about to lose it and just become an ersatz Thailand ... It's very easy for people here, especially the young people, to look to Thailand with admiring eyes. They know all the pop stars, all the movie stars.'[1]

Horrified by the greed, urban chaos and environmental devastation they see in Thailand, the leaders of the ruling Lao People's Revolutionary Party are exceptionally cautious about the inevitable process of modernization. 'The authorities here are very well aware of the problems in Thailand,' says Somsanouk. 'That's why they keep a slow pace. Laos is always called one of the poorest countries in the world, but if you travel in Laos, [you see] people have their own land, their own house and so on. They are not starving, even if they don't have a TV or a telephone.' The LPDR should not stand for Lao People's Democratic Republic, one leading Lao businessman insists, but for 'Laos – Please Don't Rush'. Like their fraternal communist allies in neighbouring Vietnam, Lao leaders have introduced some economic reforms, including privatization, since the 1980s. They have abandoned most of their socialist policies, but they fear the chaos they believe would come with free democracy or untrammelled economic liberalization. They came to power in the aftermath of the Vietnam War – during which the US dropped a staggering two million tonnes of bombs on Laos, a greater tonnage than in all its Second World War bombing missions put together – and imposed a typical communist political structure on what remains a largely rural country. Thousands of people, including Hmong tribespeople who had fought for the Americans, fled the country; others were sent to re-education camps. Today, however, socialism is barely mentioned in official speeches and the hammer and sickle has been removed from official stationery. The regime has embraced Buddhism and looks to Asian 'soft authoritarianism' as justification for its continued grip on power. Important families, some tracing their influence back to the years before 1975 and others to the revolution, dominate politics and business.[2] The army, as in other south-east Asian states, is also an important player. A reshuffled, nine-member LPRP politburo which emerged from the sixth party congress in March 1996 included six generals and a colonel.[3] The army is involved in logging and other businesses, often through the BPKP (*Bolisat Phatthana Khet Phoudoi*, or Mountainous Area Development Company), and holds a 25 per cent stake in a Malaysian-run joint venture to build a US$200 million tourist and gambling resort.[4]

However worthy the motives behind Laos's reluctance to be sucked into the free market, its tiny economy – already hampered by its remoteness and heavily dependent on foreign aid – is suffering from the dead hand of government interference. Movement across the new Mekong bridge, for example, is so tightly controlled that it is scarcely more convenient than the old ferries. A move to set up a committee of hoteliers to discuss tourism promotion and other matters of common interest was blocked by the government, apparently nervous of any organization not under its control; they were told to use the officially approved chamber of commerce. Potential foreign investors have been kept waiting for as long as three years to have their licence applications approved or rejected. Bureaucracy is nightmarish: company stamps – even those for hotels with such innocuous messages as 'complimentary breakfast' – are supposed to be approved by government ministries. South-east Asia's recent economic slowdown will make life even more difficult. One of Laos's biggest exports is hydro-electricity sold to Thailand. Laos was hoping to build many more dams on its plentiful rivers to increase income and reduce dependence on foreign aid, but forecasts for regional electricity demand have been revised sharply downwards. Only tourism may offer some financial respite.

Laos joined Asean in 1997, thus firmly establishing itself as part of south-east Asia and giving it a chance of freer trade with the rest of the region. But even this has been a traumatic step for Laos, which struggles to pay its Asean fees and lacks enough English-speakers and skilled diplomats to make an impression at the 300 yearly meetings of the organization and its various committees. Laos remains predominantly rural and undeveloped, with more than half its people surviving from subsistence agriculture, at risk of death and injury from unexploded bombs from the Vietnam war, and playing no part in the modern consumer economy. As it approaches the twenty-first century, the country is fearful of being left behind by economically more vigorous neighbours. But it is also wary of the social, cultural and political upheaval that joining the race for prosperity will probably entail. 'When I see how Thailand grows. I don't want that to happen in Laos,' says Virachit Philaphandeth, a leading businessman who heads the Lao Toyota franchise. 'They are too much into industry and Bangkok is over-developed. Income is not spread around.' Like other Lao, Virachit is concerned about the cultural invasion from across the Mekong. 'In one way you gain something, and in another way you lose something. Culture from outside will affect us a lot, but we can still preserve a lot of good Lao tradition.'[5] But even if Laos succeeds in preserving some of its distinctive culture intact, its heavy-handed political system is certain to change. Like those of neighbouring Vietnam and Cambodia, the generals and communist party leaders who run the country will find their authority challenged by a new generation of citizens more interested in democracy and freedom than in the history of a struggle that ended before they were born.

CAMBODIA
The slow recovery from 'Year Zero'

An awful shadow lies over Cambodia's modern history. Between 1975 and 1978 about 1.5 million Cambodians, a fifth of the population, were murdered or starved to death by the extreme left-wing Khmers Rouges. After overthrowing the US-backed dictator Lon Nol and seizing Phnom Penh – two weeks before the fall of Saigon to the Vietnamese communists – the Khmers Rouges established one of the most barbarous regimes the world has known. In an attempt to establish by force a quasi-Maoist, agrarian utopia, Pol Pot and his followers emptied Cambodia's towns by marching the inhabitants into the countryside, killed those with foreign connections, persecuted the educated and the skilled, and promoted the ignorant into positions of power. They officially restarted history at 'Year Zero', but within years the shadowy *Angkar* (the organization) was devouring itself in an orgy of massacres, torture and political purges. Vietnam, provoked by repeated cross-border raids by the Khmers Rouges, invaded Cambodia in 1978 and installed a government of Khmers Rouges defectors the following year. Hardly a Cambodian family had been left untouched by the horror. Some were eliminated; others were scattered across the globe, from refugee camps in Thailand to émigré communities in the US. The epitaph for Khmer Rouge rule was tinged with bathos. In 1997, Pol Pot, a former teacher who liked the French poet Verlaine and whose real name was Saloth Sar, was arrested by a rival faction in his crumbling guerrilla group in northern Cambodia. Looking frail, almost pathetic, Pol Pot blamed Vietnam for Cambodia's troubles. 'I came to carry out the struggle, not to kill people,' he told an interviewer in Anlong Veng. 'Even now, and you can look at me, am I a savage person? My conscience is clear.'[1] He died on April 15 the following year at the age of sixty-nine.

Cambodia today, however burdened with history, faces much the same challenges as its neighbours: how to increase prosperity and integrate itself into the global economy, establish political stability and avoid too much social upheaval. For the first half of the 1990s,

CAMBODIA

Capital city:	Phnom Penh
Population (1995):	10 million
Government:	Authoritarian elected
Annual per capita GNP (1996):	US$300
Real economic growth 1995:	7.6 per cent
Real economic growth 1998 (estimate):	n/a
Main language:	Khmer
Main religion:	Buddhism
Date of independence:	1953
Former colonial power:	France

Sources: ADB; World Bank; author.

it seemed that Cambodia was on track to share in south-east Asia's economic success. After a decade of isolation and guerrilla war in Cambodia, Vietnamese troops withdrew, paving the way for an international peace agreement and an election organized by the United Nations in 1993. Prince Sihanouk returned from exile, and was crowned King. For most Cambodians, life began to return to normal. Phnom Penh, increasingly busy and chaotic, started to resemble other south-east Asian cities. Middle-class Cambodians went to the seaside at weekends. Cambodians returned from overseas to visit relatives, and sometimes to stay. Taiwanese businessmen built clothing factories to take advantage of cheap labour. Hotels were built or refurbished. More tourists arrived to visit the magnificent temples of Angkor, a reminder of the period a millennium ago when Khmer civilization was at its height and Khmer rulers controlled an Asian empire. Newspapers flourished, as did bars, brothels, restaurants and video rental stores. Sunday nights in Phnom Penh, when hundreds of families on small motorcycles – sometimes five to a machine – would cruise slowly around the city's broad but potholed avenues just for the pleasure of it, became a celebration of normality.

The UN-organized election was at first glance a successful, if expensive, democratic exercise. (The whole UN peacekeeping and polling operation was at that time the biggest in the organization's history and cost US\$2 billion.) In the face of a Khmer Rouge boycott and threats of violence, the overwhelming majority of eligible Cambodians registered to vote, and almost all of them went on to cast their votes under the protection of UN troops and election monitors. What is more, most voters, having listened avidly to the popular UN radio station broadcasting in Khmer, knew exactly what they were doing and why. The royalist Funcinpec[2] party, led by Prince Norodom Ranariddh, won the largest number of seats in the new parliament. But Funcinpec, which had fought a sporadic guerrilla war in alliance with the ousted Khmers Rouges against the incumbent Vietnamese-backed government, was led largely by French-educated émigrés and had little influence over the troops, police and bureaucrats who control day-to-day life in rural Cambodia. When the Cambodian People's Party – the party of the outgoing government, which had won the second largest number of seats – threatened to reject the election results and demanded to be in a coalition, Funcinpec was obliged to agree.

The coalition, led by 'First Prime Minister' Ranariddh and 'Second Prime Minister' Hun Sen, never functioned effectively. CPP officials, especially in the lawless provinces, refused to share real power with their Funcinpec rivals. Each party competed for corrupt earnings from activities such as logging and the smuggling of liquor and consumer goods. Sam Rainsy, a former Funcinpec member and respected finance minister who had the impossible task of managing the budget, was forced out. He formed a new party, the Khmer Nation Party, and campaigned vainly for democracy, justice and workers' rights. In March 1997, he was fortunate to escape with his life when fifteen people were killed and dozens wounded by grenades thrown by unknown assailants at a demonstration he was leading to protest against the failures of the Cambodian justice system. In July of the same year, Hun Sen staged a coup d'état against Ranariddh, his fellow prime minister. Although Hun Sen promised to hold elections, as scheduled, in 1998, he and his CPP allies were back in full control of the country they had ruled since the Vietnamese invasion. Their opponents were hunted down and tortured and, according to the UN, up to sixty were killed.[3]

Hun Sen, a former Khmer Rouge commander who had lost an eye in battle and defected to Vietnam, is an authoritarian ruler suspicious of democracy and free speech. Cambodian liberals who had welcomed democracy with open arms were therefore fearful about the future. Ranariddh, then in exile, urged other countries to be tough with Hun Sen and demand proper democracy. 'To a gangster, you have to talk like a gangster,' he said.[4] But many foreign and local investors could hardly disguise their relief at the prospect of dealing with a united government: the administration of the country had been all but paralysed for more than a year by the feuding between Funcinpec and the CPP. The lesson from Cambodia, according to Singaporean, Vietnamese and other supporters of 'Asian values' and authoritarian political systems, is that liberal democracy does not work, especially in a country as poor and unsophisticated as Cambodia. Supporters of democracy, on the other hand, say it is not democracy itself which is to blame, but the refusal of the CPP to give up power after losing the election and the inability of Funcinpec to seize it after winning. A more telling point in favour of the democrats is that it was Indonesia and Asean – authoritarian warts and all – which brokered the Cambodian peace agreements, including the provision for a free election: there was no other obvious way to bring Cambodia back into the international fold or to overcome its political impasse. After the coup, Asean balked at accepting Cambodia as its tenth and final member as planned in 1997, although it did welcome Burma, perhaps because memories of the Burmese regime's worst atrocities had been dulled by the passage of time.

Hun Sen, meanwhile, remained in charge of a weak economy made even weaker by south-east Asia's economic downturn. His own soldiers had looted Phnom Penh's airport and various homes and businesses, including some of the new textile factories, in the course of the coup d'état. Cambodia depends on foreign aid – apart from the big international institutions and bilateral donors there are 200 foreign charities and other non-government organizations working in the country – but the US and other donors suspended payments as a result of the coup. The International Monetary Fund was unhappy about the continued diversion of logging revenues away from the budget and into the pockets of military officers. Indeed, the wholesale rape of Cambodia's forests bodes ill for the future of a barely industrialized country that is bound to depend on the export of natural resources and on tourism for its future economic growth. In the 1970s, more than two-thirds of Cambodia was forest. Half of that has gone, and the remainder is threatened by unscrupulous loggers from other Asian countries and greedy Cambodian soldiers: even national parks are not safe, and there is no sign of the development of a 'sustainable' timber industry. Cambodia has also earned an unenviable reputation as a centre for international heroin-trafficking and money-laundering.

A rare fragment of good news for Cambodians was that the faction-ridden Khmer Rouge organization seemed to be withering away in its jungle hideouts near the Thai border. Some reports said that by mid-1998 there was as few as 500 Khmer Rouge guerrillas left.[5] But most of the vices that the Khmers Rouges had criticized before they seized power in 1975, including rampant corruption, were back with a vengeance, and some Khmer Rouge commanders – having been officially rehabilitated by the government – were running their own fiefdoms in the provinces. As for Hun Sen, he won the biggest share of the vote in the July 1998 election, but the results were contested by the opposition and the outcome was a political deadlock. Cambodia was still squeezed between its more powerful neighbours, Thailand and Vietnam, neither of which had any compunction about plundering Cambodian natural resources or redrawing international boundaries in their favour. And the whimsical Sihanouk, who always seemed to prefer to live in China or North Korea rather than at home, once again found himself presiding over a weak and vulnerable Cambodia.

VIETNAM
Victorious but poor

There are fashions in investment, and Vietnam was all the rage among foreign investors in the early 1990s. The investors – Taiwanese, South Koreans, Australians, French and many other nationalities besides – promised to inject billions of dollars into industrial estates, factories, breweries, hotels and oil exploration. Here, they believed, was the next 'Asian tiger' – a country with a substantial population of seventy-five million people who were desperately poor but literate, hardworking and eager to succeed. The communist government was equally enthusiastic, abandoning socialist economics as the Soviet Union fell apart and adopting a vigorous economic liberalization policy known as *doi moi* (renovation). Vietnam was transformed. The southern city of Saigon, renamed Ho Chi Minh City following the defeat of US-backed South Vietnam in 1975 and the reunification of the country, bustled with entrepreneurial energy; high-rise buildings sprang up in the city centre, and acres of land were cleared and levelled in the suburbs for the new textile and clothing factories. Hanoi, the capital in the north, was once a sleepy town of wide avenues and crumbling French villas, but it too began to seethe with motorcycles, taxis and trucks. The stores were piled high with televisions and video cassette recorders, and Vietnamese entrepreneurs and students could be seen tapping away furiously at rented computers in the city's ubiquitous photocopying shops. In streets where three years before there had been no visible sign of commerce, there were hotels, bars, restaurants, karaoke rooms, massage parlours – even an Irish pub. The US economic embargo on Vietnam, maintained out of pique at the American defeat, was finally lifted. The remaining 'boat people', most of whom had fled to escape Vietnam's desperate poverty after the war, were either persuaded or forced to return home from refugee camps around Asia.

There had, meanwhile, been a flowering of Vietnamese literature, although the books rarely met with the approval of the ruling Communist Party. Slightly later than their American adversaries, the Vietnamese were struggling to come to terms with the horrors of a war

VIETNAM

Capital city:	Hanoi
Population (1995):	75 million
Government:	Communist, one-party state
Annual per capita GNP (1996):	US$290
Real economic growth 1995:	9.5 per cent
Real economic growth 1998 (estimate):	4 per cent
Main language:	Vietnamese
Main religion:	Buddhism, Taoism, Confucianism, Catholicism
Date of independence:	1954 (reunification of north and south, 1976)
Former colonial power:	France

Sources: ADB; author.

that was many times more traumatic for them than for the US. Vietnam's military record was not in doubt; under such generals as Vo Nguyen Giap, its armies had not only defeated the French in the 1950s and driven out the Americans, but had also marched into Cambodia in 1978 to overthrow the Khmers Rouges, and had given the Chinese a bloody nose when they invaded northern Vietnam in 1979. But the Vietnamese had paid a high price, and in the years of repression and poverty after the fall of Saigon, they began to wonder whether it was worth it. In the novel *Paradise of the Blind*, Duong Thu Huong tells the story of Hang, a woman whose family and village are torn apart by land reforms in the 1950s and the communist obsession with ideology, personified by the stern figure of her Uncle Chinh; by the 1980s, cynicism and corruption are everywhere and Uncle Chinh is a pathetic figure living in Moscow and using his party position to smuggle goods in and out of Vietnam.[1] Bao Ninh's grim book *The Sorrow of War* explores the disillusionment and trauma of Vietnamese soldiers after the victory in 1975. They have nightmares, they drink, and they find it hard to adapt to life in peacetime. They are unappreciated: 'As we had won, Kien thought, then that meant justice had won; that had been some consolation. Or had it? Think carefully; look at your own existence. Look carefully now at the peace we have, painful, bitter and sad. And look at who won the war.'[2] The writer Bui Tin, who was born into a family of mandarins, became a communist military officer and journalist and then rejected the system he had helped to build, put it like this: 'Walking around the streets of Hanoi in recent years, I have felt continuous mental torture. The children look thin and frequently speak in obscenities. The women are gaunt and anxious. Sewage spills here and there. Sometimes arguments explode, abuse is hurled and knives are brandished. The city teems with gamblers, thieves, pickpockets, prostitutes and opium smokers . . . So what was all the sacrifice of the Revolution about?'[3]

The rise of a new generation born after the end of the war, along with economic growth and increased prosperity, should have ushered in a new and more hopeful era for Vietnam. The first fruits of economic reform were impressive: agricultural output soared as peasants were given control of their own land, quickly making Vietnam into one of the world's biggest rice exporters. But the country's communist leaders, many of them still suspicious or ignorant about the market-based policies they have embraced, are discovering that the next stage of reform is more difficult. Having halved the number of moribund state enterprises to about 6,000, they are reluctant to close or privatize the rest – although few are profitable – for fear of antagonizing the party nominees who run them and leaving thousands of employees out of a job.[4] The armed forces, meanwhile, have sought to improve the profitability of their extensive business activities to reduce their dependence on the meagre central government budget. Among other projects, the Defence Ministry has a stake in the US$15 million Saigon Superbowl, a leisure and entertainment complex financed by a Singaporean-led consortium.[5] But many foreign investors, frustrated by bureaucracy and corruption and often obliged to enter into joint ventures with local Communist Party organizations, have lost some of their early enthusiasm for Vietnam. The rate of economic growth has started to fall.

Ordinary Vietnamese, jolted out of the dour but fairly predictable life they lived under the old village traditions and under socialism, are bewildered as well. Their expectations have been raised. They see newly rich entrepreneurs and Communist Party officials, but they themselves usually remain poor. Teenagers defy the police to race motorcycles round the lake in central Hanoi. Crime, heroin addiction and prostitution are on the increase. Some turn to religion – Buddhism, Christianity, or the unusual cult of Cao Dai-ism (its prophets and spiritual guides include Jesus, Mohammed, Confucius, Sun Yat Sen, Victor Hugo and William Shakespeare) – for consolation. 'Every day there are new phenomena,' says Professor Pham Bich San of the Institute of Sociology at the Vietnam National Centre for Social Sciences. 'For example, suicide suddenly – or drugs ... People are confused about their role in society. They don't know their exact place. Officially people are still classified as farmers, intellectuals and so on, but in reality we're starting to talk about the poor, the less poor, the middle class and the upper class.'[6]

Vietnamese politics, by contrast, seems quite straightforward. The Communist Party has absolute control. But since it has abandoned communist policies, and retained merely the framework of a traditional communist administration, it remains in power now simply because it was in power already. Vietnamese leaders boast that they avoided the sort of chaos seen in post-communist Russia because, like their Chinese counterparts, they liberalized the economy while leaving the political system intact. Eventually, however, the contradictions within an authoritarian government implementing policies that run directly counter to its ideological inheritance will have to be resolved. The communists want to delay that day for as long as possible. They have replaced some of their septuagenarian leaders and moved the economic reformer Phan Van Khai into the prime minister's job. In 1997 they allowed a record sixty-six non-communists to be elected to the 450-seat National Assembly (although all candidates are vetted by the Party) and they have permitted fairly vigorous questioning there of government ministers;[7] and they have emphasized their nationalist credentials more than their communism – they have, for example, called for a mass mobilization of volunteers to help build a new US$5 billion highway down the old Ho Chi Minh Trail, the network of tracks down the spine of the country which funnelled men and weapons down to the south during the war.

Unfortunately for the government, the young were born after the end of the war and are not as interested as their parents in the conflict, let alone in communism. 'Fewer and fewer young people want to be party members. They mock it quite a lot,' says one former party loyalist. 'Their priority now is to enrich themselves, either by working for a foreign company or going into business.'[8] The pressure for greater freedom of information, for a more open debate about the country's future and eventually for democracy, has been increasing steadily, as much from inside as from émigré opposition groups based in the US and France. But the government is nervous about losing control. It alternates between cautious liberalization (releasing the occasional dissident and permitting more freedom in the arts) and old-fashioned repression (crushing demonstrations, silencing outspoken Buddhist monks, and restricting access to satellite television and the Internet). Questioned about the future, officials regurgitate the arguments for authoritarian 'Asian values' or retreat into vague assertions about socialism. 'The goal is socialism, but what is socialism?' asks another intellectual who is convinced that the party is losing its grip. 'According to the authorities, it's so that people can be richer, the country stronger and society just and civilized. That's very vague. Political contradiction leads to economic contradictions. That's why our market economy is not completely a market economy.'[9]

The government has a difficult foreign affairs agenda as well. An increasingly confident and prosperous China – which has sought to dominate Vietnam for more than 2,000 years – has recently launched repeated incursions into what Vietnam regards as its territorial waters in the South China Sea, especially in areas dedicated to oil exploration. Vietnam's navy is no match for the Chinese, and it was with almost palpable relief that the Vietnamese finally succeeded in restoring diplomatic relations in 1995 with a reluctant United States, the ultimate guarantor of maritime security in Asia. In the same year Vietnam acceded to Asean, gathering in another set of important potential allies in any future confrontation with China: other Asean states, including the Philippines, have also suffered from China's attempts to enforce its claims in the South China Sea, and Asean has taken an unusually firm stance in telling China to stop its provocative activities and abide by international agreements to discuss territorial disputes peacefully. Since Asean was established as a thinly-veiled alliance against communism, Vietnam's inclusion – and its new relationship with the US – meant that the Cold War was finally over for Hanoi.

But the new challenges of Chinese recalcitrance, global economic competition and – above all – the growth of popular demands for a better system of government, are only just beginning to make themselves felt. General Le Ka Phieu, the army political commissar who became Communist Party general secretary at the end of 1997, faces demands for democratic reform not only from intellectuals such as Phan Dinh Dieu but also from former military stalwarts such as General Tran Do. As Le Dat, a poet expelled from the Party as far back as 1957 for his pro-democracy writings, put it recently: 'Democracy will come more and more, but its form is not certain . . . To survive, the Party must change. That's all.'[10]

MALAYSIA
Vision 2020 and the Malay dilemma

Malaysia exemplifies both the triumph and the fragility of what came to be called the Asian 'economic miracle'. Since Malaya's independence from Britain in 1957 (the Borneo states of Sabah and Sarawak joined later along with the predominantly ethnic Chinese island of Singapore to form the new federation of Malaysia, but Singapore was pushed out in 1965), the country has been transformed and enriched. Whereas once it depended largely on exports of tin, palm oil and other primary commodities, Malaysia is now among the world's biggest exporters of air conditioners and electronic products. It welcomed foreign investment – Matsushita, the Japanese electronics company, alone accounts for a substantial share of the country's gross domestic product – and promoted manufacturing and service industries. Mahathir Mohamad, the energetic, septuagenarian former doctor who has been prime minister since 1981, spurred on his people to ever greater ambitions with his determination that Malaysia should be a fully developed country by the third decade of the new millennium – a concept named 'Vision 2020'. Mahathir is immensely proud of his country's post-colonial achievements, and Malaysia's success gave him a platform from which to champion third-world and Islamic causes against what he sees as an arrogant and complacent West. By the 1990s, he was a champion of 'Asian values', rejecting the idea that there were universal standards – on such matters as human rights, liberal democracy, labour conditions or environmental protection – that could or should be applied to developing countries such as Malaysia. As far as Mahathir was concerned, these demands were usually thinly disguised attempts by the West to reduce the competitiveness of Asian economies.

Other south-east Asian countries were also industrializing and urbanizing fast and enjoying the benefits of years of continuous economic growth. But Malaysia is unusual in one important respect: its racial make-up. Whereas Thailand, Indonesia and the Philippines have relatively small ethnic Chinese minorities active in business, the proportion of Chinese in Malaysia is quite large. About 30 per cent

MALAYSIA

Capital city:	Kuala Lumpur
Population (1995):	20 million
Government:	Authoritarian elected
Annual per capita GNP (1996):	US$4,370
Real economic growth 1995:	9.5 per cent
Real economic growth 1998 (estimate):	Minus 7.5 per cent
Main language:	Malay
Main religion:	Islam
Date of independence:	Malaya, 1957; Malaysia, 1963
Former colonial power:	Britain

Sources: ADB; *Far Eastern Economic Review,* Asia Pacific Consensus Forecasts; author.

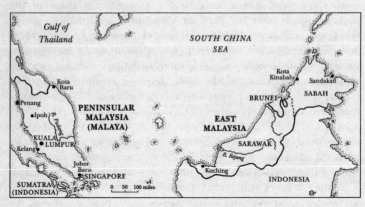

of the population are Chinese, 9 per cent are Indians, 11 per cent are the predominantly Christian and animist inhabitants of Sabah and Sarawak, and about 50 per cent are Moslem Malays. Under Malaysia's race policies – which have been aimed essentially at helping the poorer, more rural Malays to narrow the gap with the business-oriented, largely urban Chinese – the last two categories are entitled to preferential treatment and lumped together as *bumiputras* ('sons of the soil'), or 'bumis' for short.[1]

Race has always been a crucial factor in Malaysian politics, and especially so since the race riots and bloodshed of May 1969 in which scores of people were killed after a general election. Mahathir's famous book, *The Malay Dilemma*, was primarily a study of what he saw as the racial differences between the Chinese and the Malays, along with his solutions for remedying the inequalities between the two groups. 'The Malays are spiritually inclined, tolerant and easygoing. The non-Malays and especially the Chinese are materialistic, aggressive and have an appetite for work,' he wrote. 'Malaysia has far too many non-Malay citizens who can swamp the Malays the moment protection is removed. The frequent suggestion that the only way to help the Malays is to let them fight their own battles cannot therefore be seriously considered.'[2] It was not. The 'New Economic Policy' (NEP) was introduced in 1971 with the aim of increasing the Malays' share of the country's corporate assets from 2 per cent to 30 per cent by 1990. Although the figure reached in that year was only slightly more than 20 per cent, the policy was regarded as a qualified success, and it was replaced with the milder 'New Development Policy' in 1991. Malays had been subsidized, promoted and favoured in education, business and government. But the policy – like affirmative action programmes elsewhere in the world – had its critics. There were doubts as to whether it had made Malays more enterprising, by giving them new opportunities, or whether it had done the opposite, by making it clear that they would usually succeed regardless of merit. Malays granted business loans under the policy, for example, often failed to repay them.[3] Furthermore, while a few prominent Malay businessmen, especially those connected with the dominant United Malays National Organization (Umno), had profited handsomely from the policy, rural Malays and the population of Borneo had hardly benefited at all. Finally, the Chinese in Malaysia bitterly resented the discrimination; nowhere in south-east Asia is Chinese contempt for their non-Chinese fellow-citizens as frequently and scathingly expressed as in Malaysia. The policy could even make life difficult for successful Malays, because their success was inevitably attributed to favouritism rather than their own qualities. 'Even some Malays are beginning to feel these special privileges are perhaps a burden,' says Abdul Rahman Adnan, director of the Institute for Policy Research in Kuala Lumpur. The last thing Malays want is to be treated like 'pampered poodles', he says. 'We want to show we are capable of doing it.'[4]

Few Malaysians could or would claim any kind of pure racial ancestry – the author Rehman Rashid says he has cousins surnamed Halim, Aziz, Ghani, Wee, Ratnam, Khannabhiran, Arumugam, Ryan, Marshall, Rodrigues, Keese and Kuylaars – but Malaysia is still no melting pot, and most of the Chinese and Malay communities continue to exist in separate social worlds. The major political parties are racial parties in reality if not in name. Umno, the main Malay party, controls the ruling *Barisan Nasional* (the National Front), a coalition which includes the Malaysian Chinese Association and the Malaysian Indian Congress, while the main opposition parties are the (largely Chinese) Democratic Action Party and the (Malay Islamic fundamentalist) *Parti Islam se-Malaysia*; one of the few multiracial parties is the *Parti Bersatu Sabah* on Borneo, where the racial equations are different from those of peninsular Malaysia. For three decades, racial peace has been maintained and economic expansion has driven the country towards its goal of full industrialization.

Mahathir is a popular leader and a skilful politician who seems to know when to make and break alliances – sometimes suppressing Islamic fundamentalists and sometimes seeking to co-opt moderate Islamic leaders by adopting their ideas – to keep himself in power. His skills and those of his successors, however, are likely to be tested by the challenge of creating a Malaysia that is simultaneously Islamic, modern and multiracial. At present Malaysians are governed by a mixture of national law, Islamic law and customary law, depending on who they are and where they live. Moslems, for example, can be prosecuted under *sharia* for *khalwat* – close proximity between unmarried, unrelated people of the opposite sex – whereas the Chinese cannot. How are such rules to be enforced in a mixed group of teenagers, or in the modern office or factory? 'Malaysia is in a position where nobody wants to call it a secular state, because that would offend Moslems,' says Adnan. 'Neither would you want to call it an Islamic state, because that would offend non-Moslems.' He adds: 'We see Chinese girls in the skimpiest of clothing in the middle of KL [Kuala Lumpur] and no one bats an eye. But if a Malay girl did it, there would be a hue and cry and talk of moral decay.'[5] Such talk is already widespread. Faced with rising drug addiction and crime and an increased incidence of teenage sex, the Malaysian government has mounted vocal campaigns against various 'social ills'. A particular concern for the authorities is that Malays appear to be proportionately more prone to problems than other races, possibly because of the turmoil resulting from recent migration to big cities. Between 1988 and 1996, official statistics showed that 69 per cent of drug addicts, 70 per cent of HIV carriers and 90 per cent of incest victims were Malays.[6] Some Malays, though, think the problem is not that Malays are worse behaved, but that their traditional social structures are more puritanical and therefore less able to deal with the effects of modernization: people are not supposed to drink alcohol or meet girlfriends and boyfriends at home, so they take drugs and hang around in shopping malls; babies born out of wedlock are not easily accepted into the family or put out to adoption as they might be by the Chinese, so embarrassed mothers leave them to die outside the village banana plantation. 'Mahathir says it's a Malay problem,' says the film-maker Hishamuddin Rais. 'But I'm sure Malay and Chinese youth are fucking at the same rate.'[7]

While he grappled with such problems Mahathir's economic plans became increasingly ambitious. The world's tallest buildings, the Petronas Towers originally designed for Chicago and now named after the Malaysian oil company, rise elegantly over central Kuala Lumpur. A project was devised to build the world's longest building as well – the so-called Linear City of shops, entertainment centres and apartments running above and around the Klang River. A modern airport designed to serve as an Asian hub was built outside the capital. A new administrative capital, meanwhile, was to be constructed at the heart of a 750-square-kilometre 'Multimedia Super Corridor', a high-technology zone to rival the 'Silicon Valley' area in California. In Borneo, work began on the huge Bakun dam, which was to supply electricity to the Malaysian peninsula. These projects had cost, were costing or would cost billions of dollars, putting a severe strain on the country's still modest economy. Critics began to accuse Mahathir of hubris. 'He seems to have a tendency for monumentalism,' said K.S. Jomo, a professor at the University of Malaya's faculty of economics and administration. 'It is the latest decade of growth which has sired this profligacy.'[8]

Nemesis, or something close to it, was not long in coming. Thailand's economic boom collapsed in 1997, sending Asian currencies and stock markets – including Malaysia's – spiralling downwards. Although the Malaysian crisis was not at first as severe as the one in neighbouring Thailand, the two countries had many problems in common, including a property bubble based on over-enthusiastic bank lending and a lacklustre performance from the manufactured exports which had hitherto driven economic growth. Mahathir's response was characteristically defiant. He accused foreign speculators of trying to undermine successful Asian economies, traded insults with the currency speculator George Soros, recommended a ban on unnecessary foreign currency trading and even suggested that there was a Jewish 'agenda' aimed against Moslems. Anwar Ibrahim, at the time Mahathir's deputy and anointed successor (and also the finance minister),[9] had the uncomfortable task of trying to reassure foreign investors without openly contradicting his prime minister. The government bowed to the inevitable and suspended or delayed several big infrastructure projects, including the Bakun dam (which was already struggling to find financing), Linear City and the new capital city.

Malaysia, it turned out, was economically competitive, but not as competitive as Mahathir seemed to think. With almost full employment in the cities, wages had risen faster than productivity. Big projects run by the new generation of Malay entrepreneurs had based much of their success on protectionism and favouritism; the Malaysian Proton car company, for instance, profited from tariff protection and government support to seize more than half the local car market, but was unlikely to have prospered in a free market for vehicles. Some did not succeed at all. The state-run Perwaja steel company collapsed in 1996 with debts of M\$6.9 billion. Umno, meanwhile, was racked by financial and sexual scandals and allegations of corruption. Muhammad Muhammad Taib, Umno vice-president, resigned as chief minister of the state of Selangor after being accused in Australia of failing to declare the equivalent of M\$2.4 million in cash when he was leaving Brisbane airport. (There was never any question that he had the money, but an Australian court acquitted him on the grounds that he had not intended to defy the regulations.) Both Mahathir and Anwar realized that the government, although still firmly in control, was losing the respect it had earned from economic success; in one speech to Umno members about 'money politics', Mahathir wept and said he feared that corruption, if left unchecked, would 'destroy the country'.[10] Malaysian leaders, who had been among the first to extrapolate economic growth rates decades ahead and conclude that the next century would be an 'Asian' or 'Pacific' century, now realized that they would have their work cut out to build a modern, fully industrialized and multiracial society that could be an example to the Islamic world.

INDONESIA
Fin de régime – and end of empire?

For its size and importance, Indonesia is one of the least understood countries in the world. Many Europeans and Americans would have trouble finding it on a map. Yet it is the world's fourth most populous nation and the largest Moslem one, and the biggest and most influential member of Asean. It extends for more than 5,000 kilometres, consists of more than 13,000 islands and has 200 million inhabitants. There are, however, good reasons for its obscurity. Indonesia does not conjure up in the minds of foreigners, or even its own citizens, the image of a homogeneous, powerful whole. A collection of territories won from the Dutch at independence in 1949 (it was known in colonial times as the Dutch East Indies), the country embraces hundreds of languages, dialects and ethnic groups: its official motto is 'Unity in Diversity'.

But there is no doubt about the dominance of the densely populated island of Java, the country's industrial and administrative centre, which accounts for more than half the country's population. Although the Javanese wisely chose a minority language from Sumatra as the nation's *lingua franca* (known as *Bahasa Indonesia*, it is very close to Malay), they have still been accused of running a Javanese empire. Since the 1950s, millions of Javanese have been sent from their overcrowded villages to settle the outer islands, a policy called 'transmigration' which has sometimes earned the newcomers the hostility of the existing inhabitants. Moslem fundamentalists in Aceh, on the northern tip of Sumatra, have fought a sporadic separatist war against Jakarta for years and been brutally suppressed by the army for their pains. There are also separatists in the remote territory of Irian Jaya (the western side of the island of New Guinea) at the other extremity of Indonesia. And there was a bout of savage bloodletting in West Kalimantan in Borneo in 1997 involving the native Dayaks and settlers from Madura, an island off Java: hundreds of people were killed, and the Dayaks were reported to have drunk the blood of their victims, beheaded them, removed their hearts and livers and impaled the mutilated bodies on stakes by the road.[1]

INDONESIA

Capital city:	Jakarta
Population (1995):	198 million
Government:	Interim authoritarian
Annual per capita GNP (1996):	US$1,080
Real economic growth 1995:	8.2 per cent
Real economic growth 1998 (estimate):	Minus 15 per cent
Main language:	Bahasa Indonesia
Main religion:	Islam
Date of independence:	1949
Former colonial power:	Netherlands

Sources: ADB; *Financial Times*; author.

That is not to say that Indonesia's nation-building has necessarily been a failure. 'The Javanese are getting to be less Javanese and the non-Javanese are getting to be more Javanese,' says Sarwono Kusumaatmadja, the former environment minister. 'If we make a mess of ourselves, a lot of nations will suffer, so the stability of the archipelago is a global asset . . . We are too heterogeneous to break apart. We are not a society composed of big blocs of ethnicity or religious identity. We are a country of very small mosaics.'[2] But it is with its occupation of East Timor that Indonesia has the most difficulty, especially on the diplomatic front. Indonesia launched an exceptionally brutal invasion of the former Portuguese territory in 1975, after the Portuguese revolution which precipitated Lisbon's hasty abandonment of its colonies. Out of a population of some 650,000, it is estimated that more than 100,000 Timorese were killed during and after the Indonesian annexation. The United Nations has refused to recognize Indonesian jurisdiction over East Timor, and Jakarta has made little progress in winning over the overwhelmingly Roman Catholic inhabitants of the region. Indonesian troops have contained East Timor's separatist Fretilin guerrillas, and the Fretilin leader Xanana Gusmão was captured in 1992, but the colonization of East Timor remains a constant embarrassment to a country that prides itself on its anti-colonial past. Indonesia's reputation was further tarnished by a massacre in the capital Dili in 1991: soldiers gunned down and bayoneted dozens of pro-independence Timorese who had marched to a cemetery to mourn one of their colleagues killed earlier, and the violence was captured on videotape and broadcast internationally. Five years later, there was yet more embarrassment for the Indonesian government when the 1996 Nobel Peace Prize was awarded to José Ramos Horta, the most prominent East Timor independence campaigner in exile, and Carlos Ximenes Belo, the region's Roman Catholic bishop. Soon afterwards Suharto, who was then still president, visited East Timor, shook hands with Belo and inaugurated a twenty-seven-metre-high statue of Christ (the size was said to allude to the incorporation of East Timor as Indonesia's twenty-seventh province). Sporadic violence has continued, however, and by 1998 the conflict was no closer to a solution. East Timorese hoped that the uprising in Jakarta which forced Suharto to step down in May 1998 would give them a better chance of negotiating independence or winning it on the battlefield. But for the Indonesian authorities in Jakarta, it would be unthinkable to let East Timor go; that would raise the prospect of secession by other islands and the disintegration of the Indonesian nation.

By 1997, the growing middle class in the capital Jakarta was worrying more about the inevitable *fin de régime* than the more remote prospect of an end of empire. Suharto and his 'New Order' administration were credited at home and abroad with having restored political stability and promoted economic growth after the chaos of the 1960s under his predecessor Sukarno. During the murky period of history following a suspected communist coup attempt in 1965, hundreds of thousands of people, mostly ethnic Chinese, are thought to have been killed in massacres inspired by anti-communism. Shortly afterwards, the quiet but effective General Suharto removed the flamboyant Sukarno and took his place as president. Whereas Sukarno had been the Father of Independence, Suharto became known as the Father of Development. He brought in western-trained Indonesian experts, labelled the 'Berkeley mafia', to run the economy, which – helped by revenues from exports of oil and gas – they successfully did. Economic reforms encouraged foreign investors from Japan, the US and elsewhere to make Indonesia a base for low-cost production of shoes and textiles; factories sprang up where once there had been rice fields. In most of Indonesia, peace prevailed for thirty years.

But unease was growing by the time the ailing Suharto approached the end of his sixth five-year term as president in 1998. He was in his mid-seventies, but had not designated a successor to lead what everyone knew to be a fragile union of disparate cultures. Corruption was rampant, and there was widespread resentment of the extraordinary favours granted to the fast-growing business empires of his six children, not to mention his grandchildren and other relatives. They were or had been involved in a long list of lucrative activities, including toll-roads, telecommunications, petrochemicals and the importing of cars, as well as badly run monopolies in the trading of cloves and the production of urea fertilizer tablets. Suharto's associates, particularly ethnic Chinese billionaires such as Liem Sioe Liong and Mohammad 'Bob' Hasan (Hasan had converted to Islam) were also envied for their control of key business sectors such as cement and timber. What would happen to these tycoons and their businesses after Suharto had gone? Would they be protected or persecuted?

How many of their assets had they moved overseas to preserve their wealth from the possible depredations of a new regime? The nervousness was exacerbated by the realization that the anger of the poor directed against the rich was all too easily translated into explosive conflicts between Moslems and Christians, or between Javanese (or other local inhabitants) and Chinese. Ethnic Chinese account for only about 5 per cent of the population, but own most of the country's large and medium-sized businesses. In the mid-1990s there were numerous reports of Moslems burning down churches and attacking Chinese shops. Various prominent figures were touted as possible presidential candidates for the future, including Suharto's children, senior military officers, and B. J. Habibie, the research and technology minister who had secured state finding for the country's ambitious aircraft-building and ship-building projects. 'Why are 190 million people so helpless and waiting for the answer to come out from Suharto himself as to whether he wants to run [for president] or not?' complained Marsillam Simandjuntak, a prominent critic of the government. 'Why can't the 190 million people decide for themselves?'[3]

In the end, the people did decide, but not before Suharto had duly begun his seventh term and chosen B. J. Habibie as his vice-president. As the Indonesian currency reeled from the effects of the south-east Asian financial crisis (it was Indonesia that was the region's worst-hit economy) food and other prices rose and Indonesians took to the streets to protest against the corrupt rule of the Suharto family. Many of the demonstrators were students, and when troops shot six of them dead at Trisakti University in Jakarta on May 12, it was the beginning of the end for the Suharto regime. In the orgy of looting, murder and protests that followed in the capital, at least 1,188 Indonesians were killed, according to a local human-rights organization. Suharto's former political allies turned against him, and finally, on May 21, after thirty-two years in power, Suharto made a brief statement on television from his palace. 'I have decided to hereby declare that I withdraw from my position as the president of the Republic of Indonesia,' he said. 'I express my deepest sorrow if there were mistakes, failures and shortcomings.'

B. J. Habibie took over the presidency, but he was no more popular than Suharto and had strange ideas about economics that worried foreign investors. (He was notorious not just for his heavy expenditure on government industrial projects but for his 'zigzag' theory, according to which interest rates should be lowered, then raised and then lowered again to boost economic growth.) He freed some political prisoners and promised that electoral laws would be reformed and new elections held in 1999. Meanwhile, Indonesians were demanding a full accounting of the Suharto years. In particular, they wanted to trace the wealth of Suharto, his relatives and associates, no easy task when the former first family controlled some 1,200 companies spread through almost every sector of the economy.

For the first time in decades, almost anything seemed possible in Indonesian politics in the tumultuous days after Suharto's fall. The army remained strong, and saw itself as the ultimate guarantor of national unity. Megawati Sukarnoputri, the uncharismatic daughter of Sukarno who had challenged Suharto in 1997, was again named as a possible contender for political power. But leaders with Islamic agendas also emerged into the political limelight: Amien Rais, a university lecturer who heads the Muhammadiyah, the country's second biggest Moslem organization, was touted as a possible presidential candidate. Indonesia's neighbours were apprehensive. The end of the Suharto regime was much less bloody than it might have been, but the country's political direction remained uncertain and its economy was in tatters (gross domestic product was expected to shrink by as much as 10 per cent in 1998). Yet Indonesia remained by far the biggest and most important member of Asean.[4]

Politics under Suharto had been based on two pillars. One was *dwifungsi*, the 'dual function' which the armed forces had granted themselves so that they could play a sociopolitical role as well as a military one. General H. B. L. Mantiri, chief of general staff, said in 1994 that the army saw itself as the 'shepherd' of Indonesians. 'Our dual function will last for ever and ever,' he declared.[5] The other was *pancasila*, the vague 'five principles' ideology that prescribed belief in God; just and civilized humanitarianism; national unity; democracy through consultation and consensus; and social justice. On these pillars sat a superficially democratic structure allowing three political parties to participate in elections. Golkar was the government party which always won, and the opposition consisted of the Indonesian Democratic Party (PDI, which was broadly supposed to represent left-wingers) and the United Development Party (PPP, which brought together Moslem interests). However, only

425 members of the 1,000-seat People's Consultative Assembly were elected, with 500 appointed by the president and a further seventy-five nominated by the armed forces.

These arrangements, patronizing as they were, had served the Suharto government comfortably for many years with only minor adjustments. But the abuses of power permitted by the system and the lack of genuine representation that it perpetuated made the official practice of politics seem irrelevant, even ludicrous, to many Indonesians. Suharto's authoritarian government had lifted millions of Indonesians out of poverty (and raised a few to previously unimaginable wealth), but it proved unable to modernize itself to accommodate the aspirations of Indonesia's newly educated citizens. Now that Suharto was gone, the way was clear for wholesale political reform – provided the army did not step in too clumsily with its own interpretation of what was good for Indonesia.

SINGAPORE
Brutal efficiency

Abraham Isaac's downfall was engineered in the most Machiavellian manner. Melancholy now, the Singaporean Indian recalls how he lost his job as a teacher after criticizing the government's repressive methods in an article in the Teachers' Union newsletter. His accusers could not think of anything illegal about the article itself, so they framed false charges: that he had insulted his school principal and refused to teach a class. Witnesses who knew the truth were too frightened to testify ('I have a wife. I have children. I have to, you know . . . toe the line') or mysteriously unable to attend the hearing. In a final, cruel twist, an education ministry official suggested with feigned outrage that his most serious offence was to have dared to say that the government had put pressure on the principal to frame the bogus charges. The scene is low-key but sinister. It is also fiction – Abraham is the creation of the writer and lawyer Philip Jeyaretnam, the son of a disillusioned opposition leader – but it is painfully close to the truth: many a Singaporean dissident would recognize the machinations of the authorities and the mood of despair afflicting those who try to oppose the ruling People's Action Party. As Abraham laments earlier in the story after meeting a particularly smug and odious government politician: 'Is there no-one who can articulate a future other than the superficially material . . . ? Or will any such man inevitably be crushed, the immense machinery of government turned against him, while our citizens lower their heads and busy themselves, making money for the good of the nation, or else wining and dining prospective spouses in the pursuit of babies, another national duty in which I never excelled.'[1]

Unlike many other authoritarian states, Singapore is an economic success. Since its divorce from the Malaysian federation in 1965, this multiracial island (77 per cent of its three million citizens are Chinese, and most of the rest are Malays and Indians) has undergone a very rapid industrial revolution and boosted its per capita income to levels higher than that of most western countries. Singapore is a paragon of high-technology efficiency. Each year it wins a string

263

SINGAPORE

Capital city:	Singapore
Population (1995):	2.8 million
Government:	Authoritarian elected
Annual per capita GNP (1996):	US$30,550
Real economic growth 1995:	8.7 per cent
Real economic growth 1998 (estimate):	1.5 per cent
Main language:	English
Main religion:	Various
Date of independence:	1965 (separated from Malaysia)
Former colonial power:	Britain

Sources: ADB; *Financial Times*; author.

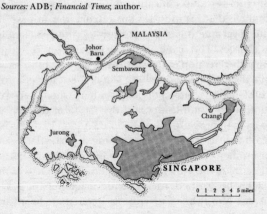

of accolades from various international bodies: most competitive country; best airport; least corrupt and least bureaucratic country in Asia. Such achievements are made possible partly by its manageable size. As George Yeo, the minister for information and the arts, once wrote, Singapore would suffer the same high crime rates, pollution and other problems of fast-growing Third World cities if it were not able to control the movement of people into the country. 'Instead of indiscriminate urban drift, we select migrants based on talent, income and other criteria,' he said.[2] Another writer commented slightly less charitably on Singapore's small size when he said that it was 'Monaco writ large, not China writ small'.[3] Yet another called it 'Disneyland with a death penalty'.[4] But there is no doubting the attractiveness of Singapore's cleanliness, efficiency, prosperity and relatively low crime rate for multinational companies, foreign tourists and for Singaporeans themselves. Basking in the economic successes of their authoritarian, materialistic vision, Singapore's leaders have become some of the most forceful proponents of 'Asian values', lecturing other Asian governments on the merits of the Singaporean method.

For Singaporeans, however, there is a less pleasant side to their economic triumphs. It is not merely that dissidents have been persecuted or driven into exile. There is also a fear of the bureaucracy and a lack of spontaneity which repels some foreigners and worries many Singaporeans. Some have emigrated; others – rather like the Arab citizens of the Gulf states – have jobs in their own country but spend as much time as possible elsewhere. Yeo once lamented that Singapore had created a 'five-star hotel' rather than an organically integrated community. Goh Chok Tong, the prime minister, mourned the fact that his school friends were in the US or Australia, 'seemingly failing to note', as one academic put it, 'that they had chosen to go to those same societies which his country's officials had typified as being morally and economically bankrupt'.[5] Fears of increased emigration may have been one of the reasons behind 'Singapore Our Best Home', an oddly named campaign to make Singapore safer than ever and create what Home Minister Wong Kan Seng called 'a society that is vibrant and confident in every sphere of life'.[6] This was only one of a torrent of government campaigns over the years urging Singaporeans to be patriotic, turn up at wedding parties on time, flush the lavatory, not be too greedy at buffets, be courteous, have fewer babies (when the population was rising fast), and now to have more babies ('Children. Life would be empty without them,' was the solemn declaration on one public poster in 1997). There is even a 'Social Development Unit', an official match-making service to promote marriage and family values. Some of the government's methods, like its housing estates of numbered tower blocks in which most Singaporeans live, have more than a hint of old-fashioned communism, even Orwellian totalitarianism. But the government insists that constant striving for greater efficiency is essential if Singapore is to survive and succeed. 'Andy Grove [former boss of the US microprocessor company Intel] titled his autobiography *Only the Paranoid Survive*,' said Lee Hsien Loong, the deputy prime minister. 'It could be Singapore's motto.'[7] Asked if Singapore was like the ancient city of Sparta, Lee replied with another classical comparison: 'Sparta is too austere. But Sisyphus – you are always pushing the stone up the hill and if you let go, it goes down again and you may never be able to push it again. You are in a special situation. If you were twenty million or a hundred million [people] then you would be different – you have a critical mass, you have land, you have resources, maybe if you're lucky a bit of oil and a bit of uranium and then if the government makes a hash of things, well you subsist and one day you have a better government. Australia is in such a position . . . but Singapore, no.' He added: 'We are perpetually wondering who's next going to come along who may eat us up.'[8]

The architect of Singapore's success since independence is Lee Kuan Yew, Lee Hsien Loong's father, who hammers home the message about vulnerability by reminding Singaporeans of the way in which Japanese troops seized the island – then a supposedly impregnable British stronghold – during the Second World War. The LSE- and Cambridge-educated elder Lee, who handed over the Prime Minister's post to Goh in 1990 and now has the title of Senior Minister, is an intelligent and arrogant man with little tolerance for opposition. 'The central mystery is, why the need for such total dominance? And it's really hard to explain that,' says one of his Singaporean critics, who requested anonymity. 'Maybe the Senior Minister believes fervently that if he lets things slip even a little bit, they will just explode.'[9] Lee and his successors have maintained the institutions of liberal democracy, including an elected parliament, and they deny accusations of nepotism and of manipulating the justice system. But since independence they have constrained both the local and foreign press, used the government's control of the housing market to cow voters into supporting the PAP, detained some political opponents without trial, driven others into exile and relentlessly pursued others with flurries of libel actions from government ministers which would not succeed in other jurisdictions. The result, according to Christopher Lingle, an American academic working in Singapore who fled back home to escape one such court action from the elder Lee, is 'phobocracy' – rule by fear. 'Paranoiac control over information, rule by fear, the imposition of paternalistic dependency, intimidation of opposition politicians and an effective propaganda campaign allows Singapore's authoritarian-capitalist regime to hide behind an unwarranted pristine image,' he wrote. 'On the basis of court rulings, almost every major political dissident in post-Independence Singapore has been found to be a tax cheat, a reprobate, a liar, a member of some international conspiracy and/or a (bankrupt) libeler.'[10] Ordinary Singaporeans grumble about the enormous salaries of government ministers (the salaries match private-sector pay and help prevent corruption, the government says) and high prices; as one author has pointed out, Singaporeans have a Swiss *cost* of living, but not a Swiss *standard* of living.[11] Yet they vote in overwhelming numbers for the ruling PAP, and only a handful of the government's opponents continue the unequal struggle. One such is the young neuropsychologist and former MP Chee Soon Juan, himself the target of various court actions, who points out that most voters are anxious not to offend the authorities. 'In Singapore, anything you do, you need a licence – taxi, lawyer, doctor – you need a licence renewable every year.' He says: 'I don't think they can victimize everybody, but nevertheless it's a significant level of fear.'[12] But the dissident who most puts the government to shame is the quiet-spoken socialist Chia Thye Poh. He refused to say what the government wanted him to say – that he was a communist – because he said it was untrue; and he therefore refused to beg for an amnesty. He was detained in jail in Singapore from 1966 for more than twenty-three years without being charged or brought to trial, followed by three years of confinement to the tourist island of Sentosa; even in 1997 he was still subject to government restrictions on political activity, although he insisted on his right to tell his own story. 'I have never been a threat to the country or the security of the country,' he said. 'It's just that I'm having a different political view to the party in power.' Even in white-ruled South Africa, he said, Nelson Mandela had been charged. 'Yet in Singapore I've never been charged or convicted of anything and I'm not a free man. And I'm not a man of Mandela's stature. I'm just a member of parliament.'[13]

But with the economy expanding rapidly, Chia's fate was of little concern to the average Singaporean. The government began to develop Singapore as a transport and services hub for Asia, not so much through laissez-faire, free-market policies that encouraged entrepreneurs (as commonly believed by outsiders who wrongly assumed that Singapore was like Hong Kong), but by means of vigorous central planning. Singapore was not quite as backward when the British left as is sometimes suggested by its promoters: it was already a significant international port, and not a primitive fishing village. But the post-independence government embarked on a vigorous programme to promote economic growth. It welcomed high-tech multinational companies, making Singapore a big exporter of disc drives; enforced high savings by its citizens and ran conservative economic policies; ensured that transport links inside Singapore and between the island and the outside world were highly efficient; raised the standard of education; and promoted tourism. This 'command economy' approach to the development of infrastructure evidently worked. The port, for example, became the busiest in the world in terms of tonnage; more than 800 ships are in Singapore at any one time and the port serves more than 360 shipping lines.[14]

By the 1990s there were three new prongs to government economic strategy. First, there was a recognition that Singapore needed to promote entrepreneurialism and gradually expose state-run corporations to market competition. 'Now there are enough people, the level of education of the people at large, the qualifications are such that you can trust the market to be able to respond effectively, and therefore the all-pervasive hand of government in the micro part [of the economy] is no longer necessary,' said Goon Kok Loon of the Port of Singapore Authority.[15] Second, there was a drive to persuade Singapore's state and private companies to invest overseas, especially in Asia and especially in sectors (such as infrastructure) where they were strong, to overcome the limitations of the island's small domestic market; billions of dollars have been invested in

China, Indonesia and elsewhere, although in many cases it is still too early to measure the success of these Singaporean projects. Third, Singapore decided to become an 'intelligent island', by which the government meant it would promote computerization as widely and deeply as possible to improve the efficiency of business and government and make life easier for its citizens.

Singapore's leaders thus hope they can perpetuate their success by adding computers and a dash of economic liberalization to the old combination of political and social engineering and state economic leadership. Some people have expressed doubts about the ability of a society so hostile to the free flow of information to produce the technical innovation and creative thinking thought to be necessary for successful competition in the information age. So far, Lee Kuan Yew and his followers have confounded their critics, and they believe they can continue to do so by remaining constantly alert for signs of weakness in the fabric of Singapore society. White South Africa was obsessed by fears of a 'total onslaught' from hostile communist outsiders, and Singapore has devised the concept of 'total defence' to include civilians as well as soldiers in the protection of the nation from military invasion and other malign foreign influences. Like South Africans, however, Singaporeans may find that the strongest pressures for change come not from outside, but from within.

BRUNEI
Sultan of swing

The small Borneo sultanate of Brunei Darussalam ('place of peace') is a political and economic misfit in modern south-east Asia. It reluctantly attained independence in 1984 at the insistence of an embarrassed Britain keen to rid itself of one of its last colonial responsibilities, and has more in common with the Islamic monarchies of the Gulf than with its neighbours. Like the Gulf states, Brunei is rich in oil and gas. The income from the oilfields developed by Shell has made Sultan Hassanal Bolkiah one of the richest men in the world and financed a lavish welfare state (known as the Shellfare state) for his subjects. As in the Gulf, there is no clear distinction between the income of the Sultan and the income of the state, the economy is dependent on foreign workers, and the secretive government makes no pretence of being democratic. Brunei, furthermore, adopts the same hypocritical mixture of public religiosity and private hedonism. Islamic codes of conduct apply inside the country. Alcohol (previously available to non-Moslems) was banned entirely in 1991. A typical item on the evening news shows a tribal village family publicly renouncing animism or Christianity and embracing Islam; they are rewarded with gifts and a visit from a senior government official such as the permanent secretary from the Ministry of Defence. Brunei's ruling family believes that a combination of Islamic chauvinism and largesse will endow them with political legitimacy and disarm any Islamic fundamentalist opponents, but their private behaviour has been called into question in a flurry of recent court cases.

Brunei's history goes back more than a thousand years. It was once a trading empire with extensive territories under its control, but the arrival of the colonial powers, and in particular the depredations of James Brooke, the white 'rajah' of Sarawak, in the nineteenth century, has left it today with two separate chunks of land surrounded by Sarawak, which is now part of Malaysia. It was fortunate for the Sultans of Brunei that oil was discovered at Seria, within the rump of their empire, in the early twentieth century. Sultan Omar, the

BRUNEI

Capital city:	Bandar Seri Begawan
Population (1995):	285,000
Government:	Authoritarian monarchy
Annual per capita income (1997, estimate):	US$17,000
Real economic growth 1995:	n/a
Real economic growth 1998 (estimate):	n/a
Main language:	Malay
Main religion:	Islam
Date of independence:	1984
Former colonial power:	Britain

Sources: World Bank; Reuters; author.

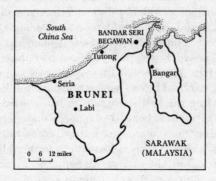

devout Moslem and anglophile who was father of the present Sultan, is credited with forging modern Brunei with the help of the early oil revenues. When the left-wing Brunei People's Party won the country's first election in 1962 and promised to introduce democracy, Sultan Omar refused to let them take power, and successfully called on the assistance of Britain's elite Gurkha troops to crush a subsequent rebellion, using emergency powers that have remained in force ever since. He abdicated and pushed his twenty-one-year-old, Sandhurst-trained son on to the throne in 1967 to defuse demands for democracy from the British Labour government of the time.

The wealth of Brunei – and of the Sultan – grew rapidly after the sharp rise in oil prices in the 1970s, allowing members of the ruling family to practise profligacy on a hitherto unimagined scale, buying the best hotels, cars, aircraft, jewels, furniture and clothes that London, Singapore or the rest of the world had to offer. The Sultan is reputed to have more than 150 Rolls-Royce cars, and the Istana Nurul Iman, the Sultan's main palace and the home of his first wife Queen Saleha, is said to have 1,788 rooms, including a throne room the size of a football pitch. His second wife, Queen Mariam, a former air hostess of mixed British and Japanese parentage, lives in the Istana Nurul Izza. Members of the royal family can afford to fly popular music stars and beauty queens to Brunei for their entertainment, and to hire the best sportsmen to teach their children the finer arts of football or snooker. Discretion is understandably much prized in Brunei, and there was intense embarrassment in the country in 1997 when Shannon Marketic, a former Miss California and Miss USA, claimed in a US sexual harassment case that she was held captive in the main palace for use as a sex slave. She said she was one of a group of women expected to act like prostitutes for a group of wealthy men attending nightly parties at the palace sports complex, and she demanded compensation from the Sultan and his brother Prince Jefri. Both men rejected the allegations and said they had never met her, and both were eventually dismissed as defendants in the suit on the basis that they were protected by the Foreign Sovereign Immunities Act. Ms Marketic, however, promptly filed another lawsuit.[1] In February 1998, Robert Manoukian, a former friend of Prince Jefri who was fighting a legal battle with him over business deals that had fallen through, told the High Court in London that the prince would pay for as many as forty prostitutes at a time to come to the Dorchester Hotel for his and his friends' entertainment. That case was settled out of court.[2]

Inevitably, the Sultan's enormous wealth has attracted the attention of unsavoury businessmen and salesmen from all over the world, and his representatives are often the first to receive a call when large sums of money are required in a hurry – whether for the rescue of a British institution such as Barings, the merchant bank which collapsed in 1995, or to finance a US undercover operation. But Brunei's chequebook diplomacy has not been a great success. The public fiasco over Brunei's contribution to US-backed Nicaraguan rebels was particularly embarrassing. The Sultan quietly donated $10 million to the cause, earning the gratitude of the US, but the cheque was deposited in the wrong account in Switzerland, to the delight of a Swiss shipping magnate. By the time the muddle was sorted out, the Iran-Contra scandal was breaking in the US and it was deemed safer to return the money to Brunei.[3]

At home, the earnings from oil and gas and Brunei's overseas investments can be used for decades to come – but not for ever – to delay political and economic reform. The government is believed to have substantial foreign exchange reserves, while the Brunei Investment Agency has estimated assets of about $50 billion. Then there is the Sultan's personal wealth – probably about $40 billion – and billions of dollars in a secretive 'Future Generations Fund', similar to the funds established in several Gulf states for the same purpose. The ruling family often buys hotels and other properties and resells them to the investment agency, and there is little clarity about the dividing lines between the various asset-holding institutions.[4] As in the Gulf, Bruneians are pampered from cradle to grave. Half the citizens of working age have easy jobs as civil servants. They pay no tax and most services are free. Per capita income is among the highest in the world. Even amusement is free of charge: the Sultan had the huge Jerudong Park playground built for Brunei's 300,000 people near his polo pitches; Bruneians and migrant workers – who do the menial jobs – can be seen playing video games, wandering among the fountains and sampling the go-karts and fairground rides each night. Most food is imported, some of it from cattle ranches in Australia that cover more territory than Brunei. 'The structure of the economy is simple,' wrote James Bartholomew, author of one of the few books on Brunei. 'Shell extracts the oil and gas, the royal family takes a large slice of the profit and the rest of the profit provides money to keep the Malay Bruneians in government sinecures. The Chinese pick up what they can by keeping the shop.'[5]

The Sultan's ample financial handouts to Bruneians have weakened the democratic political opposition to the royal family, and Brunei says it has released its last political prisoners.[6] But the combination of rapid population growth – more than 40 per cent of Bruneians are under twenty – and a stagnant economy mean that unemployment is rising and Islamic fundamentalism remains a force to be reckoned with. Political manoeuvrings remain opaque – Prince Jefri resigned as Finance Minister in 1997 and handed the portfolio to his brother the Sultan, who was already Prime Minister and Defence Minister – but Brunei has begun to make efforts to diversify its economy in order to reduce its dependence on oil and gas. Its forests are relatively unspoilt and the authorities want to promote 'eco-tourism' as an alternative source of income,[7] although logging appears to be increasing as oil revenues decline, and forest fires seem to be common. Brunei maintains close military ties with Britain and Singapore, and its currency is fixed one-to-one with the Singapore dollar. It has been a member of Asean since independence in 1984, but remains on the sidelines and rarely takes the initiative at Asean meetings.

Brunei, however, is by no means ready to compete in the world economy after the oil and gas has run out. There is an air of listlessness in the capital Bandar Seri Begawan. On a typical day, migrant workers can be seen wandering gloomily around the shops in their time off while bored Bruneians cross the border into Malaysia to find prostitutes and alcohol. In Kampong Ayer, the wooden suburb on stilts in a river estuary, Brunei residents sleepily watch satellite television while monitor lizards pick their way between discarded metal air conditioners and plastic bags in the mud below. Out in Seria, Shell's employees are in the field, in their offices or in their comfortable houses in a sprawling compound criss-crossed with pipes and adorned with the occasional old 'nodding donkey' oil well (the bigger rigs are visible out at sea); an Englishwoman and some Dutch friends are trying to find homes for stray dogs picked up by the health authorities. Change will certainly come to Brunei one day, as it will come to the Gulf states thousands of miles to the west, but neither the Sultan, nor the majority of his pampered citizens, nor his foreign workers seem in any hurry to bring about the transformation from absolute to constitutional monarchy that has already happened in Thailand and Malaysia.

THE PHILIPPINES
Chaotic democracy

'Now open: guns for the good guys', trumpets a typical weapons-shop advertisement in the *Manila Bulletin*, one of the plethora of lively daily newspapers in the Philippines. It is selling semi-automatic weapons and sub-machine guns. Another advertisement is offering 'tested reliability' in the form of a Norinco .45 calibre pistol, which 'comes with two magazines, plus cleaning kit'.[1] The Philippines is no ordinary south-east Asian country, as any traveller arriving at the chaotic Ninoy Aquino international airport – named after the politician assassinated during the reign of the dictator Ferdinand Marcos – soon finds out. Where else do restaurants boast 'singing cooks and waiters'? Where else are the streets packed with 'jeepneys', the colourful, home-made cars and vans based loosely on the wartime American Jeep? Where else do people call their politicians – and themselves – by nicknames such as 'Bongbong' and 'Baby'? Although the Philippines sees itself in economic and security terms as part of south-east Asia, Filipinos still look across the Pacific to the US for many of their cultural and political cues. Occupied by Spain in the sixteenth century (it was the Spanish King Philip II who gave the archipelago its name, and Spanish missionaries who ensured that most Filipinos today are Roman Catholic), the Philippines fell into American hands during the Spanish-American war in 1898 and thus became the only major US colony. This unusual combination of influences led to the now standard explanation for the character of the Philippines: 'Three centuries in a Roman Catholic convent and fifty years in Hollywood'. More than a million people of Filipino origin live in the US, and the US has heavily influenced the way people talk, eat and entertain themselves.

More important, perhaps, is the legacy of America's political and judicial systems. By Asian standards, Filipinos are extraordinarily litigious: to the exasperation of foreign businesses, there hardly seems to be any commercial matter of any importance, be it a price rise or a privatization contract, which is not referred to the Supreme Court. Like Americans, Filipinos also enjoy the sentimental razzmatazz of

PHILIPPINES

Capital city:	Manila
Population (1995):	68 million
Government:	Democratically elected
Annual per capita GNP (1997, estimate):	US$1,160
Real economic growth 1995:	4.8 per cent
Real economic growth 1998 (estimate):	Minus 0.5 per cent
Main language:	Tagalog, English
Main religion:	Roman Catholicism
Date of independence:	1946
Former colonial power:	US (preceded by Spain)

Sources: ADB; Asia Pacific Consensus Forecasts; author.

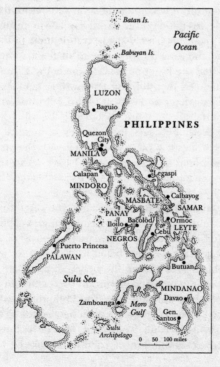

expensive election campaigns. And the people they elect have much the same problems as their American counterparts: the president and the administration are repeatedly stymied by congressmen and -women beholden to special interests. It is therefore difficult to implement political or business decisions in the Philippines. This inheritance of US-style democracy puts the Philippines in an interesting position in the debate over 'Asian values'. After independence in 1946, the Philippines was one of the richest countries in Asia, but it has since been overtaken by most of its neighbours. Authoritarians argue that the fault lies with an overdose of quarrelsome democracy, a bad idea for a developing country that may need to implement unpopular policies for the general good. 'The south-east Asian caricature of Filipinos is that if there are five at a meeting, there will be six different factions,' says political columnist Alex Magno.[2] Democrats retort that much of the Philippines' economic backwardness can be blamed on Marcos, who was popular when first elected but went on to become a dictator well before the end of his twenty-year rule; his nationalistic 'crony capitalism' protected various sectors of the economy from outside competition to the benefit of his friends and the long-term detriment of the nation. Democrats also point out that the Philippines, far from being a true democracy, is unduly influenced by a few big landowning families which have vast powers of patronage and appear to prosper whoever is in power. 'It's very personalistic and the [belief in] the whole tradition of democracy is overdone,' says Juan Flavier, a medical doctor and Senator whose honesty is often contrasted with the venality of the 'trapos' or traditional politicians.[3] 'And I have yet to see a Filipino politician lose gracefully. It's always, "I was cheated". We are not sportsmanlike, we are not statesmanlike.'[4]

Few doubt the need for firm leadership. It is often forgotten that, before he was murdered, the mercurial Benigno 'Ninoy' Aquino, now a martyr for democracy, shared Marcos's distrust of the country's chaotic political system and his belief in the need for authoritarian rule. The problem with Marcos, he believed, was that he had been authoritarian without being economically successful.[5] In recent years, there have been hopeful signs that the Philippines will be able to strike a balance between democracy and effectiveness in government, although the struggle is far from over: Marcos was overthrown in the 'people power' revolution of 1986 and replaced by Benigno's widow Corazon Aquino; she was also a member of the influential Cojuangco family and therefore the cousin of one of Marcos's cronies. Under her weak presidency, democracy was restored but there were seven attempted coups d'état and the economy was neglected. General Fidel Ramos, who had switched sides from Marcos at the last minute to help her to victory in 1986 and subsequently protected her from the soldiers who wanted to oust her, won her endorsement and went on to win the 1992 presidential election. The cigar-chomping Ramos – a cousin of Marcos – inherited an economy in tatters, but succeeded in turning it around during his six-year term. 'Steady Eddie', as he is known, presided over an urgent programme of power-station construction to end the chronic electricity shortages bequeathed by Aquino; liberalized financial markets and allowed foreign banks into the domestic banking sector; dismantled monopolies in telecommunications, oil, civil aviation, power and water; boosted electronics exports; and helped push a long overdue package of tax reforms through Congress. 'These are laws that should have been put in place forty years ago, but we are doing it now,' he said of his economic legislation. What is more, he did it through the democratic system, in spite of the scepticism of Asian authoritarians such as Lee Kuan Yew of Singapore and of other foreigners. 'I'm not experiencing the gridlock that you [foreign commentators] always accuse the Philippine leadership of having,' he said. 'The Philippines is still the model of respect for human rights and democracy in south-east Asia.'[6]

But the battle over the future of the Philippine political system continued. Having restored Philippine pride and set the country on the path towards becoming a 'tiger' economy, Ramos discreetly let it be known that he was interested in serving a second term – forbidden by the constitution to avoid a repeat of the Marcos experience. Liberals and left-wingers, including Corazon 'Cory' Aquino, campaigned vigorously against the efforts of Ramos and his supporters to do the 'cha-cha', an abbreviation of 'charter change' – in other words, they opposed the attempt to change the constitution. Some of them even suggested that Ramos had Marcos-like dictatorial tendencies. Ramos was forced to back down. Yet this in turn aroused fears that the country would suffer from the chaotic populism that lies at the other extreme of the political spectrum from dictatorship. This was seen as a particular risk because opinion polls showed the favoured candidate for the 1998 presidential election to be Vice-President Joseph 'Erap' Estrada, a hard-drinking B-movie actor and nightclub owner who seemed to have little interest in economic policy.[7] (It is one of the peculiarities of Philippine politics that the president and vice-president are elected separately, so a president can end up with a deputy who was not on his ticket.) 'I will be pro-poor and pro-country,' Estrada would say vaguely in response to such criticisms.[8] Many educated Filipinos, while dreading the possibility of another Marcos, were equally afraid that a populist president would throw away the hard-won economic gains of the 1990s. 'Look who people elect!' declared Bernadette Madrid, a paediatrician in Manila. 'They elect only actors and actresses because they cannot distinguish what is real. People think of his films and think he is that,' she said, alluding to Estrada's film roles as a Robin Hood figure who defended the poor. 'I feel we shouldn't change the constitution, but we should have a strong government. I just feel that democracy as it is practised in the United States may not be for us because we still have very naïve voters – politically immature.'[9] It certainly remains true that Filipino voters are easily dazzled, as the return from exile – and election to the Senate – of Imelda Marcos, glamorous and notorious widow of Ferdinand, makes clear. As one journalist wrote: 'Where else but the Philippines, where fact and fiction, forgiving and forgetfulness merge so seamlessly, would Imelda be able to return unvanquished, brushing aside prison sentences totalling forty-two years for corruption to take a seat in Congress?'[10] As predicted, Estrada was elected president in 1998. He quickly affirmed his commitment to the economic reforms begun by Ramos, and the business community – having watched his rise to power with mounting horror – were obliged to accept him and hope for the best.

Weak as the Philippine political system may be when it comes to decision-making, it enjoys one big advantage over its south-east Asian rivals: openness. Indeed, it is the openness which creates many of the difficulties, since every interested party demands the right to have its say and policy debates can drag on interminably. The benefit of this, according to optimistic Filipinos, is that they have already fought many of the bruising battles which other Asians, ruled by secretive and authoritarian governments in league with favoured business allies, have yet to undergo. 'When you become affluent and you can't speak and can't oppose and can't have freedom of assembly,' says Roberto Romulo, a former foreign minister and chairman of the PLDT telephone company, 'I would suggest they are going to go through a cycle which is *déjà vu* for us.' Economic liberalization – a particularly pressing issue after the 1997 financial crisis – is enacted by a process of debate and is therefore not as vulnerable as it would be in a country where it was pushed through on 'the whim of some autocrats'.[11] The Philippines was certainly less hard hit than its neighbours in the first year of the crisis. Another businessman reflecting on the violent events leading up to the resignation of President Suharto in neighbouring Indonesia, said tartly: 'We may have elected a clown to be our president, but at least we don't have dead students on the streets.'[12]

Yet several serious obtacles to the prosperity of the Philippines remain in place. First, a sense of economic nationalism that runs counter to the tide of global liberalization is never far beneath the surface, although a decade has passed since the Marcoses fled to the United States. In November 1997, the Supreme Court declared unconstitutional a law deregulating the country's oil sector, having already baffled foreign and local investors by refusing to allow the oil companies to raise the local price of imported fuel to compensate for a sharp fall in the value of the Philippine peso. Earlier in the year the Court cancelled a privatization deal to sell the government-owned Manila Hotel to a foreign-led consortium on the grounds that the hotel was part of the 'national patrimony', and awarded the contract to a local group that bid less. Other privatizations suffered from similar problems, while mining companies were discouraged from making new investments by a law protecting the rights of indigenous peoples which appeared to conflict with other legislation. Such laws and court decisions reflect the near-impossibility of persuading people to make difficult choices. To a greater degree than other democrats, it seems, Filipinos complain bitterly about power cuts, but are reluctant to pay a realistic price for electricity; insist on the right to government services, but shy away from paying taxes to finance them; and resent traffic congestion and pollution, but will take to the streets to protest against increases in the price of fuel. As the Filipino statesman Manuel Quezon remarked in the early part of the twentieth century to his fellow politician Sergio Osmeña: 'The trouble with you is that you take this game of politics too seriously. You look too far behind you and too far ahead of you. Our people do not understand that. They do not want it. All they want is to have the present problem solved, and solved with the least pain. That is all.'[13]

Another obstacle to Philippine prosperity is violence. Under Corazon Aquino and then under Ramos, the government made peace with various insurgent groups. The most notable deal was with Moslem guerrillas in the southern island of Mindanao; four provinces of the island were made into an autonomous region under Nur Misuari of the Moro National Liberation Front, peace returned, and investors started to show an interest in this hitherto neglected part of the Philippines. It was not long before a more radical group, the Moro Islamic Liberation Front, broke the peace with a series of attacks.[14] But the Philippines suffers from gangsterism and a gun culture that goes far beyond politically motivated groups. Violent crime, particularly the kidnapping of wealthy ethnic Chinese, is common, and the police who are supposed to catch the criminals are sometimes implicated in the crimes themselves. Small wonder, then, that many of the wealthier inhabitants of Manila live in guarded 'villages' isolated from the mean streets outside.

Last, but not least, of the Philippines' problems is its reluctance to control the growth of its population. This is not a fashionable topic in these anti-Malthusian days, but there are many people – including Catholic Filipinos – who point out that the fast-swelling population makes it difficult to improve per capita income and puts an intolerable strain both on urban services and on natural resources, a strain that other south-east Asian countries with more effective family planning programmes have not had to bear.[15] 'The failure of the Philippines in this area leaves a hardworking, largely literate population with an almost insurmountable burden of poverty and makes future development . . . painfully slow,' wrote one family planning advocate.[16] Given that Spaniards are now enthusiastic practitioners of family planning, it is odd that this Roman Catholic orthodoxy should be one of the most pernicious legacies of a period of Spanish colonialism that ended a century ago.

EIGHT

After the crash: The unfinished revolution

> Don't write off Asia, don't write off Asean. Asia, Asean are passing through difficult moments. These are temporary. It may take us two years. It may take us three years, but we will recover.
>
> – Goh Chok Tong, Singapore prime minister, in March 1999.[1]

> I sense a resurgence of that good old bubble feeling ... Although it is a relief from the gloom that has enveloped Asia for the past two years, the new euphoria is ill-founded and could well prove to be only the calm eye of the typhoon that presages the next storm.
>
> – Clyde Prestowitz, president of the Economic Strategy Institute in Washington.[2]

By the second half of 1999, Asian economies had started to recover rapidly from the financial crash. The prediction by Goh Chok Tong, the Singapore prime minister, that south-east Asia would emerge from the crisis within two or three years soon looked overly pessimistic. Exports increased. Wealthy Asians once again crowded into luxury goods shops to buy expensive jewellery and clothes as consumption accelerated. Most countries, except for Indonesia, appeared to be pulling out of the recession. Economists predicted that in 1999 Singapore's gross domestic product would grow 4 or 5 percent, and Malaysia's by more than 3 percent. Thailand and the Philippines were also recovering. 'I think the worst is over,' said Mahathir Mohamad, the Malaysian prime minister, as early as April 1999.[3]

After a severe but brief interruption of eighteen months, south-east

Asia's industrial revolution appeared to be confidently under way again.

The financial costs, however, were enormous. Japan alone had provided $80 billion to support struggling east Asian economies; one can only speculate how such a sum might have helped another part of the world – Africa, say – less favoured by the industrialized nations. And the panicky retreat of foreign investors had precipitated a series of Asian banking crises that have yet to be fully resolved. In mid-1999, one European investment bank forecast that Thailand's domestic bank losses from bad loans would amount to $79 billion, while for Indonesia the figure was $38 billion. Most of these losses will have to be borne by the governments of the countries concerned – in other words by their taxpayers – not by the dubious tycoons and poorly managed companies that actually owe the money. 'The banking crises in Indonesia and Thailand are likely to be among the worst ever measured,' concluded Deutsche Bank. 'The lesson of the Asia crisis is that inefficient financial institutions, typically banks, misallocate capital which eventually entails heavy capital losses ultimately born by the public sector. Avoiding another crisis requires the single-minded pursuit of efficient financial institutions, even if to the cost of slower near-term growth.'[4]

Another important lesson was that the methods of Asia's old-fashioned business executives, whether in managing their companies or doing deals with their powerful friends in government, left a lot to be desired – especially when the friends were no longer powerful. It soon became clear, for example, that the Bimantara group of 150 companies run by Bambang Trihatmodjo, son of the deposed President Suharto of Indonesia, depended more on his political connections than his management skills. He may have opened the way to government deals, but it was foreign contractors who did the hard technical work. The group turned out to be one of the biggest debtors to Indonesia's ailing banks. Bimantara Citra, the core of the group, was particularly hard hit by the Asian economic crisis and its market value fell from $2 billion in early 1997 to a mere $40 million in mid-1999.[5]

Meanwhile, Theng Bunma, the influential Cambodian business-man, ran into legal difficulties in Hong Kong, but successfully claimed diplomatic immunity after being charged with forging immigration documents.[6]

In Thailand, Dhanin Chearavanont, head of one of the country's biggest conglomerates, acknowledged that his debt-laden Charoen Pokphand group had grown too fast and that he needed to understand more about global competition. The company has since sold some of its operations and restructured its debts.[7]

Malaysian companies linked to Umno, the ruling party, also laboured under heavy debt burdens; Petronas, the state oil group, was periodically deployed to rescue favoured companies – including some shipping interests controlled by Mahathir's son Mirzan.[8]

The crisis did jolt some south-east Asian governments into overdue reforms of the protectionist laws that had shielded their economies from competition in the vital area of financial services. Singapore, for instance, launched a five-year programme of bank liberalization, lifting a 40 per cent limit on foreign shareholdings in its domestic banks. Thailand introduced a new bankruptcy law to make it easier for creditors to recover loans from recalcitrant debtors: one of the biggest obstacles to modernizing Asian economies has been the rickety framework of commercial laws and the corrupt or inefficient courts that make it hard to implement what laws there are. Foreign financial institutions such as Standard Chartered and Goldman Sachs took advantage of Asia's economic distress and the climate of reform to plunge in and buy Asian assets when prices were low. The assets bought included struggling Asian banks (previously off-limits to foreigners) and debts to Asian banks and finance houses which were sold at a discount by bank restructuring agencies. GE Capital, the US financial services group, spent $15 billion on Asian assets in 1998 and 1999.

But do the reforms go far enough? South-east Asia began to recover partly because of artificially high deficit spending by governments to 'pump-prime' their economies. Continued growth remains vulnerable to several dangers: the vital Japanese economy might suffer a downturn; US demand for Asian goods might weaken; China might devalue its currency, making its exports more competitive and thereby undermining south-east Asian export growth; and Indonesia might descend into chaos and destabilize the whole region. Even if none of these dangers materializes, south-east Asia needs to strengthen its banking systems and vigorously reform the way it does business if it wants to avoid a repeat of the crisis. Corruption is still rife in Indonesia. Malaysian conglomerates have yet to wean themselves off their cosy relationship with government. The murder in Thailand in March 1999 of Michael Wansley, an Australian auditor working for Deloitte Touche Tohmatsu, while investigating a debt-burdened sugar company, shows that the old, gangsterish ways of doing business still survive.

The idea that Asia was on the road to a full recovery was a myth, said Hong Kong businessman Ronnie Chan in mid-1999. 'Unless systemic weaknesses are adequately addressed, no recovery is sustainable. Speculative financial attacks may return, and other forces of globalization may also prove merciless,' he wrote. 'The recent crisis is the culmination of decades of operating under grossly inadequate social systems. It will take at least ten to twenty years to build the proper institutions and the associated social and cultural norms.' Other commentators took a similar view, arguing that Asia's political, judicial and education systems all needed varying degrees of modernization to ensure future progress.[9]

After the crash, several south-east Asian economies are unlikely to reach the size they attained in 1996 until about five years later in 2001, and economists say annual growth rates may never again soar to the double-digit levels seen in the 1980s and early 1990s.

One of the intriguing debates generated by the financial crisis was over Mahathir's unilateral decision in September 1998 to protect Malaysia from the vagaries of international markets by imposing controls on the flow of capital out of his country. The currency was fixed against the US dollar and ceased to trade on international markets. Foreigners were banned for a year from repatriating money invested in the Malaysian stock market, a ban subsequently replaced with a punitive 'exit tax'. Although this was anathema to free-market ideologues, and although Mahathir made his move amid his usual diatribes against foreign speculators, it was not a black-and-white issue. Some western economists were sufficiently concerned about the extreme volatility in international currency and other markets caused by short-term speculators that they too favoured some kind of control. By the third quarter of 1999, furthermore, Malaysia seemed to be recovering as well as its neighbours from the crisis.

Mahathir's government claimed the controls had worked. Others disagreed. They said it was true that Malaysia was recovering, but argued that the country would have done even better had the controls not been imposed at all. Malaysia, they said, was better placed than Thailand and Indonesia at the start of the crisis because its banks were much more solid, and because it had high foreign exchange reserves and relatively little short-term foreign debt. The government was also lucky during the crisis that commercial banks disobeyed government orders to boost their lending to Malaysian companies, which might simply have increased their pile of bad loans. What is more – insisted economists such as Merton Miller and Jeffrey Sachs – Mahathir's restrictions on capital flows were imposed only after the worst of the crisis was over and were therefore useless at best. 'Malaysia's capital controls didn't merely shut the door after the horses had bolted but when the horses were ready to come back into the barn,' wrote Sachs.[10]

More worrying was Malaysia's failure to get to grips with corporate reform. As in other south-east Asian countries, the domestic economy is dominated by local companies whose success has depended as much on ethnicity and political connections as on management skills. A controversial plan outlined by the Malaysian central bank in late July 1999 to merge 58 financial institutions into six large groups did little to inspire confidence among reformers. The six 'anchor' institutions were not the strongest banks, and excluded a bank aligned with Anwar Ibrahim, Mahathir's jailed rival and former deputy. The plan also aimed to restrict the number of institutions controlled by the ethnic Chinese community to two, leaving four for the favoured Malay majority.[11]

Malaysia's incipient recovery from the crisis, while welcome, increased concerns that the government would delay indefinitely the process of making the country's big businesses internationally competitive. 'There is a danger in equating success in stabilizing the economy with vindication of the Malaysian way – the corporatist model of terribly cosy relations between government and business,' warned investment banker Lim Say Boon.[12]

The push for better business ethics cannot be separated from the growing pressures for political reform in south-east Asia. It was no coincidence that Mahathir sacked Anwar, his deputy prime minister and finance minister, for having 'low morals' the day after imposing capital controls on the Malaysian economy. In this way, Mahathir associated himself with the new, nationalist policy and firmly linked Anwar to the painful, 'western', belt-tightening economic policies of the sort recommended by the IMF. But the disagreements went deeper than that. Anwar had advocated a democratization of Malaysia's still-authoritarian society, and Mahathir saw him as a dangerous political rival.

Anwar was accused of corruptly abusing his power to conceal sexual crimes. He was detained at first under the Internal Security Act and then charged, but the drama that followed was as much a trial of the Malaysian justice system as of Anwar himself. Anwar appeared in court bruised and with a black eye, and the former police chief was subsequently charged for the assault. The judge would not allow Anwar's lawyers to put their principal argument for the defence, namely that Anwar was the victim of a political conspiracy. In April 1999, he was found guilty and sentenced to six years in jail. From the dock he called for urgent political reform. 'I have no hope of justice,' he said. 'The charges are part of a political conspiracy to destroy me and ensure Mahathir Mohamad's continued hold on power at whatever cost.' Foreign and Malaysian observers criticized the trial. Robin Cook, the UK foreign secretary, expressed particular concern about 'the relationship between the executive and the judiciary in Malaysia'. John Howard, the Australian prime minister, said Malaysia was 'lurching towards authoritarianism'.

Anwar's second trial – for sodomy, an illegal act in Malaysia – was even more bizarre. The defence asked for the charges to be dropped after the prosecution twice changed the dates when Anwar was alleged to have sodomized his former chauffeur. On one occasion they changed the date after the defence pointed out that the building where the crime was supposed to have been committed did not exist at the time. After trying May 1994 and May 1992, the prosecution eventually plumped for some time between January and March 1993.[13]

Thousands of pro-democracy demonstrators took to the streets during Anwar's first trial, shouting 'Reformasi!' ('Reform!'), lighting bonfires and hurling chunks of pavement at the police, who dispersed the protesters with water cannon and baton charges. Wan Azizah Wan Ismail, Anwar's wife – an Irish-trained eye doctor – meanwhile decided to enter politics and formed the Parti Keadilan Nasional (the National Justice Party, or PKN). The party's manifesto called for a two-term limit for the prime minister (Mahathir has been in power since 1981 and is in his 70s) as well as the abolition of the Internal Security Act and an end to government influence over the media and the judiciary. 'Corruption has spread like a cancer, and leaders have accumulated detestable levels of wealth,' said the PKN's *Agenda for Change.* 'The voice of the majority is sidelined, silenced by the media that is controlled by the political elite and business tycoons.' The PKN pledged to continue the existing policy of preference for Malays, introduced to bring rural Malays into the economic mainstream and reduce the commercial dominance of the Chinese. But it said it would reform the programme so as to help the underprivileged, as originally intended, rather than enriching a privileged few.[14]

The angry mood in Malaysia at the time of Anwar's trial in early 1999 convinced some observers that the usually canny Mahathir had made a serious political miscalculation in hounding his former deputy. In February, students went on a protest march after the University of Malaya refused to renew the contract of Chandra Muzaffar, a professor who is a well-known Anwar supporter. When Anwar was convicted, Chandra said of Mahathir: 'Every dictator in history has, towards the end of his career, made inexplicable mistakes. He is depending on the instruments of power to keep him where he is.' Shahnon Ahmad, a leading Malaysian writer, wrote an obscene, 240-page political satire entitled simply 'Shit'. The setting is an alimentary canal where a leader called PM refuses to get out, stays for twenty years and creates a terrible stink.[15]

By September, however, it looked as if Mahathir, provided his health held out, would survive this particular political crisis. He appointed the harmless Abdullah Ahmad Badawi as his new deputy, made the most of Umno's grip on the mainstream media and resorted to the familiar tactic of criticizing foreigners. Mahathir dismissed Anwar as a 'puppet' of the US, and warned Malaysians of 'recolonization' by 'ethnic Europeans'. A billboard with the kind of Orwellian message favoured by the military junta in Burma appeared in Kuala Lumpur declaring: 'Foreign interference is a threat to national stability'. None of this was sophisticated enough to change the minds of disgruntled urban intellectuals, but Mahathir's crude nationalism has never done him any harm in the countryside from which he draws much of his support. Wan Azizah's party formed an alliance with other opposition parties in anticipation of a general election. By teaming up, they hoped to break the political dominance of the Umno-led National Front Coalition. But the opposition alliance was an odd mixture, with the Islamic fundamentalist PAS on one side, the mainly Chinese Democratic Action Party on the other and Wan Azizah's PKN in the middle. Opponents of Mahathir feared he would waste no time in attracting Chinese voters to his side by warning them – as he often has in the past – of the dangers of extremist Islam. The regional economic recovery was another factor in his favour.

Indonesia, Malaysia's bigger and more unstable neighbour, was in the throes of a more profound political upheaval following the 1998 uprising that forced Suharto to step down after three decades in power. Golkar, the ruling party, floundered in the unfamiliar climate of freedom, while new political parties and factions sprouted all over the country. Ethnic and religious violence was common. The independent media flourished. But B.J. Habibie, Suharto's interim successor, survived long enough as president to call a general election in June 1999. This, the first free election in 44 years, was a disorderly and hard-fought contest that bore little similarity to the staged, pseudo-democratic ceremonies of the Suharto era, when Golkar was assured of victory. Forty-eight parties took part this time and the counting dragged on for weeks. 'In the old days it was a lot easier because we knew the results beforehand,' said a smiling Rudini, chairman of the National Election Commission and a former minister of home affairs.[16]

As predicted, the Indonesian Democratic Party for Struggle (PDI-P), led by Megawati Sukarnoputri, won the biggest share of the vote, with 33.7 percent, while Golkar came second with 22.4 percent. Megawati, the daughter of the former Indonesian leader Sukarno, is not a charismatic figure – she resembles an uninspiring schoolteacher more than a fiery politician. But her 1998 confrontation with the Suharto regime over the future of Indonesian democracy made her the symbol of change and of the popular desire to modernize the country's politics. One of her priorities was the creation of an independent judiciary. Megawati, however was never assured of the presidency. The 700-member assembly that made the choice in October 1999 included 38 military officers and 200 appointed delegates, and Megawati showed no aptitude for striking the necessary political deals. In the end it was Abdurrahman Wahid, the ailing Moslem leader, who was elected president amid street protests by Megawati's supporters. Megawati was elected vice-president. Habibie withdrew from the race when it was clear that he had no chance of winning, but at least he could claim to have done his best to reintroduce democracy to Indonesia.

More surprising was Habibie's bold attempt to rid Indonesia of the problem of East Timor, the former Portuguese territory invaded by Indonesia in 1975 and subsequently annexed and subjected to a particularly brutal occupation. The UN has never recognized East Timor as part of Indonesia, and Ali Alatas, the Indonesian foreign minister, used to describe the problem euphemistically as a 'pebble' in the Indonesian shoe. With Suharto gone and Jakarta's authority weakened, there was unrest in several outlying parts of the Indonesian archipelago, including East Timor. Habibie called for a referendum, giving the East Timorese the choice between independence and autonomy within Indonesia. In a UN-organized poll on 30 August 1999, they voted overwhelmingly for independence, with more than 78 percent in favour. East Timor was due to become an independent state in early 2000.

The referendum campaign, however, was marred by murders and intimidation. Pro-Indonesian militiamen, apparently armed and certainly tolerated by the Indonesian military, went on the rampage immediately after the result was announced, killing and maiming innocent East Timorese, including UN workers, and setting fire to the capital Dili. Even as he welcomed the referendum result, Xanana Gusmão, the East Timorese resistance leader, warned of the dangers of a 'new genocide'. Indonesia's generals, who had carved out what they thought was a permanent political role for the armed forces under Suharto (himself a former general), were in confusion. They were particularly worried that independence for East Timor would presage the break-up of Indonesia, a collection of some 300 ethnic groups and more than 13,000 islands. Some of Indonesia's outlying peoples already regarded the country as a Javanese empire rather than a modern nation state to which they belonged. There was separatist violence in Aceh, on the north-western tip of Sumatra, and rumblings of discontent in Irian Jaya in the east. There were also outbreaks of trouble between Christians and Moslems in the Moluccan spice islands and between locals and settlers in Indonesian Borneo. The Chinese minority, including wealthy and not-so-wealthy business families, were as vulnerable as ever to rioting mobs.

Comparisons were made with the break-up of Yugoslavia, and it was not only soldiers who were worried about the integrity of the Indonesian nation. Dewi Fortuna Anwar, a political scientist who became Habibie's spokeswoman, made it clear that the government was prepared to give up East Timor but nothing more. 'The Acehnese need to understand that Aceh is not East Timor,' she said. 'Indonesia is an abstract concept, based on the former Dutch East Indies. If we start allowing different parts to break away, it will be dismembered before we know where we are.'[17]

Habibie's government said it was prepared to decentralize some powers to the provinces and allow them to spend locally a portion of the earnings from natural resources – oil, gas, fish and forests, for example – in their areas. After decades of corruption, however, it was hardly surprising that many Indonesians doubted whether Jakarta could be trusted. Suharto, denying he had any foreign assets, sued *Time* magazine over its report that he and his family had a $15 billion fortune in Indonesia and abroad.[18]

But there was never any doubt about his influence over the Indonesian economy.When the Indonesian Bank Restructuring Agency published a list of the 200 biggest debtors to state banks, no one was surprised to find that five of the top ten were linked to Suharto's family and friends.[19] A change in Indonesia, although it brought with it instability and danger, was both inevitable and long over-due.

Elsewhere in south-east Asia, the financial crisis had a less immediate impact, although it nudged along political and economic reforms. Singapore's well-managed economy weathered the storm well, and the government liberalized the banking sector to allow more competition from foreign banks. The last restrictions were lifted on dissident Chia Thye Poh, who immediately said he would campaign against the security legislation under which he had been first detained and then restricted without a trial. Lee Hsien Loong, son of Lee Kuan Yew, the founder of modern Singapore, was being groomed as a successor to Goh Chok Tong. The ruling People's Action Party maintained a tight grip on the island, but people spoke of a slight easing of Singapore's strict social and political controls. 'It's not a deliberate loosening,' said Lee Kuan Yew. 'It's a change in the generations.'[20]

Burma, with its inward-looking and poverty-stricken economy, was less directly affected by the economic crisis than its neighbours, and the military junta continued to arrest and harass its opponents. Aung San Suu Kyi, the opposition leader, said oppression had 'worsened greatly' on a scale 'the world has not yet grasped'.[21]

International pressure on the junta increased slightly, and the junta was condemned for refusing a visa to Suu Kyi's dying husband, the British academic Michael Aris. He subsequently died without seeing his wife, who refuses to leave Burma for fear that she will not be allowed back in. The European Union has stopped granting visas to Burmese officials and their families, and the International Labour Organization has banned Burma from most of its activities because the authorities use forced labour. Nine years after Suu Kyi's party won a general election, the army showed no desire to respect the result and hand over power. 'You can't cry over spilled milk now,' said Hla Min, the junta spokesman now promoted to the rank of colonel. 'If you're going to stick to demanding that the government should hand over power, I don't think that is very realistic.'[22]

President Joseph Estrada of the Philippines, helped by some well-chosen economic advisers, was praised for steering his country through the Asian financial crisis. But he was also accused of reviving the influence of business 'cronies' from the time of the Marcos dictatorship, and suspected, like his predecessor Fidel Ramos, of wanting to change the constitution for his own ends. Chuan Leekpai, the Thai prime minister, grappled with the slippery ethics of old-style politicians as he sought to introduce both financial and political reforms. In Vietnam, the Communist Party continued to stall on economic restructuring. It was anxious to attract more foreign investment but still cringed from the inevitable loss of political control that real economic freedom would entail. Tran Do, a retired general and member of the party's central committee, was expelled from the party for advocating reform and later refused permission to start a newspaper. He warned that the Communist Party was losing the confidence of the Vietnamese people and needed to change to save itself. The party, however, was adamant, insisting that no power-sharing would ever be tolerated.[23]

In Cambodia, the main factions reached an agreement in November 1998 to resolve the impasse following the election in July that year: Hun Sen became the sole prime minister and his rival Prince Ranariddh was appointed speaker of the National Assembly. The remnants of the Khmer Rouge capitulated following the death of their leader Pol Pot, who was reported to have committed suicide. Cambodians mooted plans to bring Khmer Rouge leaders to justice through some sort of tribunal as they struggled to come to terms with their gruesome past.

The financial crash will not be quickly forgotten in south-east Asia. It precipitated political crises in Indonesia and Malaysia. On the economic front, it made Asians acutely aware of global competition and the need to reform their business practices and banking systems to keep up with the rest of the world. Almost every country in the region began or accelerated a programme of economic reform, although there is still disagreement about how much more remains to be done. But in some areas – the environment, for example – there was much less progress. The victims of the environmental abuse that has accompanied south-east Asia's rapid industrialization of the past three decades continued to stage protests in 1998 and 1999: there were demonstrations against planned power stations in Thailand, a dam in Malaysia, a pulp mill in Indonesia and toxic waste dumping in Cambodia. However, some commentators argued that the poverty induced by economic recession had set back the environmentalist cause, because it pushed desperate people into illegal fishing, logging and wildlife poaching.

Worst of all, it was evident that neither Asean nor Indonesia had done anything to stop a repeat of the forest fires in Borneo and Sumatra that have regularly blanketed the region in smoke and haze since the 1980s. As the smoke returned in mid-1999 over parts of Indonesia, Malaysia and Singapore – reducing visibility in the shipping lanes of the Malacca Strait and forcing aircraft over Sumatra to be temporarily rerouted – the Malaysian government responded with its characteristic short-sightedness on environmental issues: instead of trying to get something done about the pollution, it decided to stop publishing its Air Pollution Index. Law Hieng Ding, the environment minister, shrugged off criticism of the decision and accused foreign journalists of having used the index to frighten away tourists.[24]

Asean – joined by Cambodia in April 1999 to bring the organization to its full complement of ten – did not make much headway on security co-operation either. Asean had already damaged its international standing by accepting Burma, one of the world's worst human rights abusers, as a member two years earlier; it was particularly embarrassing for Asean that in exchange for recognizing Burma it had received nothing in return from the military junta, not even a gesture towards democratization. There was not much that Asean could hope to do about such dangers as the unpredictability of North Korea or the strained relations between China and Taiwan. Although the Philippines, an Asean member, did renew its military ties with the US (with an agreement allowing joint exercises and US ship visits) Orlando Mercado, the defence minister, was only slightly exaggerating when he said his country had 'a navy that can't go out to sea and an air force that cannot fly'.[25]

But Asean could not find common cause even on matters that closely concerned its members, such as how to deal with human rights issues and how to confront China as it expanded its presence on the contested atolls of the South China Sea. Al Gore, the US vice-president, angered Asian authoritarians when he expressed support for Malaysian pro-democracy demonstrators at an Asia-Pacific Economic Co-operation summit in Kuala Lumpur; what made the statement especially galling – and rude, Asian leaders said – was that Gore said it at a dinner hosted by Mahathir. 'Among nations suffering economic crises, we continue to hear calls for democracy ... calls for *reformasi*,' said the tactless Gore. 'We hear them today, right here, right now, among the brave people of Malaysia.' Rafidah Aziz, Mahathir's trade minister, called Gore's statement 'the most disgusting speech I've heard in my life'. Joseph Estrada, the Philippine president, disagreed, calling the speech 'beautiful'. Not only did Estrada regard Anwar – sacked and persecuted by Mahathir and later sentenced to jail – as a friend. He was also maintaining a Philippine tradition of standing up for freedom and democracy in opposition to the authoritarian Asean consensus.[26]

Disagreements over human rights were not new in Asean. China's moves in the South China Sea, on the other hand, had previously brought Asean countries together in a rare show of unity: they called for peaceful settlement of rival claims and told China to stop its activities. Yet in 1999 there was scant support for Manila when it protested against renewed Chinese manoeuvres near the Philippines; among other incidents, China enlarged its outpost on Mischief Reef, where its supposed 'shelters for fishermen' looked like a cross between an airport control tower and a cheap apartment block.

Malaysia then complicated matters further by building its own large concrete structures – apparently in violation of several Asean agreements – on Investigator Shoal, also claimed by the Philippines. One Philippine analyst even suggested the move was in retaliation for Estrada's support of Anwar.[27]

Asean, in any case, was in disarray as its leaders acknowledged at a low-key meeting in Singapore in July 1999. 'Are we a force to reckon with in the region, admired and respected, or are we just passers-by, seen but not heard?' asked Surin Pitsuwan, Thai foreign minister.[28]

Neither south-east Asian disunity, nor the financial crisis, nor even the political revolution in Indonesia completely silenced the champions of 'Asian values'. Mahathir, for example, told a Tokyo conference on African development that the 'Asian way' was still the best strategy, blamed Asia's recent economic setbacks on free-market capitalism, and warned of neo-colonialism. 'True, the countries of east Asia seem to have failed recently but it is not really due to the true Asian way,' he said. 'Currency trading and raids on the stock market are not the fault of Asians or their ways or value system.'[29]

Lee Kuan Yew of Singapore continued to point out the dangers of US-style democracy as practised in the Philippines. 'It has democracy and a free press which are supposed to get rid of corruption, cronyism and nepotism,' he said. 'But by backing the right candidates with their resources in the last election, Mrs Marcos and her children are back in the political and business limelight. [President] Marcos pillaged the country but the family is back, and the loot has not been recovered.'[30]

Lee also returned to the different approaches taken by the Soviet Union and China towards economic and political development, a favourite historical comparison of 'Asian values' theorists, who argue that reformers in the Soviet Union were crazy to liberalize politics before modernizing the economy. Lee said that when he met Mikhail Gorbachev he found him 'completely bewildered' by what he had unleashed: 'He had jumped into the deep end of the pool without learning how to swim.' Deng Xiaoping's chilling strategy for stability in China made much more sense to Lee. 'I understood Deng Xiaoping when he said: if 200,000 students have to be shot, shoot them, because the alternative is China in chaos for another 100 years.'[31]

Other strands of the 'Asian values' argument – including the demonization of a western world supposedly collapsing under the weight of its own immorality and laziness – looked distinctly frayed. The US economy continued to grow faster than almost anyone had anticipated. US crime rates, in spite of occasional high-profile shooting incidents, continued to fall. More importantly, Asians themselves – in Malaysia, Indonesia, Vietnam and elsewhere – persisted in rejecting the authoritarian beliefs of their governments. Chee Soon Juan, an opponent of the Singapore government, wrote a book called *To Be Free* about six prominent Asians who have struggled for freedom in their countries, including Aung San Suu Kyi of Burma and Singapore's Chia Thye Poh.[32]

With the IMF imposing economic austerity measures and foreign investors snapping up debt-distressed Asian companies at bargain prices, it was inevitable that the financial crisis would arouse some anti-western sentiment. But the crisis, because it had exposed the failings of authoritarianism and highlighted the need for economic reform, also undermined the idea that Asia had succeeded because its peoples were culturally superior or because its governments had found a unique recipe for growth.

The ten countries of south-east Asia have participated in the quickest industrial revolution the world has yet seen, but their economic achievements owe nothing to a mysterious Asian 'miracle' or to the 'Asian values' of authoritarian politicians: broadly sensible economic policies, yes, and a favourable international climate, but not a pan-Asian cultural predisposition to success. There was never so much talk of Latin American 'miracles' or Latin American 'values' when their economies grew as fast as, or faster than, east Asia's developing economies in the 1950s, 1960s and 1970s. (It was only in the 1980s that Latin America stumbled economically, and it now seems to be recovering again.)[33]

In south-east Asia, there was an understandable tendency after three or four decades of economic expansion to assume that progress was inexorable and that the obstacles to further growth existed only in the imagination of cynical and jealous western observers. But the problems were real. In fact, both the successes and disasters of the region's industrial revolution have been remarkably similar in type and sequence to those of previous industrial transformations: rapid economic growth; an upsurge of nationalistic self-confidence; the push for political reform from an increasingly sophisticated population; migration to the cities, resulting in the erosion of traditional family ties and other social changes; the rise of unscrupulous tycoons who buy respectability for themselves and their families; pollution and other environmental damage; and the search for economic cooperation and a security framework to keep strong nation states at peace with each other. There is no reason to believe that south-east Asian countries will not continue to follow the pattern adopted by other industrializing countries, except in so far as the communications revolution and new technology is changing the situation for everyone. It is true that south-east Asia's modernization has been fast, but that is not because its inhabitants are Asian miracle-workers. It is because each industrial revolution has always been faster than the previous one. To be accurate, one should not even talk of separate industrial revolutions, but of a continuing, accelerating process of change in which each country and region eventually takes part.

South-east Asia is experiencing both the advantages and disadvantages of a late start. Its inhabitants can learn from the mistakes and successes of others and leapfrog whole stages of technological advance; there is no need to build a steam engine before driving a car or using a computer. But the speed of change and the power of technology can be bewildering and dangerous, allowing the new industrializers to abandon their old habits – and destroy their natural and man-made heritage – before they fully understand what they are doing. 'Everything is telescoped,' says the Thai scholar Ammar Siamwalla, reflecting that Thailand has undergone drastic economic and political changes in 50 years that took 150 years or more in Britain. 'I suppose there is only so much the human intellect can handle in one generation. But on the other hand, we know from your experiences how to do certain things.'[34]

In the old days, Thai living conditions were harsh, diseases such as cholera were common and superstition was rife – rather like pre-industrial Europe. Now people are richer, enjoy improved medical care and education, live longer and have better houses. But Thailand and its neighbours still face an awesome array of challenges; political, social, commercial, environmental and diplomatic. Ironically, some of the biggest of these challenges have to do with the organization of society, the area that governments are most inclined to boast about when they compare their countries with the 'decadent' West.

In politics, there are numerous signs that south-east Asian countries will – like Europe, Japan, Taiwan and South Korea before them – become more democratic as their inhabitants become better educated and more demanding. Authoritarian south-east Asian governments are resisting the inevitable liberalization of politics; so there will obviously be setbacks for democracy and there may be violent confrontations; and the forms of democracy that eventually emerge may not be the same as those found in other parts of the world. But there is no doubting the desire of millions of Burmese, Vietnamese and others to replace their old-fashioned political systems (whether military, quasi-feudal, or merely corrupt and patronising) with modern ones that represent their interests.[35] The Indonesian uprising of 1998 that ousted Suharto is only one more step in this process.

Political change is preceded by enormous social changes as millions of villagers migrate to south-east Asian cities, exchanging farm work for jobs in industry and services. This improves living standards but also leads to serious problems, including broken families, the growth of prostitution, crime, alcoholism, drug abuse and AIDS. Yet global standards of what is acceptable and what is not are so pervasive that most Malaysians or Singaporeans would be horrified if they had to witness nineteenth century English-style misery in their own countries today. In the workplace, people are quickly becoming accustomed to the curse and the blessing of modern, paid employment, the boredom and the financial rewards, and the strict and previously unrecognized division between 'work' and 'leisure'. Sweatshops employ child labour in countries such as Thailand and the Philippines, but there is scant evidence of the extreme cruelty of nineteenth century England which drove children aged seven or less to haul coal underground like beasts of burden, or to work for 16 hours a day so that they fell asleep and maimed themselves in factory machines. Education was worse in England too. In Birmingham in 1838, less than half of the children aged between five and 15 went to school.[36] Housing and health were appalling. It was estimated that half the children born in Manchester in a typical year in the 1830s died before the age of five.[37]

In many areas of life, the world's standards are higher than they were 150 years ago. But that does not mean that south-east Asian

governments can be complacent. The need for education and technical skills is greater than before, and people's expectations are higher
too. These expectations – fuelled by the lifestyles glimpsed on television and by the fact that many people have been left behind by
the first wave of enrichment – are steadily increasing the demands
made of governments. They are asked to regulate more (by limiting
working hours, setting safety standards, protecting the environment)
and to provide more services (education, healthcare, justice, pensions). This is exactly what happened in Britain, starting with the
brutal Poor Laws and culminating in the all-embracing welfare state
after the Second World War. (Indeed, welfare systems in the industrialized world expanded so fast and eventually became so expensive
that controlling their growth became one of the principal preoccupations of western governments in the 1980s and 1990s.)
Further, the modernization which south-east Asian governments are
supposed to manage is a much more daunting challenge than in
any previous era. For centuries economic growth at any rate much
above zero was an achievement; now successful developing economies are expected to grow at 6, 8, 10 or even 12 percent a year,
rates of expansion which strain human resources to the limit. Populations are much larger too. Indonesia has to deal with more than
two million new entrants to the job market each year, whereas the
entire population of England and Wales at the start of the first
industrial revolution was only about seven million.[38]

Fast-growing populations, partly the result of a sudden decline in
disease and infant mortality after the introduction of western medicine, have hitherto boosted south-east Asian economic growth
because of the rising proportion of young workers. But as birth rates
decline and populations age, there will be fewer people of working
age to support the elderly. Growth will be constrained and government budgets will be stretched. The same phenomenon has occurred
in Europe, but not at quite such a drastic speed. South-east Asia's
big demographic gift, in short, will become a big burden.[39]

In the future, managing south-east Asia's economies will not be
as easy as it was. Nor will managing its businesses. Entrepreneurs did
well for themselves and their countries during the early years of
industrialization. But much of their success was based on exploiting
rich natural resources; on doing cosy deals with their own governments to build roads and run telephone networks; and on exploiting

foreign technology and cheap local labour to make exports that they sent to eager foreign markets. Now the natural resources are depleted, their domestic markets are being opened to more foreign competition, the local labour is not so cheap, and they are being urged to innovate and finance technological advances of their own. They are also being told to curb pollution and protect the environment. Such is the price of success. South-east Asian governments must also start to pay their way. Their increased economic clout means they are expected to contribute to the general good by opening their markets in world trade negotiations and by looking after their own military security instead of hanging on to America's coattails.

In 1903, Theodore Roosevelt made a prediction about the rise of Asia. 'The Atlantic Era is now at the height of its development and must soon exhaust the resources at its command,' he said. 'The Pacific Era, destined to be the greatest of all, is just at its dawn.'[40] Ninety years later, south-east Asian leaders were making the same sort of predictions. They foretold that the twenty-first century would be the 'Pacific Century'. Their countries had an unrivalled record of economic growth. Their success, they claimed, could be attributed to strong government, hard work, and their unique values. They had a sense of community, discipline and a devotion to family sorely lacking in the weak liberal cultures and floundering economies of the West. They were at the heart of an 'Asian Renaissance'. Their success was unstoppable. Singaporeans were already among the wealthiest people in the world; Malaysia would become a fully industrialized economy by the year 2020; the others would follow.

The reality was more complicated and more mundane. South-east Asia had been economically successful, but its achievements were no more extraordinary than those of other industrial revolutions in Europe, the US and Japan. The south-east Asian experience was quicker and more dramatic because it was taking place in an era of more advanced technology and of more rapid international transfers of capital and skills. Millions of people had been catapulted from rural poverty into a modern world of houses, hospitals, schools, and factory jobs. Instead of dying of typhoid, people were killed by the modern scourges: car crashes, heart disease and cancer. Instead of worrying about the rice crop, they fretted about university education for their children. This was progress. But the changes were so quick that the unavoidable social, political and environmental challenges generated by industrialization were only beginning to emerge by the time south-east Asian leaders started boasting of their 'miracle' recipe for development. There was a dawning realization among governments that these issues were as important for long-term progress as the holy grail of next year's economic growth rate, and they would have to be tackled with vigour if development over the next twenty years was to be as spectacular as in the previous twenty.

As for the region's 500 million inhabitants, many of them had never been wholly satisfied by the official south-east Asian recipe for success. Some political leaders thought they could import the outward packaging of modern industrial societies – the prosperity, the cars, skyscrapers, airports, televisions and telephones – without the moral and political content: freedom, justice and the rule of law, qualities which they wrongly identified as 'western' rather than modern. The result was often an unstable mixture of tawdry modernity on the outside, and a moral vacuum within. It was absurd that the intensely materialistic politicians and their business allies who ran most of south-east Asia should have ever defended themselves (and even gone triumphantly on the offensive against the West) with such a grandiose moral construction as 'Asian values'. The absurdity was short-lived. It was uncovered, gradually at first, by the brave minority who dared to stand up and make 'un-Asian' demands for democracy or trade union rights or an end to corruption. Then the hollow core of the 'Asian Way' of doing business was further exposed by the collapse of shoddily-run finance houses and over-indebted companies across the region. Economic growth forecasts for the coming years were revised drastically downwards, and south-east Asian governments sought billions of dollars of help from the IMF and Japan. The economic 'miracle' had turned out to be a myth. By 1999, south-east Asia had started to recover, but few doubted that the next stage of the industrial revolution would be managed by a different set of leaders with a different set of values. The old leaders still had achievements to boast of. But in the end they had made the mistake of being arrogant, when they should have been merely proud.

Notes

Introduction: A miracle that turned sour

1 *Asia Rising,* by Jim Rohwer, p. 24. Nicholas Brealey Publishing, 1996.
2 *Asian Drama: An Inquiry into the Poverty of Nations,* by Gunnar Myrdal. Twentieth Century Fund/Pantheon Books, 1968.
3 *Contemporary Southeast Asia,* by Robert C. Bone, Jr., pp. 114–16. Random House, 1962.
4 *Emerging Asia: Changes and Challenges,* p. 11 and p. 21. Asian Development Bank, 1997; and see 'Asia's population advantage', *The Economist,* 13 September 1997.
5 See, for example, *Thai Culture in Transition,* pp. 61ff, by William Klausner. The Siam Society, Bangkok, 1997.
6 Anwar was sacked by Mahathir Mohamad, the prime minister, in late 1998 and detained after leading pro-democracy demonstrations.

Chapter 1: The rise and fall of 'Asian values'

1 *Following Ho Chi Minh: The Memoirs of a North Vietnamese Colonel,* by Bui Tin (translated and adapted by Judy Stowe and Do Van). Hurst and Co., 1995.
2 Although he focused on the near east, not the far east, the classic text on this subject is *Orientalism: Western Conceptions of the Orient,* by Edward W. Said. Penguin, 1995 (first published by Routledge and Kegan Paul, 1978).
3 As the writer Ian Buruma noted, the missionary and the libertine changed places. (*The Missionary and the Libertine.* Faber and Faber, 1996.)
4 'Culture Is Destiny; A Conversation with Lee Kuan Yew', by Fareed Zakaria, *Foreign Affairs,* March/April 1994.
5 Indonesia, for instance, won independence from the Dutch in 1949, while Malaysia (as Malaya, because it had yet to incorporate the Borneo states) became independent in 1957.
6 Published in English as *The Voice of Asia: Two Leaders Discuss the Coming Century,* by Mahathir Mohamad and Shintaro Ishihara. Kodansha International, 1995. Shintaro had already made his name with the bestselling nationalistic work, *The Japan That Can Say No.*
7 See *Japan in War and Peace: Essays on History, Culture and Race,* p. 48, by John Dower. Fontana Press, 1996.
8 *Asian Values and Modernization,* ed. Seah Chee-Meow. Singapore University Press, 1977.
9 'Politics and Cultural Myths: Democracy Asian style versus the West', by Stephanie Lawson, the *Asia-Pacific* magazine, June 1996. 'A proponent of the new model, Wu Teh Yao, claimed than an Eastern form of democracy could be arrived at through these means, producing a new model of rule called

"Consencracy". What is notably absent from this neologism is the qualifier derived from *demos* – the people. In its place we find consensus.'

10 Interview with the author, 25 April 1997.

11 'The United States: "Go East, Young Man"', by Kishore Mahbubani, *The Washington Quarterly*, Spring 1994. One of his points was that it was now the Americans whose thinking had become so rigid that they were unable to raise important questions about their own society.

12 'The 10 Values That Undergird East Asian Strength and Success', by Tommy Koh, *International Herald Tribune*, 11 December 1993.

13 *Listen to the Emerging Markets of Southeast Asia: Long-Term Strategies for Effective Partnerships*, by Corrado G. M. Letta. John Wiley and Sons, 1996.

14 'Asian Values Deserve More Respect', by Reginald Dale, *International Herald Tribune*, 17 May 1995.

15 The 'neo-Orientalist' view has been perpetuated by sociological studies which were sometimes misinterpreted by others and which sometimes concentrated on historical material that failed to take account of the rapid effects of modernization. 'Most Asians respect authority too much to share the western distrust of authority and power,' wrote Lucian Pye. '. . . people in those [Asian] cultures have positive feelings about dependency and have usually regarded a craving for autonomy as quixotic and unbecoming in civil relations.' (*Asian Power and Politics: The Cultural Dimensions of Authority*, by Lucian W. Pye, with Mary W. Pye. Belknap Press/Harvard University Press, 1985.)

16 'Singapore Flogging Defense: The "Chaos" on US Streets', by Philip Shenon, *New York Times*, 13 April 1994.

17 Interview with the author, 1 April 1997.

18 'Manila's Dirty Harry returns to the beat', by Edward Luce, *Financial Times*, 30 June 1996.

19 Interview with the author, 31 March 1997.

20 'Confucius or convenience?', by Victor Mallet, *Financial Times*, 5 March 1994.

21 Private communication with the author.

22 Interview with the author, 26 February 1997.

23 Interview with the author, 31 March 1997.

24 Interview with the author, 20 March 1997.

25 Interview with the author, 28 January 1997.

26 Interview with the author, 19 February 1997.

27 'Go East, Young Man', by Kishore Mahbubani, *Far Eastern Economic Review*, 19 May 1994.

28 'Industrial conflict in west at 50-year low', by Robert Taylor, *Financial Times*, 9 April 1996.

29 'The Uncertain States: The US should be enjoying a peace dividend rather than an unease dividend', by Gerard Baker, *Financial Times*, 29–31 March 1997; 'Major Crime Falls Again, But Why?' by Fox Butterfield, *International Herald Tribune*, 6 January 1997.

30 *Orientalism: Western Conceptions of the Orient*, p. 328 in Penguin Books edition, 1995, by Edward Said. Routledge and Kegan Paul, 1978.

31 *Corruption and Democracy in Thailand*, p. 145, by Pasuk Phongpaichit and Sungsidh Piriyarangsan. Silkworm Books, 1996. (First published in 1994 by The Political Economy Centre, Faculty of Economics, Chulalongkorn University.)

32 Speech to Rotary International 1996 Asia Regional Conference. *Bangkok Post*, 28 October 1996.

33 Speech in Singapore Legislative Assembly, 27 April 1955. Quoted in *To Catch a Tartar: A Dissident in Lee Kuan Yew's Prison*, by Francis T. Seow. Yale University Southeast Asia Studies, 1994.

34 *Far Eastern Economic Review*, passim, 1996.

35 'Society vs The Individual', by Sandra Burton, *Time*, 14 June 1993.

36 'Indonesia Warns Philippines of Deep Feelings over East Timor'. Associated Press, 16 May 1994.

37 Speaking to the author and other journalists, 22 July 1994.

38 In some ways 'constructive engagement' with Burma was even more controversial, because the junta's foreign interlocutors made little effort to speak to the government's democratic opponents – which had been part of the West's 'constructive engagement' policies towards South Africa.

39 Interview with a group of journalists, January 1994.

40 Communication with the author, February 1997.

41 Interview with the author, 18 February 1997.

42 Interview with the author, 31 March 1997.

43 Interview with the author, 19 February 1997.

44 Interview with the author, 25 March 1997.

45 Interview with the author. Date confidential.

46 'Patten's Asia: Beyond the Myths. "By Invitation" ', *The Economist*, 4 January 1997.

47 'Pacific Century: Myth or Reality?', by Morton Abramowitz, *Contemporary Southeast Asia*, December 1993, published by Institute of Southeast Asian Studies, Singapore.

48 Speech to Rotary International 1996 Asia Regional Conference. *Bangkok Post*, 28 October 1996.

49 'The Smoke Over Parts of Asia Obscures Some Profound Concerns', by Christopher Lingle, *International Herald Tribune*, 7 October 1994.

50 'Cambodia Looks All Right', by Tommy Koh, *Far Eastern Economic Review*, 29 February 1996.

51 'Of crashes and conspirators', *The Economist*, 2 August 1997.

52 Interview with the author, 31 March 1997.

53 'Asians only ones who can stand up to West', by Kwan Weng Kin, *The Straits Times*, 28 March 1997.

54 *The Asian Renaissance*, by Anwar Ibrahim. Times Books International, 1996.

55 Interview with the author, 3 March 1997.

56 Interview with the author, 20 March 1997.

57 Communication with the author.

58 'An Asian Vision of a New Asia', by Barry Wain, *The Asian Wall Street Journal*, 5 February 1994.

59 Communication with the author.

60 'West Must Remember Asia Is More Than the Next Big Market', by Tom Plate, *Los Angeles Times*, reprinted in *The Cambodia Daily*, 28 April 1997.

61 'Asia, a Civilization in the Making', by Masakazu Yamazaki, *Foreign Affairs*, July/August 1996.

62 'Is Culture Destiny? The Myth of Asia's Anti-Democratic Values', by Kim Dae-jung, *Foreign Affairs*, November/December 1994.

63 BBC television. *Newsnight*, 19 February 1997.

64 'An Asia-Pacific Consensus', by Kishore Mahbubani, *Foreign Affairs*, September–October 1997.

Notes

Chapter 2: The new democrats

1 'Singapore party celebrates victory before the election', by James Kynge, *Financial Times*, 24 December 1996.

2 'Indonesians told to play along at polls', by Manuela Saragosa, *Financial Times*, 24–25 May 1997.

3 Interview with the author, 13 February 1997.

4 Interview with the author, 24 March 1997.

5 See, for example, 'Singapore party celebrates victory before the election', by James Kynge, *Financial Times*, 24 December 1996.

6 This was extensively reported in the local and regional media at the time. See, for example, 'Politically Incorrect: Lee Kuan Yew backs down as Malaysians protest', by S. Jayasankaran and Murray Hiebert, *Far Eastern Economic Review*, 27 March 1997.

7 'The Development of Democracy in Asean', speech given at conference in Makati, 7 April 1997.

8 *Corruption and Democracy in Thailand*, p. 178, by Pasuk Phongpaichit and Sungsidh Piriyarangsan. Silkworm Books, 1996.

9 Interview with the author, 28 January 1997.

10 Interview with the author, 28 January 1997.

11 Interview with the author, 16 April 1997.

12 Interview with the author. Used in *Financial Times*, 16 March 1993.

13 *Economic Growth and Political Change in Asia*, by Graham Field. Macmillan Press, 1995.

14 He has used the phrase more than once. See, for instance, 'Let countries choose own system of democracy', by Ahmad A. Talib, *New Straits Times*, 20 May 1995.

15 'Open and Closed', by John Gittings. *Prospect* magazine, April 1996.

16 'Clinton's Stance on Rights Challenges Ties With Asia', by Michael Richardson, *International Herald Tribune*, 2 January 1997.

17 *A Malaysian Journey*, p. 253, by Rehman Rashid. Rehman Rashid, 1993.

18 'Democracy and Identity', by David Martin Jones, in *Towards Illiberal Democracy in Pacific Asia*, p. 77. Macmillan Press, 1995.

19 Interview with the author, 19 March 1997.

20 Interview with the author, 5 February 1997.

21 'Not a lot to smile about', by Jeremy Seabrook, *New Statesman & Society*, 19 January 1996.

22 *On the Eve of the Millennium*, by Conor Cruise O'Brien. The Free Press, 1996.

23 *A Malaysian Journey*, p. 242, by Rehman Rashid. Rehman Rashid, 1993.

24 'Malaysia's legal system loses its gloss', by Kieran Cooke, *Financial Times*, 5 September 1995.

25 *Indonesia's New Order*, ed. Hal Hill, p. 22. University of Hawaii Press, 1994.

26 *Thailand's Boom!* by Pasuk Phongpaichit and Chris Baker, p. 221. Silkworm Books, 1996.

27 'Judgment calls', by Sheila Coronel, *The Investigative Reporting Magazine*, January–March 1997; Macapagal's comment is from an interview with the author, 10 April 1997.

28 For a detailed assessment of one of the Jeyaretnam cases, see 'Singapore: J. B. Jeyaretnam – the use of defamation for political purposes'. Amnesty International statement, 15 October 1997.

29 See 'Pacific Asia's Rise Involves More Than Economics', by Ho Kwon Ping, *International Herald Tribune*, 11 May 1994. Such views, however, are not exclusively Asian. In the UK, more than a quarter of people questioned in a

survey thought it worse to let a guilty person go free than to convict an
innocent person – see 'Public gets tough over law and order', *Financial Times*,
19 November 1997.

30 Interview with the author, 1 April 1997.

31 This was a common sight in the official *The New Light of Myanmar* newspaper
in early 1994. See for example, 'Burmese generals still jittery after all these
years', by Victor Mallet, *Financial Times*, 22 January 1994.

32 'Sing Singapore', by Victor Mallet, *Financial Times*, 19 August 1993.

33 Among other works, see *Privatizing Malaysia: Rents, Rhetoric, Realities*, ed. Jomo
K. S., Westview Press, 1995; and *Political Business: Corporate Involvement of
Malaysian Political Parties*, by Edmund Terence Gomez. James Cook University
of North Queensland, 1994.

34 Khieu Kanharith, interview with the author, 8 February 1997.

35 Interview with the author, 28 February 1997.

36 Speech given in Makati at a regional conference on the development of
democracy in Asean, 7 April 1997.

37 Interview with the author, 19 March 1997.

38 See *Corruption & Democracy in Thailand*, by Pasuk Phongpaichit and Sungsidh
Piriyarangsan. Silkworm Books, 1996.

39 The phrase was used in Thailand by an inquiry into members of the 1988–91
government of the late Chatichai Choonhavan.

40 Interview with the author, 10 April 1997.

41 Interview with the author, 15 April 1997.

42 Interview with the author, 27 January 1997.

43 Interview with the author, 3 March 1997.

44 The analysis of the thinking within the Vietnamese government is based on
interviews with Vietnamese people who understandably wish to remain
anonymous.

45 Interview with the author, 19 February 1997.

46 Both the regulations and Lee Kuan Yew are quoted in 'Information
Technology and Political Control in Singapore', by Garry Rodan. Paper for
Japan Policy Research Institute.

47 Interview with the author, 31 March 1997.

48 Garry Rodan gave the example of CNN alerting Singapore Cable Vision of
potentially sensitive material, for example about the controversial case of the
US teenager Michael Fay, who was caned for vandalizing cars in Singapore.
'Information Technology and Political Control in Singapore', by Garry Rodan.
Paper for Japan Policy Research Institute.

49 'Invitation retracted', *Far Eastern Economic Review*, 4 September 1997.

50 The author attended the screening.

51 Interview with the author, 20 March 1997.

52 Interview with the author, 27 March 1997.

53 Interview with the author, 25 February 1997.

54 Interview with the author, 28 February 1997.

55 'Asians in Cyberia', by Gerald Segal, *The Washington Quarterly*, Summer
1995.

56 Interview with the author, 19 March 1997.

57 Interview with the author, 6 January 1997.

58 Interview with the author, 24 March 1997.

59 See *Politics Without Democracy, 1815–1914*, pp. 27–30, by Michael Bentley.
Fontana Press, 1996.

60 *The End of History and the Last Man*, p. 50, by Francis Fukuyama. Penguin Books, 1992.
61 Interview with the author, 24 January 1997.
62 *Emerging Asia: Changes and Challenges*. ADB, 1997.
63 Interview with the author, January 1997.
64 Interview with the author, 20 March 1997.

Chapter 3: Sex, drugs and religion: Social upheaval in the 1990s
1 Penguin Economic History of Britain, vol 3: *Industry and Empire*, by E. J. Hobsbawm. Penguin, 1990 (first published by Weidenfeld and Nicolson, 1968).
2 *All That Is Solid Melts into Air*, by Marshall Berman. Verso, 1983.
3 *Hard Times*, by Charles Dickens. Chapman and Hall, first published 1854.
4 The paragraphs that follow on Malaysia's drug problem are based on the author's research and interviews in Kuala Lumpur in March 1997.
5 Interview with the author, 27 February 1997.
6 Interview with the author, 27 January 1997.
7 Interview with the author, 3 March 1997.
8 Interview with the author, 24 April 1997.
9 'City Limits', by William McGurn, *Far Eastern Economic Review*, 6 February 1997.
10 *Emerging Asia: Changes and Challenges*, pp. 308–9 (quoting UN urbanization figures), Bank, May 1997.
11 'People-Centred Sustainable Cities', by Mary Racelis. Paper presented at a conference on sustainable cities, Manila, October 1996.
12 The paragraphs on life in Manila are based on the author's research and interviews in April 1997.
13 Interview with the author, 24 April 1997.
14 *The Economist*, 13 April 1996, quoting 'Income distribution and malnutrition in Thailand', by Yukio Ikemoto, *Chulalongkorn Journal of Economics*, 1993.
15 Interview with the author, 21 March 1997.
16 Interview with the author, 18 March 1997.
17 'Vietnamese club together against golf', by Jeremy Grant, *Financial Times*, 4 January 1997; 'Rural descent', *The Economist*, 13 September 1997.
18 'Implementation of Substance Abuse Prevention and Intervention and Demand Reduction Program in Thailand, 1995'. Thanyarak Hospital, Ministry of Public Health, Thailand.
19 'Anti-drug drive at schools stepped up', by Sirikul Bunnag, *Bangkok Post*, 29 January 1997.
20 Background Brief, UNDCP Subregional Programme in East Asia (quoting figures from Thailand Development Research Institute Study, 1995), October 1995.
21 UNDCP, 1997.
22 'Family Matters', by Michael Vatikiotis, *Far Eastern Economic Review*, 1 August 1996; and 'Family institution the key', *Borneo Bulletin*, 8 April 1997.
23 Interview with the author, 30 January 1997.
24 Interview with the author, 30 January 1997.
25 Personal communications with the author; all sources asked to remain anonymous.
26 Interview with the author, 25 March 1997.
27 *Emerging Asia: Changes and Challenges*, pp. 168–9, ADB, May 1997.

28 'Myanmar's secret plague', *The Economist*, 23 August 1997; 'Blind in Rangoon', by Bertil and Hseng Noung Lintner, *Far Eastern Economic Review*, 1 August 1996.

29 'Developing Effective HIV/AIDS programs for transsexuals working as sex workers', by Khartini Slamah, Pink Triangle Malaysia.

30 Communication with the author.

31 'Philippines law and order under fire', by Edward Luce, *Financial Times*, 22 December 1995.

32 'Sumatran town lives in thrall to gangsters', by Victor Mallet, *Financial Times*, 17 May 1994.

33 The figures are from market research by A. C. Nielsen SRG, 1996.

34 A. C. Nielsen SRG. Figures for the Philippines, for example, showed a 60 per cent increase in baby diaper sales between 1993 and 1994.

35 I am grateful to Peter Weldon of A. C. Nielsen SRG for emphasizing this point.

36 *Indonesia's New Order: The Dynamics of Socio-economic Transformation*, p. 261, ed. Hal Hill. University of Hawaii Press, 1994.

37 *Thailand's Boom!*, by Pasuk Phongpaichit and Chris Baker, p. 125. Silkworm Books, 1996.

38 'Fishing for the Green', *The Nation* (Thailand), 30 April 1997.

39 The film, made by Prince Chatri Chalerm Yukhon, was given the English name 'Little Angels 1' and won a prize at the 1997 South-east Asian Film Festival in Phnom Penh. Agence France Presse, in *Borneo Bulletin*, 7 April 1997.

40 'New Play Examines Modern Khmer Society', by Vanna Ross and James Grant-Morris. Via Camnews internet service, 24 October 1997.

41 Remarks to the Foreign Correspondents' Club of Thailand, 22 January 1997.

42 Interview with the author, 20 March 1997.

43 The examples come from 'War of the Words: Speak Singlish, can or not? That is the question', by Murray Hiebert, *Far Eastern Economic Review*, 21 March 1996.

44 Interview with the author, 16 April 1997. The linguistic examples are also his.

45 *Indonesia's New Order: The Dynamics of Socioeconomic Transformation*, p. 289, ed. Hal Hill. University of Hawaii Press, 1994.

46 'Thai Personal Pronouns: A Linguistic Labyrinth', in *Thai Culture in Transition*, by William Klausner. The Siam Society, 1997.

47 Communication with the author.

48 Interview with the author, 11 February 1997.

49 Interview with the author, 29 January 1997.

50 Interview with the author, 19 March 1997.

51 *Emerging Asia: Changes and Challenges*, p. 278. ADB, May 1997.

52 I am grateful to Seng Teak, a Russian-educated official of the Cambodian environment ministry, for the young man's marriage anecdote and for the analysis of favoured spouses.

53 *Emerging Asia: Changes and Challenges*, p. 28 and p. 312. ADB, May 1997.

54 Chulalongkorn University's Institute of Population Studies, quoted in 'Family Matters', by Michael Vatikiotis, *Far Eastern Economic Review*, 1 August 1996.

55 *Emerging Asia: Changes and Challenges*, p. 29. ADB, May 1997.

56 'The widow and her power of prayer', by Edward Luce, *Financial Times*, 15 March 1996.

Notes

57 *Emerging Asia: Changes and Challenges*, pp. 312–15. ADB, May 1997.

58 Author's observations.

59 *No Money, No Honey! Sex-for-sale in Singapore*, by David Brazil. Angsana Books, 1996.

60 A similar process has been occurring in Japan, where the writer Banana Yoshimoto has made her name with books about young, unmarried women. 'Our lives are the result of Japan's rapid industrialization that has filled our world with material richness and captured our hearts with the American concepts of freedom and individualism,' she said in an interview. ('Mirror, mirror', by Suvendrini Kakuchi, *Far Eastern Economic Review*, 4 December 1997.)

61 'An arid Christmas. Fay Khoo laments the dearth of good, hard men come Yuletide', *Men's Review*, December 1996.

62 'Children will suffer from Rajabhat ban', *Bangkok Post*, 23 January 1997.

63 I am grateful to William Klausner of the Ford Foundation, a long-time resident of Thailand, for pointing out this aspect of the sexual revolution.

64 'Gays take a tentative step out of the closet', by Katya Robinson of Reuters, *The Nation* (Bangkok), 31 January 1997.

65 Khartini Slamah, Pink Triangle. Interview with the author, 4 March 1997.

66 *No Money, No Honey! Sex-for-sale in Singapore*, by David Brazil. Angsana Books, 1996. See also *Goddesses of the Lust Triangle: An Excursion into Manila's Erotic Dance Industry*, by Arnel F. de Guzman. The Media Gallery, 1996.

67 Estimates are inevitably vague, but see, for example, 'Travel executives urge crackdown on child sex industry', Agence France Presse, 1 April 1998.

68 Among other reports, see 'Children sold into sex slavery on Street of Flowers', by Nick Daniel, *Sunday Telegraph* (UK), 1 December 1996; and 'Asia's Plantations of the '90s', by Nicholas D. Kristof (*New York Times*), *International Herald Tribune*, 15 April 1996.

69 'Manila hails child sex case', by Nick Cumming-Bruce, *Guardian* (UK), 14 February 1996.

70 'Hanoi alarmed at rise in cases of child sex abuse', Agence France Presse. *The Nation* (Bangkok), 25 January 1997; and 'Experts urge action to end child abuse', *The Nation*, 29 January 1997.

71 'Family matters', by Michael Vatikiotis, *Far Eastern Economic Review*, 1 August 1996.

72 Interview with the author, 25 February 1997.

73 See 'Young and insolent', *The Economist*, 27 April 1996.

74 See *Indonesia's New Order: The Dynamics of Socioeconomic Transformation*, ed. Hal Hill. University of Hawaii Press, 1994.

75 *Thailand's Boom!*, pp. 117–18, by Pasuk Phongpaichit and Chris Baker. Silkworm Books, 1996.

76 *Men's Review*, March 1997.

77 Interview with the author, 29 January 1997.

78 'I find the accusation that Phra Yantra had sex with a woman factually impossible,' said Phra Dharmaratanobhas, 'because normally, in sexual intercourse on board a cruiser in very cold weather, Yantra's penis would contract so much that it could not function normally as mistakenly reported by the press.' Quoted in 'Sex and the saffron robe', by Philip Sherwell, *Sunday Telegraph* [UK], 10 April 1994. See also, 'The criminals who hide behind their saffron robes in Thai temples', by Philip Sherwell, *Daily Telegraph*, 17 January 1996.

Notes

79 Associate Professor Suwanna Satha-anandha of Chulalongkorn University's Department of Philosophy, quoted in 'Religion is now little more than convenience', *The Nation* (Bangkok), 30 January 1997.

80 For further details of such Thai cults, see *Thailand's Boom!*, pp. 127–33, by Pasuk Phongpaichit and Chris Baker. Silkworm Books, 1996.

81 'Christian revival perturbs Singapore', by Victor Mallet, *Financial Times*, 7 April 1992.

82 Interview with the author, 25 March 1997.

83 'Whose Religion?' by S. Jayasankaran, *Far Eastern Economic Review*, 11 September 1997. See also 'Islam turns SE Asia's secular heads', by Victor Mallet, *Financial Times*, 3 September 1993.

84 Interview with the author.

85 Quoted in 'A Woman's Place', by Murray Hiebert, *Far Eastern Economic Review*, 18 December 1997.

86 Communication with the author.

87 Interview with the author, 20 March 1997.

88 'Islam: real and symbolic concessions', by Victor Mallet, *Financial Times*, 24 June 1992.

89 'Emerging mass-groups point up discontent with Suharto regime', by Manuela Saragosa, *Financial Times*, 16 January 1996.

90 Interview with the author, 26 February 1997.

91 Interview with the author, 28 February 1997.

92 'Trying to save Thai tradition', by Yvan Cohen, *Christian Science Monitor*, reprinted in *South China Morning Post*. Undated.

93 Interview with the author, 31 March 1997.

Chapter 4: The day of the robber barons

1 See 'Malaysia 97: A technological transformation', by James Kynge, *Financial Times*, 19 May 1997.

2 'Thais close 56 finance companies', by Ted Bardacke, *Financial Times*, 9 December 1997.

3 Interview with the author, 24 March 1997.

4 For details of the Bre-X saga, see 'Crumbled to gold dust', by Kenneth Gooding, *Financial Times* 29–30 March 1997; 'Gold at Busang Is Called "Insignificant"', by Mark Heinzl and Richard Borsuk, *Asian Wall Street Journal*, 27 March 1997; 'Digging deep in Busang', *The Economist*, 18 January 1997; 'Gold Sealed', by John McBeth, *Far Eastern Economic Review*, 27 February 1997; 'Bre-X "salting" went on for three years', by Clay Harris, *Financial Times*, 9 October 1997; 'Gold fever strikes in Jakarta', by Andreas Harsono, *The Nation* (Bangkok), 24 January 1997; 'All in the game to Suharto clan', by Manuela Saragosa, *Financial Times*, 8 May 1997; 'Empty Motherlode?', by John McBeth, *Far Eastern Economic Review*, 10 April 1997.

5 Numerous books and papers have been written about east Asia's long period of economic growth, many of them based on the World Bank's *The East Asian Miracle: Economic Growth and Public Policy*. World Bank/OUP, 1993.

6 Among them Paul Krugman, Christopher Lingle, Michael Porter and various south-east Asian academics who struggled to make themselves heard above the din of praise for the continuing 'miracle'.

7 'The Myth of Asia's Miracle', by Paul Krugman, *Foreign Affairs*, November/December 1994. Interestingly, the World Bank had made a similar comment in its famous report on Asian 'miracle' economies. 'In this sense there is little

that is "miraculous" about the HPAEs' [High-performing Asian economies'] superior record of growth; it is largely due to superior accumulation of physical and human capital.' *The East Asian Miracle*, p. 5. World Bank/OUP, 1993.

8 'US ports feel winds of change', by Christopher Parkes and Anne Counsell, *Financial Times*, 5 November 1996.

9 'Lessons from the Thais', by Jeff Sachs, *Financial Times*, 30 July 1997.

10 The poem by an anonymous author or authors received wide distribution over the Internet.

11 'Fragility of Mahathir's vision is exposed', by James Kynge, *Financial Times*, 5 September 1997.

12 'Thai efforts on economy "satisfy IMF"', by Robert Chote, *Financial Times*, 19 September 1997.

13 'And South-East Asia thinks it's all over', *The Economist*, 8 November 1997; 'Jakarta set for radical reform – IMF chief', by Sander Thoenes, *Financial Times*, 13 November 1997; 'Indonesia's turn', *Financial Times*, 3 November 1997; 'Suharto relatives defiant over bank closures', by Sander Thoenes, *Financial Times*, 5 November 1997.

14 'The rise and fall of Thailand's technocrats', by Ben Davies, *Asiamoney*, February 1997.

15 'Lessons from the Thais', by Jeff Sachs, *Financial Times*, 30 July 1997.

16 'Malaysia model in need of update', by James Kynge, *Financial Times*, 10 October 1997.

17 These exchanges were widely reported. For a summary, see 'Complacency gives way to contagion', by John Ridding and James Kynge, *Financial Times*, 13 January 1998.

18 Actual deals were commoner in South Korea than in south-east Asia, where foreign investors remained wary well into 1998 in spite of the cheapness of the assets on offer. But foreign investors were negotiating for stakes in various Thai banks, and Tesco, the UK food retailer, was reported to be planning to pay £150 million for a Thai hypermarket operator.

19 'Toyota halts car output in Thailand', by Ted Bardacke and Michiyo Nakamoto, *Financial Times*, 6 November 1997.

20 'Bargains aplenty at Bangkok's bizarre bazaar', by John Ridding and Ted Bardacke, *Financial Times* 8–9 November 1997; 'Fire-sale, Thai-style', *The Economist*, 8 November 1997.

21 'Asian turmoil hits Ladbroke', by Scheherazade Daneshkhu, *Financial Times*, 14 November 1997.

22 *Emerging Asia: Changes and Challenges*, p. 96. ADB, 1997.

23 'How the World Works', by James Fallows, *The Atlantic Monthly*, December 1993. Fallows warned the West that east Asian economies were growing strongly because they were playing by different (non free market) rules, but he failed to appreciate the concomitant weaknesses of Asian economic and corporate management.

24 'First in, first out? Thailand is tackling its crisis by focusing on structural reform', by Ted Bardacke, *Financial Times*, 25 February 1998. Thirty-two professions are restricted to Thais.

25 'A potentially explosive brew', by Victor Mallet, *Financial Times*, 11 November 1993.

26 Interview with the author, 27 January 1997.

27 'Kumagai sells stake in Thai expressway', by Victor Mallet, *Financial Times*, 15

March 1994; 'Thailand reneges on $1bn contract', by Victor Mallet, *Financial Times*, 12 May 1993.

28 'Malaysia model in need of update', by James Kynge, *Financial Times*, 10 October 1997.

29 'Bambang's Challenge', by Henny Sender, *Far Eastern Economic Review*, 5 September 1996.

30 'Indonesia car project wins $690m loan', by Greg Earl, *Financial Times*, 13 August 1997; 'US joins Timor car dispute', *Financial Times*, 26 June 1997.

31 'Fishing for Suharto's hidden wealth', by Nick Cumming-Bruce (*Guardian*), reprinted in *Mail & Guardian* (South Africa), 5–11 June 1998.

32 *A Nation in Waiting: Indonesia in the 1990s*, p. 110, by Adam Schwarz. Allen and Unwin, 1994.

33 'Indonesia's Uncle Bob', *The Economist*, 29 March 1997.

34 Interview with the author, March 1997.

35 Interview with the author, 21 March 1997.

36 'Gone With the Wind', by John McBeth, *Far Eastern Economic Review*, 23 May 1996; 'Jail escape angers Indonesians', by Manuela Saragosa, *Financial Times*, 14 May 1996.

37 'Forest fund aids Suharto associate's company', by Manuela Saragosa, *Financial Times*, 30 January 1997.

38 Interview with the author, 24 March 1997.

39 'Dubious donor', by Nate Thayer, *Far Eastern Economic Review*, 7 August 1997; 'Narco-Nexus', by Nate Thayer, *Far Eastern Economic Review*, 24 April 1997.

40 'Too Fast, Too Loose', by Faith Keenan, *Far Eastern Economic Review*, 4 September 1997.

41 'Europe is doomed,' he told the author once at a cocktail party in Bangkok.

42 'Business briefing: Room to Move', *Far Eastern Economic Review*, 18 September 1997.

43 'Tarnishing the Image', by Sheryll Stothard, *Far Eastern Economic Review*, 4 September 1997.

44 Quoted in: 'How Optimism Built – and Doomed – A Thai Empire', by Raphael Pura, *Asian Wall Street Journal*, 31 March 1997.

45 There is much literature on the ethnic Chinese business community in Asia. One of the more recent books is *The New Taipans*, by Claudia Cragg. Century, 1995.

46 Interview with the author, quoted in 'Secrets of cultivating $5bn in sales', by Victor Mallet, *Financial Times*, 22 October 1993.

47 'CP unit reviews financial position', by Louise Lucas and William Barnes, *Financial Times*, 23 April 1998; and 'CP Group seeks strategy for survival in China', by Ted Bardacke, *Financial Times*, 27 March 1998.

48 'It's time to grow up', interview by Adi Ignatius and Gordon Fairclough, *Far Eastern Economic Review*, 14 March 1996.

49 'The search for the Asian manager: A survey of business in Asia', p. 15, by John Micklethwait, *The Economist*, 9 March 1996.

50 Interview with the author, 22 April 1997.

51 Interview with the author, quoted in 'Silk flowers and chips', by Victor Mallet, *Financial Times*, 30 November 1993.

52 David Roche of London-based Independent Strategy, quoted in 'The search for the Asian manager: a survey of business in Asia', p. 26, by John Micklethwait, *The Economist*, 9 March 1996.

53 'A Question of Class', by Michelle Zack, *Far Eastern Economic Review*, 4 December 1997.

54 Press conference, Bangkok, 24 January 1997.

55 Interview with the author, 29 March 1997.

56 'Efficiency, hard work . . . now for a spot of creativity', by James Kynge, *Financial Times*, 26–27 October 1997.

57 Interview with the author, 2 April 1997.

58 Interview with the author, 1 April 1997.

59 *Emerging Asia: Changes and Challenges*, pp. 44–5. ADB, May 1997.

60 'The real lesson from Asia', by Martin Wolf, *Financial Times*, 2 September 1997. The figures used for Thailand are calculated using the purchasing power parity method.

61 'Patten's Asia: Beyond the myths', by Chris Patten, *The Economist*, 4 January 1997.

62 'Bearish American Wisdom, or Why Failure Is Good for You', by James Grant, *International Herald Tribune*, 11 October 1996; 'East Asia: Don't Look Now, but Europeans Are Catching Up', by Gerald Segal, *International Herald Tribune*, 9 October 1996.

63 'East Asian shipwreck', *Financial Times*, 16 February 1998.

64 Interview in Forbes magazine, quoted in 'SM Lee sees Asian crisis as a setback, not end of a miracle', *New Straits Times*, 14 March 1998.

Chapter 5: Nature in retreat: South-east Asia's environmental disaster

1 *Hard Times*, by Charles Dickens. Chapman and Hall, 1854.

2 *A Malaysian Journey*, by Rehman Rashid. Rehman Rashid, 1993.

3 *WWF News*, Winter 1997/98.

4 These arguments and those in the following paragraph have been discussed in several UN and other reports, including: *Toward an Environmental Strategy for Asia*, World Bank, 1993; and pp. 199ff of *Emerging Asia: Changes and Challenges*, Bank, 1997.

5 *The Changing Geography of Asia*, p. 101, ed. Graham P. Chapman and Kathleen M. Baker, for the Department of Geography at SOAS, Routledge, 1992.

6 *Emerging Asia: Changes and Challenges*, p. 249. ADB, 1997.

7 Interview with the author, 29 January 1997.

8 'When the smoke clears in Asia', *The Economist*, 4 October 1997.

9 'Fire in the sky', *Far Eastern Economic Review*, 9 October 1997.

10 Among those concerned were experts from the Palm Oil Institute of Malaysia.

11 *WWF News*, Winter 1997/98.

12 El Niño, a current of warm water in the eastern Pacific, appears every few years and has a variety of effects on the world's weather. Among other things, it is linked to droughts in Indonesia.

13 'Where There's Smoke . . .', by Margot Cohen and Murray Hiebert, *Far Eastern Economic Review*, 2 October 1997.

14 'Trial by Fire', by Murray Hiebert and John McBeth, *Far Eastern Economic Review*, 16 October 1997; 'Indonesia given promises of help to fight fires', by Sander Thoenes, *Financial Times*, 26 September 1997.

15 See, for example, 'Suharto apologizes for smoke', by Greg Earl, *Financial Times*, 17 September 1997. Suharto cited 'obstacles that are not easy to overcome' in dealing with the fires.

16 'South-east Asian smog stumps meteorologists', by Stephen Fidler and Alexander Nicoll, *Financial Times*, 11 October 1991.

17 *The Changing Geography of Asia*, p. 100, ed. Graham P. Chapman and Kathleen M. Baker. Routledge, 1992.

Notes

18 'Skies darken over SE Asia', by James Fahn, *The Nation* (Bangkok), 3 October 1997.

19 *The Nation* (Bangkok) quoted in 'Regional tolerance of fires diminishing', Aprenet, via email, 27 September–10 October 1997.

20 'Trial by Fire', by Murray Hiebert and John McBeth, *Far Eastern Economic Review*, 16 October 1997.

21 'Malaysia gags research reports on smog', by James Kynge, *Financial Times*, 7 November 1997.

22 'Observer' column, *Financial Times*, 4 June 1998.

23 'A patchy record', by Victor Mallet, *Financial Times*, 24 June 1992. The figures came from a draft biodiversity action plan for Indonesia.

24 *Indonesia's New Order: The Dynamics of Socio-economic Transformation*, pp. 181ff, ed. Hal Hill. University of Hawaii Press, 1994.

25 *Marine Fisheries and Environment in the ASEAN Region*, by Suraphol Sudara, Dept of Marine Science, Chulalongkorn University, Bangkok, 1997.

26 In 1992, the so-called Vu Quang ox was discovered. Other previously unknown mammals have also been identified in Vietnam, including a deer-like animal known as the Truong Son muntjac. See 'New mammal discovered in Vietnam's lost world', by Adrian Edwards, Reuters, 21 August 1997.

27 'A patchy record', by Victor Mallet, *Financial Times*, 24 June 1992.

28 *Indonesia's New Order: The Dynamics of Socio-economic Transformation*, p. 65, ed. Hal Hill. University of Hawaii Press, 1994.

29 *Emerging Asia: Changes and Challenges*, pp. 222–3. ADB, 1997.

30 These and the paragraphs that follow are based on several articles written at the time: 'The city now standing still', by Victor Mallet, *Financial Times*, 27 November 1993; 'Third world city, first world smog', by Victor Mallet, *Financial Times*, 25 March 1992; 'Bangkok driven potty as traffic jams grow longer', by Victor Mallet, *Financial Times*, 1 August 1992; 'Asian city pollution "at danger levels"', by Victor Mallet, *Financial Times*, 25 October 1993.

31 UN Economic and Social Commission for Asia and the Pacific (Escap).

32 The report came from Professor Thephanom Muangman, dean of the environment and resources faculty at Mahidol University.

33 The Taiwan problem was described in 'Crowded island swamped by growing sea of rubbish', by Laura Tyson, *Financial Times*, 14 September 1996.

34 *Emerging Asia: Changes and Challenges*, p. 217. ADB, 1997.

35 'Stagnant rivers and poisoned seas', by Victor Mallet, *Financial Times*, 31 March 1993.

36 Interview with the author, 25 March 1997.

37 'Asian cities choking themselves to death', by Tom Wright, Reuters, 13 December 1996.

38 'The Soul of Cities', by Khoo Salma Nasution, *Far Eastern Economic Review*, 21 August 1997.

39 Most of the details on Chiang Mai are drawn from 'Bangkok in miniature: Chiang Mai, Thailand's northern capital', by Victor Mallet, *Financial Times*, 7 December 1993.

40 Interview with the author, 3 March 1997.

41 'Bangkok's new mayor sweeps city clean', by Chris Gelken, Gemini News, run in *Borneo Bulletin*, 7 April 1997.

42 '*Mu'ang* and *pa*: Elite views of nature in a changing Thailand', by Philip Stott, in *Thai Constructions of Knowledge*, ed. Manas Chitakasem and Andrew Turton. SOAS, 1991.

43 'Man and Nature in Malaysia: Attitudes to Wildlife and Conservation', by Adrian G. Marshall, in *Nature and Man in South East Asia*, ed P. A. Stott. SOAS, 1978.

44 A notorious example is Khao Sam Roi Yot National Park in Thailand, where the supposedly protected wetlands were devastated by the construction of commercial prawn farms in the early 1990s.

45 Interview with the author near Kapit, 17 August 1992.

46 For more details, see *Thailand's Boom!* by Pasuk Phongpaichit and Chris Baker. Silkworm Books, 1996.

47 'High-flyer's dam project swamped by doubts', by Kieran Cooke, *Financial Times*, 20 September 1995; 'Investors sought for Malaysia hydroelectric dam', by Kieran Cooke, *Financial Times*, 13 December 1995.

48 Lester Brown of the Worldwatch Institute in Washington has been one of the chief pessimists about the ability of Asia – especially China – to feed itself in the future.

49 *Emerging Asia: Changes and Challenges*, p. 207. ADB, 1997.

50 'When condom use becomes a cardinal sin', by Edward Luce, *Financial Times*, 23 September 1995; and 'Filipinos demonstrate against birth control', Reuters, 15 August 1994.

51 Interview with the author, 16 April 1997; 'Filipinos wrestle with message of birth control', by Victor Mallet, *Financial Times*, 11 August 1994.

52 'Palawan, Philippines' final frontier, fights to cement its green credentials', by Edward Luce, *Financial Times*, 9 November 1995; 'Policing Asia's last frontier', by Edward Luce, *Financial Times*, 18 November 1995; 'Protection for a final frontier', by Victor Mallet, *Financial Times*, 25 May 1993.

53 Mahathir used the words in a speech at an Asean summit in Singapore on 27 January 1992.

54 'Malaysia ridicules enemies of timber trade', by Victor Mallet, *Financial Times*, 12 February 1992.

55 'Cambodian tycoon acquires major timber concession', Reuter, 2 October 1997. For detailed accounts of the skulduggery surrounding the Cambodian timber trade, see the regular reports of the London-based NGO Global Witness.

56 'K. Kong Logging Rise Cited', by Kay Kimsong, *The Cambodia Daily*, 23 April 1997.

57 'Dancing With the Dragon', by Bruce Gilley, *Far Eastern Economic Review*, 11 December 1997.

58 Interview with the author, 5 February 1997.

59 Jonathan Rigg and Philip Stott in *The Changing Geography of Asia*, p. 97, ed. Graham P. Chapman and Kathleen M. Baker. Routledge, 1992; Philip Stott in *Thai Constructions of Knowledge*, p. 151, ed. Manas Chitakasem and Andrew Turton. SOAS, 1991.

60 'Rules must be right, and upheld', by Victor Mallet, *Financial Times*, 13 May 1993; 'Indonesia says improving logging practices', by Jim Della-Giacoma, Reuters, 20 May 1996; *Emerging Asia: Changes and Challenges*, p. 211. ADB, 1997.

61 'Guarding a dwindling asset', by Victor Mallet, *Financial Times*, 28 August 1992.

62 For a comprehensive history of the Philippine logging industry and an account of the Ormoc disaster, see *Power from the Forest: the politics of logging*, by Marites Danguilan Vitug. Philippine Center for Investigative Journalism, 1993.

Notes

63 *A Malaysian Journey*, pp. 142–3, by Rehman Rashid. Rehman Rashid, 1993.
64 Interview with the author, 30 January 1997.
65 'Fish war crisis brings Thai and Malaysian PMs to the table', by Ted Bardacke, *Financial Times*, 14 December 1995.
66 Similar scarcities have occurred in the West, it need hardly be said. Cod, for example, have been heavily overfished.
67 Other sources for the section on the marine environment include: interviews with Tan Kim Hooi and Jenny Wong of the Maritime Institute of Malaysia, 6 March 1997; *Marine Fisheries and Environment in the ASEAN Region*, by Suraphol Sudara, October 1996; *Environmental Strategy for Thailand*, by Mingsarn Kaosa-ard and Sunil S. Pednekar, Thailand Development Research Institute, September 1996; *Current issues on marine and coastal affairs in Malaysia*, by B. A. Hamzah and Jenny Wong, MIMA, October 1996; MIMA Bulletin 2/96; *Fisheries and Environment [in Sabah]*, by Junaidi Payne. World Wide Fund for Nature, Malaysia, June 1994; 'Fishing for Trouble', by Trish Saywell, and 'Floating Flashpoint', by Gordon Fairclough, both in *Far Eastern Economic Review*, 13 March 1997.
68 'Northern farmers do not oppose logging by influential persons due to concern over loss of biodiversity or fear of global warming,' wrote one academic about Thailand. 'They are more immediately worried about threats to the water supplies upon which they depend for wet rice cultivation if upper watershed areas are cleared.' 'Political Economy of Environment in Thailand', p. 3, by Philip Hirsch, *Journal of Contemporary Asia Publishers*, Manila, 1993.
69 'Asians, Too, Want Good Environment', by Tommy Koh, *International Herald Tribune*, 1 February 1994.
70 *A Malaysian Journey*, pp. 272–3, by Rehman Rashid. Rehman Rashid, 1993.
71 Interview with the author, 15 April 1997.
72 *Emerging Asia: Changes and Challenges*, pp. 199 and 261. ADB, 1997.

Chapter 6: Enemies outside and in: The 'Balkans of the Orient' and the great powers
1 'In Other Words', *Far Eastern Economic Review*, 19 June 1997.
2 'An Asia-Pacific Consensus', by Kishore Mahbubani, *Foreign Affairs*, September/ October 1997.
3 'Burma Road', by Bertil Lintner, *Far Eastern Economic Review*, 6 November 1997.
4 There were several examples of this in the 1990s. On March 7 1997, for example, China moved an exploration rig into an area off the coast of central Vietnam already set aside by the Vietnamese for exploration under their jurisdiction, and ignored Vietnamese protests. See 'Drawn to The Fray', *Far Eastern Economic Review*, 3 April 1997.
5 In March 1997, Admiral Joseph Prueher of the US Pacific Command visited Vietnam and spoke of a 'nascent military relationship'. See 'China's Creeping Assertiveness', by Gerald Segal, *Asian Wall Street Journal*, 27 March 1997.
6 Chinese military expenditure is notoriously difficult to estimate from official figures. But according to the International Institute for Strategic Studies, China's defence budget rose steadily from US$18.8 billion in 1991 to US$28.5 billion in 1994. (Quoted in *Asia's Deadly Triangle*, p. 140, by Kent E. Calder. Nicholas Brealey Publishing, 1996.)
7 *Asia's Deadly Triangle*, p. 120 by Kent E. Calder. Nicholas Brealey Publishing, 1996.
8 'Spratly spat moves into murkier water', by Victor Mallet, *Financial Times*, 28 July 1992. The US company was Crestone Energy of Denver.

9 'Towards one Southeast Asia', by José Almonte, *The Sunday Chronicle*, 14 March 1993, from a paper presented to a seminar on south-east Asian unity at Chulalongkorn University in Bangkok.

10 'Law of the Seize', by Andrew Sherry and Rigoberto Tiglao, *Far Eastern Economic Review*, 12 June 1997.

11 'Drawn to The Fray', by Michael Vatikiotis, Murray Hiebert, Nigel Holloway and Matt Forney, *Far Eastern Economic Review*, 3 April 1997.

12 'China's Creeping Assertiveness', by Gerald Segal, *Asian Wall Street Journal*, 27 March 1997.

13 See 'US–Singapore base deal', Reuters, in *Financial Times*, 16 January 1998, and *The International Politics of the Asia-Pacific, 1945–1995*, p. 144, by Michael Yahuda. Routledge, 1996.

14 'Accommodate this ambition: China must be induced to develop a stake in the Asia-Pacific status quo', by José Almonte, *Financial Times*, 24 April 1996.

15 'Not so fast', *The Economist*, 18 January 1997.

16 The 1967 Bangkok Declaration at the founding of Asean said that one of the aims of the group was 'to promote regional peace and stability through abiding respect for justice and the rule of law in the relationship among countries of the region and adherence to the principles of the United Nations Charter'.

17 Commenting on regional economic integration, the Thai MP Surin Pitsuwan said as an aside: 'Effectively, southern China will be part of Asean' (interview with the author, 29 January 1997). One can imagine the horror in south-east Asia if a Chinese official had suggested that Asean would effectively be part of China.

18 *Dictionary of the Modern Politics of South-East Asia*, p. 1, by Michael Leifer. Routledge, 1996.

19 Interview with the author, 1 April 1997.

20 'Burma Road', by Bertil Lintner, *Far Eastern Economic Review*, 6 November 1997.

21 Interview with the author, 31 March 1997.

22 Interview with the author, 6 March 1997.

23 'An Asia-Pacific Consensus', by Kishore Mahbubani, *Foreign Affairs*, September/ October 1997. He emphasized the importance of economic growth, political stability and education as measures of good governance, but went on to say: 'Private conversations also reveal a common aspiration to live in a society marked by the rule of law. Most people in the Asia-Pacific welcome the principle of equality under the law, which is the foundation of Western societies.'

24 'US starts to dance in tune with Asean music', by James Kynge, *Financial Times*, 30 July 1997.

25 Communication with the author.

26 The meeting was held in Manila on 22–3 August 1996 and the text published by Southeast Asia Beyond 2000. Interestingly the participants paid special tribute to Anwar Ibrahim, Malaysia's Deputy Prime Minister, as well as to President Ramos of the Philippines.

27 Speech given at the 1996 Gwinganna Forum of the Asia–Australia Institute of New South Wales in Beijing, October 1996.

28 *Arms, Transparency and Security in South-east Asia*, p. 41, ed. Bates Gill and J. N. Mak. Stockholm International Peace Research Institute/Oxford University Press, 1997.

29 'Which direction for Asean?' by Walden Bello, *The Nation* [Bangkok], 30 April 1997.

30 Interview with the author, 29 January 1997.

31 Interview with the author, 28 January 1997.

32 'Never mind the quality', *The Economist*, 1 March 1997; 'In other words', *Far Eastern Economic Review*, 6 March 1997.

33 *Arms, Transparency and Security in South-east Asia*, pp. 38–43, ed. Bates Gill and J. N. Mak. Stockholm International Peace Research Institute/Oxford University Press, 1997.

34 *The International Politics of the Asia-Pacific, 1945–1995*, p. 13, by Michael Yahuda. Routledge, 1996.

35 Communication with the author.

36 Interview with the author, 29 January 1997.

37 'Power vacuum danger', by Kieran Cooke, *Financial Times*, 5 December 1995.

38 SIPRI figures, quoted in 'Bear Market', by Charles Bickers, *Far Eastern Economic Review*, 4 September 1997.

39 'World arms sales growth put at 8 per cent', by Alexander Nicoll, *Financial Times*, 15 October 1997.

40 'Changing Modalities of Southeast Asian Security', by Dewi Fortuna Anwar, published in *The Indonesian Quarterly*, fourth quarter 1996, Centre for Strategic and International Studies, Jakarta.

41 'Pointless?', *The Economist*, 27 July 1996. See also: 'All ARF and No Bite', by Michael Vatikiotis, *Far Eastern Economic Review*, 2 May 1996; and 'China's Creeping Assertiveness', by Gerald Segal, *Asian Wall Street Journal*, 27 March 1997.

42 Interview with the author, 29 January 1997.

Chapter 7: Ten troubled tigers: The nations of south-east Asia
BURMA: Democracy delayed

1 Private communication with the author by foreign aid worker, February 1997.

2 'Health in Myanmar. An Interpretive Review of Data Sources Collected with the Assistance of Unicef-Myanmar, the Myanmar Ministry of Health, World Vision International-Myanmar, and other Organizations', by David Chandler, 1997.

3 'Velvet Glove', by Bertil Lintner, *Far Eastern Economic Review*, 7 May 1998.

4 'Burma's junta in move to bolster image', by William Barnes, *Financial Times*, 17 November 1997. The person quoted is Debbie Stothard, Malaysian co-ordinator of the Alternative Asean Network on Burma.

5 Quoted in *The Economist*, 1 June 1996.

6 Interview with the author, 18 February 1997.

7 *Foreign Economic Trends Report: Burma*, US Embassy, Rangoon, July 1996.

8 Interview with the author, 18 February 1997.

9 Major Hla Min, interview with the author, 19 February 1997.

10 Madeleine Albright, US Secretary of State, was among those who raised the issue. See 'Safe at Home', by Bertil Lintner, *Far Eastern Economic Review*, 14 August 1997.

11 'Diehard Optimist', by Flemming Ytzen, *Far Eastern Economic Review*, 7 May 1998.

THAILAND: The smile that faded

1 The diplomat's name is Mohammed Said Khoja. See 'Thai police bend rule of law,' by Victor Mallet, *Financial Times*, 29 November 1994.

2 *Thailand's Boom!*, p. 221, by Pasuk Phongpaichit and Chris Baker. Silkworm Books, 1996.

Notes

3 It is difficult to convey the flavour of Bernard Trink's column by quoting brief excerpts. It is an extraordinary hodge-podge of recommendations, warnings and observations about go-go bars, restaurants and everyday Bangkok life.

4 'Bachelor party no fun for Thai MPs', by Victor Mallet, *Financial Times*, 2 August 1993.

5 The slogan of General Chatichai Choonhavan, prime minister from 1988 until a coup d'état in 1991.

6 The figure is from the story 'Opponents blast prime minister's stand on corruption', Associated Press, 11 December 1996, quoting the Thai Farmers Bank Research Center.

7 Interview with the author, 27 January 1997.

8 Interview with the author, 24 January 1997.

9 Banharn Silpa-archa and Chavalit Yongchaiyudh.

10 'Thais back constitution for open government', by Ted Bardacke, *Financial Times*, 29 September 1997.

11 'Danger Ahead: Economic crisis aggravates constitutional debate', by Michael Vatikiotis and Rodney Tasker, *Far Eastern Economic Review*, 11 September 1997.

LAOS: No escape from modernity

1 Interview with the author, 13 February 1997.

2 For further discussion on this point, see *Lao Peasants under Socialism and Post-socialism*, p.xix, by Grant Evans. Silkworm Books, 1995.

3 'Change of Face', by Bertil Lintner, *Far Eastern Economic Review*, 18 April 1996.

4 'Lakeside resort taps top-end of tourism market', *Vientiane Times*, 10–16 May 1996.

5 Much of the section on Laos was based on interviews with the author during a visit to Laos in February 1997. However, most interviewees asked to remain anonymous.

CAMBODIA: The slow recovery from 'Year Zero'

1 This was Nate Thayer's historic interview with Pol Pot in Khmer Rouge-held northern Cambodia. 'On the Stand', *Far Eastern Economic Review*, 30 October 1997.

2 The acronym is from the French, meaning the United National Front for an Independent, Neutral, Peaceful and Co-operative Cambodia.

3 'Cambodia's many-headed monster', *The Economist*, 1 November 1997.

4 'Cambodian Leaders in Exile Seek International Monitoring of New Elections', by Barbara Crossette, *New York Times*, 28 September 1997.

5 See, for instance, 'Khmer Rouge defectors swap Mao-style caps for army kit', by Ted Bardacke, *Financial Times*, 6 June 1997.

VIETNAM: Victorious but poor

1 *Paradise of the Blind*, by Duong Thu Huong, translated by Phan Huy Duong and Nina McPherson. Penguin Books, 1994.

2 *The Sorrow of War*, by Bao Ninh. English version by Frank Palmos, based on the translation from the Vietnamese by Vo Bang Thanh and Phan Thanh Hao, with Katerina Pierce. Martin Secker and Warburg, 1993.

3 *Following Ho Chi Minh: The Memoirs of a North Vietnamese Colonel*, by Bui Tin, translated and adapted by Judy Stowe and Do Van. Hurst and Co., 1995.

4 'Vietnam premier backs reform', by Jeremy Grant, *Financial Times*, 29 October

1997; and 'Vietnam reforms run into heavy weather', by Jeremy Grant, *Financial Times*, 9 July 1997.

5 'Vietnam's army makes a lucky strike in leisure', by Jeremy Grant, *Financial Times*, 10 June 1996; and 'Saigon on a Roll', by Adam Schwarz, *Far Eastern Economic Review*, 7 November 1996.

6 Interview with the author, 24 April 1997.

7 'Hanoi keeps grip on power', by Jeremy Grant, *Financial Times*, 29 July 1997.

8 Interview with the author, April 1997. Like many Vietnamese, the interviewee asked to remain anonymous.

9 Interview with the author, April 1997. Again, it is not possible to name the person concerned.

10 'Steam rises: Corruption galvanizes pressure for political reform', by Faith Keenam, *Far Eastern Economic Review*, 2 April 1998.

MALAYSIA: Vision 2020 and the Malay dilemma

1 Doubt has been cast on the accuracy of such population statistics because of their extreme political sensitivity, but most estimates are in this range. These figures are from 'Malaysian Dilemmas', by S. Jayasankaran and Murray Hiebert, *Far Eastern Economic Review*, 4 September 1997.

2 *The Malay Dilemma*, by Mahathir bin Mohamad. Times Books International, 1970.

3 'The Malay wanted it all, and wanted it NOW,' wrote the author Rehman Rashid. 'In 1983, it was somewhat sheepishly admitted that of the 55,000 loans MARA [an NEP lending institution] had given to Malay businesses by then, nearly 90 per cent had not been repaid when due.' (*A Malaysian Journey*, by Rehman Rashid. Rehman Rashid, 1993.)

4 Interview with the author, 3 March 1997.

5 Interview with the author, 3 March 1997.

6 'Students the biggest buyers of condoms', *The Straits Times* (Singapore), 10 March 1997. The newspaper was quoting from reports in Malaysian newspapers.

7 Interview with the author, 26 February 1997.

8 'Mahathir's whitewater ride', by James Kynge, *Financial Times*, 26 August 1997. The same article quoted Mahathir as saying: 'Massive and rapid growth is a wonderful buffer. Like a river in flood it hides the rocks on the river bed.' It suggested that the rocks on the river bed were starting to threaten Mahathir's achievements.

9 He was later sacked and detained after Mahathir imposed capital controls on the economy, and became the focus of a political reform movement.

10 'Credible clean-up', by S. Jayasankaran, *Far Eastern Economic Review*, 19 June 1997.

INDONESIA: Fin de régime – and end of empire?

1 'Worlds Apart', by John McBeth, *Far Eastern Economic Review*, 24 July 1997.

2 Interview with the author, 25 March 1997.

3 Interview with the author, 20 March 1997.

4 The account of the end of Suharto's rule is drawn from the numerous news reports of the time, including those in the *Financial Times*, *The Economist* and the *Washington Post*.

5 'Unlikely champion of free trade', by Victor Mallet, *Financial Times*, 3 November 1994.

Notes

SINGAPORE: Brutal efficiency

1 *Abraham's Promise*, by Philip Jeyaretnam. Times Editions, 1995.
2 'In Asia and Elsewhere, Smaller Will Be the Better Way to Govern', by George Yeo, *International Herald Tribune*, 22 June 1994.
3 *The World in 2020*, p. 258, by Hamish McRae. HarperCollins, 1995.
4 William Gibson, quoted in 'Citizens who are failing to be paragons of virtue', by Edward Luce, *Financial Times*, 4 May 1996.
5 The Yeo quotation, and the comment on Goh, come from 'Human rights, democracy and development: the debate in east Asia', by Rosemary Foot. This was an academic paper originally prepared for a series of seminars at St Antony's College, Oxford.
6 'Singaporean Home Minister Aims for Haven of Security', Associated Press story published in *Cambodia Daily*, 26 February 1997.
7 'The 10% that's crucial to S'pore success', by Chua Mui Hoong. *The Straits Times* [Singapore], 1 April 1997.
8 Interview with the author, 1 April 1997.
9 Communication with the author.
10 *Singapore's Authoritarian Capitalism*, p. 93–5, by Christopher Lingle. Edicions Sirocco/The Locke Institute, 1996. For more details on these matters, see chapter 2.
11 *Economic Growth and Political Change in Asia*, by Graham Field. Macmillan Press, 1995.
12 Interview with the author, 2 April 1997.
13 Interview with the author, 27 March 1997.
14 Source: Port Authority of Singapore, February 1997.
15 Interview with the author, 29 March 1997.

BRUNEI: Sultan of swing

1 'Sultan's brother denies owning Asprey', by Clay Harris, *Financial Times*, 22 November 1997; 'Brunei sultan invokes sovereign immunity in sex raps', Agence France Presse in *Philippine Star*, 9 April 1997; 'Brunei Denies Holding US Beauty Queen as Sex Slave', Associated Press in *The Cambodia Daily*, 7 March 1997; 'Former Miss USA files another suit in battle against sultan', Associated Press, 27 March 1998.
2 'Prince used 40 prostitutes, UK court told', AFP, reprinted in *The Citizen* newspaper, 20 February 1998. 'Secret deal ends prince's £180m High Court feud', by Nick Pryer, *Evening Standard*, 17 March 1998.
3 *The Richest Man in the World*, by James Bartholomew, pp. 186–90. Viking Penguin, 1989.
4 'Sultan's swing to reform', by Kieran Cooke, *Financial Times*, 4 August 1995.
5 *The Richest Man in the World*, by James Bartholomew, p. 124. Viking Penguin, 1989.
6 'Brunei frets about youths as govt aims for diverse economy', by Bill Tarrant. Reuters, in *Jakarta Post*, 22 March 1997.
7 'Brunei frets about youths as govt aims for diverse economy', by Bill Tarrant. Reuters, in *Jakarta Post*, 22 March 1997.

THE PHILIPPINES: Chaotic democracy

1 *Manila Bulletin*, 10 April 1997.
2 Interview with the author, 16 April 1997.
3 '*Trapo*' also means a rag.

4 Interview with the author, 16 April 1997.

5 *In Our Image: America's Empire in the Philippines*, by Stanley Karnow, p. 360 and p. 390. Random House, 1989.

6 Interview with the author, in 'Tiger cub starts to find its feet', by Victor Mallet, *Financial Times*, 3 June 1994.

7 The superficial similarities between Estrada and former film actor and US President Ronald Reagan did not go unnoticed.

8 'B-Movie Actor Is Rising Star of Philippines Politics', by Seth Mydans, *New York Times*, 3 October 1997.

9 Interview with the author, 10 April 1997.

10 'One more time for the cameras, Imelda', by Justin Marozzi, *Financial Times*, 4–5 October 1997.

11 Interview with the author, 15 April 1997.

12 Quoted in 'A swansong performer', by Justin Marozzi, *Financial Times*, 28 May 1998.

13 *In Our Image: America's Empire in the Philippines*, by Stanley Karnow, p. 232. Random House, 1989.

14 'Return to arms', by Rigoberto Tiglao, *Far Eastern Economic Review*, 24 July 1997.

15 As noted elsewhere in this book, most Filipinos are keen to practise family planning but the Catholic church and its Opus Dei sect (dubbed 'Octopus Dei' by Senator Juan Flavier, the family planning advocate) make it difficult by applying pressure on the central government.

16 Malcolm Potts, International Family Planning, in a letter to *The Economist*, 8 June 1996.

Chapter 8: After the crash: The unfinished revolution

1 'It may take us three years, but we will recover', by Sheila McNulty, *Financial Times*, 30 March 1999.

2 'The coming Asian Crisis', by Clyde Prestowitz, *Far Eastern Economic Review*, 19 August 1999.

3 'The worst is over, says Mahathir', by Sheila McNulty, *Financial Times*, 23 April 1999.

4 'Is Asia's recovery sustainable?', by Angus Armstrong and Michael Spencer, Deutsche Bank global emerging markets report, May 1999. *The Economist* magazine phrased it slightly differently, saying that 'for far too long, money was lent by banks that did not care about credit risk to companies that cared even less. Bad loans were replaced with fresh ones like so much dirty linen. Worse, many banks were part of bigger business groups, into which they funnelled bank deposits, unhampered by regulatory checks'. – 'Asia's economies: on their feet again?', *The Economist*, 21 August 1999.

5 'Things Fall Apart', by Dan Murphy, *Far Eastern Economic Review*, 13 May 1999.

6 'Tycoon granted diplomatic protection against charges', *Hong Kong Standard*, 13 May 1999.

7 'Back to school', by Dan Biers, Michael Vatikiotis, Rodney Tasker and Prangtip Daorueng, *Far Eastern Economic Review*, 8 April 1999.

8 'Saviour complex', by S. Jayasankaran, *Far Eastern Economic Review*, 12 August 1999.

9 'The Asian myths', by Ronnie Chan, *Financial Times*, 24 June 1999. Other analysts who made similar points included Jeffrey Sachs, the economics professor who heads the Harvard International Institute of Development. See

'Missing Pieces', by Jeffrey Sachs, *Far Eastern Economic Review*, 25 February 1999.

10 Miller told a conference in Singapore that the good news on the capital controls was that the experiment was 'at best useless. The bad news is that the episode was actually harmful to Malaysia and its citizens'. – from 'Malaysian lending remains weak, by Sheila McNulty, *Financial Times*, 9 July 1999.

11 'Reforms leave Malaysian banks in dark', by Sheila McNulty, *Financial Times*, 5 August 1999.

12 'Shelter from the storm', by Peter Montagnon and Sheila McNulty, *Financial Times*, 4 August 1999.

13 Both trials were widely reported. Among other articles, see 'Guilty as Charged', by Murray Hiebert and Simon Elegant, *Far Eastern Economic Review*, 22 April 1999; 'Anwar is jailed for six years' and 'Anwar awakens Malaysians' political awareness', both by Sheila McNulty, *Financial Times*, 15 April 1999; Charges changed as Anwar trial begins, by Sheila McNulty, *Financial Times*, 8 June 1999; and 'The verdict on Malaysia', *The Economist*, 17 April 1999.

14 'Malaysia opposition party seeks widespread reforms', by Sheila McNulty, *Financial Times*, 2 July 1999.

15 See 'Below the belt', by S. Jayasankaran, *Far Eastern Economic Review*, 13 May 1999; 'Eye of The Storm', by S. Jayasankaran, *Far Eastern Economic Review*, 11 March 1999; and 'Anwar awakens Malaysians' political awareness', by Sheila McNulty, *Financial Times*, 15 April 1999.

16 'Free at last', by John McBeth, Dan Murphy and Margot Cohen, *Far Eastern Economic Review*, 17 June 1999.

17 'Fraying at the edges', *The Economist*, 21 August 1999.

18 'All in the family', *Time*, 24 May 1999.

19 'Jakarta names 200 top state bank debtors', by Sander Thoenes, *Financial Times*, 2 June 1999.

20 'On the loose in Singapore', *The Economist*, 29 May 1999.

21 'Rangoon Moves to Wipe Out Opposition', by Kevin Sullivan, *International Herald Tribune*, 25 May 1999. Suu Kyi made the statement in a videotape sent to the UN.

22 'Burma junta keeps tight grip on power', by Ted Bardacke, *Financial Times*, 27 May 1999.

23 'Vietnam party expels dissident', by Jonathan Birchall, *Financial Times*, 8 January 1999; and 'Party 'must tighten grip', Reuters report in *Financial Times*, 31 July 1999.

24 'Indonesian haze rolls over neighbours', by Sander Thoenes and Sheila McNulty, *Financial Times*, 7–8 August 1999; 'Through the glass, darkly', *The Economist*, 14 August 1999, and 'Environment-Asia-Smog' by Claudia Gazzini, Reuters, 6 August 1999.

25 'GIs come back?', *The Economist*, 24 April 1999.

26 'APEC's family feud', *The Economist*, 21 November 1998; 'Gore complaint rocks Apec summit' and 'Gore speech raises fears of backlash', both by Sheila McNulty and Peter Montagnon, *Financial Times*, 18 November 1998.

27 'Seaside Boom', by Rigoberto Tiglao, *Far Eastern Economic Review*, 8 July 1999.

28 'Asean ponders its modest role', by Sheila McNulty, *Financial Times*, 27 July 1999.

29 Quoted in 'Mahathir tells Africa to follow Asia's development model', by Angela Quintal, South African Press Association, 19 October 1999.

Notes

30 'Don't expect too much', by Peter Montagnon and Sheila McNulty, *Financial Times*, 17 November 1998.

31 'Veteran Asian leader scorns US policy', by Richard Lambert, Peter Montagnon and Will Dawkins, *Financial Times*, 19 May 1999.

32 The book is published by the Monash Asia Institute, Australia.

33 See 'Might Asia lose a decade?' by Stephen Fidler, and the accompanying graph, *Financial Times*, 27 November 1997. Graham Field, in his book *Economic Growth and Political Change in Asia* (Macmillan Press, 1995) made the point that Brazil grew at 8 percent a year between 1965 and 1980 and was once expected to be one of the world's biggest economies because of its 'broad social strengths', as opposed to the narrow economic focus of South Korea and Japan. At the time he wrote his book, analysts were taking the opposite view and predicting indefinite Asian growth for the opposite reason, in other words, because of east Asia's concentration on economic matters.

34 Interview with the author, 28 January 1997.

35 The modernizing of politics and society always makes for turbulence, disagreement and nostalgia. As G.P. Jones and A.G. Pool wrote of Britain: 'The one school deplored the passing of chivalry; the other was glad to be rid of servility and monopoly; and Sir Walter Scott made a fortune by recreating the old unreal world of romance for those who lived in the new grim world of reform.' (*A Hundred Years of Economic Development in Great Britain (1840–1940)*. Duckworth, 1940.)

36 *A Hundred Years of Economic Development in Great Britain (1840–1940)*, by G.P. Jones and A.G. Pool. Duckworth, 1940.

37 *The Making of the English Working Class*, by E.P. Thompson. Penguin 1991 (first published by Victor Gollancz, 1963).

38 *Penguin Economic History of Britain, vol 3: Industry and Empire*, by E.J. Hobsbawm. Penguin, 1990 (first published by Weidenfeld and Nicolson, 1968).

39 See *Emerging Asia: Changes and Challenges*, pp142–197. ADB, 1997.

40 Quoted in *The International Politics of the Asia-Pacific, 1945–1995*, by Michael Yahuda. Routledge, 1996.

Select Bibliography

Anwar Ibrahim. 1996. *The Asian Renaissance*. Times Books International, Kuala Lumpur.

Asian Development Bank. 1997. *Emerging Asia: Changes and Challenges*. ADB, Manila.

Bartholomew, James. 1989. *The Richest Man in the World*. Viking Penguin, London.

Bentley, Michael. 1996. *Politics Without Democracy 1815–1914: Perception and Preoccupation in British Government*. Fontana Press, London.

Berman, Marshall. 1983. *All That is Solid Melts into Air*. Verso, London.

Bone, Robert C. 1966. *Contemporary Southeast Asia*. Random House, New York.

Brazil, David. 1996. *No Money, No Honey! A candid look at sex-for-sale in Singapore*. Angsana Books, Singapore.

Brown, David. 1996. *The State and Ethnic Politics in Southeast Asia*. Routledge, London.

Buruma, Ian. 1996. *The Missionary and the Libertine*. Faber and Faber, London.

Calder, Kent E. 1996. *Asia's Deadly Triangle: How Arms, Energy and Growth Threaten to Destabilise Asia-Pacific*. Nicholas Brealey Publishing, London.

Campos, José Edgardo and Hilton L. Root. 1996. *The Key to the Asian Miracle: Making Shared Growth Credible*. The Brookings Institution, Washington DC.

Chanda, Nayan. 1986. *Brother Enemy: The War After the War – A History of Indochina Since the Fall of Saigon*. Macmillan Publishing, New York.

Chandler, David. 1992. *Brother Number One: A Political Biography of Pol Pot*. Westview Press, Boulder, Colorado.

Chapman, Graham P. and Kathleen Baker (eds). 1992. *The Changing Geography of Asia*. Routledge, London.

Chitakasem, Manas and Andrew Turton (eds). 1991. *Thai Constructions of Knowledge*. SOAS, London.

Chong, Alan. 1991. *Goh Chok Tong: Singapore's New Premier*. Pelanduk Publications, Malaysia.

Communist Party of Vietnam. 1996. *Eighth National Congress documents*. The Gioi Publishers, Hanoi.

Confucius. Translated by D.C. Lau. 1979. *The Analects*. Penguin Books, London.

Cragg, Claudia. 1995. *The New Taipans: A Vital Source Book on the People and Business of the Pacific Rim*. Random House, London.

Da Cunha, Derek (ed.). 1996. *Debating Singapore: Reflective Essays*. Institute of Southeast Asian Studies, Singapore.

De Guzman, Arnel F. 1996. *Goddesses of the Lust Triangle: An Excursion into Manila's Erotic Dance Industry*. The Media Gallery, the Philippines.

Dickens, Charles. 1854. *Hard Times*. Chapman and Hall, London.

Dobbs-Higginson, Michael S. 1995. *Asia Pacific: Its Role in the New World Disorder*. Mandarin, London.

Dostaler, Gilles et al (eds). 1992. *Gunnar Myrdal and His Works*. Harvest House, Montreal.

Dower, John. 1996. *Japan in War and Peace: Essays on History, Culture and Race*. HarperCollins, London.

Evans, Grant. 1995. *Lao Peasants under Socialism and Post-socialism*. Silkworm Books, Bangkok.

Fallows, James. 1995. *Looking at the Sun: The Rise of the New East Asian Economic and Political System*. Vintage Books, New York.

Fan Yew Teng. 1989. *The UMNO Drama: Power Struggles in Malaysia*. Egret Publications, Kuala Lumpur.

Field, Graham. 1995. *Economic Growth and Political Change in Asia*. Macmillan Press, London.

Fukuyama, Francis. 1992. *The End of History and the Last Man*. Penguin Books, London.

Gill, Bates and J.N. Mak (eds). 1997. *Arms, Transparency and Security in South-East Asia*. SIPRI/Oxford University Press.

Gomez, Edmund Terence. 1991. *Money Politics in the Barisan Nasional*. Forum, Kuala Lumpur.

Gomez, Edmund Terence. 1994. *Political Business: Corporate Involvement of Malaysian Political Parties*. James Cook University of North Queensland.

Government of Singapore. 1991. *Singapore: The Next Lap*. Times Editions, Singapore.

Graham, Mark and Philip Round. 1994. *Thailand's Vanishing Flora and Fauna*. Finance One, Bangkok.

Hayslip, Le Ly, with Jay Wurts. 1990. *When Heaven and Earth Changed*

Places: A Vietnamese Woman's Journey from War to Peace. Penguin Books, New York.

Hewison, Kevin (ed.). 1997. *Political Change in Thailand: Democracy and Participation*. Routledge, London.

Hill, Hal (ed.). 1994. *Indonesia's New Order: The Dynamics of Socio-Economic Transformation*. University of Hawaii Press.

Hirsch, Philip. 1993. *Political Economy of Environment in Thailand*. Journal of Contemporary Asian Publishers, Manila.

Hobsbawm, E. J. 1990. Penguin Economic History of Britain, vol 3: *Industry and Empire*. Penguin Books, London.

Huong, Duong Thu. 1994. *Paradise of the Blind*. Translated by Phan Huy Duong and Nina McPherson. Penguin Books, London.

Jeyaretnam, Philip. 1995. *Abraham's Promise*. Times Books International, Singapore.

Jomo, K. S. (ed.). 1995. *Privatizing Malaysia: Rents, Rhetoric, Realities*. Westview Press, Boulder, Colorado.

Jones, G. P. and A. G. Pool. 1940. *A Hundred Years of Economic Development in Great Britain (1840–1940)*. Duckworth, England.

Karnow, Stanley. 1989. *In Our Image: America's Empire in the Philippines*. Random House, New York.

Karnow, Stanley. 1991. *Vietnam: A History*. Penguin Books, New York.

Khoo Boo Teik. 1996. *Paradoxes of Mahathirism: An Intellectual Biography of Mahathir Mohamad*. Oxford University Press, Kuala Lumpur.

Kiernan, Ben. 1996. *The Pol Pot Regime: Race, Power, and Genocide in Cambodia under the Khmer Rouge, 1975–79*. Yale University Press, Connecticut.

Klausner, William J. 1997. *Thai Culture in Transition*. The Siam Society, Bangkok.

Krugman, Paul. 1996. *Pop Internationalism*. MIT Press, Cambridge, Massachusetts.

Leifer, Michael. 1995. *Dictionary of the Modern Politics of South-East Asia*. Routledge, London.

Letta, Corrado. 1996. *Listen to the Emerging Markets of Southeast Asia: Long-term Strategies for Effective Partnerships*. John Wiley and Sons, Chichester.

Lingle, Christopher. 1996. *Singapore's Authoritarian Capitalism: Asian Values, Free Market Illusions and Political Dependency*. Sirocco, Barcelona.

Lintner, Bertil. 1990. *Outrage: Burma's Struggle for Democracy*. White Lotus, Bangkok.

Lintner, Bertil. 1990. *Land of Jade*. White Lotus, Bangkok.

Macdonald, Peter. 1993. *Giap: The Victor in Vietnam.* Fourth Estate, London.

McRae, Hamish. 1995. *The World in 2020: Power, Culture and Prosperity: A Vision of the Future.* HarperCollins, London.

Mahathir Mohamad. 1996. *The Malay Dilemma.* Times Books International, Kuala Lumpur.

Mahathir Mohamad. 1995. *The Challenge.* Pelanduk Publications, Malaysia.

Mahathir Mohamad and Shintaro Ishihara. 1995. *The Voice of Asia: Two Leaders Discuss the Coming Century.* Kodansha International, Tokyo.

Mayhew, Henry. 1985. *London Labour and the London Poor* (selection). Penguin, London.

Minchin, James. 1990. *No Man is an Island: A portrait of Singapore's Lee Kuan Yew.* Allen & Unwin, Australia.

Ninh, Bao. 1993. *The Sorrow of War. English version by Frank Palmos* based on the translation from the Vietnamese by Vo Bang Thanh and Phan Thanh Hao, with Katerina Pierce. Secker & Warburg, London.

O'Brien, Niall. 1994. *Island of Tears, Island of Hope: Living the Gospel in a Revolutionary Situation.* Claretian Publications, Philippines.

Orwell, George. 1934. *Burmese Days.* Penguin Books, London.

Osborne, Milton. 1995. *Southeast Asia: An Introductory History.* Allen & Unwin, Australia.

Osborne, Milton. 1994. *Sihanouk: Prince of Light, Prince of Darkness.* Silkworm Books, Thailand.

Phongpaichit, Pasuk and Sungsidh Piriyarangsan. 1996. *Corruption and Democracy in Thailand.* Silkworm Books, Thailand.

Phongpaichit, Pasuk and Chris Baker. 1996. *Thailand's Boom!* Silkworm Books, Thailand.

Pye, Lucian W., with Mary W. Pye. 1985. *Asian Power and Politics: The Cultural Dimensions of Authority.* Belknap Press/Harvard University Press, Cambridge, Massachusetts.

Quah, Jon S. T. (ed.). 1990. *In Search of Singapore's National Values.* Times Academic Press, Singapore.

Ramage, Douglas E. 1995. *Politics in Indonesia: Democracy, Islam and the Ideology of Tolerance.* Routledge, London.

Ramos, Fidel V. 1994. *Time for Takeoff: The Philippines is Ready for Competitive Performance in the Asia-Pacific.* Friends of Steady Eddie, Manila.

Raslan, Karim. 1996. *Ceritalah: Malaysia in Transition.* Times Books International, Kuala Lumpur.

Rehman Rashid. 1996. *A Malaysian Journey*. Rehman Rashid, Malaysia.

Robison, Richard and David S. G. Goodman (eds). 1996. *The New Rich in Asia: Mobile Phones, McDonald's and Middle-class Revolution*. Routledge, London.

Rodan, Garry (ed.). 1996. *Political Oppositions in Industrialising Asia*. Routledge, London.

Rohwer, Jim. 1996. *Asia Rising: How History's Biggest Middle Class Will Change the World*. Nicholas Brealey Publishing, London.

Said, Edward W. 1995. *Orientalism: Western Conceptions of the Orient*. Penguin Books, London.

Schwarz, Adam. 1994. *A Nation in Waiting: Indonesia in the 1990s*. Allen & Unwin, Australia.

Seah Chee-Meow (ed.). 1977. *Asian Values and Modernization*. Singapore University Press.

Selvan, T. S. 1990. *Singapore: The Ultimate Island (Lee Kuan Yew's Untold Story)*. Freeway Books, Australia.

Seow, Francis T. 1994. *To Catch a Tartar: A Dissident in Lee Kuan Yew's Prison*. Yale University Southeast Asia Studies, Connecticut.

Sesser, Stan. 1993. *The Lands of Charm and Cruelty: Travels in Southeast Asia*. Vintage Books, New York.

Shawcross, William. 1986. *Sideshow: Kissinger, Nixon and the Destruction of Cambodia*. The Hogarth Press, London.

Sheehan, Neil. 1992. *After the War Was Over: Hanoi and Saigon*. Vintage Books, New York.

Sheehan, Neil. 1990. *A Bright Shining Lie*. Picador, London.

Sheridan, Greg. 1997. *Tigers: Leaders of the New Asia-Pacific*. Allen & Unwin, Australia.

Soeharto. 1991. *My Thoughts, Words and Deeds: An Autobiography*. As told to G. Dwipayana and Ramadhan K. H. PT Citra Lamtoro Gung Persada, Indonesia.

Stott, P. A. (ed.). 1978. *Nature and Man in South East Asia*. SOAS, London.

Sudham, Pira. 1989. *People of Esarn*. Shire Books, Thailand.

Suu Kyi, Aung San. 1991. *Freedom from Fear and other writings*. Penguin Books, London.

Taylor, R. H. (ed.). 1996. *The Politics of Elections in Southeast Asia*. Woodrow Wilson Center Press and Cambridge University Press.

Thiep, Nguyen Huy. 1992. *The General Retires and other stories*. Translated by Greg Lockhart. Oxford University Press, Singapore.

Thompson, E. P. 1963. *The Making of the English Working Class*. Penguin, London.

Tin, Bui. 1995. *Following Ho Chi Minh: The Memoirs of a North*

Vietnamese Colonel. Translated and adapted by Judy Stowe and Do
Van. Hurst and Co, London.

Vatikiotis, Michael R. J. 1994. *Indonesian Politics under Suharto: Order,
development and pressure for change.* Routledge, London.

Vatikiotis, Michael R. J. 1996. *Political Change in Southeast Asia:
Trimming the Banyan Tree.* Routledge, London.

Vitug, Marites Danguilan. 1993. *The Politics of Logging: Power from the
Forest.* Philippine Center for Investigative Journalism.

Williams, Michael C. 1992. *Vietnam at the Crossroads.* The Royal
Institute of International Affairs/Pinter Publishers, London.

World Bank. 1993. *The East Asian Miracle: Economic Growth and Public
Policy.* Oxford University Press.

Wright, Joseph J. Jr. 1991. *The Balancing Act: A History of Modern
Thailand.* Asia Books, Bangkok.

Yahuda, Michael. 1996. *The International Politics of the Asia-Pacific
1945–1995.* Routledge, London.

Index

Index

[Handwritten annotations:]

one off growth & → lab
exploitation not resources
catch up p162

where do we stand

- SL
- GS
- Biotechnology
- Dollar + Kraay
- role of projects

p104
Asian growth
free + flexible markets
(v exporters.
maintained some
domestic tariffs.

pre industrial   values   - extended families
hierarchies   hard work   respect elders
powerful communities   strict moral code

individual rights   - Asian values or
       transitional   (russia vs china)

divorce
breakdown family ties   + ↑ aging pop

346

GS dangers

- domino economics — effect of tigers
  on Lat America p143

- single issue groups

  retribalising hyphenation
- nationalism - Fiji

                    corruption p80
- pollution , crime , social disorder
  cultural confusion, need to build
  effective political institutes , drug abuse

- demands for democracy , independent judiciary
  religious + sexual freedom, free trade unions
  p7. or Asian values

- relative deprivation

    street children   alienating middle class youth
    religion decline + growth fundamentalism

- agnosticism, irrationalism, fundamentalism
  magical bank religions